Change Your Brain, Change Your Life

Healing Anxiety and Depression,
with Lisa Routh, M.D., Putnam, 2003

New Skills for Frazzled Parents,
MindWorks, 2003

Healing the Hardware of the Soul,
Free Press, 2002

Images of Human Behavior: A Brain SPECT Atlas,
MindWorks, 2003

How to Get Out of Your Own Way,
MindWorks, 2000

ADD in Intimate Relationships,
MindWorks, 1997

A Teenager's Guide to ADD,
with Antony Amen and Sharon Johnson,
MindWorks, 1995

Mind Coach: Teaching Kids to Think Positive and Feel Good,
MindWorks, 1994

The Most Important Thing in Life I Learned from a Penguin,
MindWorks, 1994

Change Your Brain, Change Your Life

REVISED AND EXPANDED

*The Breakthrough Program for Conquering
Anxiety, Depression, Obsessiveness, Lack of Focus,
Anger, and Memory Problems*

Daniel G. Amen, M.D.

HARMONY
BOOKS · NEW YORK

MEDICAL DISCLAIMER
The information presented in this book is the result of years of practice experience and clinical research by the author. The information in this book, by necessity, is of a general nature and not a substitute for an evaluation or treatment by a competent medical specialist. If you believe you are in need of medical interventions please see a medical practitioner as soon as possible. The stories in this book are true. The names and circumstances of the stories have been changed to protect the anonymity of patients.

Springer and Neuropsychology Review, Volume 2, January 1991, "Analysis of the elements
of attention: A neuropsychological approach" by Allan F. Mirsky, Figure 1, is given to the
publication in which the material was originally published, with kind permission from
Springer Science and Business Media.

Oxford University Press and Schizophrenia Bulletin, Volume 20, Issue 4, January 1994,
"Geographic Correlation of Schizophrenia to Ticks and Tick-Borne Encephalitis" by
James S. Brown, Jr., with permission from Oxford University Press.

Library of Congress Cataloging-in-Publication Data
Amen, Daniel G.
Change your brain, change your life : the breakthrough program for conquering anxiety,
depression, obsessiveness, lack of focus, anger, and memory problems / Daniel G. Amen,
M.D.—2 [edition], revised and expanded.
pages cm
1. Mental illness—Physiological aspects.   2. Brain—Pathophysiology.
3. Neuropsychiatry—Popular works.   4. Mental illness—Chemotherapy.   I. Title.
RC455.4.B5A43 2015
616.89—dc23   2015024175

ISBN 978-1-101-90464-0
eBook ISBN 978-1-101-90498-5

Printed in the United States of America

Book design by Meighan Cavanaugh
Cover design by Kalena Schoen

10 9 8 7 6 5

Revised Edition

To all our patients at Amen Clinics,

who taught me how important it is

to continue to do this work

and to tell the world about it

CONTENTS

Part Two

Know and Heal the Brain Systems
That Run Your Life

Part Three

The Brain Warrior's Way

PREFACE TO THE NEW EDITION

Since *Change Your Brain, Change Your Life* was first published in 1998, so much has changed both in the field of neuroscience and at Amen Clinics. Our clinical experience in diagnosing, treating, and optimizing the brain has grown exponentially. We've expanded from one local clinic serving the people in Northern California to a nationwide group of clinics treating children, teenagers, and adults from 111 countries. Our database of brain SPECT (single photon emission computed tomography) studies, the primary functional brain imaging study we use at Amen Clinics, has grown from about five thousand scans in 1998 to well over one hundred thousand scans in 2015, making us one of the world leaders in applying brain imaging science to help people who struggle with emotional issues such as anxiety, depression, and bipolar disorder; behavioral challenges like addictions, weight control, or anger; cognitive problems, such as brain fog or memory issues; and learning challenges, including attention deficit disorder (ADD), also called attention deficit hyperactivity disorder (ADHD).

When *Change Your Brain, Change Your Life* was first written, the medical staff at Amen Clinics prescribed more psychiatric medications than we do today. Whenever feasible, we choose more natural ways to heal and support the brain, such as supplements and lifestyle interventions (nutrition, exercise, new learning, and so forth). While we still use medications when needed and believe they save lives when used appropriately, we firmly believe that treatment providers should *first do no harm* and *use the least toxic, most effective treatments*. It's not uncommon that a new patient will come for their first visit at Amen Clinics on four, five, or eight different medications—and, unsurprisingly, they're still suffering. One child actually came to our Reston, Virginia clinic on *seventeen* different medications. We spend more time taking people off medications than putting them on new ones. Most of our new patients have never been offered healthy lifestyle or natural supplement options before coming to see us.

At the time of this writing, Amen Clinics has published more than sixty scientific studies since the first edition of this book, on a wide range of topics from traumatic brain injury in professional football players to brain trauma, obesity, suicide, predicting treatment response for patients with ADHD, meditation, and the impact of nutritional supplements on the brain. In 2014 alone we published or presented twenty new studies.

Some of the concepts I wrote about in the original version of this book have changed as our experience has expanded and new research has been published. Of course, the core belief of the original book is still as valid today as it was in 1998—*you are not stuck with the brain you have, you can make it better, you can change your brain and your life.* In the last seventeen years, we've developed and refined the method we use at Amen Clinics (the Amen Clinics Method), which I'll explain in detail so you can benefit from it without ever stepping through the door of one of our clinics.

One of my favorite examples of how you can "change your brain, change your life" is our work with professional football players. Starting in 2009, Amen Clinics performed the first and still-largest brain imaging study on active and retired NFL players, at a time when most people were ignoring this critical issue. Our research demonstrated high levels of damage in players (1), which was not a big surprise. Most thoughtful nine-year-olds would probably think it is a bad idea to repeatedly hit the organ that runs your life, even with a helmet on. But what really excited us was that on the Amen Clinics Brain Smart Program, the same one I'll discuss in this book, 80 percent of our players showed significant improvement, especially in the areas of blood flow, mood, and memory (2).

In 2010, Pastor Rick Warren asked me and Dr. Mark Hyman to collaborate on creating a health program for Saddleback Church, which has one of the largest congregations in the world. Pastor Warren had seen me on public television talking about the "dinosaur syndrome," a term I coined to describe new research that reported "as your weight goes up, the actual physical size and function of your brain goes down. Big body, little brain, you are going to become extinct if you don't get your weight under control." That got Pastor Warren's attention.

Together, the three of us created The Daniel Plan, a revolutionary five-step program to get the world healthy through religious organizations (Faith, Food, Fitness, Focus, and Friends). The first week, fifteen thousand people signed up for our program. Over the first year, they lost over a quarter of a million pounds combined—more than a space shuttle weighs. Even better, participants reported better energy, focus, creativity, sleep, memory, and mood, along with reductions in stress, blood pressure, blood sugar, sexual dysfunction, and many medications. The Daniel Plan is now being implemented in thousands of churches around the world, from Hong Kong to Johannesburg, Manila to São Paulo. Another new feature of this edition is a focus on getting you physically healthy. I don't want you to be a dinosaur.

In addition, we developed the "brain warrior" concept, which you'll read about throughout the book. As I work to get myself and those I serve truly healthy, it is clear to me that we are in a war for the health of our brains. Virtually everywhere we go, someone is tempting us with bad food that will kill us early, putting toxic thoughts in our minds by pushing us to watch horrific news events over and over, or working to addict us to the latest gadgets that interfere with our relationships. To achieve optimal mental performance, we have to have the mind-set of a brain warrior.

Over the last seventeen years I have had the opportunity to present the information in this book to millions of people. My ten national public television specials have aired more than eighty thousand times across North America. I've also been blessed to talk to medical and mental health professionals, judges, and government officials around the world, including those at the National Security Agency (NSA), the National Science Foundation (NSF), Harvard's Learning & the Brain Conference, the Department of the Interior, the National Council of Juvenile and Family Court Judges, and the Supreme Courts of Delaware, Ohio, and Wyoming. I've spoken at medical schools and participated in debates about brain imaging at national medical meetings.

This edition of *Change Your Brain, Change Your Life* offers you the latest research and thinking at Amen Clinics to help boost your brain and the brains of those you love, which in turn will improve everything in your life and theirs.

Part One

How Imaging
Changes Everything

Your Brain

A Brief Primer

Your brain is the most amazing organ in the universe. It is the organ responsible for learning, strategizing, loving, creating, and behaving. As such, it's important to know about it, love it, and maybe even be a bit obsessed with it. The human brain typically weighs about three pounds and is the consistency of soft butter. It is housed in a really hard skull that has multiple sharp bony ridges. Therefore, it might not surprise you to learn that your brain was not designed to be inside a cranium that hits soccer balls or in a ring with a mixed martial artist who wants to pound it senseless against the canvas.

The brain is an integrated whole, a symphony of parts that work together to create and sustain a life. Specific parts of the brain are designed to do certain things, but its functions are rarely simple. With that in mind, some generalizations can help you learn about your brain.

The largest structure in the human brain is the cerebral cortex, the wrinkly walnut-shaped mass that sits atop and covers the rest of the brain. The cerebral cortex has four main areas, or lobes, on each side of the brain: frontal, temporal, parietal, and occipital.

The frontal lobes consist of the motor cortex, which is in charge of directing movement; the premotor cortex, which helps to plan movement; and the prefrontal cortex (PFC), which is considered the executive part of the brain. The PFC is the most evolved part of the human brain and is involved with focus, forethought, judgment, organization, planning, impulse

Outside View of the Brain

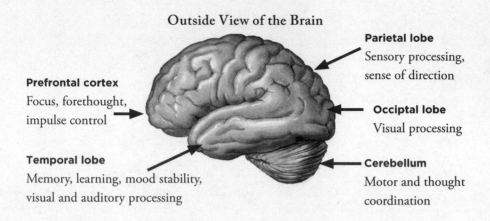

Parietal lobe
Sensory processing,
sense of direction

Prefrontal cortex
Focus, forethought,
impulse control

Occiptal lobe
Visual processing

Temporal lobe
Memory, learning, mood stability,
visual and auditory processing

Cerebellum
Motor and thought
coordination

Inside View of the Brain

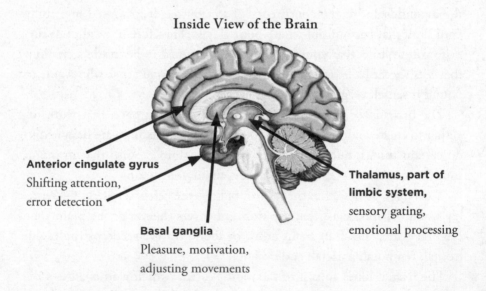

Anterior cingulate gyrus
Shifting attention,
error detection

**Thalamus, part of
limbic system,**
sensory gating,
emotional processing

Basal ganglia
Pleasure, motivation,
adjusting movements

control, empathy, and learning from mistakes. It makes up about 30 percent of the human brain, compared with just 11 percent for chimpanzees, 7 percent for dogs, 3 percent for cats (perhaps why they need nine lives), and 1 percent for mice (which is why they are eaten by cats). Deep in your frontal lobes is the anterior cingulate gyrus (ACG), a structure involved with error detection and shifting attention.

The temporal lobes, located underneath your temples and behind your eyes, are involved in mood stability, emotional reactions, temper control, learning, moving memories into long-term storage, and auditory processing. The temporal lobes have been called the "what pathway," because they name "what" things are.

The parietal lobes, at the top side and back of the brain, are the centers for sensory processing (touch), perception, and sense of direction. Called the "where pathway" because they help us know where things are in space, they're also involved in manipulating numbers, dressing, and grooming. The occipital lobes, at the back of the cortex, are concerned primarily with vision and visual processing.

Sitting underneath the cerebral cortex is the limbic or emotional system: the part of the brain that colors our emotions and is involved with bonding, nesting, feeding, sexuality, and emotions. Also underneath the cortex are structures called the basal ganglia, involved with motivation, pleasure, and smoothing motor movements.

The cerebellum—at the back bottom part of the brain—is involved with motor and thought coordination. It is essential for processing complex information.

The cortex is divided into two hemispheres, left and right. While the two sides significantly overlap in function, the left side in right-handed people is generally the seat of language, and tends to be the analytical, logical, detail-oriented part of the brain, while the right hemisphere sees the big picture and is likely involved more with hunches and intuition. It is often opposite in left-handed people.

Information from the world enters your brain through your limbic or emotional system, where it tags the information as meaningful, safe, or dangerous, then it travels to the back part of the brain (temporal, parietal, and occipital lobes), where it is initially processed and compared with past experience, and then to the front part of the brain for you to consider and then act on it. The transmission of information from the outside world to your conscious awareness in the front part of your brain happens almost instantaneously.

Introduction

The Single Most Important Lesson I've Learned
from Looking at More Than 100,000 Brains

To start the book, I'd like to share the single most important lesson I've learned from looking at more than one hundred thousand brain scans, but first, let me put it into a little context.

I am in the middle of seven children. When I was growing up my father called me a maverick, which to him was *not* a good thing. In 1972, the army called my draft number and I was trained as an infantry medic, which gave birth to my love of medicine. I quickly learned that I hated the thought of being shot at or sleeping in the mud, so I got myself retrained as an X-ray technician, and developed a passion for medical imaging. As our professors used to say, "How do you know unless you look?"

In 1979, when I was a second-year medical student, someone in my family tried to kill herself and I took her to see a wonderful psychiatrist. I came to realize that if he helped her— which he did—it would not only save her life, but it could also help her children, and even her future grandchildren, as they would be shaped by someone who was happier and more stable. This realization helped me fall in love with psychiatry, because I recognized its potential to change generations of people.

Fast-forward to 1991, when I attended my first lecture on brain SPECT (single photon emission computed tomography) imaging, given by Dr. Jack Paldi, the chief of medicine at our local hospital. At the time I was in private practice in Northern California and the director of a psychiatric addiction-treatment program. Dr. Paldi presented SPECT as a tool that could give psychiatrists more information about the brain to help them better diagnose and treat their patients.

SPECT is a nuclear medicine study that looks at blood flow and activity. It's different from traditional CT and MRI scans, which are anatomy studies that look at the brain's structure. SPECT looks at brain function and basically tells us three things about its activity: good activity, too little activity, or too much activity. It also helps to show if the brain has been hurt from physical trauma or if it has been exposed to toxins or infections.

For illustration purposes in this book I will show you two types of SPECT images: surface views and active views. Surface views look at the outside surface of the brain and show areas of healthy and low activity. Active views show areas of high or increased activity in the inner areas of the brain. Throughout the book you will see dozens of brain SPECT images, which will help you visualize how disease and trauma affect our brains. Images I.1 and I.2 show a healthy set of SPECT scans. The surface image on the left (I.1) shows full, even, symmetrical activity. The surface scans look at the top 45 percent of brain activity. Anything below that threshold shows up as a hole or a dent. The scan images with "holes" that you will see throughout the book are generally not missing parts of the brain; rather the holes indicate low activity in those regions. The white in the image on the

Images I.1 and I.2: Healthy SPECT Scans

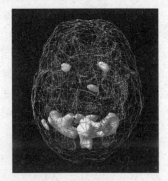

SURFACE

Full, even, symmetrical activity

ACTIVE

White equals the most active part of the brain, typically in the cerebellum in the back, bottom area

right (I.2) shows the areas of increased activity. In a healthy scan the back part of the brain is typically the most active.

Compare the healthy scan to someone who had two strokes (I.3). See the holes of low activity.

Image I.3: 2 Strokes

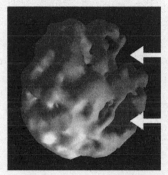

Arrows point to areas of brain damage after two strokes.

Image I.4 shows the SPECT scan of someone with Alzheimer's disease, where the back half of the brain is deteriorating.

Image I.4: Alzheimer's Disease

Severe decreases in the back half of the brain

Image I.5 shows the brain SPECT scan of a person with traumatic brain injury. As you know, your brain is soft and your skull is really hard. When you hit your head, your brain slams into the bony ridges on the inside of the skull.

Image I.5: Traumatic Brain Injury

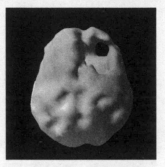

*Damage to the right
front side*

Image I.6 shows a scan of someone with a substance abuse problem. Beyond the myriad of problems drug use can cause, it also results in brain damage.

Image I.6: Drug Abuse

*Damage seen across the
cortex of the brain*

Image I.7 is of a person with obsessive-compulsive disorder. Here there is typically too much activity in the front part of the brain, so people have trouble turning off their thoughts.

Image I.7: Obsessive-Compulsive Disorder

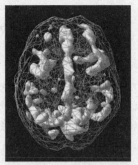

*High activity in the front
part of the brain*

Image I.8 is a scan of a person with epilepsy, a condition where we often see focal areas of increased activity.

Image I.8: Epilepsy

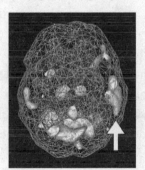

*Focal increase on the right
side of the brain*

In 1992 I attended an all-day lecture on "Brain SPECT Imaging in Psychiatry," given by physicians at Creighton University and sponsored by the American Psychiatric Association. The experience was amazing and the results they shared mirrored my own early experience with SPECT. Yet, at the same conference researchers complained loudly that clinical psychiatrists like me *should not* be using the scans in their practices, they were only for research purposes. Being a maverick, I didn't hesitate to speak up and challenge their position.

Psychiatrists then and even now are the only medical specialists who virtually never look at the organ they treat. Think about it. Cardiologists, neurologists, gastroenterologists, orthopedic doctors—in fact, every other medical specialist—look; psychiatrists guess. Before imaging, I was throwing medication-tipped darts in the dark at my patients and had unintentionally hurt some of them, which horrified me. There is a reason that most psychiatric medications have black box warnings. Give them to the wrong person and you can precipitate a disaster.

Without the benefit of looking, psychiatric outcomes have not improved in decades. Thomas Insel, director of the National Institute of Mental Health, wrote, "The unfortunate reality is that current medications help too few people to get better and very few people to get well . . . For the antidepressants . . . the rate of response continues to be slow and low. In the largest effectiveness study to date, with more than 4,000 patients with major depressive disorder in primary care and community settings, only 31% were in remission after 14 weeks of optimal treatment. In most double-blind trials of antidepressants, the placebo response rate hovers around 30% . . . The unfortunate reality is that current medications help too few people to get better and very few people to get well" (3). In fact, recent studies that looked at the published data from the pharmaceutical companies on antidepressant trials and the unpublished data obtained from the Freedom of Information Act and the pharmaceutical companies found that antidepressants, except for the most severely depressed patients, worked no better than placebos or sugar pills (4).

Without imaging, psychiatrists are forced to make diagnoses like they did in 1840 when Abraham Lincoln was depressed. I love Lincoln for his psychological mindedness and his perseverance despite many failures. Most people don't know that when Lincoln was ten years old, he was kicked in the head by a horse and knocked unconscious for hours. People thought he was dead (5). Subsequently, and perhaps relatedly, Lincoln suffered severe bouts of depression in his life, even to the point of being suicidal. After personal and political setbacks in the winter of 1840, Lincoln went to see his physician, Anson Henry. **How did Dr. Henry diagnose Lincoln's**

melancholy? He used tools that were state-of-the-art in 1840. He talked to him, observed him, and looked for symptom clusters to try to understand what was wrong. This is exactly how most psychiatric diagnoses are made in 2015, 175 years later, using a "symptom cluster" manual called the *Diagnostic and Statistical Manual* (*DSM*), published by the American Psychiatric Association.

In most family physician, pediatrician, psychiatrist, psychologist, or therapist offices patients report symptoms and doctors give them a diagnosis based on those symptoms. For example, if a patient says, "I'm depressed," they are likely going to get a diagnosis of depression and be prescribed an antidepressant medication or psychotherapy for depression. If a patient complains of being anxious, he or she will likely get an anxiety disorder diagnosis and medicine or therapy for anxiety. Or, if a patient has attentional problems, he or she often gets a diagnosis of ADD or ADHD and is put on medicine to help with focus or impulse control. Or, my favorite diagnosis to explain this diagnostic phenomenon is that if a patient tells the doctor that he or she has temper problems or explodes intermittently, he or she often gets a diagnosis called "intermittent explosive disorder" (I.E.D.— the acronym is ironic, like "improvised explosive device" in war) and is put in anger management classes. **None of these diagnostic labels tells us one thing about the underlying biology of these problems, and so people end up with one-size-fits-all treatment plans, which is the cause of many treatment failures.**

In a major lecture in 2005 to the American Psychiatric Association, Insel said, "The current way psychiatrists diagnose patients using the *DSM* **is 100% reliable**, meaning that if you diagnose someone using the *DSM* criteria today, you will likely diagnose them the same way tomorrow, **but it is 0% valid**, because it is not based on any underlying neuroscience." Essentially, Insel was saying that the emperor of psychiatric diagnosis, the *DSM*, had no clothes. This statement struck a chord with me, because at Amen Clinics we were already working beyond the *DSM* with good results. The imaging work we were doing taught us so many important lessons.

One of the first lessons was that symptom clusters like ADD/ADHD, anxiety, depression, and addictions are *not* single or simple disorders in the brain, and they all have multiple types. Images I.9 and I.10 are of two different people with depression who had virtually the same symptoms, but radically different brain scans. One had low activity, the other high activity. Do you think they'll respond to the same treatment? Of course not! Treatment needs to be tailored to individual brains, not a cluster of symptoms. Over the years, I have described seven types of ADD/ADHD, seven types of anxiety and depression, six types of addicts, and five types of overeaters (see chapter 16).

Images I.9 and I.10: Two Patients with Depression

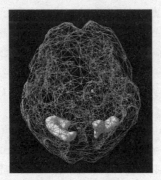
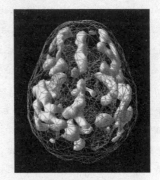

UNDERSIDE SURFACE   UNDERSIDE ACTIVE
Low overall activity   *High overall activity*

Another important early lesson was that mild traumatic brain injuries are a major cause of psychiatric illness that ruin people's lives, and very few people knew about it . . . because only a handful of psychiatrists ever look at the brains of their patients. Image I.11 is a SPECT scan of a fifteen-year-old boy who fell down a flight of stairs at the age of three. Even though he was unconscious for only a few minutes and was given a diagnosis of mild traumatic brain injury, there was *nothing* mild about the enduring effect the injury had on his life. I met him after he had been kicked out of his third residential treatment program for violence. Neither medication nor behavior therapy was the answer—he needed a brain rehabilitation program, which I will discuss in part 3.

Through our imaging work I've discovered that many people forget they had significant brain injuries and I have to ask them the "Did you ever have a brain injury?" question five to ten times to uncover if they had one or not.

Image I.11: 15-Year-Old Teen with Traumatic Brain Injury

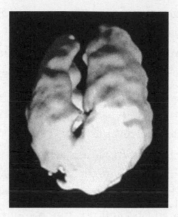

Damage to left hemisphere

I have to specifically ask people if they have ever fallen out of a tree, dove into a shallow pool, fell off a fence head first, been in a car accident, or had concussions playing sports. I was shocked by the percentage of people who initially said no to the question about brain injury, but when we saw evidence of an injury on a scan and prodded them, they begin to remember all sorts of incidents like going through a windshield of a car, falling off a cliff, or falling out of a third-story window.

As we continued our work with SPECT, the criticism from researchers grew louder, but so did the lessons. Judges and defense attorneys sought our help in trying to understand criminal behavior. To date we have scanned over five hundred convicted felons, including ninety murderers. Our work taught us that **many people who do bad things often have troubled brains . . . that was not a surprise . . . but what did surprise us was that many of these people had brains that could be rehabilitated.** Here is a radical idea I recently discussed with a group of judges in Georgia. What if we evaluated and treated troubled brains, rather than simply warehousing them in toxic, stressful environments? In my experience we could potentially save tremendous amounts of money by making a significant percentage of these people more functional, so that when they got out of prison they could work, support their families, and pay taxes. Dostoyevsky once said, "A society should be judged not by how it treats its outstanding citizens, but by how it treats its criminals." Instead of just crime and punishment, SPECT imaging taught me that we should also be thinking about crime, evaluation, and treatment.

After a quarter century and more than one hundred thousand SPECT scans, the single most important lesson my colleagues and I have learned is this: you can literally change people's brains, and when you do you change their lives. You are not stuck with the brain you have; you can make it better, and we can prove it.

Image I.12 is the scan of an ADD teenager who had been cutting herself, failing in school, and fighting with her parents. With the right treatment the low activity in her brain (Image I.13) became much better and she went from D's and F's to A's and B's and was much more emotionally stable.

Images I.12 and I.13: From Failure to Success: Underside View

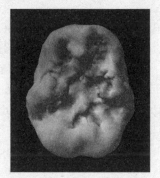 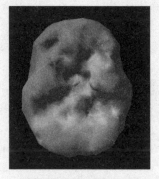

UNDERSIDE SURFACE
Low frontal lobe activity

UNDERSIDE SURFACE
Marked overall improvement

RAY AND NANCY

Ray came to see us as part of our NFL study. He played linebacker for the San Diego Chargers in the early 1970s. Part of Ray's motivation for participating in our study was that his wife, Nancy, had been recently diagnosed with frontal temporal lobe dementia and he wanted us to evaluate her as well. He was upset at the physician who diagnosed Nancy, because he told Ray that within a year she would not know who he was or his name.

When we evaluated Ray he showed evidence of brain trauma, as did almost all of our retired players, plus he was overweight. Nancy's scan was a disaster. She had severe decreased activity in the front part of her brain, consistent with the diagnosis of frontal temporal lobe dementia. When we sat down to review their scans, it was very emotional for Ray and Nancy—and for me too. From our clinical experience, we knew we could help Ray. But there is still no known effective treatment for frontal temporal lobe dementia.

Our strategy with cases like Nancy's is to do everything we can to try to slow or reverse the dementia process. And, certainly, it does not always work. I told Ray and Nancy that it was critical to immediately start our brain rehabilitation program, which will be outlined in part 3 of the book. Ten weeks later I saw them back for their first follow-up visit. Nancy's follow-up scan showed dramatic improvement. Nancy had followed through on all of our recommendations. In addition to her improved scan, her memory and cognitive function were better. Ray joked that we had to slow down, because soon enough she would be smarter than he was. In addition, Ray had lost thirty pounds! He said his motivation was helping his wife. If

Images I.14 and I.15: Nancy:
Frontal Temporal Lobe Dementia Before and After

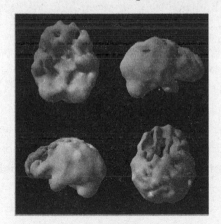 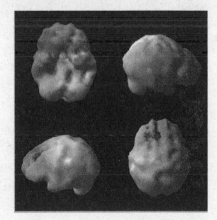

BEFORE   AFTER 10 WEEKS

he did everything we suggested, then she would too. They would do it as a couple. Sometimes motivation is about love. Ray loved Nancy.

Nancy's scans took place in early February and May of 2010. Five years later, Nancy still knows Ray's name. I have no doubt we are in a war for the health of her brain. Both Ray and Nancy have become brain warriors.

BECOMING A BRAIN WARRIOR

Helping to pioneer the clinical application of brain imaging in psychiatry has been the greatest personal and professional challenge of my life. In 1993, when I first started to talk at medical meetings about the discoveries we were making at Amen Clinics, many of my colleagues criticized and belittled me. The lack of focus on this exciting technology bothered me deeply, but did not dissuade me from using it in my work. What I was seeing in the brain was real, and the new knowledge changed the lives of many of my patients. But I hated the fight. In 1994, I decided to start keeping a low profile, expecting others would do the research and move the profession forward. Then, in April 1995, nine-year-old Andrew came into my clinic.

Andrew had been a happy, sweet boy until about a year and a half before he came to see me. Then, his personality changed. He appeared depressed. He had aggressive outbursts and he complained to his mother of both suicidal and homicidal thoughts (very abnormal for a nine-year-old). He drew pictures of himself hanging from a tree and shooting other children. When he attacked a little girl on the baseball field for no particular reason, his mother, Sherrie, called in tears. Andrew was Columbine, Aurora, and Sandy Hook waiting to happen. I told Sherrie to bring Andrew in the next day, and they bundled into the car for an eight-hour drive.

As I sat with Andrew's parents and then with Andrew I knew something wasn't right. He looked angry and sad. He had no explanations for his behavior. He did not report any form of abuse. Other children were not bullying him. There was no family history of serious psychiatric illnesses. He had not sustained a recent head injury. The vast majority of my psychiatric colleagues would have placed Andrew on some sort of medication and sent him to a counselor for psychotherapy, as they did for the Columbine shooter Eric Harris or the Springfield, Oregon, killer Kip Kinkel. Having performed more than a thousand SPECT studies by that time, I first wanted a picture of Andrew's brain. I wanted to know what we were dealing with. But with the criticism from my colleagues swirling in my own brain, I did wonder if Andrew's problems weren't completely psychological. Perhaps there was a family problem that I just didn't know about. Maybe Andrew was acting out because his older brother was a "perfect" child who did well in school and was very athletic. Maybe Andrew had these thoughts and behaviors to ward off feelings of insecurity related to being the second son in a family (I had personal knowledge of this scenario). Maybe Andrew wanted to feel powerful and these behaviors were associated with issues of control. Then logic took over my brain. Nine-year-old children do not normally think about suicide or homicide. They do not attack little girls for no apparent reason. I needed to scan his brain. If it was normal, then we would look further for underlying emotional problems.

I went with Andrew to the imaging center and held his hand while he held his teddy bear and got scanned. As his brain appeared on the computer screen, I thought there had been a technical mistake. The image of Andrew's brain had *no* left temporal lobe! Upon quick examination of the complete study, I realized the quality of the scan was fine. He was indeed missing his left temporal lobe. Did he have a cyst, a tumor, a prior stroke? A part of me felt fear for him as I looked at the monitor. But the diagnostician in me felt relieved that we had some explanation for his aggressive behavior. My research and the research of others had implicated left temporal lobe problems with aggression. The next day Andrew had an MRI (an anatomical brain study), which showed a cyst (a fluid-filled sac) about the size of a golf ball occupying the space where his left temporal lobe should have been, pushing it inside and raising his intracranial pressure. I knew the cyst had to be removed. However, getting other medical professionals to take this seriously proved very frustrating.

ANDREW AND HIS MISSING LEFT TEMPORAL LOBE

The day of the MRI I called Andrew's pediatrician and informed him of the clinical situation and brain findings. I told him to find the best person

Image I.16: Andrew (age 9)

Andrew and Buster, his dog

Image I.17

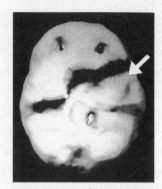

Underside surface scan

possible to drain the cyst. He contacted three pediatric neurologists. All of them said that Andrew's negative behavior was probably not in any way related to the cyst in his brain and they would not recommend operating on him until he had "real symptoms." When the pediatrician relayed this information, I became furious. *Real symptoms!* I had a child with homicidal and suicidal thoughts who was losing control over his behavior and attacking people. I contacted a pediatric neurologist in San Francisco who told me the same thing. I then called a friend of mine at Harvard Medical School, also a pediatric neurologist, who told me the same thing. She even used the words "real symptoms." I practically jumped down her throat; how could Andrew's symptoms be more real? "Oh, Dr. Amen," the neurologist replied, "when I say 'real symptoms,' I mean symptoms like seizures or speech problems." Could the medical profession really not connect the brain to behavior? I was appalled! But I wasn't going to wait until Andrew killed himself or someone else. My next call was to pediatric neurosurgeon Jorge Lazareff at UCLA, who told me that he had operated on three other children with left temporal lobe cysts who had all been aggressive. He had wondered if it was related. Thankfully, after evaluating Andrew, he agreed to remove the cyst.

After the surgery, I received two calls. The first one was from Sherrie. She told me that the surgery went well and when Andrew woke up he smiled at her. It was the first time he had smiled in a year. The next call was from Dr.

Image 1.18: Andrew after Surgery

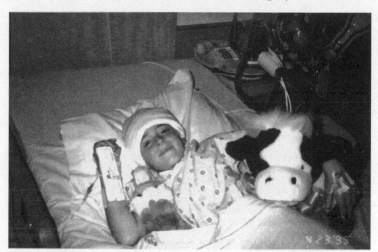

Lazareff, who said, "Oh my God, Dr. Amen, the cyst was so aggressive and had put so much pressure on Andrew's brain that it had actually thinned the bone over his left temporal lobe. If Andrew had been hit in the head by a ball it would have killed him instantly. Either way, in six months he would have been dead." It's a day I'll never forget, not just because I fought for a patient, but because Andrew is my nephew and godson.

A year later, Andrew and I were on vacation together with our families in Hawaii. After an afternoon of snorkeling we stopped at a local place for something to drink. As he was sipping from a straw, Andrew looked up at me with his beautiful brown eyes and long curly hair and asked me why he had the cyst. Our family has deeply rooted spiritual beliefs, and when Andrew asked why, I started to cry. In my soul, I felt I knew why it happened to him: so I would stop being so damned anxious, scared, and worried about what others thought of me and just do the work I was given to do. There were too many children, teenagers, and adults like Andrew who had clear brain abnormalities, whom society was just writing off as bad human beings. Since Andrew, I have helped forty-three other children and young adults with temporal lobe cysts, many of whom exhibited aggressive or violent behavior.

Andrew was blessed in the sense that he had someone who loved him paying attention to his brain when his behavior was off. Now, eighteen years later, Andrew is employed, owns his own home, and pays taxes. Because someone looked at his brain, he has been a wonderful son, and will be a better husband, father, and grandfather.

When you have the privilege of changing someone's brain, you not only improve his or her life, you have the opportunity to affect generations to come.

Image I.19: Andrew 18 Years Later with His Uncle

This book will teach you that human behavior is more complex than society's damning labels would have us believe. We are far too quick to attribute people's actions to a bad character, when the source of their actions may not be their choice at all, but a problem with brain physiology. One young man, for example, who was brought in to see me after being released from prison for violent outbursts, had a temporal lobe problem that responded positively to targeted treatment. How many "bad people" sitting in prison would prove to be perfectly nice people with the right treatment? Sometimes people aren't being loving, industrious, cheerful, peaceful, obedient, or kind, not because they wouldn't like to be, but because something is wrong with their brain—something that is potentially fixable.

Until the late 1980s, physicians had no sophisticated tools for evaluating a working brain. Standard brain MRI (magnetic resonance imaging) scans and

CAT (computerized axial tomography) scans, available since the 1970s, are anatomical studies, and although they can evaluate what a brain looks like physically, they cannot provide information on how well the brain is working. Functional brain imaging studies like SPECT, positron emission tomography (PET), functional MRI (fMRI), and quantitative EEGs (qEEGs) give more useful information. Each of these functional studies have advantages and disadvantages. At this time, in my opinion, due to cost, ease of use, and our more than one-hundred-thousand-scan database, SPECT is our diagnostic tool of choice.

It is important to note that having an abnormal SPECT scan is not an excuse for "bad behavior." SPECT adds to our knowledge about and understanding of behavior, but it does not provide all the answers. Many people who have difficulties in their brains never do anything harmful or destructive to others. Each scan needs to be interpreted in the context of each individual life.

Not all scientists will agree with every finding in this book. The information here is based largely on our extensive clinical experience and research. In this edition, I provide hundreds of references, sources, and additional reading for those interested.

You don't need a SPECT scan to benefit from this book. In fact, if you go to a medical center that has little experience with SPECT, the results are not likely to mean much to your doctor. My goal is to show you what we have learned from SPECT to help explain a wide variety of human behaviors. Many problems long thought of as psychological in nature—depression, panic disorders, ADD/ADHD—have, at least in part, biological roots that need to be addressed with an effective treatment plan. I hope that by providing new insights into how the brain works, you'll gain a deeper understanding of your own feelings and behaviors and the feelings and behaviors of others. To help you be more effective in your day-to-day life, I hope you will use the brain-based "prescriptions" that are relevant for your brain issues or brain type.

1

12 Principles to
Change Your Brain
and Your Life

At Amen Clinics we have twelve core principles that provide the foundation for our work with patients suffering from a range of issues as well as those looking to optimize their brains. They are incredibly simple, but don't let that fool you. They are also extremely powerful and will change everything in your life if you read, understand, and apply them.

1. **Your brain is involved in everything you do and everything you are,** including how you think, how you feel, how you act, and how well you get along with other people. Your brain is the organ behind your intelligence, character, personality, and every single decision you make. This is not a new idea. In about 400 BC, Hippocrates wrote, "And men ought to know that from the brain, and from the brain only, arise our pleasures, joy, laughter, and jests, as well as our sorrows, pains, despondency, and tears. And by this, in a special manner, we acquire wisdom and knowledge, and see and hear, and know what is foul and what is fair, what is bad and what is good, what is sweet, and what is unsavory . . . And by the same organ we become mad and delirious, where fears and terrors assail us . . . All these things we endure from the brain, when it is not healthy . . . In these ways I am of the opinion that the brain exercises the greatest power in the man. This is the interpreter to us of those things which emanate from the air, when the brain happens to be in a sound state." (6)

It is your brain that decides whether you should get married and if you get divorced. It is your brain that manages your money and helps you be successful at work. And it is your brain that pushes you away from the table, telling you that you have had enough (or that gives you permission to have the third bowl of ice cream). Yet most people never really think about their brains, which is a huge mistake, because success in anything you do starts with a healthy brain.

2. **When your brain works right, you work right. But when your brain is troubled, you are much more likely to have trouble in your life.** With a healthy brain you are happier, physically healthier (because you make better decisions), wealthier (also because you make better decisions), and more successful in everything you do. When your brain is unhealthy, for whatever reason (brain injuries, drug abuse, obesity, sleep apnea, mold toxicity, etc.), you are sadder, sicker, poorer, and less successful. In all the books about success on the shelf at your local bookstore, virtually none of them talk about optimizing the physical health of your brain. Based on our work with tens of thousands of people, we believe it is always the first place to start.

Image 1.1

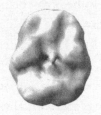

HEALTHY BRAIN	UNHEALTHY BRAIN
Happier	Sadder
Healthier	Sicker
Wealthier	Poorer
More Successful	Less Successful

If you really understand principle number 2 it can be disturbing, because it directly challenges the notion of free will. Most people think of free will as black or white: you have it or you don't. Our imaging work has taught me that free will is a gray concept. Some of us have great overall brain function and likely have a very high percentage of free will; while others, often through no fault of their own, such as having been in a car accident, have less healthy brains, leading to less free will and more troubled lives.

3. **Your brain is the most amazing, energy-hungry organ in the universe.** It is estimated that your brain has one hundred billion cells, with each one connected to other cells by up to ten thousand individual connections. It has also been estimated that you have more connections in your brain than there are stars in the universe. Let's put this in binge-watching television terms: it's been estimated that the brain has the storage capacity of three million hours of TV shows (7).

   Even though your brain is only about 2 percent of your body's weight (about three pounds), it uses 20 to 30 percent of the calories you consume and 20 percent of your body's blood flow. Take a moment to consider that. Your brain is the most metabolically expensive real estate in your body. This is important to understand, because any form of oxygen deprivation state, from a scary event like a near-drowning episode to the seemingly commonplace, like having sleep apnea, can damage your brain.

4. **Your brain is the consistency of soft butter and housed in a really hard skull with multiple sharp bony ridges, making it easily injured.** Think of something that falls in between Jell-O and egg whites on the softness spectrum—that's your brain. For extra credit, visit this link to watch a video of a newly autopsied brain, so you can see how soft it really is: https://m.youtube.com/watch?v=jHxyP-nUhUY. Now imagine it encased in a really hard skull with many sharp bony ridges (see Image 1:2). Jarring motions and head injuries can cause the brain to slam into the hard interior of the skull, causing brain injuries that can ruin lives.

   Soft brain + hard skull with sharp ridges = trouble

Image 1.2: Inside the Skull

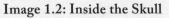

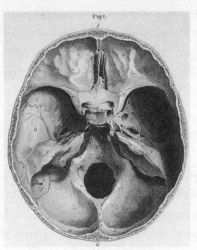

Notice the sharp bony ridges.

Traumatic brain injuries (TBIs) are a major cause of psychiatric illness and few people know this, because most psychiatrists never look at the brain. TBI has been linked to homelessness, drug and alcohol abuse, anxiety, panic attacks, depression, ADD/ADHD, learning problems, school failure, murder, suicide, domestic violence, job failure, and incarceration. In a study I did at Sierra Tucson, a psychiatric hospital in Arizona, 44 percent of new admissions had a significant history of brain injury. In another study of homeless people in Toronto, 58 percent of the men and 42 percent of the women had had a significant brain injury before becoming homeless.

At the time of this writing, more than three hundred thousand veterans have sustained a TBI since 2000 (8); the effects of such injuries can follow people for the rest of their lives, indicating that it's likely those veterans and society will feel the consequences for many decades to come.

Two million new TBIs occur each year as a result of falls, accidents, and concussions. We have to do a much better job of preventing TBIs and repairing the brain once they occur. When President Barack

Obama and LeBron James, both huge sports fans, said they would not let their children play tackle football, it was a sign that awareness about the effects of TBI are starting to become part of our cultural fabric.

5. **Many things hurt the brain.** Obviously, drugs, too much alcohol, infections, environmental toxins, and traumatic head injuries are bad for your brain. But research also tells us that obesity (9); sleep apnea (10); hypertension (11, 12), and even high normal blood pressure levels; diabetes (13, 14), prediabetes, and even high normal blood sugar levels; many medications, such as benzodiazepines (15, 16); the Standard American Diet (SAD), filled with processed foods, pesticides (17, 18), sugar, and artificial colors and sweeteners; unbalanced hormone levels; chronic stress (19, 20); negative thinking; even spending time with unhealthy people are all bad for the brain. Take a moment to think how many of these factors might be affecting you.

6. **Many things help the brain.** The exciting news is that many things are also good for your brain and can boost its function, such as learning new things; great nutrition; coordination exercises; meditation; loving relationships; and certain nutrients, including vitamins B6, B12, and D, methyltetrahydrofolate (MTHF), omega-3 fatty acids, and phosphatidylserine. In many ways, the best thing you can do for your brain is to spend time with healthy people. As we will see, they are contagious. I often say the fastest way to get healthy is to find the healthiest person you can stand and then spend as much time around him or her as possible. Chapters 19 and 20 give a detailed description of what you can do to enhance your brain.

7. **Certain systems in the brain tend to do specific things, and problems in these systems tend to cause symptoms that can benefit from targeted treatments.** Knowing about your brain can help you understand yourself and others. This is one of the main areas of focus for this book. You'll learn about the five major brain systems involved with feelings, thinking, and behavior, including the limbic or emotional

brain (mood and bonding), basal ganglia (motivation, pleasure, and anxiety), prefrontal cortex (the brain's CEO—focus, forethought, and judgment), anterior cingulate gyrus (detects errors and helps shift attention), and the temporal lobes (memory, learning, and mood stability). Specifically, we will look at the latest research about what each system does, what happens when things go wrong, and how to help them.

8. **Looking at the brain gives us the opportunity for many powerful insights not possible by just listening to symptoms alone.** After looking at more than one hundred thousand brain scans we know that if you don't look at how the brain functions in individual patients, you are really just guessing at what's wrong with them. Without imaging an individual's brain, physicians miss important causes of cognitive, emotional, or behavioral problems, such as brain injuries, toxic exposures, or infections. People end up misdiagnosed and mistreated.

   Adrianna, age sixteen, went on a mountain vacation with her family. When they arrived at their cabin they were surrounded by six deer. It was a beautiful moment. Ten days later Adrianna became agitated and started having auditory hallucinations. Her parents sought help for Adrianna, who was admitted to a psychiatric hospital and prescribed antipsychotic medications, which didn't help. The next three months were a torturous road of different doctors and multiple medications, at a cost of nearly $100,000. Adrianna had become a shadow of her former self. Desperate, her parents brought Adrianna in for a scan, which showed areas of unusually high activity. It caused us to look deeper at the potential causes of her symptoms, such as an infection or toxicity. It turned out Adrianna had Lyme disease, an infection, often caused by deer ticks. Treatment with antibiotics helped her get her life back.

   Imaging immediately decreases stigma as people begin to see their problems as medical and not moral. We have nothing else in psychiatry that is this powerful or immediate. Imaging increases treatment compliance, because people want a better brain so they can have a better life.

Steve

After I gave a lecture to a group called the National Alliance for the Mentally Ill (NAMI), one of the NAMI officers brought her son, who had paranoid schizophrenia and addiction issues, to one of our clinics. Steve had been living on the streets of San Francisco and could not live at home because of his violent, erratic behavior and his refusal to get treatment. During his clinical interview, our historian knocked on my door and told me she didn't feel comfortable seeing Steve alone; he scared her. As I introduced myself to Steve it was clear he was psychotic and was agitated being at the clinic. He told me in a loud voice that he would not take medication and I couldn't make him. To settle the tension, I asked if I could get him a cup of water.

As we talked, I told him I didn't want him to do anything he didn't want to do, but wondered if it would be okay to scan his brain. Seeing the brain SPECT scans on the walls of the clinic, he was curious and agreed to be scanned. After his scan we looked at it together. It showed high levels of damage. When I showed him a healthy scan (Image 1.3) compared to his scan (Image 1.4), he just stared at them without saying a word.

After about five minutes Steve looked at me, which was the first time we actually had eye contact, and he asked if I could help him. The scans helped him make the shift from being angry and in denial to being open to

Images 1.3 Healthy and 1.4: Steve's SPECT Scan

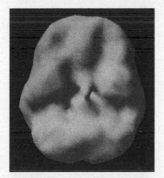 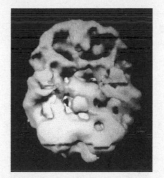

UNDERSIDE SURFACE OF
HEALTHY BRAIN
Full, even, symmetrical activity

STEVE
*Overall low blood flow
and activity*

working with me to get a better brain. This was a pivotal moment—one that the scans had given us with our patients thousands of times before. I told him we had better medications than the ones he had been on in the past and prescribed a low dose of a newer antipsychotic medication. I then gave him an appointment for three weeks later.

A week later I walked into my waiting room to get a new patient and saw Steve's mother sitting there and wondered to myself why she was at the clinic without an appointment. All of a sudden she stood up, grabbed me, and kissed me on the cheek.

"Thank you," I said, a little bewildered. "Why did you do that?"

"You can't believe how much better Steve is," she said. "He is not hallucinating, he's not aggressive, and we can have him at home. I am so grateful."

A few weeks later I saw Steve for his first follow-up visit. He was remorseful for his prior behavior and grateful he was feeling better. We did a follow-up scan, which was dramatically better. I put his original scan next to his new one and asked him, "Which brain do you want?"

He said, "I want the healthy one."

"Then you have to take your medication," I replied.

The scans made all the difference for Steve and those he loved. Imaging completely changes the discussion around mental health:

What If Mental Health Was Really Brain Health?

Images 1.5 and 1.6: Steve's SPECT Scans Before and After Treatment

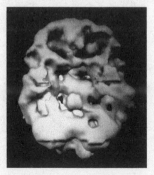
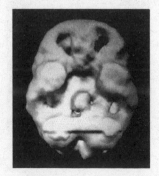

Overall low blood flow and activity   *Marked improvement*

With the pervasive stigma around mental health issues, few people want to see a psychiatrist, but almost everyone wants a better brain! Imaging helps to create brain envy. When people see their own brains, they usually want it to be better, like Steve, so they treat it better. Know better, do better.

9. **Psychiatric illnesses are not single or simple disorders in the brain. Each one has multiple types that require unique treatments. One treatment will never work for everyone.** Based on our imaging work, it is very clear that giving someone the diagnosis of depression is exactly like giving them a diagnosis of chest pain. No doctor would do that, because it doesn't tell you what is causing it or what to do for it. The same thing is true for psychiatric illnesses. Depression is a cluster of symptoms, not a disease. It has too many causes and each requires its own treatment. Rather than simply give you a diagnostic label based on symptoms, we need to understand why you are anxious or have attention problems or temper issues. Based on our imaging work, I've described seven types of anxiety and depression, seven types of ADD, six types of addicts and five types of overeaters.

10. **Brain aging is optional. Work to boost your brain's reserve.** On average, we lose about eighty-five thousand neurons a day. Little kids usually have very active brains and older people have significantly less brain activity. While our skin withers as we age, the same process typically happens in the brain. Image 1.7 is a graph of a study we performed on thirty thousand people, showing that with age the cortex or surface of the brain typically gets less and less active.

    Your day-to-day behavior is either accelerating this process or it is decelerating it. Brain aging is optional if you diligently use the right strategies. One of my favorite ways to explain this is through the lens of "brain reserve," which is the extra cushion of brain function you have to help you deal with whatever stresses come your way. The more reserve you have, the more resilient you are and the less impact aging has on your life.

    Image 1.8 is a graph on "brain reserve" that I often draw on the whiteboard in my office for my patients. At some point along the line in the graph, you cross a certain threshold, indicating that your reserve

Image 1.7: Brain Activity with Age

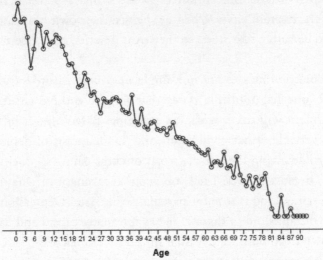

Cerebral flow to the brain's cortex throughout the life cycle

is gone and symptoms like depression, anxiety, memory problems, brain fog, or temper problems start to occur.

When you were conceived, your brain had a lot of potential for reserve, but if your mom smoked, ate bad food, was chronically stressed, or had

Image 1.8: Brain Reserve

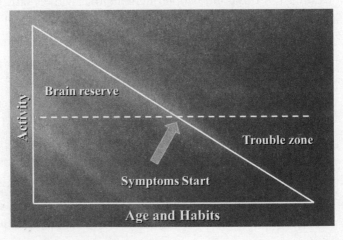

infections, your reserve was being depleted, even before you were born. If, on the other hand, your mother was healthy, ate well, took her vitamins, and was not terribly stressed, she was helping to increase your reserve. And, the rest of your life you are either increasing or decreasing your reserve. For example, if you fell down a flight of stairs at age three and hit your head, even though you had no symptoms you decreased your reserve. If you started smoking marijuana as a teenager you decreased your reserve further, then if you played tackle football or hit a lot of soccer balls with your head, there was even less reserve, even though you might not yet be symptomatic.

Think of it this way: Take two soldiers who are in a war; they're in the same tank and are both exposed to the same blast injury at the same angles. One of them walks away unharmed, the other one is permanently disabled. Why? See Image 1.9. It depends on the level of brain reserve that they had prior to the accident. One soldier had more reserve, because he took good care of his brain, his parents fed him well, he had lots of educational opportunities, and they didn't let him play football. The other soldier started lower on the line with less reserve. They're both effective at their jobs, but they started at different places and even though the blast diminished both of their reserves, the one with more reserve remained functional. Aging is the same way.

**Image 1.9: Why Some Walk Away from
Injuries Unharmed and Others Do Not**

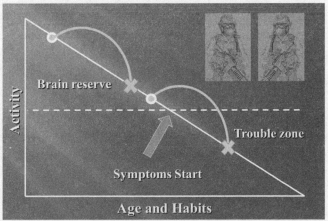

Most of the people we see at Amen Clinics start below the dotted line and are symptomatic. Getting well is not just about becoming symptom-free, it's also about boosting brain reserve and getting back above the line, which requires three simple strategies:

Brain envy (you have to really care about it)
Avoiding anything that hurts your brain
Engaging in regular brain-healthy habits

Every day you are either boosting or stealing your brain's reserve; you are either aging or rejuvenating your brain. When you truly understand this concept, you have a lot more influence in how fast your brain ages.

11. **You can change your brain and change your life.** You are not stuck with the brain you have; you can make it better, and we have proven this in scientific studies and in our clinical practice on thousands of patients. There are many smart ways to enhance, treat, and optimize the brain, including diet, exercise, supplements, medications, psychotherapy, new learning, transcranial magnetic stimulation, neurofeedback, and more. The rest of this book will give you the tools we use at Amen Clinics to help our patients change their brains and their lives. For now, here is one of my favorite stories.

    Holly worked as a chef; she was a very talented woman with a big heart. However, her boss noticed that she was moody, prone to tears, and overly sensitive when given feedback. Her sensitivity and moodiness caused stress in the workplace. Rather than terminate her employment, her boss paid for her to be scanned and evaluated at Amen Clinics. Her SPECT scan showed low overall activity, especially in her prefrontal, temporal, parietal, and occipital lobes (Image 1.10). The low activity was in a pattern commonly seen after multiple brain traumas. During her childhood she was physically and emotionally abused and was in a car accident as an adult. Based on her history and SPECT findings, Holly was put on a group of brain-supportive supplements, including a high-quality multiple vitamin, 5.6 grams of fish oil, and vinpocetine, gingko, and phosphatidylserine. After a month, Holly's employer noticed a marked improvement in her mood, focus, humor, and overall attitude. She became an indispensable employee. After three months, Holly also noticed the difference and was able to more quickly pay off her debts, because she was making better decisions. Holly's follow-up scan was also improved (Image 1.11). Underperformance at work can devastate a person's life and waste valuable resources. Virtually no employer ever thinks about their most valuable asset, the collective health of the brains of their employees. Thankfully, for Holly and her family, the brain was part of their everyday consciousness. You are not stuck with the brain you have; you can make it better.

1.10 and 1.11: Holly Before and After Treatment: Underside Surface View

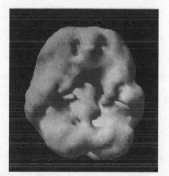 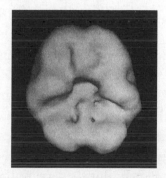

BEFORE TREATMENT   AFTER TREATMENT

12. **Get it. Give it away. Keep it forever. Change the world.** *Who* you spend time with matters. Both healthy and unhealthy habits are contagious. Research published in the *New England Journal of Medicine* found that one of the strongest associations of obesity was the people with whom you spent the most time. This multigenerational heart study looked at data from over twelve thousand subjects over a thirty-year period. Subjects who had a friend that was obese had a 57 percent chance of also being obese. If the two individuals identified each other as being strong friends the figure shot up to 171 percent. And this relationship held even if the subjects didn't live in the same area. Sibling relationships also proved important. Having

an obese sibling was related to a 40 percent increase in the chance of obesity (21).

Clearly, we influence each other, both for good and bad. Take this as a powerful motivator to be a good role model and a positive influence on the people you love. We know that when health-conscious friends improve their own health, their friends' health also improves. You can be the one who encourages others to do better by doing better yourself. And the more you help others, the more you will help yourself. I like to think of it this way: *Get it, give it away, keep it forever, change the world.*

Laurie Heiselman is a great example of this principle. She was the director of the Salvation Army's largest drug treatment program in Anaheim, California. She followed my work for many years and came to value brain health. The more she learned the more she realized she had to get her own health under control, and she took my wife's health class at the clinic. Laurie ended up losing fifty-five pounds and a litany of her own health challenges, such as rosacea and irritable bowel issues. As she got better, her husband started to engage in better health habits, as did her children and grandchildren. One of my favorite pictures is of Laurie drinking a green drink with her five-year-old grandson.

Laurie got healthy, and gave that health to her husband, children, and grandchildren. But then she realized that she interacted with hundreds of substance abusers and staff at the Salvation Army who also needed brain health, so she proceeded, despite opposition, to create a brain-healthy treatment program with the help of my wife, Tana, and myself that included classes on brain health and much of what you'll learn in this book. The results were truly spectacular. Many of the drug addicts showed improvement in their moods, mental clarity, and judgment. We saw fewer relapses and more overall success. Because Laurie became a brain warrior she not only felt better, she created brain health in her family and in those she served. Two of Laurie's favorite stories are William and Tomas.

William said, "As the days went by my mind began to clear, plus my focus, memory, and even speaking abilities were better. And I lost weight and now I have a six-pack, the kind that will not get me arrested."

1.12: Laurie sharing brain health with her 5-year-old grandson

Tomas said, "When I first came to the program I was depressed, hopeless, no future, overweight, gloomy, and foggy, all the negative things you can think of. I had failed my GED three times. Now, by putting these principles into my life my mind is clearer, faster, and energized and I have passed the GED." I love how he concluded his letter to us:

> *My life was a mess, now it is a message.*
> *I have been tested, now I have a testimony.*
> *I was a victim, now I am victorious.*
> *I went through trials, now I am triumphant.*

You can be triumphant too, by obtaining brain envy and putting these principles into your life. *This is how you can be the agent for change.* Reaching out to others so you can get brain healthy together can create a brain-healthy system. And there are many benefits to your brain health—your well-being, the way you look and feel, and the quality of your relationships. It's a win-win for everyone—*and it all starts with you.*

BUT IT'S NOT JUST ABOUT YOU . . .
IT'S ABOUT GENERATIONS OF YOU

A new field of genetics, called epigenetics, has grown up in the last twenty years. Epigenetic means "above or on top of the gene," and refers to the recent discovery that your habits and emotions can impact your biology so deeply that it causes changes in the genes that are transmitted to the next several generations. It is these epigenetic "marks" that tell your genes to switch on or off or to express themselves loudly or softly. It is through epigenetics that immediate environmental factors like diet, stress, toxins, and prenatal nutrition can affect the genes that are passed to your offspring and beyond.

It is not just about you, it is about generations of you. For instance, a 2006 study showed that boys who started smoking cigarettes before puberty (say, at age eleven or twelve) increased the risk of obesity in their children (22). This means that a dumb decision at age eleven can cause disastrous results for later generations. And obesity is just the beginning. Some researchers believe that epigenetics holds the key to understanding certain cancers (23–25), forms of dementia (26, 27), schizophrenia (28, 29), autism (30), obesity (31), and diabetes (32, 33). Clearly, your behavior matters beyond yourself and is an important reason to get healthy *now*.

I am not a big believer in baby steps. I think for you to get healthy and stay that way you need to make a serious commitment. My wife, Tana, who is my partner in helping people get well, says that to get really healthy people have to jump the canyon, which you cannot do in baby steps. It takes a leap to leave behind a toxic lifestyle.

SUMMARY OF THE 12 PRINCIPLES OF THE AMEN CLINICS
1. Your brain is involved in everything you do and everything you are.
2. When your brain works right, you work right, and when your brain is troubled you are much more likely to have trouble in your life.
3. Your brain is the most amazing, energy-hungry organ in the universe.
4. Your brain is the consistency of soft butter and housed in a really hard skull with multiple sharp bony ridges, making it easily injured.
5. Many things hurt the brain.
6. Many things help the brain.

7. Certain systems in the brain are designed to do certain things, and problems in these systems tend to cause specific symptoms that can benefit from specific treatments.
8. Looking at the brain gives many powerful insights not possible through listening to symptoms alone.
9. All psychiatric illnesses are not single or simple disorders in the brain. Each one has multiple types that require unique treatments. One treatment will never work for everyone.
10. Brain aging is optional. Work to boost your brain's reserve.
11. You can change your brain and change your life.
12. Get it. Give it away. Keep it forever. Change the world.

2

Stop Flying Blind,
Start Feeling Better

An Introduction to the Amen Clinics Method

The definition of insanity is doing the same thing over and over and expecting a different result.

(ATTRIBUTED TO ALBERT EINSTEIN)

Our largest referral network to Amen Clinics is our own patients and their families. People come from all over the world for our help because our method is very different from those of our colleagues. In this chapter I'll outline the step-by-step process we use, called the Amen Clinics Method, and help you apply it in your own life. Since 2010, we have studied the success rates of our new patients. As described below, we do a thorough evaluation, and then give each person a treatment plan targeted to his or her individual brain. Then we called them at six weeks, three months, and six months for follow up. At six months, we asked them to rate their progress (better, same, worse) and how compliant they were with our recommendations (very, somewhat, not at all).

The study made it crystal clear that, in general, we see people with complex issues who have failed **with** multiple health-care providers. On average, the first 2,500 patients had:

4.2 diagnoses (such as a combination of ADD, depression, anxiety, and addictions)
failed with 3.3 medical or mental health providers before coming to us, and tried 6 different medications.

After six months, 77 percent of our patients reported they were better. The number went up to 84 percent when accounting for the patients who allowed one of our doctors to do their follow-up treatment at Amen Clinics. Eighty-five percent reported an improved quality of life. Our study was published in the peer-reviewed medical journal *Advances in Mind-Body Medicine* (34). In a 2014 Canadian study, non-Amen Clinics clinicians and researchers using our method found that psychiatric patients who underwent SPECT-guided treatment improved significantly more than patients who did not (35).

Image 2.1: The Amen Clinics Method

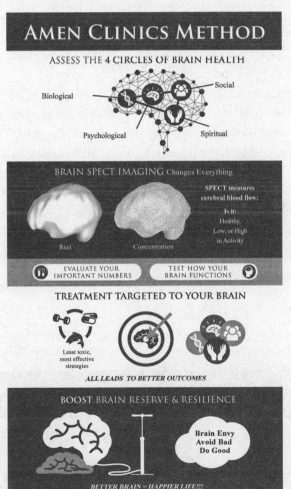

THE AMEN CLINICS METHOD IN 7 EASY STEPS

Step One: Know the 4 Circles

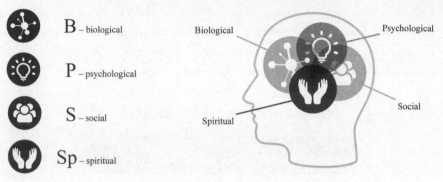

Even though we are known for our brain SPECT-imaging work, the fact is that we gather detailed clinical information on all of our patients, assessing the "four circles" of brain health: biological, psychological, social, and spiritual. People don't get sick or better in isolation. Understanding the four circles helps us understand each person from a whole person perspective. It also gives us important directions for treatment and brain optimization, which also occur in these four circles. A detailed explanation of each circle will be discussed in chapter 3. Throughout the book I will use the above symbols to describe each of the four circles.

Step Two: Know Your Brain

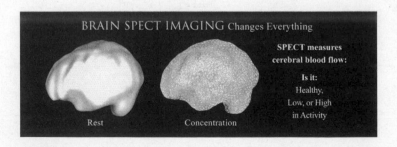

We gather information on how your brain physically functions through our work with brain SPECT imaging and possibly other tests, such as quantitative EEG (qEEG). This has been one of the biggest breakthroughs of our work. Without looking at how your brain functions, professionals are really just guessing, and even though they're educated guesses, it is often not good enough for people who are suffering with treatment-resistant ADD, depression, panic disorder, temper problems, obsessions, compulsions, or addictions.

We generally do two SPECT studies on patients, including one performed while doing a concentration task and one at rest. We have found doing both studies is very helpful, just like doing a stress test of the heart. Some issues show up better when you push the brain to work, some show up better at rest.

For those who cannot get scanned, we also use the Amen Clinics Brain Health Assessment to help predict what the SPECT study might look like. You can take it online at www.amenclinics.com. The assessment is not as accurate as a scan, but it can be very useful in helping to target treatment and is used by medical and mental health professionals around the world. You can learn more about our work with imaging in chapter 4.

Step Three: Test Your Brain

At Amen Clinics, step three involves assessing the function of our patients' brains using a sophisticated computerized neuropsychological test, called WebNeuro, that takes about thirty-five minutes to complete. The test also gives us an overall brain health score, and provides us with an objective measure of how your brain works, especially in the areas of:

- motor coordination,
- processing speed,
- sustained and controlled attention,
- flexibility,
- inhibition (self-control),
- memory, and
- executive function (judgment).

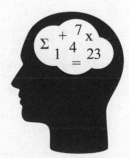

In addition, the test measures:

- stress,
- anxiety,
- mood, and
- your ability to read emotions.

Scores are also obtained on:

- emotional resilience,
- social capacity, and
- one's tendency to be positive or negative.

Example of WebNeuro Results

Overall Brain Health Score 4.4

Thinking 4.9

CAPACITY	SCALE	SCORE
Motor Coordination	expected range	7
Processing Speed	above	7.5
Sustained Attention	expected range	4.5
Controlled Attention	expected range	4.5
Flexibility	below	3
Inhibition	expected range	4
Working Memory	below	3
Recall Memory	expected range	6
Executive Function	expected range	5

Emotion 3.5

CAPACITY	SCALE	SCORE
Identifying Emotions	expected range	4.5
Emotion Bias	below	2.5

Feeling 4.3

CAPACITY	SCALE	SCORE
Stress Level	expected range	4
Anxiety Level	expected range	4
Depressed Mood Level	expected range	5

Self Regulation 4.7

CAPACITY	SCALE	SCORE
Positivity-Negativity Bias	expected range	5
Resilience	expected range	6.5
Social Capacity	below	2.5

I really like this test because it lets us know where each person is starting from. I often repeat this test on patients after to two to six months to see if we are making the progress we want. You can take this test in our brain warrior community, Brain Fit Life (www. mybrainfitlife .com). I recommend people take it as they start reading the book and then again every few months to see their progress.

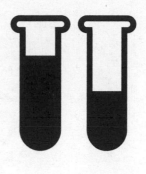

Step Four: Know Your Important Numbers

It is essential to know your important health numbers, such as body mass index, height-to-waist ratio, vitamin D, testosterone, and thyroid levels. If your important numbers are not optimal, your brain won't be either. We'll talk about how you can improve your numbers in chapter 5.

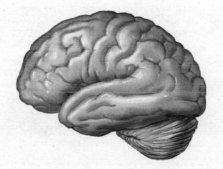

Step Five: Know the Brain Systems That Run Your Life

This is another innovation of our work. If you know which brain system or systems might be working too hard or not hard enough, then we can target treatment specifically to what your brain needs. I'll discuss five brain systems (limbic, basal ganglia, prefrontal cortex, anterior cingulate gyrus, temporal lobes), what they do, what happens when things go wrong, and how to balance them in chapters 6 through 15. Using this information on brain systems, chapter 16 will discuss the seven types of ADD, seven types of anxiety and depression, six types of addictions, and five types of overeaters.

Step Six: A Personalized Program
Targeted to Your Brain

TREATMENT TARGETED TO YOUR BRAIN

Least toxic,
most effective
strategies

ALL LEADS TO BETTER OUTCOMES

Taken together, all of this information leads to a targeted four-circles understanding of the problems and now a four-circles plan to optimize your brain and your life, as will be discussed throughout the book.

Step Seven: Boost Brain Reserve

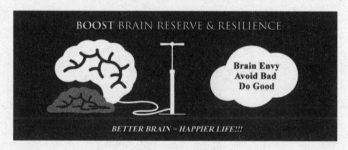

Step seven addresses how you can boost brain reserve, increase your resilience, reverse illness, and significantly decrease your risk of Alzheimer's by becoming a brain warrior for life. We'll cover this in detail in chapters 19 and 20.

You CAN WATCH an animation of the Amen Clinics Method here: http://www.amenclinics.com/the-science/see-the-process/.

3

Assess and Optimize the
4 Circles of Your Life

When I was a first-year medical student at Oral Roberts University in Tulsa, Oklahoma, our dean, Dr. Sid Garrett, gave one of our first lectures. That lecture, on how to help people of any age for any problem, has stayed with me for the last thirty-seven years. Dr. Garrett told us, "Always think of people as whole beings, never just as their symptoms." He insisted that whenever we evaluated and treated anyone, we should take into consideration the four circles of health and illness:

B—Biological: how your physical body functions (body)
P—Psychological: developmental issues and how you think (mind)
S—Social: social support and your current life situation (connections)
Sp—Spiritual: your sense of meaning and purpose (spirit)

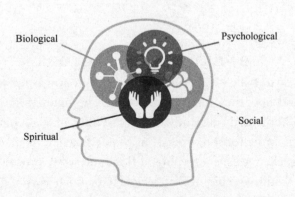

At the Amen Clinics we use these four circles to take a balanced, comprehensive approach to assessment and healing. These principles have impacted my own life and career, and once you understand them, they can help you heal in the most balanced way possible.

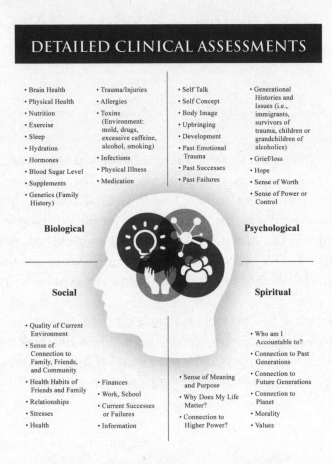

DETAILED CLINICAL ASSESSMENTS

Biological

- Brain Health
- Physical Health
- Nutrition
- Exercise
- Sleep
- Hydration
- Hormones
- Blood Sugar Level
- Supplements
- Genetics (Family History)

- Trauma/Injuries
- Allergies
- Toxins (Environment: mold, drugs, excessive caffeine, alcohol, smoking)
- Infections
- Physical Illness
- Medication

Psychological

- Self Talk
- Self Concept
- Body Image
- Upbringing
- Development
- Past Emotional Trauma
- Past Successes
- Past Failures

- Generational Histories and Issues (i.e., immigrants, survivors of trauma, children or grandchildren of alcoholics)
- Grief/loss
- Hope
- Sense of Worth
- Sense of Power or Control

Social

- Quality of Current Environment
- Sense of Connection to Family, Friends, and Community
- Health Habits of Friends and Family
- Relationships
- Stresses
- Health

- Finances
- Work, School
- Current Successes or Failures
- Information

Spiritual

- Sense of Meaning and Purpose
- Why Does My Life Matter?
- Connection to Higher Power?

- Who am I Accountable to?
- Connection to Past Generations
- Connection to Future Generations
- Connection to Planet
- Morality
- Values

B—BIOLOGICAL FACTORS

The first circle to evaluate is your biology: the physical aspects of your brain and body and how they function together. The brain is like a supercomputer, with both hardware and software. Think of your biology as your hardware—in order for it to operate at peak efficiency, its machinery (cells, connections, chemicals, energy, blood flow, and waste processing) needs to work right. Within the biology circle are factors such as your genetics, over-

DETAILED CLINICAL ASSESSMENTS

Biological

- Brain Health
- Physical Health
- Nutrition
- Exercise
- Sleep
- Hydration
- Hormones
- Blood Sugar Level
- Supplements
- Genetics (Family History)
- Trauma/Injuries
- Allergies
- Toxins (Environment: mold, drugs, excessive caffeine, alcohol, smoking)
- Infections
- Physical Illness
- Medication

all physical health, nutrition, exercise, sleep, and hormones, as well as infections and environmental issues, such as exposure to toxins. When the brain's biology is healthy, all of these factors work together to maximize your success and sense of well-being. When trauma, toxins, illness, or infections affect your biology, you are more likely to suffer with various symptoms.

For example, when you don't get enough sleep, you have overall decreased blood flow to your brain, which disrupts thinking, memory, and concentration. Likewise, a brain injury hurts the machinery of the brain, causing you to struggle with depression, thinking and memory issues, and temper problems. When you eat a high-sugar or simple carbohydrate diet, your blood sugar often becomes unbalanced, causing you to feel sluggish and foggy-headed.

P—PSYCHOLOGICAL FACTORS

Psychological factors fall into the second circle. This includes how we think and talk to ourselves, the running dialogue that goes on in our minds, as well as our self-concept, body image, past traumas, overall upbringing, and significant developmental events. Being raised in a reasonably happy home,

DETAILED CLINICAL ASSESSMENTS

Psychological

- Self Talk
- Self Concept
- Body Image
- Upbringing
- Development
- Past Emotional Trauma
- Past Successes
- Past Failures
- Sense of Worth
- Sense of Power or Control
- Generational Histories and Issues (i.e., immigrants, survivors of trauma, children or grandchildren of alcoholics)
- Grief/loss
- Hope

getting positive messages growing up, and feeling confident with our abilities and comfortable in our bodies all contribute to good psychological health. When we struggle in any of these areas, we are less likely to be successful. If we perceive ourselves as unattractive as or somehow less able than our peers, trouble starts to brew. If our thinking patterns are excessively negative, harsh, or critical, that will have a negative impact on our moods, anxiety levels, and, ultimately, our ability to focus.

Developmental issues, such as being adopted, having been neglected or abused, or experiencing a significant loss or trauma as a child, are also significant. Children often believe that they are the center of the universe, so if something bad happens during childhood, such as a child's mother dying of cancer, the child may think it is his fault and spend the rest of his life racked with guilt. Past successes and failures are a part of this circle, as are hope and a sense of worth and personal power or control.

S—THE SOCIAL CIRCLE

The social circle is next. It includes the quality of one's relationships and any current life stressors. When we have great relationships, good health, a

DETAILED CLINICAL ASSESSMENTS

Social

- Quality of Current Environment
- Sense of Connection to Family, Friends, and Community
- Work, School
- Relationships
- Stresses
- Health
- Finances
- Current Successes or Failures
- Information
- Health Habits of Friends and Family

job or endeavor we love, and enough money, our brains tend to do much better than when any of these areas are troubled. Dealing with difficult life circumstances elevates stress hormones and makes us more vulnerable to illness. Depression is often triggered by stressful life events, such as school failure, marital problems, family dysfunction, financial difficulties, health problems, work-related struggles, or losses. And as we've touched upon, the health habits of the people with whom you spend time have a dramatic impact on your own health and habits.

SP—THE SPIRITUAL CIRCLE

Beyond the biological, psychological, and social aspects of our lives, we are also spiritual beings. To fully heal and be our best, it is important to recognize that we are more than just our bodies, minds, brains, and social connections. We must ask ourselves deep questions, such as:

What does my life mean?
What is my purpose?
Why am I here?
What are my values?

DETAILED CLINICAL ASSESSMENTS

Spiritual

- Sense of Meaning and Purpose
- Why Does My Life Matter?
- Values
- Morality
- Who am I Accountable to?
- Connection to Past Generations

- Connection to Future Generations
- Connection to Planet
- Connection to Higher Power?

Do I believe in God or a Higher Power?

How does that manifest in my life?

What is my connection to past generations, future generations, and the planet?

Having a sense of purpose, as well as connections to past and future generations, allows us to reach beyond ourselves to affirm that our lives matter. Without a spiritual connection, many people experience an underlying sense of despair or meaninglessness. Morality, values, and a spiritual connection to others and the universe are critical for many people to feel a sense of wholeness and connection. Research from multiple sources reports that having a sense of meaning and purpose helps you be healthier and live longer (36–38).

AMEN CLINICS 4-CIRCLES TREATMENT: BIOLOGICAL, PSYCHOLOGICAL, SOCIAL, AND SPIRITUAL

Our treatment plans are directed toward optimizing the four circles. For example:

B—Biological interventions may include diet, exercise, supplements, medication, neurofeedback, transcranial magnetic stimulation, sleep apnea evaluations and treatment, hyperbaric oxygen, and others.

P—Psychological strategies may include different forms of psychotherapy, including cognitive therapy, or not believing every stupid thought you have, hypnosis, meditation, interpersonal psychotherapy, and dealing with past traumas or other emotional issues.

S—Social interventions may include appropriate school or work accommodations, relationship counseling, parenting classes, and social skills training.

Sp—Spiritual interventions include an in-depth conversation on what your life means, why you are here, and major life goals. In addition, it may also include discovering connections to past and future generations and the planet.

4

How Imaging Changes Everything

Stories from the Revolution (From Miracles and Meat Cleavers to Flashers, Tooth Fairies, and Trains)

Y ou can understand the four circles of your life and still completely miss getting the right help. It is also important to understand how your brain functions. At Amen Clinics, we have three ways to evaluate brain function:

1. Brain imaging—either with SPECT or another tool such as quantitative EEG (qEEG)

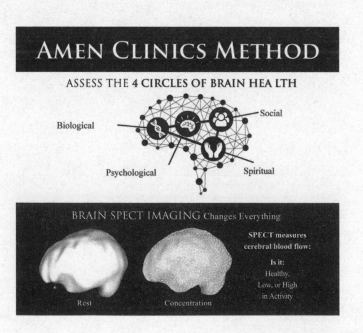

AMEN CLINICS METHOD

ASSESS THE **4 CIRCLES OF BRAIN HEA LTH**

Biological — Social

Psychological — Spiritual

BRAIN SPECT IMAGING Changes Everything

SPECT measures cerebral blood flow:

Is it:
Healthy,
Low, or High
in Activity

Rest — Concentration

2. Amen Clinics Brain Health Assessment
3. Neuropsychological assessments

As mentioned, we do a study called brain SPECT imaging, which evaluates blood flow and activity patterns. SPECT gives a direct look at how the brain works. In a scientific study we recently published, getting a SPECT scan changed the diagnosis or treatment plan in nearly eight out of ten patients (39). Having a scan allows us to see what is happening in the brain that may be the cause of someone's emotional and cognitive struggles, such as when the brain works too hard or not hard enough, or if it has patterns consistent with trauma or toxic exposure.

> *Without a scan or another measure of brain function,*
> *it is like throwing medication-tipped darts in the*
> *dark at someone's brain.*

Despite the intense criticism I received from colleagues early on for doing something outside the box of psychiatry's standard of care, I persisted in ordering SPECT scans because of the amazing outcomes this technology allowed me to witness. In this chapter I will share some of my favorite stories and ten lessons they taught me.

1. **Daniel: Seeing my own brain created brain envy. I had to have a better brain.**
   Most people never think about their brains because they never look at them. We worry about the wrinkles in our skin, because we can see them. Or maybe you fret about your waistline because you hate how it looks in the mirror. Our eyes give us feedback when we aren't looking optimal. Your brain, on the other hand, only gives you indirect clues that something is not right—perhaps your mood is off, you can't sleep, or you start forgetting words that used to roll off your tongue.
   I never really cared much about my own brain until I started looking at the brain. I had no problem doing jumps on my bicycle when I was ten and falling on my head. That's what tough boys did; you just got up. I played tackle football, using my helmet as a spear. The helmet

made me feel invincible. I never gave a thought to the first bout of viral meningitis (a brain infection) I had at age eighteen when I was in basic training in the army or to the second bout during my medical internship ten years later. I didn't see any problem with drinking a half gallon of soda a day, carrying extra weight, or being constantly stressed in medical school and beyond, surviving on four hours of sleep a night. I was tough! Even as I progressed through my psychiatric training, military work, and starting a private practice, I never really thought about my own brain. If a physician who specializes in diseases of the brain doesn't really think about his brain, why would you?

It all changed in the spring of 1991 when I started working with SPECT. Over the course of a few months I ordered many SPECT scans on my patients and found them extremely useful. They were so valuable that I started scanning people in my own family: my aunt who had a panic disorder, a cousin who was suicidal and depressed, my mother, my children, and then myself. Like many men, I had the belief that I was 100 percent normal, maybe even a little better than normal. Despite my history of playing football and meningitis, I expected to see a very healthy brain. After all, I had never done drugs, didn't smoke, and rarely drank alcohol. Yet, my brain did not look healthy. In fact, it looked like the brain of an older man. "Yuck," I thought. "I need to do better."

That same week I scanned my sixty-year-old mother, Dorie, who had an unbelievably beautiful brain. In fact, she became our "poster" example of a healthy brain. Her brain was full, even, and symmetrical, and showed healthy activity throughout. Her beautiful brain function was reflected in the myriad healthy activities and relationships she had. My mom has always been the best friend to her seven kids, twenty-two grandkids, and now twenty-two great-grandkids. I had brain envy. I wanted my brain to be like hers.

Since then, I have thought about ways to optimize my brain and the brains of my patients, readers, family, and friends. Working to improve my own brain function eventually led me to have a better body. With better function in the front part of my brain that houses judgment and impulse control, my decisions were better, as were my forward-thinking skills. As you'll see, a scan I had twenty-two years after that first one was much better too.

Brain envy made my life better and I want the same for you.

Here are my own current four-circles interventions: **B**—great nutrition, exercise, sleep, and supplements; **P**—work hard to not believe every stupid thought I have and get therapy when I need it; **S**—have a supportive spouse and staff at Amen Clinics; **Sp**—focus on a deep sense of purpose for my family and work.

Image 4.1: My Mother's Beautiful SPECT Scan at 60

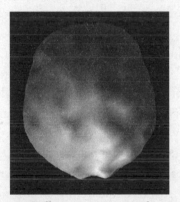

*Full, even, symmetrical,
healthy appearance*

Image 4.2: Daniel Before   **Image 4.3: Daniel 20 Years Later**

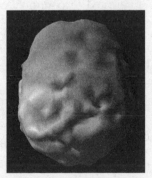 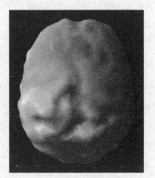

Bumpy, toxic appearance   *Much healthier*

It is clear that our society is going the wrong way
in terms of brain health.

Most people just don't care about their brains. We let our kids play football, hit soccer balls with their heads, and do dangerous gymnastic routines. There is little brain envy, because most people never look at or think about their brains. Since most people never get their brains scanned or tested they have no idea when the trouble starts.

When our patients see their own brain scans, they often develop brain envy and want their brain to be better. I once treated a sixteen-year-old boy who frequently abused drugs, including cocaine. But when he saw what the cocaine was doing to his brain, he immediately stopped! When I told him that his brain would not finish developing until he was twenty-five and that his drug abuse might permanently delay his development, he said, "Oh, I don't want that!" and just stopped using. That was a sign of intelligent life.

2. **Sally: Self-Forgiveness, "You Mean, It's Not All My Fault?"**
   Sally, a forty-year-old woman, had been hospitalized under my care for depression, anxiety, and suicidal ideas. In my clinical interview with her, I discovered that she had many adult ADD symptoms (such as short attention span, distractibility, disorganization, and restlessness). She had an ADD son (a frequent tip to diagnosing ADD in adults); had never finished college, despite having an IQ of 140; and she was employed below her ability. When I talked to her about the possibility of having ADD, she didn't think the diagnosis applied to her, because she could concentrate if she was really interested (a common misconception among people with ADD). She was resistant to treatment. Since just that morning I had heard my first lecture on SPECT, I asked Sally if we could look at her brain. She enthusiastically said yes, and was interested in getting more information to understand herself. We scanned Sally at rest and then again the next day while she performed a concentration task. Her results were abnormal. At rest, she had good overall brain activity, especially in the prefrontal cortex, but when she tried to focus her brain actually *dropped* in activity, especially in the prefrontal cortex.

When I laid the pictures on the table in her hospital room and explained them to her she started to cry and said, "You mean, it's not all my fault?" This is something I've heard a lot over the years.

"Right," I said, taking the glasses I wear when I drive out of my pocket and said, "Having ADD is just like needing glasses. People who wear glasses aren't dumb, crazy, or stupid. Our eyeballs are shaped funny and we wear glasses to focus. Likewise, people who have ADD aren't dumb, crazy, or stupid. Their frontal lobes shut down when they're supposed to turn on. And they need help to turn them back on so they can focus. In fact, as you can see, the harder you try, the worse it gets."

This discovery helped Sally make sense of her life and she had a wonderful response to the four-circles treatment plan: **B**—great nutrition, exercise, sleep, medication; **P**—psychotherapy to deal with disappointments from the past; **S**—couples therapy and parent training; **Sp**—focus on a deep sense of purpose for her life. In a short time, Sally felt calmer and more focused. She went back to school and finished her degree. Her relationship with her husband and son were better and she no longer thought of herself as a failure, but rather as someone who needed help for a medical problem. When you understand ADD this way, you realize that not treating it really amounts to neglect. It's like withholding glasses from someone who cannot see.

Images 4.4 and 4.5: Sally's SPECT Studies (Underside Surface Views)

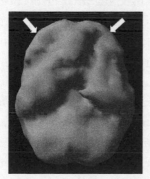 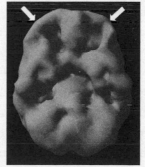

AT REST
Good prefrontal activity
(arrows)

DURING CONCENTRATION
Drop-off of prefrontal activity
(arrows)

With Sally's positive response to treatment fresh in my mind I ordered more SPECT studies on my most treatment-resistant patients.

3. **Kate: Be Very Careful with Psychiatric Medications**
Kate, a minister's wife, went to her family doctor and told him she was stressed and depressed and couldn't sleep. After a seven-minute appointment, she left his office with three prescriptions: a selective serotonin reuptake inhibitor (SSRI—fluoxetine/Prozac) for depression, a benzodiazepine (alprazolam/Xanax) for her anxiety, and a sleeping pill (zolpidem/Ambien), all prescriptions that suppress overall brain activity. Within three days Kate started to feel better. After a week she was feeling really great.

Then, while stopped at a traffic light, a man in a truck pulled up beside her. He winked at her, which was not unusual as Kate was an attractive woman. But what happened next was very unusual. Kate proceeded to unbutton her blouse and showed the man her breasts. Horrified at her own behavior she sped off, and of course he tried to follow her. She stopped taking the medicines and came to see us. As part of her evaluation, we scanned Kate after she had been off those medications for several weeks. Her scan showed low overall activity, especially in the front part of her brain. The three medications she was given had all decreased her brain activity further, thereby disinhibiting her judgment, leading to the incident with the unbuttoned blouse.

Without looking there is no way to know if a person needs more brain stimulation or less. Symptoms don't always equate to underlying function. Kate's brain needed more activity. Learning this information helped Kate understand her disturbing behavior and she got much better with a targeted plan: B—great nutrition; exercise; stimulating supplements, including rhodiola, ginseng, and green tea to support her mood; and melatonin and magnesium for sleep; P—psychotherapy to learn how to deal with the stress of being a pastor's wife; S—reconnecting with her husband; Sp—prayers for understanding and forgiveness about her past behavior and reconnecting with her sense of mission.

When I first started performing SPECT scans, I was often concerned by the visible effects some psychiatric medications had on the brain, particularly benzodiazepines, sleeping medications, and pain pills like hydrocodone and oxycodone. They suppressed brain function in many patients—it was evident on their scans. This evidence was one of the main reasons I started to research natural ways to heal the brain. Recently, there has been a group of published articles that substantiate my observations about these medications, especially benzodiazepines, which increase the risk of Alzheimer's disease and other types of dementia (40–42), which are all conditions known to be associated with low blood flow to the brain.

Aside from increasing the risk of dementia, a significant issue illustrated by Kate's story is that giving someone the wrong or unnecessary medication can cause negative behaviors that put that person in a dangerous situation—costing them relationships, financial security, or even their lives. When I first started our imaging work there was great controversy around research studies that suggested certain medications increased the risk of violence and suicide. Having been in clinical practice for over a decade at the time, I had exactly the same concern, and scans like Kate's were helping me understand why and who would respond to which medications and diminished the risk of prescribing the wrong ones.

4. **Willie: A Short Fuse on a Stick of Dynamite: When Someone's Personality Changes, Think About the Brain**
Willie was the kind of guy who got along with everyone. An A student, he had a college scholarship waiting for him, and his future seemed altogether promising—until his head collided with the dashboard of his car during an accident. Although Willie felt dazed, he seemed to be okay by the next day. Three months later he got into another accident when he swerved to avoid hitting a dog that had run out into the street. His head hit the windshield even harder, and this time he had to be sent to an emergency room. After examining Willie, the doctor told him he had nothing to worry about; he had only a "minor concussion." In the months that followed, this "minor concussion" wreaked havoc on Willie's life. His whole attitude and demeanor began to change. Normally a friendly person, he found himself suddenly losing his tem-

per at the smallest things. Where he had once been patient, he now had a short fuse. Where he had once been amiable and calm, he was now always angry. His irritability and constant flares of temper began to alienate his friends and family.

The brunt of his anger came to rest on his college roommate and, strangely, began to center around food. Inexplicably, Willie's appetite had also changed. In just three months, he had put on seventy pounds, and he was hungry all the time, often eating all the food in his home. By this time he was at college and living with a roommate, who finally got fed up and asked Willie to eat only the food he bought himself. Willie felt that his roommate was actually trying to hurt him by depriving him of the food he thought he needed. He became consumed with negative, paranoid thoughts, and in his mind, the only way to protect himself was to "hurt this enemy."

One afternoon, Willie took a huge meat cleaver and a butcher knife and waited at the front door for his roommate, a man who used to be his friend. "He was going to be instantaneously dissolved," Willie told me later.

Yet even as he was gripped by paranoia, some part of Willie's mind was still sane. He saw himself, as if from above, standing behind the door holding these weapons. He knew he was out of control and that he had to stop himself before it was too late. He went to the telephone and called a friend, who then gave him my telephone number, and the immediate crisis was averted.

Willie described for me his two accidents and the severity of his personality changes. I immediately ordered a brain SPECT study, which showed three abnormalities: his anterior cingulate gyrus was working too hard, so he tended to get stuck on negative thoughts; his left temporal lobe was low in activity, which is often associated with paranoia and violent thoughts; and his prefrontal cortex was low, meaning he had trouble controlling the violent thoughts he got stuck on. The minute I saw Willie's brain study, it clearly explained for me the changes that had been occurring in his personality: paranoia, fiery temper, and persistent uncontrollable negative thoughts about his roommate.

Images 4.6 and 4.7: Willie's Brain, Affected by Head Trauma

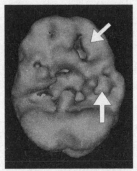 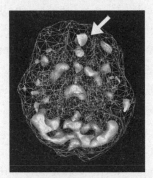

Damage to left PFC
(top arrow) temporal lobe
(bottom arrow)

Increased anterior
cingulate gyrus
(arrow)

The next step was clear. I knew I had to balance Willie's brain to help him get back control of his life. Here was Willie's four-circles plan: **B**—I prescribed an antiseizure medication for the temporal lobe abnormality and an antiobsessive antidepressant to help him get "unstuck" from negative thoughts. I taught him about nutrition to get his cravings under control (eat protein at each meal to balance his blood sugar and decrease high-glycemic foods), and we also worked on his sleep and exercise; **P**—psychotherapy to give him a reality check and help him come to grips with his violent thoughts; **S**—communicate with his girlfriend to make sure he had the support he needed; **Sp**—talk with Willie about living his sense of purpose.

After several weeks of treatment, the results were dramatic. Willie began to regain his sense of humor and reconnect with his friends and family. Once his brain was properly balanced, he reclaimed his sweet disposition and returned to being one of the nicest human beings you will ever meet.

5. **Brian and the Tooth Fairy: Sometimes Thoughts Really Can Get Stuck in Your Head**

Brian, age six, was very excited the day he lost his first tooth. That night, the tooth was secure under his pillow in a special pouch for the tooth fairy. The next morning, Brian was ecstatic when he found a dollar in the pouch. All day long he thought and thought and thought about the tooth fairy. In fact, he was so happy that he secretly pulled out another tooth after school. His mother, who was surprised by the second tooth, went through the tooth fairy ritual again. Two days later, Brian tried to pull out a third tooth. His mother, who saw him tugging at a tooth she knew wasn't loose, started to worry. She told him that the tooth fairy doesn't come if you pull out your own teeth and not to do it anymore, but Brian knew better. Over the next month, Brian couldn't get the thought of the tooth fairy out of his head and he pulled out three more teeth. His mother then brought him to me for an evaluation.

In Brian's family there was a history of alcohol abuse, depression, and obsessive-compulsive disorder. We discovered that behavioral interventions were not successful in keeping Brian's hands out of his mouth. Additionally, Brian was oppositional and had trouble at school. The teacher said he "always got stuck on certain thoughts" and could not pay attention to his classwork. After several months, individual therapy was not progressing. I ordered a brain SPECT study to better understand the functional pattern of Brian's brain. His study revealed marked increased activity in his frontal lobes. When this part of the

Image 4.8: Brian's Brain

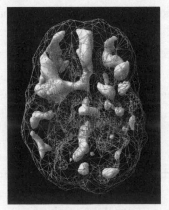

Note markedly overactive
frontal lobes.

brain is overactive, people may end up getting "stuck" on certain thoughts and behaviors.

Brian's four-circles plan: **B**—Given the intense level of overactivity of his frontal lobes, I put Brian on a low dose of a medicine to increase serotonin and calm this part of the brain. Today, I would have started with a more natural treatment to do the same thing, by using 5-HTP or St. John's wort; **P**—psychotherapy to teach Brian self-soothing strategies when he felt out of control; **S**—working with his parents to make sure Brian had the support he needed; **Sp**—talking to Brian about what his special purpose in life might be.

6. **Margaret: Differentiate Between Two Problems with Similar Symptoms**
I first met Margaret when she was sixty-eight years old. Her appearance was ragged and unkempt. She lived alone, and her family was worried because she appeared to have symptoms of serious dementia. They had finally admitted her to the psychiatric hospital where I worked after she nearly burned the house down by leaving a stove burner on. When I consulted with the family, I also found out that Margaret often forgot the names of her own children and frequently got lost when driving her car. Her driving habits had deteriorated to the point where the Department of Motor Vehicles had to take away her license after four minor accidents in a six-month period. By the time I came into the picture, some of Margaret's family had had enough and were ready to put her into a supervised living situation. Other family members, however, were against the idea and wanted her hospitalized for further evaluation.

While at first glance it may have appeared that Margaret was indeed suffering from Alzheimer's disease, the results of her SPECT study showed full activity in her parietal and temporal lobes. If she had Alzheimer's, there should have been evidence of decreased blood flow in those areas. Instead, the only abnormal activity shown on Margaret's SPECT was increased activity in her limbic system at the center of the brain. Often, this is a finding in people suffering from depression. Sometimes in the elderly it's difficult to distinguish between Alzheimer's disease and depression because the symptoms can be similar. However, with *pseudodementia* (depression or another condition masquerading as dementia), a person may appear demented yet not be at all. This is a critical distinction, because a diagnosis, prognosis, and treatment of Alzheimer's disease is different from depression in many important ways. The results of Margaret's SPECT study convinced me to aggressively treat her for depression. Her four circles plan included: **B**—the stimulating antidepressant bupropion (Wellbutrin); **P**—psychotherapy, which centered around the loss of her husband; **S**—working with her family to be patient with the treatment process and give her the support she needed; **Sp**—talking with Margaret about her most important contributions in her life and her spiritual beliefs, which were very important to her. After three weeks, she was talkative, well groomed, and eager to socialize with the other patients. After a month in the hospital she was released to go home. Before discharge she asked if I would write a letter to the DMV to help her get her driver's license back. Since I drove on the same highways she did, I was a bit hesitant, and told her that if in six months she remained improved and remained compliant with treatment, I would write to the DMV for her. Six months later she was still doing great, and I repeated her SPECT study. It was completely normal. I wrote the letter to the DMV, and she eventually got her license back!

7. Michelle: PMS Is Real and Can Wreak Havoc in the Lives of Women and Couples

On three separate occasions, Michelle, a thirty-five-year-old nurse, left her husband within the week before the onset of her menstrual period. On the third occasion, her irritability, anger, and irrational behavior escalated to the point where she attacked him with a knife over a minor disagreement before she left. The next morning, her husband called my office. When I first met Michelle, it was several days after her menstrual period had started and things had significantly settled down, as her severe temper outbursts were usually over by the third day after her period started. In my office, she appeared to be a gentle, soft-spoken, contrite woman. It was hard for me to imagine that only days before this woman had gone after her husband with a carving knife. Because her actions were so serious, I decided to perform two SPECT studies on her. We did the first one four days before the onset of her next period—during the roughest time in her cycle—and the second one eleven days later—during the best time of her cycle.

The SPECT study done right before the onset of her period showed increased activity in the limbic system, the brain's emotional center, and in the anterior cingulate gyrus, which I think of as the brain's gear shifter. This combination caused her to feel negative and have trouble letting go of negative thoughts. Michelle also had low activity in her temporal lobes, which is associated with mood instability and misperceiving new information, as well as low activity in her prefrontal cortex, which is the part of your brain that helps you control your impulses. There was a dramatic change on the SPECT scan done eleven days later, where her brain looked much more normal.

Contrary to the beliefs of some naysayers, PMS, or premenstrual syndrome, is real. Women with PMS are *not* imagining things; the chemistry of their brain has been hijacked and produces reactions that are hard to manage. The limbic system has a higher density of estrogen receptors than other parts of the brain, making it more vulnerable, in some women, to the estrogen changes that occur at puberty, before the onset of menses, after a baby is born, or during menopause. Sometimes these changes can produce dramatic effects. For women like Michelle, PMS can be debilitating or even dangerous.

Michelle's four-circles plan included: **B**—At the time (1991), I used medication to help balance Michelle's brain. Today I would prescribe progesterone cream to use during the last week or two of her cycle, in addition to a combination of supplements to balance the brain, especially calcium, magnesium, and vitamin B6. I encouraged Michelle to exercise and decrease her intake of sugar and alcohol. **P**—Psychotherapy was essential for Michelle to help give her more self-regulation skills; **S**—I worked with the couple to improve understanding and communication; **Sp**—We explored Michelle's deepest sense of meaning and purpose, which centered around holding her family together for herself, her husband, and her children. The treatment evened out her moods and she felt closer to her husband.

4.9 and 4.10: Michelle's PMS-Affected Brain (Before and After)

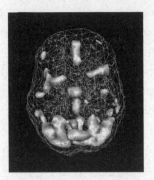 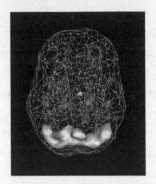

DURING WORST TIME
OF CYCLE
*Increased limbic and
cingulate activity*

DURING BEST TIME
OF CYCLE
Calmer overall activity

8. Bob and Betsy: When Your Marriage Is in Trouble, Think About the Brain

I was a psychiatrist for nearly a decade before I started looking at the brain. I loved being a psychiatrist, but I was often frustrated, because we had so little objectively useful information to help our patients. This was especially true of the difficult couples I saw in my practice. When I was faced with an angry couple, it was hard to know: if she was too rigid or he was just insensitive; if she overelaborated or he couldn't pay attention; if she was too sexually withholding or he was too demanding. The whole process seemed too soft, too arbitrary, and I had to rely on what the couples told me and my own clinical intuition, rather than on any hard biological information. When I decided to scan my first couple I discovered something that would forever change the way I look at relationships.

Bob and Betsy initially brought their son and daughter to see me for school-related problems. Their daughter struggled with concentration, while her brother was hyperactive and oppositional. The girl got much better with treatment, but the boy did not. After a few sessions alone with their son it was clear to me why he wasn't getting better. His mom and dad hated each other and he was suffering from the chronic stress and turmoil at home. I often say that children are like violins—they play out the stress between their parents with their behavior. So I suggested that the couple see me for counseling. They told me that they had already seen four other therapists and it almost always made things worse. But, if they were hurting their children they would try again.

At the time I had two blue leather couches in my office. On their first visit they sat on the opposite ends of each couch. That is a bad sign in marital therapy, and it went downhill from there. After about three months, I started to dread seeing this couple. Betsy had a PhD in grudge holding. She would go on and on, and talk about the same things over and over. She seemed unable to let go of any hurts. She talked about things his mother had done to upset her fifteen years earlier. I once thought to myself that she would not only beat things to death, she would probably beat them into the afterlife.

Betsy was married to a man I called "the sniper." Bob rarely seemed to pay attention. But whenever Betsy would settle down and become more open to the therapeutic process he would say something so evil, so awful, so nasty—seemingly just to get her going again.

After six months, I started to have physical stress symptoms whenever I would see them on my schedule. My stomach would hurt and I would start to get a headache. One day, after nine months of seeing them, I was in the shower getting ready for work and I realized that they were on my schedule. My stomach started to hurt. "Oh no!" I thought, "THESE PEOPLE ARE IN MY SHOWER. Today I am going to tell them to get divorced." I had actually had that thought for several months. Research shows that it is better for children to be from divorced families than to live with chronic conflict (43). My problem with the thought about divorce, however, was that I grew up very Catholic. Not just a little Catholic, a lot Catholic! I often joke that I was going to be a priest until I realized I was going to be called Father Amen and I just thought no one would believe it.

Now, only the Catholics who are reading this will understand what happened next. After I had the thought "Today I am going to tell them to get divorced," the Catholic voice inside my head yelled at me, "WHAT?! BECAUSE YOU ARE NOT A GOOD ENOUGH THERAPIST, YOU ARE GOING TO TELL THESE PEOPLE TO

GET DIVORCED AND DAMN THEIR ETERNAL SOULS TO HELL?" I just stood there and stared at the showerhead, wondering, "How much therapy will it take for me to get over this?"

I got out of the shower, dried off, and went to the phone and called Dr. Paldi, the physician who owned the brain imaging center. It was 1991 and we had just started our work together. "Hey, Jack," I said, "will you give me two scans for the price of one?"

"Why?" he said,

"Jack, I have this couple that I have been seeing for nine months and I have no idea how to help them."

"Couple?" he said. "You want to scan a couple. How interesting! You know I have been married twice and I can't figure it out. Maybe we could even start a dating service and match people's brains."

When I brought up the idea of brain imaging to Bob and Betsy they were very interested. They knew our work together wasn't going in a positive direction, but they wanted to be better. The scans literally changed their lives.

Betsy's scan showed marked increased activity in the anterior cingulate gyrus, again the area involved in shifting attention. When it is overactive, people tend to get stuck on negative thoughts and to be rigid

Image 4.11: Betsy's Overfocused Brain

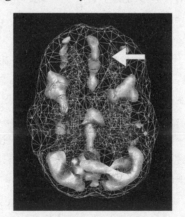

Increased anterior
cingulate gyrus

and argumentative and hold grudges. Just by random chance (if you believe in random chance), the night before Betsy's scan I read an article in the *American Journal of Psychiatry* that reported that fluoxetine (Prozac) calms down this part of the brain (44), so I put Betsy on it.

Bob's scan showed low activity in the front part of his brain when he tried to concentrate, a finding consistent with attention deficit disorder and conflict-seeking behavior, so I put Bob on treatment for ADD.

Image 4.12: Bob's ADD-Affected Brain

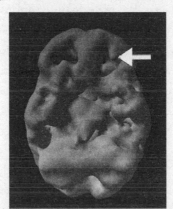

Low prefrontal cortex activity
with concentration

Then, I told the couple that I did not want to see them for a month. I wanted to give the medicines time to work, plus, my poor stomach needed a break.

When they came back a month later, they sat on the same couch for the first time. Betsy had her hand on Bob's leg—a good sign in marital therapy. Twenty-four years later they are still married and the children did much better after Bob and Betsy got effective treatment. I call this better marriage through biochemistry.

Here are some important points to remember from this story: chronic conflict may be a sign of underlying brain dysfunction; frequent fighting between parents can harm your children's brains; and, with proper diagnosis and treatment, there is hope to change your brain and dramatically improve your relationships.

The four-circles plan that eventually worked for Bob and Betsy included: **B**—medication targeted to their individual brains. Today I would have also given them the option of supplements. **P**—The psychological interventions were much more effective once their brains were balanced; **S**—couples work and parent training to help them be more effective with the children; **Sp**—We explored Bob's and Betsy's deepest sense of meaning and purpose for themselves and their children.

Since Bob and Betsy, we have scanned more than a thousand couples, many of whom were experiencing terrible relationship problems. In my experience, knowing the individual brain patterns of people who struggle in relationships can be very helpful. There will be more on this topic in chapter 17.

9. **Leslie: If You Knew a Train Was Going to Hit You, Would You Get Out of the Way?**
I start many of my lectures with a terrifying video of two women who became trapped on an eighty-foot-high railroad bridge with a freight train barreling toward them. Obviously, the train surprised them as they walked along the tracks. You can see the video here: https://www.youtube.com/watch?v=nAkKcZh6Q-4. Ultimately, the women survived by lying down flat in the middle of the tracks. I show this video because it reminds me of how blind most people are to the health of their brains. If you know brain health troubles are coming, would you get out of the way? Or, would you be like these two women, oblivious to the pitfalls of walking on a railway bridge with no escape?

Leslie got out of the way. At the age of forty-four, she started to notice she was a bit forgetful. Initially, she attributed it to a lack of sleep and stress at work. But after reading my book *Use Your Brain to Change Your Age*, she became concerned. Both her mother and grandmother had died with Alzheimer's disease, and she read that because of this she was genetically predisposed to it. When we scanned Leslie, she already had low activity in her temporal lobes, making her more vulnerable to the potential of Alzheimer's. Rather than let the findings paralyze her with fear, she developed brain envy and began to take her brain health extremely seriously and included each of the four-circles interventions: **B**—She started a brain healthy diet and lost thirty pounds, started taking ten thousand steps a day and lifting weights twice a week, improved her sleep, and took supportive supplements, including gingko, phosphatidylserine, vitamin D, and omega-3 fatty acids; **P**—meditation, stress reduction, and questioning her negative and frightening thoughts; **S**—She planted brain-healthy habits at home, because she knew her children had a high genetic risk of Alzheimer's; **Sp**—She developed a clearer sense of meaning and purpose to enhance the health of those she loved—plus she did not want to be a burden to her family in the future. Within weeks, she noticed better energy and memory and a year later her brain looked healthier and younger than before.

In 2014, a study sponsored by General Electric found that 75 percent of the population would want to know if they had a pending neurological problem, such as dementia or Alzheimer's, even if there was nothing they could do about it (45). In our experience, if you get serious about it, there is a lot you can do to take care of your brain.

Images 4.13 and 4.14: Leslie Before and After Scans

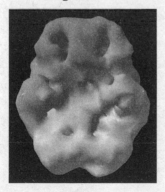

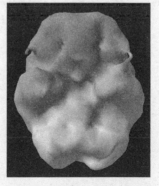

BEFORE

Low frontal and temporal lobe activity

AFTER

Overall improved activity

10. **Carlos: You Are Not Stuck with the Brain You Have. You Can Make It Better and We Can Prove It.**

When we first saw Carlos, he was forty-eight years old and filled with worries, negative thinking, depression, anger, and trouble focusing. He had undiagnosed dyslexia as a child and had struggled with heavy drinking in the past. His health habits were terrible, he weighed 266 pounds, and his brain was in trouble, all of which were not helping his emotional issues.

Carlos completely committed himself to the four-circles program we laid out for him. He is an analytical man, and the logic of the program made sense to him. After ten weeks, he lost twenty-four pounds and after thirty weeks he was down fifty pounds. More important, his mood, energy, and memory were better as well. Plus, he looked and felt ten years younger.

By taking to heart the steps in the Amen Clinics Method, Carlos stopped overeating as a way to medicate his sadness and irritability. And by eating brain-healthy foods at frequent enough intervals, he no longer had the energy crashes that made him so vulnerable to stress. He looks like a different person on the outside, but we saw a dramatic

 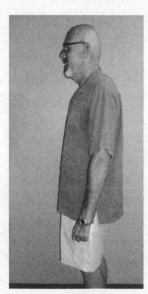 

266 lbs.   *243 lbs.*   *216 lbs.*

difference on the inside as well. His follow-up SPECT scan showed overall increased activity. Carlos changed his brain and in the process changed his life!

This is the part I love most about Carlos's story. After seeing Carlos's success, his wife, who was not overweight, started our program to learn about creating a brain-healthy family and ended up losing ten pounds herself. Then their fourteen-year-old daughter took the program. Carlos's success influenced everyone he loved. Several years later I saw Carlos in our waiting room and he still looked fabulous. I asked him how he kept it going. "It's not hard," he said. "I have the program dialed in."

You can do this too. None of what I will ask you to do is hard. It just takes consistent effort.

Images 4.15 and 4.16: Carlos's Before and After Scans

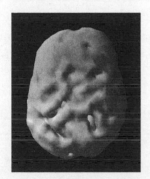 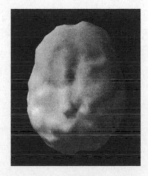

BEFORE
Overall decreased activity

AFTER
Overall improved activity

Hope

Whenever someone asks me to sign one of my books, I sign it "With hope." This is a meaningful phrase to me. The scans have given me more hope to help my patients. Most people are not a short fuse on a stick of dynamite like Willie before his treatment or Michelle during the worst time of her cycle. We do not use meat cleavers or carving knives to deal with others who irritate us. Most of us are warm, kind, and reasonable people who want to form meaningful relationships and be successful in our day-to-day lives. When our brain patterns are normal and balanced, we are generally able to do all these things. When behavior becomes abnormal, however, as in the cases above, often something is wrong with the patterns in the brain. These case histories demonstrate that *the physical patterns in our brains have a dramatic impact on how we think, feel, and behave.* Only recently have we discovered how to recognize those patterns and how to treat them in four circles.

AMEN CLINICS BRAIN HEALTH ASSESSMENT

A long time ago I realized that not everyone can get a scan, either because of cost or a lack of availability in your area. My books are translated into over thirty languages, so if you read one in China or Brazil, odds are you're not going to get a scan. So, based on thousands of scans, I developed an assessment to help people predict what their scans might look like if they could get one. The assessment is not as effective as getting a SPECT scan, especially when there are complex issues, but many people find them helpful, and they're used by thousands of mental health professionals around the world. The assessment can be found online at www.amenclinics.com.

5

Know Your Important Numbers

You Cannot Change What You Do Not Measure

A key component of the Amen Clinics Method is to know your important health numbers. A critical principle in business management is that "you cannot change what you do not measure." This same principle also applies to your health. This chapter describes the key health numbers you should know about yourself.

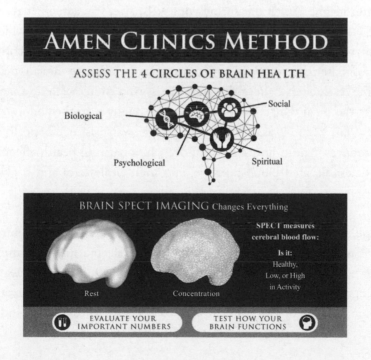

AMEN CLINICS METHOD

ASSESS THE 4 CIRCLES OF BRAIN HEALTH

Biological

Social

Psychological

Spiritual

BRAIN SPECT IMAGING Changes Everything

SPECT measures
cerebral blood flow:

Is it:
Healthy,
Low, or High
in Activity

Rest

Concentration

EVALUATE YOUR
IMPORTANT NUMBERS

TEST HOW YOUR
BRAIN FUNCTIONS

BMI or Body Mass Index is a measure of your weight compared with your height. A normal BMI is between 18.5 and 25; the overweight range falls between 25 and 30; and a BMI greater than 30 indicates obesity. You can find a simple BMI calculator on the Web. Knowing your BMI is important because being overweight or obese has been associated with having less brain tissue and lower brain activity—this isn't an association you want to keep. Plus, obesity doubles the risk for Alzheimer's disease (46, 47) and depression (48). There are probably several mechanisms that cause this, including the fact that fat cells produce inflammatory chemicals and store toxic materials in the body. Knowing your BMI will help you put your weight in perspective.

Waist to Height Ratio (WHtR). Another way to measure the health of your weight is with your waist-to-height ratio. The WHtR is calculated by dividing waist size by height. For an example, a female with a 32-inch waist who is 5'10" (70 inches) would divide 32 by 70 to get a WHtR of 45.7 percent. Generally speaking, it's healthy to stay under the fiftieth percentile—in other words, your waist size in inches should be less than half your height. When measuring your waist size, you actually have to use a tape measure! Don't hazard a guess or rely on your pants size, which can vary between manufacturers. In my experience, 90 percent of people will underestimate their waist circumference. Get an accurate measurement.

Some researchers believe this number is even more accurate than BMI because the most dangerous place to carry weight is in the abdomen. Abdominal fat, which is associated with a larger waist, is metabolically active and produces various hormones that can cause harmful health effects, such as diabetes, elevated blood pressure, and high cholesterol and triglyceride levels.

Average number of hours you sleep. One of the fastest ways to hurt your brain is to get less than seven or eight hours of sleep at night. Chronic insomnia triples your risk of death from all causes (49, 50) and is associated with cognitive decline (51, 52). Getting less than six hours of sleep at night has been associated with lower overall blood flow to the brain, and hurts your mood, focus, and memory for days after. Teenagers who average an hour less sleep than their peers have a higher incidence of depression and suicide (53). When you sleep less, you eat more and are more likely to be obese (54). The negative effects of sleep deprivation are so great that people who are drunk outperform those lacking sleep (55).

Fascinating new research has shown that the brain actually cleans or washes itself only during sleep (56). The brain has a specialized fluid system that helps to rid it of toxins that build up during the day, including beta-amyloid plaques thought to be involved in Alzheimer's disease. During the day the brain is so metabolically active managing our lives that this cleaning system is inactive. It only turns on when we're sleeping. Without healthy sleep, this waste clearance system doesn't have enough time to operate, thus allowing toxins to build up over time, which can cause cognitive and emotional problems. Think of sleep deprivation's effect on your brain as what your home or office might look like if no one bothered to take out the trash for a month.

Make sleep a priority and strive to get seven to eight hours a night. Our website www.mybrainfitlife.com has hypnosis audios that help with sleep. To help promote good sleep: eliminate or limit caffeine and alcohol; exercise in the morning rather than at night; turn off all blue-light-emitting devices (cell phones, tablets, e-readers, etc.) at night, and leave anything else that will disrupt your sleep outside the bedroom; make sure your bedroom is cool and as dark as possible. While I don't advocate sleeping pills, supplements like melatonin and magnesium can be helpful for better sleep.

Blood pressure. Good blood pressure is critical for brain health. High blood pressure and even blood pressure at the higher end of the normal range (pre-hypertension) is associated with lower overall brain function (57), which means more bad decisions. Here are the numbers you should know:

Below 120 over 80: optimal
120–139 over 80–89: prehypertension
140 (or above) over 90 (or above): hypertension

Check your blood pressure or have your doctor check it on a regular basis. If your blood pressure is high, make sure to take it seriously. Some behaviors that can help lower your blood pressure include losing weight, daily exercise, fish oil supplements, and, if needed, medication.

Low blood pressure can also be a problem. As with many numbers, there is a healthy range.

GET KEY LABORATORY TESTS

Laboratory tests will provide another set of important numbers to know. Ask your health-care professional to order them, or you can even order them for yourself at websites like www.saveonlabs.com. If your numbers are abnormal, please work with your health-care professional to get them into optimal ranges. Here are the key lab tests you should get:

CBC (Complete Blood Count). This is a blood draw that checks the health of your blood, including red and white blood cells. People with a low red blood cell count can feel anxious, tired, and have significant memory problems.

General metabolic panel with fasting blood sugar and lipid panel (blood test). This test checks the health of your liver, kidneys, fasting blood sugar, cholesterol, and triglycerides. Fasting blood sugar is especially important.

Normal is between 70–105 mg/dL;
Optimal is between 70–85 mg/dL;
Prediabetes is between 105–125 mg/dL; and
Diabetes is 126 mg/dL or higher.

Why is **high fasting blood sugar** a problem? High blood sugar causes vascular problems throughout your whole body, including your brain. Over time, it causes blood vessels to become brittle and vulnerable to breakage. It leads not only to diabetes, but heart disease, strokes, visual impairment, impaired wound healing, wrinkled skin, and cognitive problems. Diabetes doubles the risk for Alzheimer's disease. According to a large study from Kaiser Permanente, for every point above 85 patients had an additional 6 percent increased risk of developing diabetes in the next ten years (86 = 6 percent increased risk, 87 = 12 percent increased risk, 88 = 18 percent increased risk, etc.). Those who had a fasting blood sugar above 90 already had vascular (blood vessel) damage and were at risk for having damage to kidneys and eyes.

Cholesterol and triglycerides are also important, not least because 60 percent of the solid weight of the brain is fat. Both too-high and too-low cholesterol is bad for the brain. According to the American Heart Association, optimal levels are as follows:

- Total Cholesterol (135–200 mg/dL, yet below 160 has been associated with depression, so I think optimal is 160–200 mg/dL)
- HDL (>= 60 mg/dL)
- LDL (<100 mg/dL)
- Triglycerides (<100 mg/dl)

Knowing the particle size of LDL cholesterol (your health-care professional can order this test) is important because large particles are less toxic than smaller particles. If cholesterol is a concern for you, I recommend you read *The Great Cholesterol Myth* by Steve Sinatra and Jonny Bowden. To optimize your cholesterol levels make sure to get your diet under control, as well as taking fish oil and exercising regularly. Of course, you should consult with your physician about any changes you make to your diet or lifestyle.

Hemoglobin A1C (HbA1C—blood test). This test shows your average blood sugar levels over the previous two to three months and is used to diagnose diabetes and prediabetes. Normal results for a nondiabetic person are in the range of 4–5.6 percent. Prediabetes is indicated by levels in the 5.7 to 6.4 percent range. Higher numbers may indicate diabetes. The dietary advice later in the book will help you get your blood sugar under control.

Vitamin D (blood test). Low levels of vitamin D have been associated with obesity (58), depression (59), cognitive impairment (60, 61), heart disease (62, 63), reduced immunity (64, 65), cancer (66), psychosis (67), and all causes of mortality (68, 69). A healthy vitamin D level is between 30–100ng/dL, with the most optimal range between 50–100ng/dL. The blood test is called 25-hydroxy vitamin D level; if your levels are low get more sunshine in a safe way and/or take a vitamin D3 supplement. Personally, I never wanted to be in the bottom of any class I was ever in. Two-thirds of the U.S. population is low in vitamin D—the same percentage of residents who are overweight or obese. According to one study, when vitamin D is low, the hormone leptin, which tells us to stop eating, is not effective. One of the reasons for the dramatic rise in vitamin D deficiency is that people are wearing more sunscreen when outside and spending more time inside while working or sitting in front of the television or computer.

Thyroid panel (blood test). Abnormal thyroid hormone levels are a common cause of anxiety, depression, forgetfulness, confusion, and lethargy. Having low thyroid levels decreases overall brain activity, which can impair your thinking, judgment, and self-control, and make it very hard for you to feel good. Low thyroid functioning can make it nearly impossible to manage weight effectively. To know your thyroid levels, you need to know:

- TSH (thyroid stimulating hormone): .4–3.0 milli-international units per liter (mIU/L)
- Free T3: 100–200 nanograms per deciliter (ng/dL)
- Free T4: 4.5–11.2 micrograms per deciliter (mcg/dL)
- Thyroid antibodies: thyroid peroxidase <9.0 IU/Ml and thyroglobulin antibodies <4.0 IU/mL

Unfortunately, there is no single symptom or test result that will properly diagnose low thyroid function or hypothyroidism. The key is to gather your symptoms and your blood test results and consult with your physician. Symptoms of low thyroid include fatigue, depression, mental fog, dry skin, hair loss (especially the outer third of your eyebrows), feeling cold when others feel normal, constipation, hoarse voice, and weight gain. Most doctors do not check thyroid antibodies unless the TSH is high. I think this is a mistake. Many people have autoimmunity against their thyroid, which makes it function poorly, even while their TSH is "normal." Because of this disparity, I think measuring thyroid antibodies should also be part of routine screening.

Consider Bernadette's story.

Hi Dr. Amen:

I am a healthy, active thirty-two-year-old female who is very adamant on getting my yearly health checkups and blood work. I have recently listened to (and read) Change Your Brain, Change Your Body *and took your suggestion and had the more in-depth preliminary blood tests done (thyroid, hormones, vitamins, etc.) even though I was questioned by my doctor about why I wanted these ancillary tests when there was no apparent reason for conducting such research. I stated that I wanted to understand my numbers. I found that my "thyroglobulin antibodies" were high, indicating there was a problem. I immediately saw an endocrinologist, who found a growth on my thyroid, which turned out to be cancerous and spread to my lymph nodes. If it hadn't been for your advice, this issue may have gone undiagnosed for some time and worsened my prognosis. Without reading your book, I may not have had a chance to write this e-mail. Thank you so much for what you do!*

Sincerely, Bernadette

C-reactive protein (CRP). This is a very good blood test for inflammation. It measures the general level of inflammation, although it does not tell you what has caused it.

Elevated inflammation is linked with a number of diseases and conditions that are associated with mood problems, aging, and cognitive impairment (70–72). A healthy range is between 0.0–1.0 mg/dL.

Fat cells produce chemicals that increase inflammation, which is a pressing reason to monitor weight and belly fat. The most common cause of elevated C-reactive protein is metabolic syndrome or insulin resistance. The second most common is some sort of reaction to food: either a true allergy, a food sensitivity, or an autoimmune reaction such as occurs with gluten. High CRP levels can also indicate hidden infections.

Homocysteine (blood test). Elevated homocysteine levels (>10 micromoles/liter) in the blood have been associated with damage to the lining of arteries and atherosclerosis (hardening and narrowing of the arteries) as well as an increased risk of heart attacks, strokes, blood clot formation, and possibly Alzheimer's disease. This is a sensitive marker for B vitamin deficiency, including folic acid deficiency. Replacing these vitamins often helps return the homocysteine level to normal.

Ferritin (blood test). This is a measure of iron stores, a number that increases with inflammation and insulin resistance. Levels between 40–80 ng/mL are ideal. Women often have lower iron stores than men, due to blood loss from menstruation. Some theorize that this is one of the reasons that women tend to live longer than men. However, you don't want ferritin levels that are too low, as this is associated with anemia, restless legs, ADD, and low motivation and energy. High iron stores have been associated with stiffer blood vessels and vascular disease. Some research suggests that donating blood to lower high ferritin levels may enhance blood vessel flexibility and help decrease the risk of heart disease. Plus, when you give blood you are being altruistic, which is also good for your mind and body.

Free and total serum testosterone (blood test). For both men and women, low levels of testosterone have been associated with low energy, cardiovascular disease, obesity, low libido, depression, and Alzheimer's disease.

DHEA-S (blood test). This is an adrenal gland hormone related to stress that is also a precursor, or building block, for other hormones.

Estrogen and progesterone for women. Depending on the circumstances, these are measured in blood or saliva. Menstruating women are usually tested on day 21 of the cycle while postmenopausal women can be measured anytime. Estrogen is responsible for vaginal lubrication, helps with libido and memory—and so much more. Progesterone calms emotions, contributes to a restful sleep, and acts as a diuretic.

Knowing and optimizing these numbers is critical to helping your brain work right. If any of them are abnormal, the function of your brain can be troubled too. Work with your local health-care provider to help get these numbers into the most optimal range possible.

Part Two

Know and Heal the Brain Systems That Run Your Life

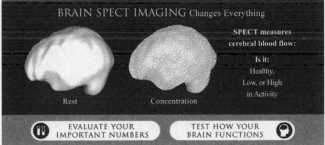

AMEN CLINICS METHOD

ASSESS THE 4 CIRCLES OF BRAIN HEALTH

Biological

Social

Psychological

Spiritual

BRAIN SPECT IMAGING Changes Everything

SPECT measures
cerebral blood flow:

Is it:
Healthy,
Low, or High
in Activity

Rest

Concentration

EVALUATE YOUR
IMPORTANT NUMBERS

TEST HOW YOUR
BRAIN FUNCTIONS

TREATMENT TARGETED TO YOUR BRAIN

Least toxic,
most effective
strategies

ALL LEADS TO BETTER OUTCOMES

6

Looking into Love and Depression

The Limbic System

FUNCTIONS OF THE LIMBIC SYSTEM (LS)

sets the emotional tone of the mind
filters external events through internal states (creates emotional
   coloring)
tags events as internally important
stores highly charged emotional memories
modulates motivation
controls appetite and sleep cycles
promotes bonding
directly processes the sense of smell
modulates libido

In a paper published in 1878, French neurologist Paul Broca noted that deep in the middle of the brain all mammals possess a group of areas that are different from the surrounding cerebral cortex. Using the Latin word for "border," *limbus*, Broca named this collection of brain areas the **limbic lobe**, because they form a ring or border around the brain stem below the cortex (73). In the 1930s, scientific evidence suggested this area was involved with emotion; the American neurologist James Papez proposed a circuit (now known as the Papez circuit) of connected structures within the limbic lobe that facilitate the experience of emotion (74).

In the 1960s, neuroscientist Paul MacLean described the triune brain, a

Papez Circuit

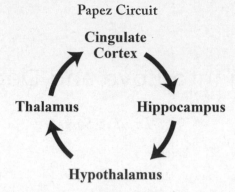

concept he popularized in his 1990 book, *The Triune Brain in Evolution* (75), which described the limbic system as between the older reptilian brain and the newer neocortex. He believed the limbic system was responsible for motivation and emotion involved in feeding, reproduction, and parenting.

Image 6.1: Triune Brain

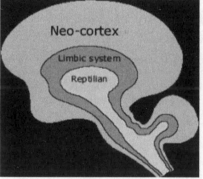

Over time it has been recognized that emotion is not just located in these deep areas of the brain, but rather in multiple areas that are widely distributed and interconnected. The limbic system is one of the most interesting and critical parts of being human and is power-packed with functions, all of which are critical for human behavior and survival (76). From an evolutionary standpoint, this is an "older" part of the mammalian brain that enabled animals to experience and express emotions. It freed them from the primitive behaviors dictated by the brain stem, found in the older "reptilian" brain. The subsequent development of the surrounding cerebral cortex in higher animals, especially humans, gave us the capacity for problem solving, planning, organization, and rational thought. Yet in order for these functions to have an effect in the world, one must have passion, emotion, drive, and the desire to make something happen. The limbic brain adds the emotional fuel in this process.

The limbic system (LS) typically includes the:

- thalamus—a large structure deep in the center of the brain that relays information to and from the outside world and the cerebral cortex.
- amygdala—an almond shaped structure in the temporal lobes; involved in emotional and fear responses.
- hippocampus—a seahorse-shaped structure that helps memories get into long-term storage.
- hypothalamus—about the size of a pearl; is an important emotional center, controlling the chemicals that make you feel hungry, sexual, sleepy, exhilarated, angry, or unhappy.
- olfactory cortex—our sense of smell, which connects to emotional and memory centers.

Many scientists also include the anterior cingulate gyrus and portions of the prefrontal cortex as part of the limbic brain. I leave them out here as they will be discussed in their own chapters. In our experience at Amen Clinics, when the LS is less active, there is generally a positive, more hopeful state of mind. When it is overactive, sadness and negativity can take over. This finding actually surprised my colleagues and me. We thought that excessive activity in the part of the brain that controlled emotion might correlate with enhanced feelings of all kinds, not solely negative ones. Yet we noticed again and again that when this area was overactive on SPECT, it often correlated with the subject's tendency toward being negative or feelings of sadness. In a study of more than fifteen thousand patients, we saw a significant correlation between increased activity in the LS and the question we ask of patients' "frequent feelings of sadness."

Emotional shading is the filter through which you interpret the events of the day, coloring them in ways that reflect your emotional state of mind. When the LS is overactive, you are likely to interpret neutral events through a negative filter: negative emotional shading. For example, if you have a neutral or even positive conversation with someone whose LS is overactive or "negatively set," he or she is likely to interpret the conversation in a negative way. When this part of the brain is less active, a neutral or positive interpretation of events is more likely to occur. Emotional tagging of events (whether positive or negative) is critical to survival. The valence or charge we give to certain events in our lives drives us to action (such as approaching a desired mate) or causes avoidant behavior (withdrawing from someone who has hurt us in the past).

Premenstrual syndrome (PMS), discussed in chapter 4, is a classic example of this emotional shading principle. As mentioned, in our study of PMS within five to ten days before the onset of menstruation, the LS becomes more activated with this shift in hormones and can color events in a more negative way. A friend's wife has a fairly severe case of PMS. He tells me that during the first week of her cycle, she looks at him with love and affection, and almost anything he does seems to be right. Ten days before her period, things are dramatically different. She doesn't want to be touched. She "has a different look," which he describes as a combination of a scowl and a "don't mess with me" expression. He can barely do anything right in her eyes. She emotionally colors most events in a negative way. Then, a few days after her cycle starts, she's back to being more positive, loving, and affectionate.

The hippocampus, located on the medial or inside of the temporal lobes, has also been reported to be involved in storing highly charged emotional memories, both positive and negative. If you have been traumatized by a dramatic event, such as being in a car accident or watching your house burn down, or if you have been abused by a parent or a spouse, the emotional component of the memory is stored in the limbic system of your brain. And if you have won the lottery, graduated magna cum laude, or watched your child's birth, those emotional memories are stored there as well. The total experience of our emotional memories is responsible, in part, for the emotional tone of our mind. The more stable, positive experiences we have, the more positive we are likely to feel; the more trauma in our lives, the more emotionally set we become in a negative way. These emotional memories are intimately involved in the emotional tags we impose on the day's events.

The LS also affects motivation and drive. It helps get you going in the morning and encourages you to move throughout the day. In our experience, overactivity in the LS is associated with lowered motivation and drive, which is often seen in depression. The limbic system, especially the hypothalamus, controls the sleep and appetite cycles of the body. Healthy sleep and appetite are essential to maintaining a proper internal milieu. However, disruptions in the limbic system can negatively affect sleep and appetite, which may mean an inclination toward too much or too little of either. For example, during typical depressive episodes, people have been known to lose their appetites and have trouble sleeping despite being chronically tired, but in *atypical* depression they usually sleep and eat excessively.

The LS structures are also intimately involved with bonding and social connectedness. When the LS of animals is damaged, they do not properly bond with their young. In one study of rats, when the limbic structures were damaged, mothers would not feed and nurture the young but would drag them around the cage as if they were inanimate objects. The LS affects the bonding mechanism that enables you to connect socially with other people; in turn, your ability to do this successfully influences your moods. We are social animals. When we are bonded to people in a positive way, we feel better about ourselves and our lives. This capacity to bond then plays a significant role in the tone and quality of our moods.

The LS also directly processes the sense of smell. The olfactory system is the only one of the five sensory systems that goes directly from the sensory organ to where it is processed in the brain. The messages from all the other senses (sight, hearing, touch, and taste) are sent to a "relay station" before they are sent to their final destination in different parts of the brain. Because your sense of smell goes directly to the LS, it is easy to understand why smells can have such a powerful impact on our feeling states. The multibillion-dollar perfume and deodorant industries count on this fact: beautiful smells evoke pleasant feelings and draw people toward you; unpleasant smells repel them.

I learned about the limbic–smell connection firsthand when I was sixteen years old and dating a good Catholic girl who had a lot of self-control. As a typical teenage boy, I had less of it. One night, I ran out of my aftershave and borrowed my brother's English Leather. When I picked her up for our date, I noticed a difference. I had a car with a bench seat in the front. Usually, she sat across the car near the passenger door. That night she sat in the middle seat next to me. She took my hand before I reached for hers. She was cuddlier and more affectionate than before. From then on, English Leather was the only scent I wore.

Bonding, smells, sexuality, and the LS are intimately connected. Napoleon once wrote to Josephine to ask her not to bathe for two weeks before he came home from a battle. He wanted her scent to be powerful, because it sexually excited him.

Limbic overactivity, often associated with depression, frequently results in decreased sexual interest. For many years, I have hypothesized that decreased sexual activity is associated with increased limbic activity and more vulnerability to depression. I studied this phenomenon in a man who had problems with depression and increased activity in his limbic system on SPECT. I asked him to make passionate love with his wife. I then rescanned him within an hour. His limbic activity was significantly decreased. Orgasm has been described as a mini-seizure of the limbic system and tends to release or lessen limbic activity. Sexuality is good for the bonded human brain with a committed partner.

Whenever a person is sexually involved with another person, neurochemical changes occur in both their brains that encourage limbic, emotional bonding. Yet limbic bonding is the reason casual sex doesn't really work for many people on a whole mind and body level. Two people may decide to have sex "just for the fun of it," yet something is occurring on another level they might not have decided on at all: sex is enhancing an emotional bond between them whether they want it or not. One person, often the woman, is bound to form an attachment and will be hurt when a casual affair ends. One reason it is usually the woman who is hurt more is that the female limbic system is larger than the male's. One likely consequence is that she will become more limbically connected.

I once treated a patient named Renee who had a high sex drive. She was not sexually satisfied by her husband. For years, other men flirted with her and she remained faithful, until one day she decided, out of pure frustration, to have an affair with a coworker. From the outset, they agreed that they were going to have friendly sex, just for fun, just for the pleasure, and in the first two months that seemed to work. Then Renee felt herself wanting to see him more often. She tried to get him to meet with her twice a week instead of once a week, as they had originally agreed. Instead of responding positively, her lover pulled away. The more attached she became, the more detached he became. Although Renee and her lover had been on the same wavelength in the beginning, in the end she had changed and he hadn't, and she felt used. It is important to understand how your body and psyche work. In this case, Renee would have been wise to realize that her limbic system was not quite as open to casual sex as she wanted it to be. She would have been better off staying with her husband and working things out sexually with him, rather than picking a casual acquaintance for a sexual liaison.

As mentioned above, current research has demonstrated that females, on average, have a larger LS than males. This gives females several advantages and disadvantages. Because of their larger limbic brain, women are more in touch with their feelings, and they are generally better able to express their feelings than men. They have an increased ability to bond and be connected to others (which is why women are usually the primary caretakers of children—there is no society on earth where men are primary caretakers of children). Females even have a more acute sense of smell, which is likely to have developed from an evolutionary need for the mother to recognize her young. Having a larger LS leaves a female somewhat more susceptible to depression, especially at times of significant hormonal changes such as the onset of puberty, before menses, after the birth of a child, and at menopause.

The LS, especially the hypothalamus at the base of the brain, is responsible for translating our emotional state into physical feelings of relaxation or tension. The front half of the hypothalamus sends calming signals to the body through the parasympathetic nervous system. The back half of the hypothalamus sends stimulating or fear signals to the body through the sympathetic nervous system and is responsible for the fight-or-flight response—a primitive state that gets us ready to fight or flee when we are threatened or scared. This "hardwired response" happens automatically upon activation, such as witnessing or experiencing an emotional or physical threat: the heart beats faster, breathing rate and blood pressure increase, the hands and feet become cooler to shunt blood from the extremities to the big muscles (to fight or run away), and the pupils dilate (to see better). This limbic translation of emotion is powerful and immediate. It happens with overt physical threats as well as with more covert emotional threats. This part of the brain is intimately connected to the prefrontal cortex and seems to acts as a switching station between running on emotion (the LS) and rational thought and problem solving using our cortex. When the limbic system is turned on, emotions tend to take over. When it is cooled down, more activation is possible in the cortex. Current research shows a correlation between depression and increased limbic system activity and shutdown in the prefrontal cortex, especially on the left side.

PROBLEMS IN THE LIMBIC SYSTEM

sadness
clinical depression
increased negative thinking
negative perception of events
flood of negative emotions, such as hopelessness, helplessness, and guilt
appetite and sleep problems
decreased or increased sexual responsiveness
social isolation
pain

The problems in the limbic system (as in all the other systems) generally correspond to their functions. Do you know people who see every situation in a bad light? That pessimism actually could be a LS problem because, as mentioned, when this part of the brain is working too hard, the emotional filter is colored by negativity. One person could walk away from an interaction that ten others would have labeled as positive, but which he or she considers negative. There can also be a flood of negative emotion, such as hopeless, helplessness, and guilt. What makes this negative mind-set even more challenging is that research has shown that depressive thoughts actually interfere with day-to-day memory function and concentration (77).

There are three problems caused by abnormalities of the LS that warrant their own sections: bonding disruption, mood disorders, and pain.

BONDING DISRUPTION

Bonding and limbic problems often go hand in hand. One of the most fundamental bonds in the human universe is the mother-infant bond. Hormonal changes shortly after childbirth, however, can cause limbic or emotional problems in the mother. They are called the "baby blues" when they are mild, and postpartum depression or psychosis when they are severe. When these problems arise, the LS of the mother's brain shows abnormally high activity (this phenomenon has been detected in animals as well as humans). In turn, significant bonding problems may occur. The mother may emotionally withdraw from the baby, preventing the baby from developing normally. For instance, babies who experience "failure to thrive" or who have low weight or delayed development often have mothers who are emotionally unattached; thus it can be said that the abnormal activity of the mother's LS causes developmental problems for the baby. Conversely, problems in the LS can be caused by outside events that disrupt the human bonding process. This can occur at any stage in life. Here are three of the most common.

Death

The death of a parent, spouse, or child causes intense sadness and grief. In these familial relationships, there is often a tight neurochemical bond (from the myriad of stored emotional memories and experiences). When it is broken, the activity of the LS is disrupted. Many who experience grief say the pain actually feels physical. This sensation is not imaginary. Grief often activates the pain centers in the brain, which are housed near the limbic system. It is interesting to note that the people who had a good relationship with the person who died often heal their grief much more easily than those whose relationship with the deceased was filled with turmoil, bitterness, or disappointment. The reason for this is that a positive relationship is associated with good memories, and remembering and reprocessing these memories helps in the healing process. But when people who had a bad relationship with the deceased person reflect, they have to relive the pain. In their mind, they may still be trying to fix what was wrong and to heal the wound, but they can't. In addition, the guilt they may carry with them impairs the healing process. Donna is an example of this.

Donna and her mother had had a stormy relationship, fighting constantly over things that were seemingly insignificant. Yet in spite of their problems, the year following her mother's death was the hardest of Donna's life. Her husband could not understand the magnitude of her grief; all he had ever heard her do was complain that her mother was selfish and uninterested in her. What he failed to understand was that Donna had to grieve not only her mother's death, but also the fact that now she would never have the mother-daughter bond she had always wanted. Death had ended all her hopes.

Losing a spouse or a lover is traumatic in a different way from losing any other loved one. Once you have made love with a person on a regular basis, a partner's death can be extraordinarily painful because the limbic connection has been broken. A spouse or lover becomes part of the chemical bond of this part of the brain, and it takes time for that bond to dissolve. Your limbic system misses the person's touch, voice, and smell.

Limbic connection doesn't depend just on sexual intimacy. Another often overlooked "limbic loss" is the loss of a family pet. Many people become as attached to their pets as they do to the significant people in their lives. Pets often give unconditional love and connect with our innermost caring selves. I have often felt that holding one of my cats or petting my dog during a scan would have a positive "limbic cooling" effect. Unfortunately, while I was writing the first edition of this book my dog, Samantha, died of cancer. The sadness in my family was great, with many tears—

especially from my daughters. We all had problems sleeping, no one felt like eating, and anything that reminded us of Samantha would quickly bring up tears and feelings of intense sadness and loss. I have known some pet owners who became so depressed after a pet died that they felt suicidal and even paranoid. Appreciating this significant grief is often necessary to healing.

Divorce

Divorce can be a source of the most severe kind of stress possible for a human being to experience. For many, it actually causes more anguish to lose a spouse through divorce than it does through death. As stated above, people who are "limbically connected" have a very powerful bond, and I believe this phenomenon may be one of the major reasons women often don't leave abusive men. They shared their beds and homes with them, and in many cases have had children with these men. To break that bond, which is at the core of their limbic brain, causes a severe rupture that can make the woman feel fragmented, as if she were not quite whole without the man. She may be plagued by sleep and appetite problems, depression, irritability, and social isolation. I once treated a woman who was married to a controlling, angry man whom she could never please. On the day he told her he was leaving her for another woman, he caused a severe limbic injury in her and she became so depressed that she put her head in the oven and turned on the gas. Fortunately she was rescued and taken to the hospital. It wasn't until her LS began to heal and she could experience her own autonomy that she realized she didn't even like her husband, and in any case, it certainly wasn't worth killing herself over a man who cheated on her.

Even the partner who initiates a separation suffers distress and often goes through a period of depression, because the "chemical limbic bonds" break for everyone involved in the separation. The one who is walking out the door may fail to realize this and not anticipate the grief period that will likely follow. For some, divorce is so devastating that it can trigger enormous anger and vengefulness. In fact, I have never seen two people more cruel to each other than those going through a messy divorce. They lose all sense of fairness and rationality and do everything possible to hurt each other. What ignites such negative responses? Breaking the chemical connection activates the LS, causing people to become not only depressed and negative but also oversensitive, taking every little thing the wrong way. Anger quickly follows. They know they have to separate, and unconsciously they use the anger and aggression as a way to do it. Another cause of perpetual fighting in divorce situations is related to overactivity in the anterior cingulate gyrus, where people get stuck on their negative thoughts and behaviors (see chapter 12).

The Empty Nest Syndrome

When children leave home, parents often feel intensely sad and bereft. Many lose their appetite and have trouble sleeping. Something is missing. This may be confusing, because the parents remember how arduous it was struggling through the growing pains of their offsprings' adolescence, and they assumed it would be a relief when the teenagers were finally out of the house and off to their own lives. (Of note, it has been suggested that the discordant nature of the parent-child relationship during adolescence may be nature's way of helping parents and teens make the transition from the close bond of childhood to the total independence of young adulthood.) Yet no matter how difficult those adolescent years were for both sides, a tremendous bond still exists, and breaking it is stressful.

I once treated a man who developed a clinical depression after his only daughter left home for college. Even though he was happily married, enjoyed his work, and was otherwise healthy, he felt sad, cried easily, had trouble sleeping, became more irritable, and had concentration problems—all symptoms of depression. Another woman I treated, whose two sons went off to college one year after the other, became so depressed and felt so lonely and unimportant that she resorted to having an affair as a way to deal with her pain. She lost her marriage over the affair, became suicidal, and almost lost her life.

DEPRESSION

Lack of bonding and depression are frequently related. People who are depressed often do not feel like being around others and consequently isolate themselves. The social isolation tends to perpetuate itself: The more isolated a person becomes the less bonding activity occurs. This worsens the depression and increases the likelihood of further isolation.

Depression is associated with low levels of certain neurotransmitters, especially norepinephrine, dopamine, and serotonin. In our experience, these deficits can cause increased activity in the LS, which in turn causes many of the problems associated with depression. Since the LS is intimately tied to moods, when it is overactive the ensuing problems with depression may snowball and affect all the other LS functions.

Ariel came to see me because she had been experiencing symptoms of depression for over two years. She was tired, suffered from sleeplessness and negative thinking, had no motivation, and had begun to have suicidal thoughts. The symptom that was most difficult for her husband, however, was her complete loss of interest in sex. He was ready to leave her because he thought she wasn't interested in him anymore as a man. Why else, he thought, had it been such a long time since she had wanted to touch him? After I had her brain scanned, I was not surprised to find that her limbic system was working way too hard. Giving this information to her husband was a powerful tool in helping him to view the situation objectively: his wife wasn't neglecting him because she didn't like him, but rather because something was off balance in her brain. Most important of all, the problem was rectifiable using a four-circles approach. We'll discuss how to put four-circles plans into action in more depth in chapter 7.

BIPOLAR DISORDER

Sandy

Sandy was fifty-three years old when she was admitted to the hospital under my care. The month before, her family had had her committed to another psychiatric hospital for delusional thinking and bizarre behavior—she had actually ripped out all the electrical wiring in her home because she heard voices coming from the walls. In addition to the above symptoms, she was barely getting any sleep, her thoughts raced wildly, and she was irritable. Her doctor had diagnosed bipolar disorder (a cyclical mood disorder) and placed her on lithium (an antimanic medication) and an antianxiety medication. After responding well, she was sent home. But Sandy did not want to believe that anything was wrong with her, and she stopped taking both medications. Her belief was actually supported by some members of her family, who openly told her she didn't need pills and that doctors prescribe them only to force patients into numerous follow-up visits. Yet their advice was ill-fated, for within weeks of stopping the treatment, Sandy's bizarre behavior returned. This was when her family brought her to the hospital where I worked. When I first saw Sandy, she was extremely paranoid. Believing that everyone was trying to hurt her, she was always looking for ways to escape from the hospital. Again her thoughts were delusional; she believed she had special powers and that others were trying to take them from her. At times, she also appeared very "spacy." In an attempt to understand what was going on with her for myself, and to convince her that at least part of her problems were biological, I ordered a SPECT study.

Carrying this out did not prove to be easy. Our clinic tried to scan her on three separate occasions. The first two times she ripped out the intravenous line, saying we were trying to poison her. The third time was a success because her sister stayed with her and calmed her down by talking her through the experience. The SPECT scans revealed increased activity in her LS and patchy increased activity overall. In other words, some areas showed

Image 6.2: Sandy's Bipolar Brain

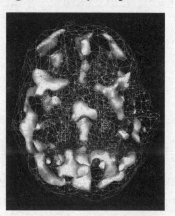

Note overall increased activity
throughout the cortex.

increased activity and some showed decreased. My experience told me that cyclic mood disorders often correlate with focal areas of increased activity in the LS specifically as well as too much activity across the surface of the brain.

For Sandy's family, this was powerful evidence that her problems were biological, so that when she refused medication, they were now willing to encourage her to take it. After she accepted their advice, her behavior normalized again. Once I knew she was feeling better and more in control, I showed her the brain studies. Through a better understanding of the problem she was able to agree to our four-circles approach, including medication.

Sandy's case illustrates one of the most clinically significant problems in people diagnosed with bipolar disorder. This illness is usually responsive to medication. In fact, I have not seen supplements alone fully treat this particular disorder in very many cases. Here, as in true schizophrenia, I am a huge fan of medication therapy. The problem is that when people afflicted by bipolar disorder improve, many feel so normal they do not believe they ever had a problem to begin with. It is difficult for them to accept that they have to keep taking medication when they think they no longer have a problem. Yet as we have seen, prematurely stopping medication actually increases the chances of relapsing. Through the use of brain-imaging studies, I have been able to decrease the relapse rate of my patients by visually demonstrating the biological nature of their disorders and the need to treat them as such—a great asset in encouraging patients to cooperate in their own healing. In addition to that, SPECT-imaging studies have helped me persuade patients to stop blaming themselves for their symptoms.

Pain

In my experience, people who experience chronic pain often have high activity in the thalamus, which is part of the limbic system. This is especially true with issues like fibromyalgia (chronic muscle pain). A number of antidepressants, such as duloxetine (Cymbalta) and amitriptyline (Elavil), have been found to be successful in alleviating pain syndromes, as have mood-supporting supplements like S-adenosylmethionine (SAMe) and fish oil.

LIMBIC SYSTEM CHECKLIST

Please read this list of behaviors and rate yourself (or the person you are evaluating) on each behavior listed. Use the following scale and place the appropriate number next to the item. Five or more symptoms marked 3 or 4 indicate a high likelihood of limbic system issues.

0 = never
1 = rarely
2 = occasionally
3 = frequently
4 = very frequently

___ 1. Feelings of sadness
___ 2. Moodiness
___ 3. Low energy
___ 4. Excessive guilt
___ 5. Crying spells
___ 6. Lowered interest in things usually considered fun
___ 7. Low self-esteem
___ 8. Decreased interest in sex
___ 9. Negative sensitivity to smells/odors
___ 10. Forgetfulness
___ 11. Poor concentration
___ 12. My feelings are often or easily hurt
___ 13. Feeling overwhelmed by the tasks of daily living
___ 14. Sensitive to criticism
___ 15. Lacking confidence in own abilities

7

Feel Better Fast

Limbic System Prescriptions

Finally, brethren, whatever is true, whatever is honorable, whatever is right, whatever is pure, whatever is lovely, whatever is of good repute, if there is any excellence and if there is anything worthy of praise, let your mind dwell on these things.

—PHILIPPIANS 4:8

As discussed in chapter 6, the limbic system processes our sense of smell, stores highly charged emotional memories, and affects sleep and appetite cycles, moods, sexuality, and bonding. To optimize and support limbic system issues, we have the options of a number of diverse four-circles Limbic Prescriptions, based on research and my own personal clinical experience:

B—Supplements and medications, aromatherapy, acupuncture, transcranial magnetic stimulation, cranial electric stimulation, neurofeedback, physical exercise, and nutrition

P—ANT therapy, the Work in 4 Questions, and practicing gratitude and appreciation

S—Surrounding yourself with people who provide positive bonding, protecting your children with limbic bonding, building people skills, and having healthy physical contact

Sp—Finding purpose and passion, and doing random acts of kindness

BIOLOGICAL LIMBIC PRESCRIPTIONS

B—Consider Limbic Supplements or Medications from the Amen Clinics Method Algorithm

In the Amen Clinics Method Algorithm we do not just prescribe supplements or medications based on symptom clusters alone, but rather consider the symptom clusters (i.e., depression, anxiety, ADD) along with the area of the brain we're concerned about. At Amen Clinics we use the following algorithm when we see high activity in the limbic system (LS) plus symptom clusters of depression, cyclic mood issues, or pain.

> **Supplements for high LS + mood issues**—My favorite two supplements to support a healthy mood are omega-3 fatty acids, especially those that contain a higher EPA content, and S-adenosylmethionine (SAMe). In a review of fifteen trials involving 916 participants on omega-3 fatty acids for depression, supplements that had greater than 60 percent EPA showed significantly more benefit on depression scores versus supplements with <60 percent EPA (78). The dosage range was 200 to 2,200 mg a day of EPA (78, 79). SAMe has over forty studies validating its use to support mood (80). MedlinePlus, the National Institutes of Health website, which gives scientific evidence rating for natural supplements, reports that SAMe is likely effective for both depression and osteoarthritis. The dosage of SAMe is between 200 to 400 mg two to four times a day (half that for children). *People who have bipolar disorder should not take SAMe.* There have been a number of reported cases of SAMe causing manic or hypomanic episodes (excessively up or happy moods, extreme impulsivity in sexuality or spending money, pressured speech, or decreased need for sleep).
>
> **Medications for high LS + depressive symptoms**—bupropion (Wellbutrin).
>
> **Supplements for high LS + cyclic mood changes**—omega-3 fatty acids in a balance between EPA and DHA.
>
> **Medications for high LS + cyclic mood changes**—lithium or anticonvulsants, such as lamotrigine (Lamictal) or valproate (Depakote).
>
> **Supplements for high LS + pain**—SAMe or omega-3 fatty acids

Medications for high LS + pain—duloxetine (Cymbalta), amitriptyline (Elavil), or gabapentin (Neurontin).

See chapter 16 to learn more about the seven types of anxiety and depression, and what to do for them. To get the best results with supplements or medication, I use them together with the other Limbic Prescriptions described in this chapter.

B—Surround Yourself with Soothing Scents

Your limbic system is the part of your brain that directly processes your sense of smell. That is why perfumes and wonderful-smelling soaps are attractive and unpleasant body odors are repellent. In the British journal *The Lancet*, a study was reported on the benefits of aromatherapy using the oil from lavender flowers. When used properly, lavender oil aroma helped people to feel less stressed and less depressed. It also enhanced sleep. In aromatherapy, special fragrances are used in a steam machine, in the bath, on the pillow, and in potpourris. The right smells likely "cool" the limbic system. Pleasing fragrances are like an anti-inflammatory. By surrounding yourself with flowers, sweet fragrances, and other pleasant smells, you affect the working of your brain in a powerful and positive way. However, there is a difference between ingesting the substance and smelling it. When you ingest something, it goes to the stomach and is processed by the digestive system. Moreover, many essential oils, including lavender, are dangerous if ingested.

Consider cinnamon, commonly used for cooking in countries throughout the world. Being of Lebanese descent, my mother used to put cinnamon in many dishes, including stuffed grape leaves—one of my favorites. When I recently told her that the scent of cooked cinnamon is considered a natural aphrodisiac for men, she put her hand on her forehead and said, "That's why I have seven kids; your father would never leave me alone."

B—Acupuncture

The ancient Chinese medical art of acupuncture has been shown to have multiple mental health benefits, including helping with mood (81, 82), addiction (83), and pain (84). Brain-imaging studies have shown that acupuncture increases blood flow to the brain (85) and helps to calm the limbic system at the same time (86). It appears that acupuncture works through a completely different mechanism than do typical antidepressants. It has been shown to work through the endorphin system (the brain's natural pain-killing mechanism). If a person has been resistant to typical antidepressants, but gets relief from their mood problems from opiate-like drugs such as morphine or hydrocodone (Vicodin), that is an indication to me that acupuncture might be helpful.

B—Repetitive Transcranial Magnetic Stimulation (rTMS)

rTMS is an FDA approved treatment for depression. A powerful magnet is placed usually over the left front part of the brain to stimulate the brain. This therapy has been found to boost blood flow and activity patterns in this part of the brain, and subsequently calm the limbic system. rTMS is a clinically proven treatment for depression (87). We use it at Amen Clinics; in our experience, it has about an 80 percent success rate with few side effects. rTMS is also being used for other conditions not approved by the FDA, including pain, addictions, obsessive-compulsive disorder, and autism. In my experience, it is important to have a baseline brain scan to have an idea of exactly where the brain should be treated with rTMS.

B—Cranial Electric Stimulation (CES)

CES is another electrical stimulation treatment for the brain that I believe has a limbic action. This treatment is less expensive than rTMS, but has supportive scientific literature (88, 89), especially in the areas of mood enhancement, sleep, and pain.

B—Neurofeedback

Neurofeedback is a treatment where brain-wave activity is measured and then optimized through training regimens with patients. There are studies suggesting neurofeedback can help with mood and pain (90, 91), as well as solid scientific evidence that it can help for ADD/ADHD (92, 93).

B—Physical Exercise

A head-to-head study comparing exercise with antidepressant medication found that after twelve weeks, both therapies were equally effective (94). At ten months, exercise was actually more effective—and it has no side effects. See chapter 19 for the best brain-healthy physical exercises.

B—Nutrition

There is a powerful connection between food and mood. Inflammation-promoting diets are associated with depression and dementia, while anti-inflammatory diets are associated with improved mood, memory, and energy. Chapter 20 will discuss the Brain Warrior Diet, as well as the brain–gut connection.

PSYCHOLOGICAL LIMBIC PRESCRIPTIONS

P—ANT Therapy

One of the limbic techniques that is a mainstay of helping our patients at the Amen Clinics is what I call ANT therapy, or learning how to kill the ANTs (Automatic Negative Thoughts). I coined this term in the early 1990s after a hard day at the office, during which I had several very difficult sessions with suicidal patients, teenagers in turmoil, and a married couple who hated each other. When I got home that evening I found thousands of ants in my kitchen. It was gross. As I started to clean them up, the acronym came to me. I thought of my patients from that day—like my infested kitchen, my patients' brains were also infested by the negative thoughts that were robbing them of their joy and stealing their happiness. The next day, I brought a can of ant spray to work as a visual aid and have been working diligently ever since to help my patients eradicate their ANTs.

Here are the actual "ANT Killing" principles that we use at Amen Clinics with people of all ages. Truly learning these principles will help you gain more control over your feelings and behavior.

1. **Did you know . . . every time you have a thought, your brain releases chemicals?** That's how our brains work.

   you have a thought
   your brain releases chemicals
   an electrical transmission goes across your brain and
       you become aware of what you're thinking.

   Thoughts are real and they have a direct impact on how you feel and
       how you behave.

2. Every time you have a mad thought, an unkind thought, a sad thought, or a cranky thought, your brain releases negative chemicals that activate your limbic system and make your mind and body feel bad. Think about the last time you were mad. How did you feel physically? When most people are mad, their muscles get tense, their heart beats faster, their hands start to sweat, and they may even begin to feel a little dizzy. Your body reacts to every negative thought you have.

3. Every time you have a good thought, a happy thought, a hopeful thought, or a kind thought, your brain releases chemicals that make your body feel good. Think about the last time you had a really happy thought (such as when you went on a great date or cuddled a child). What did you feel inside your body? When most people are happy their muscles relax; their heartbeat and breath slow. Your body also reacts to your good thoughts.

4. **Your body reacts to every thought you have!** We know this from polygraphs or lie detector tests. During a lie detector test, you are hooked up to equipment that measures:

   hand temperature
   heart rate
   blood pressure
   breathing rate
   muscle tension, and
   how much the hands sweat

The tester then asks questions such as "Did you do that thing?" If you did the bad thing, your body is likely to have a "stress" response that might manifest in the following ways:

hands get colder
heart goes faster
blood pressure goes up
breathing gets faster
muscles get tight
hands sweat more

Almost immediately, the body reacts to your thoughts, whether you say anything or not. Now, the opposite is also true. If you did not do what they are asking you about it is likely that your body will experience a "relaxation" response and react in the following ways:

hands will become warmer
heart rate will slow
blood pressure goes down
breathing becomes slower and deeper
muscles become more relaxed, and
hands become drier

Again, almost immediately, your body reacts to what you think. This happens regardless of whether you are telling the truth or lying—your body reacts to every thought you have, whether it is about school, friends, family, or anything else.

5. Thoughts are very powerful! They can make your mind and body feel good or they can make you feel bad. Every cell in your body is affected by every thought you have. That is why when people get emotionally upset they often develop physical symptoms, such as headaches or stomachaches. **If you can think about good things, you will feel better.** Did you know that Abraham Lincoln had periods of bad depression well into adulthood? He even thought about killing himself and

had some days when he didn't get out of bed. In his later life, however, he learned to treat his bad feelings with laughter. He became a very good storyteller and loved to tell jokes. He learned that when he laughed, he felt better.

6. Your automatic thoughts do not always tell you the truth. I once knew a boy who thought he was stupid because he didn't do well on tests. When we tested his IQ, however, we discovered that he was close to being a genius! **You don't have to believe every thought that goes through your head.** It's important to think about your thoughts to see if they help you or they hurt you. Unfortunately, if you never challenge your thoughts, you just "believe them" as if they were true. These negative thoughts invade your mind like ants at a picnic (or in my kitchen). One negative thought, like one ant at a picnic, is not a big deal. Two or three negative thoughts, like two or three ants at a picnic, become more irritating. And ten or twenty negative thoughts can cause real problems.

7. **You can train your thoughts to be positive and hopeful** or you can just allow them to be negative and upset you. Once you learn about your thoughts, you can choose to think good thoughts and feel good, or you can choose to think bad thoughts and feel lousy. That's right, it's up to you. Research has even shown that positive emotions—especially a sense of awe—can reduce inflammation that might otherwise adversely affect your health (95). You can learn how to change your thoughts and you can learn to change the way you feel.

   One way to learn how to change your thoughts is to notice them when they are negative and talk back to them. If you can correct negative thoughts, you take away their power over you. When you just think a negative thought without challenging it, your mind believes it and your body reacts to it.

   Learning how to not believe every stupid thought you have is a critical skill to ending unnecessary suffering. ANTs pop up in your brain automatically, seemingly out of nowhere, and when left unchallenged, they bite, nibble, torture, and infest your mind. When the

ANTs are left unchecked they steal your happiness and literally make you feel old, fat, depressed, and feeble-minded.

Whenever you notice these automatic negative thoughts or ANTs you need to crush them or they'll begin to ruin your whole day. One way to crush these ANTs is to write down the negative thought and talk back to it. For example, if you think, "Other people will laugh at me when I give my speech," write it down and then write a positive response; something like: "Others may find it interesting." Doing this helps take away their power and will help you feel better. Some people tell me they have trouble talking back to these negative thoughts because they feel that they are lying to themselves. They believe that the thoughts that go through their minds first are the truth. Remember, thoughts sometimes lie to you. It's important to check them out before you just believe them!

Here are nine different ways that our thoughts lie to us and make situations out to be worse than they really are. Think of these nine ways as different species or types of ANTs. When you can identify the type of ANT, you begin to take away the power it has over you. I have labeled some of these ANTs as red, because they are particularly harmful to you. Notice and exterminate ANTs whenever possible.

ANT #1: All-or-nothing thinking: these thoughts happen when you make something out to be all good or all bad. There's nothing in between. You see everything in black or white terms. If a baseball player strikes out, he may think he's the worst player ever, rather than saying to himself, "The best baseball players make an out seven times out of ten. Next time will be better."

ANT #2: "Always" thinking: this happens when you think something that happened will "always" repeat itself. For example, if your wife is irritable and she gets upset you might think to yourself, "She's always yelling at me," even though she yells only once in a while. But just the thought "She's always yelling at me" is so negative that it makes you feel sad and upset. Whenever you think in words like *always, never, no one, everyone, every time,* or *everything,* you're falling prey to "always" thinking, which isn't usually accurate. There are many examples of "always" thinking: "No one ever calls me." "Everyone is always picking on me at work." "You never listen to me." This type of ANT is very common. Watch out for it.

ANT #3 (red ANT): Focusing on the negative: this occurs when your thoughts only see the bad in a situation and ignore any of the good that might happen. For example, let's say you gave a presentation at work. Most of your coworkers told you that you did a great job, but one person fell asleep during the talk and now all you can think about was how boring it must have been. If you want to keep your mind healthy, it's very important to focus on the good parts of your life more than you do the bad parts. I once helped a child who was depressed. In the beginning, he could only think about the bad things that happened to him. He had recently moved and told me that he would never make new friends (even though he already had several). He thought he would do poorly in his new school (even though he got mostly good grades), and that he would never have any fun (even though his new house was near a bay and an amusement park). By focusing on the negative in his new situation, he was making it very hard on himself to adjust. He would have been much better off if he looked at all the positives in the situation rather than the negatives. After three weeks of ANT therapy, he told me, "It's an ANT ghost town in my head."

ANT #4 (red ANT): Fortune telling: this is where you predict the worst possible outcome to a situation. For example, let's say you just started a vacation and the hotel had trouble checking you in. You immediately think that this is a sign that everything else will go wrong. The first negative thing that happens can put you into a depression spiral.

ANT #5 (red ANT): Mind reading: this happens when you believe that you know what another person is thinking when they haven't even told you. Many people do this, and more often than not it gets them into trouble. It's a major reason why people have trouble in relationships. I tell people, "Please don't read my mind; I have enough trouble reading it myself!"

You know you're mind reading when you have thoughts such as "Those people are mad at me. They don't like me. They're talking about me."

ANT #6: Thinking with your feelings: this occurs when you believe your negative feelings without ever questioning them. Feelings are very complex, and as I mentioned above, they sometimes lie to you. But many people believe their feelings even if there's no evidence for them. "Thinking with your feelings" thoughts usually start with the words *I feel*. For example, "I feel like you don't love me." "I feel stupid." "I feel like a failure." "I feel nobody will ever trust me." Whenever you have a strong negative feeling, check it out. Look for the evidence behind the feeling. Do you have real reasons to feel that way? Or are your feelings based on events, insecurities, or things from the past?

ANT #7: Guilt beatings: Guilt is typically not a helpful emotion. In fact, guilt often causes you to do things that you don't want to do. Guilt beatings happen when you think with words like *should, must, ought,* or *have to.* Here are some examples: "I must never lie." "I ought to call my grandmother." "I have to pay my bills." Because of human nature, whenever we think that we "must" do something, no matter what it is, we don't want to do it. Remember the story of Adam and Eve. The only restriction that God put on them when he gave them the Garden of Eden was that they shouldn't eat from the Tree of Knowledge. Almost immediately after God told them what they "shouldn't do," they started to wonder why they shouldn't do it. Well, you know how the rest of the story turned out.

It is better to replace guilt beatings with phrases like "I want to do this," "It fits my goals to do that," "It would be helpful to do this," etc. So in our examples above, it would be more productive to rephrase those thoughts to: "It's helpful for me not to lie, because people will trust me." "I want to call my grandmother." "It's in my best interest to pay my bills."

ANT #8: Labeling: whenever you attach a negative label to yourself or to someone else you inhibit your ability to take a clear look at the situation. Some examples of negative labels are *nerd, jerk, idiot, spoiled brat,* and *clown.* Negative labels are very harmful. Whenever you call yourself or someone else a spoiled brat or an idiot you lump that person in your mind with all of the "spoiled brats" or "idiots" that you've ever known and you become unable to deal with them in a reasonable way. Stay away from negative labels—for yourself and others.

ANT #9 (the most poisonous red ANT): Blaming: where you blame others for the problems in your life. Typically, you'll hear yourself thinking:

"It wasn't my fault that . . ."
"That wouldn't have happened if you had . . ."
"How was I supposed to know . . ."
"It's your fault that . . ."

Blaming others starts early. I have four children. When my next-to-youngest daughter, Katie, was eighteen months old she would blame her brother, who was eleven, for any trouble she might be in. Her nickname for him was Didi, and "Didi did it," even if he wasn't home. One day she spilled a drink at the table while her mother's back was turned. When she turned around and saw the mess, Katie told her, "Didi spilled my drink." When her mother told her that her brother was at a friend's house, Katie continued to insist her brother had done it.

Whenever you blame someone else for the problems in your life, you become powerless to change anything. Many of us play the blame game, but it rarely helps us. Stay away from blaming thoughts and take personal responsibility for changing the problems you have.

SUMMARY OF ANT TYPES:

1. All-or-nothing thinking: thoughts that things are all good or all bad.
2. "Always" thinking: thinking in words like *always, never, no one, everyone, every time,* or *everything.*
3. Focusing on the negative: only seeing the bad in a situation.

4. Fortune telling: predicting the worst possible outcome to a situation with little or no evidence for it.
5. Mind reading: believing that you know what another person is thinking even though they haven't told you.
6. Thinking with your feelings: believing negative feelings without ever questioning them.
7. Guilt beatings: thinking in words like *should, must, ought,* or *have to.*
8. Labeling: attaching a negative label to yourself or to someone else.
9. Blaming: blaming someone else for the problems you have.

Train yourself to recognize ANTs whenever one enters your mind and write them down. When you write down your ANTs and talk back to them, you begin to take away their power and gain control over your moods.

Here are some examples of ways to kill these ANTs:

ANT	SPECIES OF ANT	KILL THE ANT
There's nothing to do.	All or Nothing	There are probably lots of things to do if I think about it for a while.
No one will ever want to date me.	Always Thinking	That's silly; be patient and put myself in situations where I can meet people.
The boss doesn't like me.	Mind Reading	I don't know that. Maybe she's just having a bad day. Bosses are people too.
I'm stupid.	Labeling	Sometimes I do things that aren't too smart, but I'm not stupid.
It's my wife's fault.	Blaming	I need to look at my part of the problem and look for ways I can make the situation better.

Your thoughts matter. Kill the ANTs and train your thoughts to be positive and it will benefit your mind, mood, and body.

P—The Work in 4 Questions

Another technique that I teach all of my patients is called the Work. It was developed by my friend Byron Katie and is explained so well in her book *Loving What Is* (96). Katie, as her friends call her, describes her own experience suffering from suicidal depression. She was a young mother, businesswoman, and wife in the high desert of Southern California who became severely depressed at the age of thirty-three. For ten years, she sank deeper and deeper into self-loathing, rage, and despair, with constant thoughts of suicide and paranoia. For the last two years, she was often unable to leave her bedroom or care for herself or her family. Then one morning in 1986, out of nowhere, Katie woke up in a state of amazement, transformed by the realization that when she believed her thoughts, she suffered, but when she questioned her thoughts, she didn't suffer.

Katie's great insight is that it is not life or other people that make us feel depressed, angry, stressed, abandoned, and despairing: it is our own thoughts that make us feel that way. In other words, we can live in a hell of our own making, or we can live in a heaven of our own making.

Katie developed a simple method of inquiry to help people question their thoughts. It consists of writing down any thoughts that are bothering us, or any in which we are judging other people. Then we ask ourselves four questions, and do what Katie calls a "turnaround." The goal is not so much positive thinking as accurate thinking. The four questions are:

1. Is it true? (Is the stressful or negative thought true?)
2. Can I absolutely know that it's true?
3. How do I react when I believe that thought?
4. Who would I be without the thought? Or, how would I feel if I didn't have the thought?

The "turnaround": after you answer the four questions, take the original thought and completely turn it around to its opposite, and ask yourself whether this new version of the thought that is causing your suffering is not true, or even truer than the original thought. In my office I frequently find myself at my whiteboard, writing these four questions and helping people talk back to the thoughts that make them suffer.

Rosemary's husband of thirty-four years died of cancer. Rosemary was the alumni director at my college and we have been friends for many years. After John's death she was very sad and lonely, and I helped her work through her grief. Two years after John died, Rosemary wanted to start dating again. She loved being in a close relationship, but she told me, "No one would ever want a seventy-five-year-old woman." So we worked on that thought.

- Question #1: Is it true that no one would ever want a seventy-five-year-old woman?
  "Yes," she said. "I am too old to date."
- Okay . . . Question #2: Can you ABSOLUTELY know that it is true that no one would ever want a seventy-five-year-old woman?
  "No," she said. "Of course, I can't know that for sure."
- Question #3: How do you feel when you have the thought "No one would ever want a seventy-five-year-old woman?"
  "I feel sad, hopeless, angry at God, and overwhelmed by my loneliness."
- Question #4: Who would you be or how would you feel if you didn't have the thought "No one would ever want a seventy-five-year-old woman?"
  "Well, I would feel much happier, more optimistic. I would feel like my usual self," she said.
- Okay . . . now turn the original thought around: "No one would ever want a seventy-five-year-old woman." What is the opposite?
  "Someone will want a seventy-five-year-old woman."
  Okay . . . which is truer? "I don't know," she said, "but if I act like no one will want me, then no one will want me." After our exercise Rosemary started dating again. A year later she met Jack. When I sat with Rosemary and Jack for the first time it felt like I was with two fifteen-year-olds who had just fallen in love. It was so cool. They were married May 4, 2007.

All of us need a way to correct our thoughts. Just think about what would have happened to Rosemary if she didn't kill the ANTs that were

Image 7.1: Rosemary and Jack

stealing her happiness and robbing her joy. I have seen these four questions dramatically change people's lives, including my own.

Byron Katie's own brain provides the most powerful evidence of this technique. As I wrote above, before she found the ability to question her mind, she suffered for many years. But the four questions gave her peace.

P—Gratitude and Appreciation

When you bring your attention to the things you are grateful for in your life, your brain actually works better. Psychologist Noelle Nelson and I did a study on gratitude and appreciation. While she was working on a book called *The Power of Appreciation*, she underwent two SPECT scans. The first time, she was scanned after thirty minutes of meditating on all the things she was thankful for in her life. Her brain looked very healthy after this "appreciation meditation." Then she was scanned several days later after focusing on the major fears in her life. Noelle took the exercise very seriously, and let flow a string of frightening thoughts.

"If my dog got sick I couldn't go to work because I would have to stay home to care for him."

"If I didn't go to work, however, I would lose my job."

"If I lost my job, I wouldn't have enough money to take my dog to the vet and he would likely die."

"If the dog died I would be so depressed I still wouldn't be able to go back to work."

"Then I would lose my home, and become homeless."

Then I scanned her brain. Her frightened brain looked very different from her gratitude brain. She had seriously decreased activity in two parts of her brain. Her cerebellum was completely shut down. If you recall, the cerebellum is known to be involved in physical coordination, such as walking or playing sports. New research also suggests that the cerebellum is involved in processing speed—in other words, how quickly we can integrate new

Images 7.2–5

Grateful 7.2   Fearful 7.3

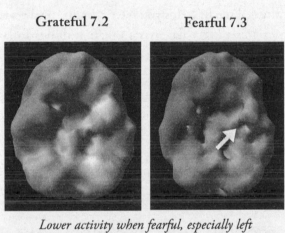

Lower activity when fearful, especially left
temporal lobe (arrow)

Grateful 7.4   Fearful 7.5

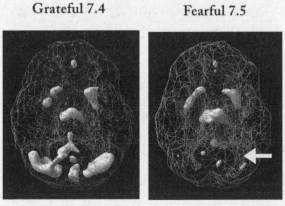

Drop out of cerebellum when fearful (arrow)

information. When the cerebellum is low in activity people tend to be clumsier and less likely to think their ways out of problems. They think and process information more slowly and they get confused more easily. When I saw Noelle's second scan, I thought, "This is why negative thinking is involved in athletic slumps." If an athlete thinks he will fail, likely he will. I now had proof that negative thinking actually shuts down the coordination part of the brain. Noelle's "fear meditation" had also reduced activity in her temporal lobes, which are involved with mood, memory, and temper control. Problems in this part of the brain are associated with some forms of depression, but also dark thoughts, violence, and memory problems. Negative thought patterns change the brain in a negative way, but conversely, practicing gratitude literally helps you have a brain to be grateful for.

Here is an exercise: every day, write out five things for which you are grateful. The act of writing helps to solidify them in your brain. In my experience, when depressed patients do this exercise every day they get better faster. Other researchers have found that people who express gratitude on a regular basis are healthier, more optimistic, make more progress toward their goals, have a greater sense of well-being, and are more helpful to others. Doctors who regularly practice gratitude are actually better at making correct diagnoses on their patients.

SOCIAL LIMBIC PRESCRIPTIONS

S—Surround Yourself with People Who Provide Positive Bonding

Have you ever picked up a container that had ants crawling on it? Within seconds they've crawled onto your body and you are hurriedly trying to brush them off. If you spend a lot of time with negative people, the same thing will happen. You may walk into a room in a buoyant mood, but before long their ANTs are going to rub off on you. Their ANTs will hang out and mate with your ANTs! That's not what you want—so surround yourself with positive people as much as possible.

Look at your life as it is now. What kind of people are around you? Do they believe in you and make you feel good about yourself, or are they constantly putting you down and denigrating your ideas, hopes, and dreams? List the ten people you spend the most time with. Make a note of how much they support you and the ways in which you would like to be supported more.

In my second year of college, I got the bright idea that I wanted to go to medical school. I was on the speech team, and one day I told my speech coach about my dream to become a physician. The first thing out of her mouth was that she had a brother at Michigan State who hadn't made it into medical school. "And," she added, "he was much smarter than you are." The message was clear: you don't have a chance. Making a big decision like that was hard enough to do with encouragement; the disheartening comment from the coach was a blow to my confidence I did not need. I went home with my spirits considerably dampened. Later that evening when I told my father what had happened, he just shook his head and said, "Listen, you can do whatever you put your mind to. And if I were you, I wouldn't spend much time with that coach."

If you think of your life as an obstacle course, it is easy to understand that the fewer obstacles in the road, the better off you will be. Negative people present unnecessary obstacles for you to overcome, because you have to push your will to succeed over their doubts, objections, and cynicism. Spending time with people who believe you'll never really amount to anything will dampen your enthusiasm for pursuing your goals and make it difficult to move through life in the direction you want to go. On the other hand, people who instill confidence in you with a can-do attitude and people whose spirits are uplifting will help breathe life into your plans and dreams.

It cannot be overemphasized how contagious the attitudes of others are and how much hidden influence they can exert. The reason so many people feel good about attending a positive-thinking seminar is that they have been in a room full of people who were all reaffirming the best in one another. But let one of those people go home and walk into a house where someone makes fun of his efforts and says he's wasting his time and will never get anywhere anyway, and watch how fast the positive effects of the seminar wear off!

When you spend a lot of time with people, you bond with them in certain ways, and as I mentioned earlier, the moods and thoughts of others directly affect your limbic system. If you go out with someone for dinner and after the first half hour you're beginning to feel bad about yourself, and then you remember that you always feel bad about yourself when you have dinner with this person, you are not imagining it; your limbic system is actually being affected by him or her. Deciding that you don't want to spend time with people who are going to have an adverse effect on you doesn't mean you have to blame them for the way they are. It simply means that you have the right to choose a better life for yourself.

I believe that limbic bonding is one of the key principles behind the success of support groups like Alcoholics Anonymous. For years, clinicians have known that one of the best ways to help people with serious problems like alcoholism is to get them to connect with others who have the same problem. By seeing how others have learned from their experiences and gotten through tough times in positive ways, alcoholics can find the way out of their own plight. While gaining information about their disease is helpful, forming new relationships and connections with others may be the critical link in the chain of recovery. How our limbic system functions is essential to life itself. Choose to spend time with people who enhance the quality of your limbic system rather than those who cause it to become inflamed.

S—Protect Your Children with Limbic Bonding

In a study published in the *Journal of the American Medical Association*, researcher Michael Resnick, PhD, and colleagues at the University of Minnesota reported that teenagers who felt loved and connected to their parents had a significantly lower incidence of teenage pregnancy, drug use, violence, and suicide (97). So important is the bonding between children and parents that it overrides other factors traditionally linked to problem behavior, such as living in a single-parent home or spending less time with a child. The article concluded that the degree of connection (limbic bonding) that teenagers feel with parents and teachers is the most important determinant of whether they will engage in risky sexual activity, substance abuse, violence, or suicidal behavior.

Another study reported that "on average, parents spend less than seven minutes a week talking with their children." It is not possible to "limbically bond" and have much of a relationship in such little time. Children need actual physical time with their parents. Think about the times your parents spent positive one-on-one time with you. Did that make you feel important, special?

Some parents complain that their children are too busy or are not interested in spending time with them. When this happens, I recommend that parents force the issue with their kids, telling them that they're important to them and that they need to spend time with them. Of course, the way in which you spend time with them is critical. If you spend the time lecturing or interrogating them, neither of you will find it very enjoyable and both of you will look for ways to avoid contact in the future.

Here is an exercise that I've found extremely powerful in improving the quality of time you have with your child. The exercise is called "special time." Special time works. It will improve the quality of your relationship with your child in a very short period of time. It also works for older children and teens. Here are the directions.

1. Spend twenty minutes a day with the child doing something that he or she would like to do. It's important to approach the child in a positive way and say something like "I feel we have not had enough time together and you're important to me. Let's spend some special time together every day. What would you like to do?" It's important to remember that the purpose of this time is to build the limbic bond and relationship with your child. Keep it as positive as possible.

2. During special time there are to be no parental commands, no questions, and no directions. This is very important. This is a time to build the relationship, not discipline difficult behavior. If, for example, you're playing a game and the child starts to cheat, you can reframe her behavior. You can say something like "I see you've changed the rules of the game, and I'll play by your rules." Remember, the goal of special time is to improve the relationship between you and your child, not to teach. Of course, at other times, if the child cheats it is important to deal straightforwardly with it.

3. Notice as many positive behaviors as you can. Noticing the good is much more effective in shaping behavior than noticing the bad.

4. Do much more listening than talking.

I once received a phone call from a friend of mine who complained that his eighteen-month-old daughter did not want anything to do with him when he came home from work. He told me that he thought it must be "one of those mother-daughter things" and that she'd probably grow out of it. I told him that it probably meant he wasn't spending enough time with his daughter and that if he did special time with his daughter she would become much more open and affectionate with him. My friend took my advice. He spent twenty minutes a day doing something that his daughter chose (usually playing with blocks in her room). He spent the time listening to her and feeding back what he heard her say. Within three weeks, his daughter's behavior dramatically changed. Whenever my friend would come home from work, his daughter would run to hug him, and she would hang on to his leg all evening.

Remember, spending actual physical daily time with your child will have a powerfully positive effect on your relationship and protect your child from many of the potential problems in life.

S—Build People Skills to Enhance Limbic Bonds

It has been shown that enhancing emotional bonds between people will help heal the limbic system. In one large study in which patients were treated for major depression (98), the National Institutes of Health compared three approaches: antidepressant medication, cognitive therapy (similar to my ANT therapy), and interpersonal psychotherapy (enhancing relationship skills). Researchers were surprised to find that each of the treatments was equally effective in treating depression; many people in the medical community think that the benefits of medication far outweigh the benefits of therapy. Not surprising was the fact that combining all three treatments had an even more powerful effect. So not only were pharmaceuticals and professional therapists helpful, but patients played a significant role in helping each other. How you get along with other people can either help or hurt your limbic system! The better you get along with those around you, the better you will feel.

I teach my patients the following seven principles to help keep their relationships healthy and rewarding:

1. Take responsibility for keeping your important relationships strong. Don't be the type of person who blames other people for the problems in your life. It will take you down the rabbit hole of victimhood. Take responsibility for making your key relationships better and look for ways to improve them today. If you do this, your relationships will improve almost immediately.

2. Never take relationships for granted. They need to be constantly nurtured, like plants need water.

3. Protect your relationship. A surefire way to doom a relationship is to discount, belittle, or degrade other people. Protect your relationships by building those people up.

4. Clarify any hurts early. Whenever there is a question of motivation or intention, check with them about their behavior or motives. You cannot read other people's minds.

5. Notice what you like more than what you don't. It's very easy to notice what you do not like about a relationship, but when you spend more time noticing the positive aspects of the relationship, you're more likely to see an increase in positive behavior.

6. Maintain and protect trust. So many relationships fall apart after there has been a major violation of trust, such as an affair or other form of dishonesty. Once a violation has occurred, try to understand why it happened.

7. Deal with difficult issues. Whenever you give in to another person to avoid a fight, you give away a little of your power. If you do this over time, you give away a lot of power and begin to resent the relationship. Avoiding conflict in the short run often has devastating long-term effects. In a firm but kind way, stick up for what you think is right. It will help keep the relationship balanced.

B/S—Recognize the Importance of Physical Contact

The limbic system is not only involved in emotional bonding, it is also involved in physical bonding. Touch is critical to life itself. In a barbaric thirteenth-century experiment, the German emperor Frederick II wanted to know what language and words children would speak if they were raised without hearing any words at all. He took a number of infants from their homes and put them with people who fed them but had strict instructions not to touch, cuddle, or talk to them. The babies never spoke a word. They all died before they could speak. Salimbene, a historian of the time, wrote of the experiment in 1248, "They could not live without petting." This powerful finding has been rediscovered over and over. In the early 1990s thousands of Romanian infants were orphaned and warehoused without touch, sometimes years at a time. PET studies (similar to SPECT studies) of a number of these deprived infants have shown marked overall decreased activity across the whole brain (99).

Physical connection is also a critical element in the parent-infant bonding process. The caressing, kissing, sweet words, and eye contact from the baby's mother and father give it the pleasure, love, trust, and security it needs to develop healthy limbic pathways. From this, a bond or connectedness between the parents and the baby can begin to grow. Without love and affection, the baby does not develop appropriate limbic connectedness and thus never learns to trust or connect to others. The baby feels lonely and insecure, and becomes irritable and unresponsive.

Bonding is a two-way street. A naturally unresponsive baby may inadvertently receive less love from its parents. The mother and father, misreading their baby's naturally reserved behavior, may feel hurt and rejected and therefore less encouraged to lavish care and affection on their child. A classic example of this problem is illustrated by autistic children. Psychiatrists used to label the mothers of autistic children "cold"; they believed the mother's lack of responsiveness caused the autism. In recent times, however, it has been shown in numerous research studies that autism *is* biological (100, 101) and precedes any relationship. The mothers of autistic children in their studies started out warm, but actually became more reserved when they did not get positive feedback from their children. The kind of love that is critical to making the parent-infant bond work is reciprocal.

Love between adults is similar. For proper bonding to occur, couples need to hold and kiss each other, say sweet words, and make affectionate eye contact. It is not enough for one side to give and the other to passively receive. Physical manifestations of love need to be reciprocated or the other partner feels hurt and rejected, which ultimately causes the bond to erode.

Journalists George Howe Colt and Anne Hollister cite numerous incidents of the healing power of touch: "Studies have shown massage to have positive effects on conditions from colic to hyperactivity to diabetes to migraines, in fact, every malady TRI [Touch Research Institute, in Miami, Florida] has studied thus far." They report that "massage, it seems, helps asthmatics breathe easier, boosts immune function in HIV-positive patients, improves autistic children's ability to concentrate, lowers anxiety in depressed adolescents, and reduces apprehension in burn victims about to undergo debridement. . . . Even in the elderly, elders exhibited less depression, lower stress hormones, and less loneliness. They had fewer doctor visits, drank less coffee, and made more social phone calls."

Healthy touch is essential to our humanity. Yet, in our standoffish, litigious society, touch is becoming less and less frequent. Touch your children, your spouse, your loved ones regularly. Giving and receiving massages on a regular basis will enhance limbic health and limbic bonding.

SPIRITUAL LIMBIC PRESCRIPTIONS

Sp—Passion and Purpose

Having a sense of purpose in life may help you live longer, no matter what your age.

Researchers evaluated data from over six thousand participants, focusing on their self-reported purpose in life (e.g., "Some people wander aimlessly through life, but I am not one of them") and other psychological variables. Over a fourteen-year follow-up period, 569 participants died (about 9 percent of the sample). Those who had died had reported lower purpose in life and fewer positive relations than did survivors. Greater purpose in life consistently predicted lower mortality risk across the lifespan (36). Similar findings were concluded in a review of ten studies of 137,142 subjects: researchers found that those with a higher sense of purpose in life had a lower risk of dying from any disease, including cardiovascular events (38).

Barbara Bush is a great example of this (102). In her early fifties, the former first lady went through a period of depression, when she felt like crying every day and had really dark thoughts. Like so many people, she was ashamed to seek help. She found that when she started to volunteer and direct her attention to help others, she started to feel much better. When she had a reason to get up and a purpose to her day, it had a healing effect.

What is important to you? What do you care deeply about? What makes your brain sing? Answering these questions can help your mood; they can also help you live a longer, fuller life.

Sp—Random Acts of Kindness

Can being kind to others make a meaningful difference in your level of happiness? Psychologist Sonja Lyubomirsky, from the University of California, Riverside, decided to put this question to the test with a controlled study that asked students to carry out five weekly "random acts of kindness" of their choice, anything from buying food for a homeless person to helping a younger sibling with schoolwork. The students reported higher levels of happiness than the control group, with students who performed all five kind acts in one day feeling the best by the end of the six-week study period. Before this, other studies had found that altruistic people tend to be happy, but Dr. Lyubomirsky established that good deeds are actually a direct cause of an increase in well-being and can decrease depressive symptoms (103).

In another study, researchers at the University of Wisconsin–Madison discovered that human kindness is teachable, and can change how the brain works in the process (104). Helen Weng and colleagues trained young adults to engage in a compassion meditation, an ancient Buddhist technique to increase feelings of empathy and compassion for people who are stressed and suffering. Participants focused on a time when someone else had suffered and then practiced praying that his or her suffering was relieved. They repeated phrases to help them focus on compassionate feelings, such as "May you be free from suffering." The participants in the study first chose a person on whom it might be easiest to practice compassion, such as a family member or a friend. They then practiced expanding compassionate feelings to a stranger, and even to themselves. Finally, they were trained how to extend these feelings to a "difficult person" in their lives.

Dr. Weng is quoted: "It's kind of like weight training. Using this systematic approach, we found that people can actually build up their compassion 'muscle' and respond to others' suffering with care and a desire to help." Brain-imaging studies found that compassion training actually boosted the function in several areas of the brain, including the prefrontal cortex, which is involved with empathy.

How many people can you show kindness to today?

8

Looking into Anxiety and Fear

The Basal Ganglia and More

FUNCTIONS OF THE BASAL GANGLIA

integrates feeling and movement
shifts and steadies fine motor movements
suppresses unwanted motor behaviors
helps to set the body's anxiety level
involved in forming habits
modulates motivation and drive
mediates pleasure/ecstasy

The basal ganglia are a set of large structures toward the center of the brain that surround the limbic system. They are involved with integrating feelings, thoughts, and movement, along with helping to shift and smooth motor behavior. Research suggests the basal ganglia are involved in forming habits (105, 106). At Amen Clinics, we've noticed they are also involved with setting the body's anxiety level. In addition, the basal ganglia help to modulate motivation (106) and are involved with feelings of pleasure and ecstasy (which is why drugs like cocaine and methamphetamines work in this part of the brain). Let's look at each of these functions in more depth.

The integration of feelings, thoughts, and movement in the basal ganglia causes you to jump when you get excited, tremble when you're nervous, freeze when you're scared, or get tongue-tied when the boss is chewing you out. The basal ganglia allow for a smooth integration of emotions, thoughts, and physical movement, and when there is too much input, they tend to lock up. A patient of mine was badly burned in a motorcycle accident in San Francisco. As he lay burning on the ground, people stood nearby, frozen with fear, unable to move to help him. For years he was confounded by their actions, wondering why no one had moved to help him. "Didn't they care? Was I not worth trying to help?" he wondered. For years this man lived with both the physical pain from the accident and the emotional pain of feeling that others did not care enough to help him. He was relieved to learn a new interpretation of the situation: the intensity of emotion caused by the fiery accident had overwhelmed the onlookers' basal ganglia and they had become unable to move, even though most of them probably wanted to help.

Image 8.1: The Basal Ganglia System

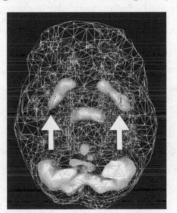

Underside active view (arrows point to basal ganglia)

When the basal ganglia are overactive (as we have seen in the case of people with anxiety tendencies or disorders), people are more likely to be overwhelmed by stressful situations and have a tendency to freeze or become immobile (in thoughts or actions). When their basal ganglia are underactive (as we have seen in people who have attention deficit disorder [ADD]), often a stressful situation moves them to action. People with ADD are frequently the first ones on the scene of an accident, and they respond to stressful situations without fear.

One day, my wife, Tana, and I were out for a walk, when a pit bull came running toward us. I froze (unsurprising, as my basal ganglia are always working overtime). But Tana rushed at the pit bull and scared him away. If you'll remember, Tana has ADD. She's also a neurosurgical intensive care nurse who's very competent in crises. Don't ask her to remember to close cabinet doors or focus when she isn't interested, but she is the one you want in an emergency. To have her in my life, I'll happily close the cabinet doors behind her.

Shifting and smoothing fine motor behavior is another function of the basal ganglia and is essential to handwriting and motor coordination. Again, let's use the example of ADD, which tends to show low activity in the basal ganglia, as well as the prefrontal cortex and cerebellum. Many children and adults with ADD have very poor handwriting. The act of handwriting is difficult and often stressful for them. Their writing may be choppy or sloppy (107). In fact, many teens and adults with ADD print rather than write in cursive. They find printing easier because it is not a smooth, continuous motor movement, but rather a start-and-stop motor activity. Many people with ADD also complain that they have trouble getting their thoughts out of their head and onto paper, a term called finger agnosia (the fingers cannot tell what the brain is thinking). We know that the medications that help ADD, such as the psychostimulants Ritalin, Dexedrine, and Adderall, work by enhancing the production of the neurotransmitter dopamine in the basal ganglia. These medications sometimes improve handwriting and enhance a person's ability to get his or her thoughts onto paper to an amazing extent. In addition, many people with ADD say that their overall motor coordination is improved by these medications. Below is an example from one of my patients.

Another clue about the motor control functions of the basal ganglia comes from the understanding of two other illnesses, Parkinson's disease (PD) and Tourette's syndrome (TS). PD is caused by a deficiency of dopamine within the basal ganglia system. It is characterized by a "pill rolling" hand tremor, muscle rigidity, cogwheeling (jerky, stop-and-start movements

Hello, my name is Tommy.

Tommy, age fourteen, handwriting, no medication

Hello, my name is Tommy.

Tommy's handwriting after ADD diagnosis and treatment with stimulant medication

when trying to rotate a joint), loss of agility, loss of facial expression, and slow movements. Often, giving persons dopamine-enhancing drugs, such as L-dopa, helps these symptoms by facilitating smoother motor movements. The basal ganglia are also involved in suppressing unwanted motor activity. When there are abnormalities in this part of the brain, people are more at risk for Tourette's syndrome, which is a combination of motor and vocal tics (more on TS later in the chapter).

In our brain-imaging work, we have seen that the basal ganglia are also involved in setting your anxiety level. Overactive basal ganglia are often associated with anxiety, tension, increased awareness, and heightened fear (108). Underactive basal ganglia can cause problems with motivation and energy. The basal ganglia have also been reported to be involved in learning, habit formation, and repetitive behaviors (109, 110). In our research, one of the strongest statistical findings associated with increased activity in the basal ganglia is nail biting, which is usually a habitual expression of anxiety. With my overactive basal ganglia, it's no surprise that I used to bite my nails until my fingers bled.

Interestingly, some of the most highly motivated individuals we've scanned, such as entrepreneurs and corporate CEOs, have significant increased activity in this part of the brain. We theorize that some people can use this increased activity in the form of motivation to become "movers" in society. My mother, for example, who like me has increased activity in this part of the brain, does tend to be a bit anxious, but she is a woman on the go. She raised seven children without appearing stressed, and at the age of eighty-four plays golf several times a week and is always up "doing something" for other people. I believe that using the additional energy and drive from increased basal ganglia activity helps ward off anxiety. In our database, we have seen a strong association of "excessive motivation" with high basal ganglia activity.

Another interesting finding about this part of the brain is that the basal ganglia are likely involved in the pleasure control loops of the brain. One brain-imaging study performed by Nora Volkow's group at the Brookhaven National Laboratory in Upton, New York, looked at where cocaine and Ritalin work in the brain. Both were taken up mostly by the basal ganglia (111). While cocaine is an addictive substance, Ritalin (in doses prescribed for ADD) typically is not. The study clearly showed why. Cocaine is a powerful enhancer of dopamine availability in the brain, and it has both very fast uptake and clearance from the brain. It comes on strong in a powerful wave, and then it's gone. The user gets a high, and when it's gone, he or she wants more. In contrast, while Ritalin also increases the availability of dopamine to the basal ganglia, its effects are less powerful and it clears from the brain at a much slower rate. Dr. Volkow's group postulated that activation of the basal ganglia by cocaine perpetuates the compulsive desire for the drug. Ritalin, on the other hand, enhances motivation, focus, and follow-through, but does not give users a high or an intense desire to use more (unless at much higher doses than clinically prescribed). In fact, one of the biggest clinical problems I have with teenagers who have ADD is that they forget to take their medication.

Intense romantic love can also have a cocaine-like effect on the brain, robustly releasing dopamine in the basal ganglia. Love has real physical effects. I had the opportunity to scan a close friend, Bill, shortly after he had met a new woman. He was head over heels for her. After their third date, when they spent the day at the beach in each other's arms, my friend came by my office to tell me about his newfound love. He was so happy he almost seemed to have a drug high. By coincidence, while Bill was talking, my nuclear technician came into my office and told me we had an extra dose of the isotope and could do another scan if I had someone who needed one. Since I had an earlier scan of Bill's brain as part of our normal control group, I decided we'd scan him again and get a look at the brain of new love. To my amazement, his brain looked as if he had just taken a lot of cocaine. The activity in both the right and left basal ganglia was very intense, almost to the point of resembling seizure activity. Love has real effects on the brain that are as powerful as addictive drugs.

Image 8.2: Bill's Love-Affected Scan

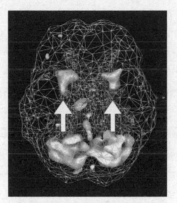

*Increased left and right basal
ganglia activity (arrows)*

PROBLEMS WITH THE BASAL GANGLIA

anxiety, nervousness (112, 113)
physical sensations of anxiety
tendency to predict the worst
conflict avoidance (114)
risk aversion (115)
Tourette's syndrome/tics (116)
muscle tension, soreness
tremors
fine motor problems
low/excessive motivation
sensitivity to rejection (117)
social anxiety (118, 119)

ANXIETY

Any discussion about anxiety must start with the good aspects of it. People with really low levels of anxiety are constantly late, often die early from preventable health-related problems, and are more likely to go to jail. As you can see, some anxiety is good. Appropriate levels of anxiety prevent you from driving too fast on a rainy night, get you to pay your taxes on time, and stop you from having an affair when you want to stay married. In one of the most important studies, in 1921, researchers from Stanford University evaluated 1,548 ten-year-old children, looking for the traits that were associated with health, success, and longevity. They then continued to follow them over the next ninety years. The results were fascinating. Longevity was not associated with happiness or a lack of worry. In fact, the don't-worry-be-happy people died the earliest from accidents and preventable illnesses, because they tended to underestimate risks. The trait most associated with longevity was conscientiousness, which meant if you said you were going to do something—and you actually consistently followed through—you lived longer than did others (120). Of course, balance is important. You want to have enough anxiety to do the right things, but not so much that it causes you to suffer.

When researchers look at the brains of anxious subjects they often find a number of areas of the brain with heightened activity, including the:

- basal ganglia
- amygdala and hippocampus in the medial areas of the temporal lobes
- insular cortex (between temporal lobes and prefrontal cortex)
- areas of the prefrontal cortex, especially on the right side

Many of the patients we have treated with anxiety disorders have had heightened activity in these areas of the brain. Here's one of the first patients I scanned who had a severe struggle with lifelong anxiety.

Gary

Gary went to his doctor complaining of back pain. The doctor examined Gary's back and found a tender spot over his kidneys. He asked Gary to get a kidney X-ray. As soon as the doctor asked him to get an X-ray, Gary's thoughts took off: "The doctor is going to find out I have cancer." (Notice this little leap in logic!) But his thoughts didn't stop there. Ten seconds later, he'd already put himself into treatment. "The doctor's going to find out I have cancer. I'm going to have to have chemotherapy. I'm going to vomit my guts out, lose all my hair, be in a tremendous amount of pain, and then I'm going to die!" His mind took him down the rabbit hole of a futuristic hell—all in a span of about thirty seconds. Then Gary had a panic attack. His heart began to race; his hands became cold; he started to hyperventilate; and he broke out in a sweat. He turned to the doctor and said, "I can't have that X-ray."

Bewildered, the doctor replied, "What do you mean? You came to see me to get help. I need this X-ray so I can figure out—"

Gary said, "No, you don't understand! I can't have the X-ray!"

The doctor found my number, called me, and said, "Daniel, please help me with this guy."

As Gary told me this story, I knew that he had a lifelong panic disorder. Gary was an expert at predicting the worst, which was driving his panic symptoms. In treating Gary, I taught him the Basal Ganglia Prescriptions given in the next chapter. I even went with him to have the kidney X-rays, because it was important to have it done quickly. I hypnotized him, enabling him to be calm through the procedure. He did wonderfully. He breathed in a relaxed way, and he went through the procedure without any problems—until the X-ray technician came back into the room with a worried look on his face and asked Gary which side of his back was giving him pain. Gary grabbed his chest and looked at me like "You SOB! I knew you were lying to me about this! I'm going to die!" I patted him on the leg and said, "Look, Gary, before you die, let me take a look at the X-ray" (psychiatrists are also medical doctors). As I looked at his X-ray I could see that Gary had a big kidney stone, which can be terribly painful—but kidney stones don't usually kill anybody! Gary's basal ganglia, as well as the other areas described above, were working too hard, putting him through tremendous emotional pain by causing him to predict the worst possible outcome to situations. Anxious thoughts can make pain worse. As Gary became more upset about his pain, the anxiety signals caused his muscles to contract; the smooth muscles in the ureter (the tube from the kidneys to the bladder) contracted, clamping down on the stone and intensifying the pain.

Over time, Gary's four-circles interventions included: **B**—the anticonvulsant medication gabapentin (Neurontin) to calm the anxiety (today I would have started with the supplements magnesium, GABA, theanine, and Relora to help soothe the anxiety), omega-3 fatty acids, and diaphragmatic breathing exercises; **P**—meditation, hypnosis, and ANT therapy to question the automatic negative thoughts; **S**—group therapy to enhance his social skills; **Sp**—an extended discussion to help Gary develop a clear sense of meaning and purpose.

Anxiety-provoking situations also cause many people with overactive basal ganglia to become frozen with fear and unable to leave their homes, a condition called agoraphobia (fear of being in public). I have treated many people who have been housebound for years (one woman for forty years) because of fear of having a panic attack.

Marsha

Marsha, a critical care nurse, was forced into treatment by her husband. She was thirty-six years old when she first began experiencing panic attacks. She was in a grocery store when all of a sudden she felt dizzy and short of breath, with a racing heart and a terrible sense of impending doom. She left her cart in the store and ran to her car, where she cried for over an hour. After her first episode, the panic attacks increased in frequency to the point where she stopped going out of her house, fearing that she'd have an attack and be unable to get help. She stopped working and made her husband take the children to and from school. She was opposed to any medication, because in the past her mother, in attempting to treat her own panic attacks, had become addicted to Valium and had often been quite mean to Marsha. Marsha did not want to see herself as being in any way like her mother. She believed that she "should" be able to control these attacks. Her husband, seeing her dysfunction only worsen, took her to see a family counselor. The counselor taught her relaxation exercises and how to talk back to her negative thoughts, but it didn't help. Her condition worsened, and her husband brought her to see me. Given her resistance to treatment, I decided to order a SPECT study to evaluate Marsha's brain so I could discuss it with her.

Image 8.3: Marsha's Panic-Disorder-Affected Brain

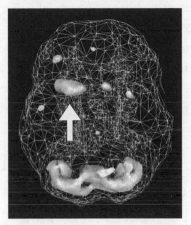

3-D UNDERSIDE ACTIVE VIEW
*Note increased right basal ganglia
activity (arrow).*

Her SPECT study revealed marked increased focal activity in the right side of her basal ganglia. Interestingly, the findings on her scan convinced Marsha to try medication. Her four-circles interventions included: **B**—gabapentin (Neurontin) to quiet her basal ganglia, omega-3 fatty acids, and diaphragmatic breathing exercises; **P**—hypnosis and ANT therapy; **S**—family therapy to help her family understand her illness; **Sp**—reconnecting with her sense of purpose, which had been very high as a mother, wife, and nurse. After two months of treatment she was able to leave her house, go back to work, and resume her life. Several years later she was able to completely stop her medication and has remained panic-free.

POSTTRAUMATIC STRESS DISORDER

Posttraumatic stress disorder (PTSD) occurs after experiencing a traumatic event that resets the brain to a perpetually more active state. Our published work on over one thousand patients with PTSD demonstrates increased limbic, basal ganglia, and anterior cingulate gyrus activity in what looks like a diamond pattern (see Image 8.4). Common PTSD symptoms also associated with increased activity in these areas are:

- recurrent upsetting thoughts or dreams of a past traumatic event (molestation, accident, fire, etc.)
- panicked or fearful response to experiences that resemble that past event
- efforts to avoid thoughts or feelings associated with a past trauma
- feeling that your future is shortened
- being easily startled
- constant anxiety or fear of future bad events

Image 8.4: PTSD and the Diamond Pattern

Increased anterior cingulate (top of diamond), thalamus (bottom of diamond), left and right basal ganglia (sides of diamond), right lateral temporal lobe (arrow on viewer's left indicates right temporal lobe)

In 2005, my colleagues and I evaluated and treated six police officers who had been involved in on-the-job shootings, developed PTSD, and were placed on medical leave. The "diamond pattern" was seen in all of their brain scans. After treatment with a special psychotherapeutic technique called EMDR (eye movement desensitization and reprocessing), they each reported significant improvement and all six officers went back to work. Their follow-up scans all showed calming of the hyperactive areas.

PTSD can be acute or chronic. It can occur right after a terrible event, or even appear years after the fact. It can also be chronic after years of abuse or growing up in an unpredictable and stressful home, such as with an alcoholic or drug-abusing parent. During my psychiatric training, I studied children and grandchildren of alcoholics. It was clear that persistent early childhood trauma could reset the activity in children's brains to a higher-than-normal level, setting them up for emotional problems later in life.

CONFLICT AVOIDANCE

Anxiety is, by definition, very uncomfortable. Thus, people who are anxious tend to avoid any situations that might make them more uncomfortable, especially dealing with conflict. People who have basal ganglia problems tend to be frozen by conflict, and consequently do what they can to avoid it. Unfortunately, conflict avoidance can have a serious negative impact on your life.

Loren

Loren, the owner of a neighborhood deli, hated conflict. He also had problems with chronic feelings of tension and anxiety. His fear of confrontation prevented him from firing employees who were not good for his business. It also caused him to be overly nice to people who were negative to him, so Loren grew to resent his own lack of assertiveness. His problems even caused marital difficulties. For years Loren wouldn't talk about the things in his marriage that made him unhappy. He would just hold them in until he finally exploded. Learning to deal with conflict was the centerpiece of his treatment.

TOURETTE'S SYNDROME (TS)

TS is a very interesting disorder that provides the bridge between the basal ganglia and two seemingly opposite disorders, attention deficit disorder (ADD) and obsessive-compulsive disorder (OCD). TS is characterized by motor and vocal tics lasting more than a year. Motor tics are involuntary physical movements such as eye blinking, head jerking, shoulder shrugging, and arm or leg jerking. Vocal tics typically involve making involuntary noises such as coughing, puffing, blowing, barking, and sometimes swearing (coprolalia). TS runs in families and may be associated with several genetic abnormalities found in the dopamine family of genes. SPECT studies of TS patients, by the Amen Clinics and others, have found abnormalities in the basal ganglia. One of the most fascinating aspects of TS is its high association with both ADD and OCD. It is estimated that 60 percent of people with TS have ADD and 50 percent have OCD. On the surface it would appear that these are opposing disorders. People with ADD have trouble paying attention, while people with OCD pay too much attention to their negative thoughts (obsessions) or behaviors (compulsions). In looking further at patients with both ADD and OCD, I have found a high association of each disease in their family histories. So, for example, people with ADD often have relatives with OCD-like features and people with OCD have people in their families with ADD. There is even a subtype of ADD that has been termed overfocused ADD; affected people have symptoms of both inattention and overfocus.

A crash course in the neurotransmitters (chemical messengers that help the brain to function) dopamine and serotonin is necessary here. In the brain there tends to be a balancing mechanism between dopamine and serotonin. This balance, however, tends to be played out in the basal ganglia. Dopamine is involved with motor movements, motivation, attention span, and setting the body's idle speed, while serotonin is more involved with mood control, shifting attention, and cognitive flexibility. When something happens in the brain to raise dopamine levels, serotonin becomes less effective; and when serotonin levels are raised, dopamine becomes less effective. For example, when I give someone a psychostimulant to treat ADD, it works by effectively raising the availability of dopamine in the basal ganglia. This helps with focus, follow-through, and motivation. If I give him too much, he may become obsessive, moody, and inflexible (symptoms of too little serotonin). Likewise, if I give someone who has ADD a medication that enhances serotonin availability in the brain, such as a selective serotonin reuptake inhibitor (SSRI), his ADD symptoms are likely to become worse, but he won't care that they are worse and will also show lowered motivation.

Since the basal ganglia are involved with dopamine production (low in ADD) and have been found to be overactive in OCD (in conjunction with the anterior cingulate gyrus), the basal ganglia are likely significantly involved in all three of these disorders. Blocking dopamine with certain antipsychotic medications like risperidone (Risperdal) helps to suppress tics but makes ADD symptoms worse; psychostimulants, such as Ritalin (methylphenidate) or Adderall (a combination of amphetamine salts), help ADD symptoms but have a variable effect on tics (they may make them better or worse). Also as mentioned, psychostimulants tend to exacerbate OCD symptoms and cause people to focus more on the thoughts or behaviors that bother them. An interference mechanism in the basal ganglia is likely to be part of the picture, upsetting the dopamine-serotonin balance in the brain.

I once gave a keynote lecture to the Tourette Syndrome Foundation of Canada. I was in a room with four hundred people with TS, many of whom exhibited both motor tics (head shaking, shoulder shrugs, etc.) and vocal tics (such as honking, barking, and in some cases swearing). About halfway through my lecture someone yelled loudly, "Fuck you!," which made me catch my breath. No one had said that to me since my first wife. I chose to ignore the comment, hoping it wouldn't recur. Then about three minutes later, "Fuck you!" came again from the audience. Now I started to sweat, but still didn't say anything. Then a few minutes later the f-bomb filled the air. I stopped the lecture and found the person who was shouting out and asked, "Is that a tic or don't you like the lecture?" He turned red and replied, "I'm so sorry. I like the lecture." But how did I really know?

FINE MOTOR PROBLEMS

As discussed earlier, fine motor problems, like handwriting issues, are often associated with low basal ganglia activity. Another interesting connection that is probably related to basal ganglia hyperactivity is the development of fine motor tremors when we become anxious. When I was a young lecturer in front of an audience, I didn't hold papers in my hands because I was concerned the paper might start to rattle or shake in response to the anxiety I felt. When the basal ganglia are overactive, we are more at risk for increased muscle tension or tremors. In my practice I have often prescribed the medication propranolol to calm the tremors musicians get during a performance.

Increased muscle tension related to overactive basal ganglia activity is often associated with headaches. I have noticed that a number of people with resistant headaches have intense focal areas of increased activity in the basal ganglia. This seems to occur with both muscle contraction headaches (often described as a pain in the back of the neck or as a tight band around the forehead) and migraines (usually one-sided throbbing headaches that may be preceded by a visual aura or other warning phenomena). Interestingly, anticonvulsant medication such as topiramate (Topamax), which decreases areas of overactivity in the brain, is often helpful in decreasing some types of headaches.

LOW AND HIGH MOTIVATION

As stated earlier, motivation tends to be low in dopamine-deficient states, such as in ADD. However, when serotonin levels are raised too high, decreased motivation also becomes a problem. Physicians know that if a dose of serotonin-enhancing antidepressants is too high, lowered motivation is often the result. Many people have told me they stopped these medications because with them, they stopped doing things that were important to their business or home life. One CEO told me he had stopped taking his SSRI because he realized he wasn't keeping up with his paperwork and he really didn't care. "That's not like me," he said.

Heightened dopamine or basal ganglia states may also cause increased or even excessive motivation. As I mentioned earlier, we found that many CEOs of corporations have enhanced basal ganglia activity. They also tend to work excessive hours. In fact, weekends tend to be the hardest time for these people. During the week, they charge through each day, getting things done. On the weekend, during unstructured time, they often complain of feeling restless, anxious, and out of sorts. Relaxation is foreign to them. In fact, it is downright uncomfortable. Workaholics may be made in the basal ganglia. Their internal idle speed or energy level doesn't allow them to rest. Of course, there is a positive correlate. Many of the people in society who make things happen are driven by basal ganglia that keep them working for long periods of time.

BASAL GANGLIA CHECKLIST

Here is a basal ganglia system checklist. Please read this list of behaviors and rate yourself (or the person you are evaluating) on each behavior listed. Use the following scale and place the appropriate number next to the item. Five or more symptoms marked 3 or 4 indicate a high likelihood of basal ganglia issues.

0 = never
1 = rarely
2 = occasionally
3 = frequently
4 = very frequently

___ 1. Feelings of nervousness or anxiety
___ 2. Symptoms of heightened muscle tension (headaches, sore muscles, hand tremor)
___ 3. Feeling keyed up or on edge
___ 4. Quick to startle
___ 5. Tendency to freeze in anxiety-provoking situations
___ 6. Excessive fear of being judged or scrutinized by others
___ 7. Conflict avoidance
___ 8. Lacking confidence
___ 9. Sensitive to criticism
___ 10. Biting fingernails or picking at skin
___ 11. Always watching for bad things to happen
___ 12. Excessive motivation
___ 13. Tics
___ 14. Poor handwriting

9

Stop Feeling Nervous Now

Basal Ganglia Prescriptions

4 WAYS TO BREAK AN ANXIETY ATTACK:
I SHOULD KNOW

In 1989, I wrote an article for *Parade* magazine called "How to Get Out of
Your Own Way." After the article was published, my office received more
than ten thousand letters asking for more information about how to stop
self-defeating behavior. CNN even asked me to be on one of their shows. It
was to be my first time on TV, and while I was in the greenroom waiting to
go on, I started to feel very anxious. I had trouble breathing and my heart
started to race; I felt so uncomfortable I wanted to run out of the studio.
Fortunately, the little voice in my head started to laugh at me and said,
"You treat people who have this problem. What do you tell *them* to do?"
There are four simple steps: in fact, I often write them on a memo pad and
hand it to my patients.

1. "Breathe! Slow down your breathing." During anxiety attacks breathing becomes erratic, shallow, and rapid. Your brain is the most metabolically active organ in your body. Any state that lowers oxygen will
   trigger fear and panic. By taking slow, deep breaths you'll boost oxygen
   to your brain and start to regain control over how you feel. When I was
   in the greenroom, I did that and felt calmer. We'll discuss breathing
   techniques in more detail later in the chapter.

2. "Don't leave." If I had left the studio, I wouldn't have gone back and
   might have never accepted another invitation to appear on TV again.
   So I didn't leave.

Image 9.1: Panic Prescription

3. "Write down your thoughts." If your thoughts are distorted, talk back to them. My first thought was "I am going to forget my name." Now, that was funny, because it was unlikely they would ask my name—they already knew it, they had invited me. Then I thought, "I am going to stutter. Two million people are going to think I am an idiot." I chuckled to myself. No wonder I wanted to run out of the studio—my brain was playing a horror film with me as the main victim.

Fortunately for me, I knew how to talk back to these thoughts. So, right there in the CNN studio in Los Angeles, I took out a piece of paper and did the ANTeater exercise. I drew two lines vertically down the paper, dividing it into three columns. In the first column I wrote down the thoughts, unedited as they occurred in my brain. In the second column I wrote down what type of ANT it was (see chapter 7 for a refresher on this exercise). In the third column, I killed the ANTs by talking back to them.

So, in the first column I wrote the initial thought, "I am going to forget my name." In the middle column I wrote "fortune telling," where I was predicting the worst, the most common ANT among people who have panic attacks. In the third column, I wrote, "I've never forgotten my name. But if I do, I have my driver's license in my wallet." Playing with the thoughts helps to see how absurd they can be.

Below the first ANT I wrote out the second one, "I am going to stutter." In the middle column I wrote "fortune telling," because I was still predicting disaster in the future. And, in the third column, I wrote, "Probably not. I usually don't stutter, but if I do there will be people who stutter in the audience who will now have a doctor they can relate to." Having fun with the thoughts helps you disarm them.

Then I wrote the last thought, "Two million people will think you are an idiot." In the middle column I wrote "mind reading." Again I was predicting the worst. In the third column, I wrote, "Maybe so."

Next to it I wrote three numbers: 18–40–60, which stands for a rule I teach my patients, called the 18–40–60 rule. It says that when you are eighteen, you worry about what everyone thinks of you; when you are forty, you don't give a damn what anyone thinks about you; and when you're sixty, you realize no one has been thinking about you at all. People spend their days worrying and thinking about themselves, not you.

4. Take calming supplements or medications to help, if needed. Remember that this is the last step—to be used if the first three aren't effective.

    This five-minute exercise helped me relax and I was able to go on the show and do well. If I had run out of the studio, I probably never would have gone back and it would have dramatically changed my life and career. Now, my television programs have aired over eighty thousand times across North America. Don't let your ANTs steal your dreams and your ability to do good things in the world.

    The following prescriptions will help you soothe stress and enhance your overall sense of calm and relaxation. They are based on what we have learned about the basal ganglia and other areas of the brain that generate anxiety and angst (such as the amygdala and insular cortex), as well as my clinical experience with patients.

B—diaphragmatic breathing, hand warming, heart rate variability training, supplements and medications, nutritional interventions

P—ANT therapy (especially for fortune-telling ANTs), self-hypnosis and guided imagery, meditation, relaxation response, EMDR

S—learning how to deal with conflict

Sp—finding your purpose and passion

BIOLOGICAL BASAL GANGLIA PRESCRIPTIONS

B—Diaphragmatic Breathing 5 x 2 = 10

Breathe slowly and deeply, mostly with your belly, taking 5 seconds to inhale, then holding it for 2 seconds, then 5 seconds to exhale, and 2 more seconds to hold your exhalation. Repeat for 10 breaths. This is one of the main exercises I teach patients who have panic disorders. The purpose of breathing is to get oxygen from the air into your body and to blow off waste products such as carbon dioxide. Every cell in your body needs oxygen in order to function. Brain cells are particularly sensitive to oxygen, as they start to die within minutes when they are deprived of it. Slight changes in oxygen content in the brain can alter the way a person feels and behaves. When a person gets angry, his or her breathing pattern changes almost immediately. Breathing becomes shallower and significantly faster. This breathing pattern is inefficient, and the oxygen content in the angry person's blood is lowered. Subsequently there is less oxygen available to a person's brain and he or she may become more irritable, impulsive, confused, and prone to negative behavior (such as yelling, threatening, or hitting another person).

Let your breath relax you. Sit in a chair. Get comfortable. Close your eyes. Put one hand on your chest and one hand on your belly. Then, for several minutes, feel the rhythm of your breathing. Do you breathe mostly with your chest? Mostly with your belly? Or with both your chest and belly? The way you breathe has a huge impact on how you feel. Have you ever watched a baby breathe? Or a puppy? They breathe almost exclusively with their bellies. They move their upper chest very little in breathing. Yet most adults breathe almost totally from the upper part of their chest.

To correct this negative breathing pattern, lie on your back and place a small book on your belly. When you breathe in, make the book go up, and when you breathe out, make the book go down. Shifting the center of breathing lower in your body will help you feel more relaxed and in better control of yourself. Practice this diaphragmatic breathing in the 5 x 2 = 10 pattern several times a day to help you develop a deeper sense of calm and peace.

This has been one of the most helpful exercises for me personally. When I first learned how to breathe diaphragmatically, I discovered that my baseline breathing rate was twenty-four breaths a minute and I breathed mostly with my upper chest. I had spent ten years in the military, being taught to stick my chest out and suck my gut in (the opposite of what is good for breathing). Learning how to quiet my breathing helped calm my anxiety and helped me feel more settled overall. I still use it to calm my

Diaphragmatic Breathing Diagram

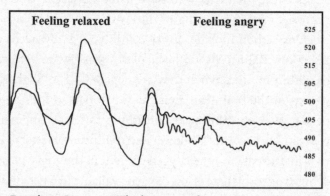

Breathing Diagram: The large waveform is a measurement of abdominal or belly breathing, by a gauge attached around the belly. The smaller waveform is a measurement of chest breathing, by a gauge attached around the upper chest. At rest, this person breathes mostly with his belly (a good pattern), but when he thinks about an angry situation his breathing pattern deteriorates, markedly decreasing the oxygen to his brain (common to anger outbursts). No wonder people who have anger outbursts often seem irrational!

nerves before tough meetings, speaking engagements, and media appearances. I also use it, in conjunction with self-hypnosis, to help me sleep when I feel stressed. My current baseline breathing rate is less than ten times a minute.

B—Hand Warming

A fascinating technique that supports relaxation is learning how to warm your hands with your brain. By using mental images of activities that warm the hands, such as putting your hands in front of a warm fire, holding a cup of hot green tea, touching your partner's warm skin, or sitting in a hot tub, many people can actually increase the temperature in their hands and induce a generalized relaxed brain and body state.

Whenever we are stressed, our hands get cold because blood is being shunted away from the hands and feet to the large muscles of our shoulders and hips (preparing us to fight or flee). Even though you might be feeling stressed about a big project at work or a fight you had with a friend, your body reacts in some ways as it would have when your biggest stressor was encountering a saber-toothed tiger. Warming your hands counteracts the stress response and increases parasympathetic tone and relaxation. There are a number of studies that report lowered blood pressure with hand warming (121). In one study from Korea, it was used to treat patients with hypertension. A significant decline of the systolic and diastolic blood pressure was observed in the treatment group (122).

B—Heart Rate Variability (HRV) Training

HRV training is another important way to lower stress and increase a sense of peace. HRV is the beat-to-beat variation in heart rhythm. Most people think that a healthy heart rhythm is perfectly regular. Not so. Even under normal, healthy conditions, our heart rhythm bounces around. High HRV has been associated with heart and brain health, while low HRV has been associated with illness.

HRV issues can become apparent when mothers deliver babies. Obstetricians typically monitor the baby's HRV before delivery with scalp monitors.

In a healthy baby, the heart rate varies significantly. If the baby's heart rate becomes too steady, the baby is considered to be in trouble. Lower HRV is a sign of distress, whether we are about to be born or are adults. HRV has been found to predict survival after heart attack. Over a half dozen well-designed studies have shown that reduced HRV predicts sudden death in patients who have had a heart attack (123, 124). Studies also suggest that lower HRV may predict risk of death even among individuals free of heart disease (125). Knowing what you now know about the relationship between our brains and our physical health, it might not surprise you to learn that studies also show a relationship between high levels of anxiety and heart disease.

Many other studies have suggested a link between negative emotions (such as anxiety and hostility) and reduced HRV (126, 127). One research group reported an association between anxiety and reduced HRV in 581 men, while another group observed lower HRV in individuals who were "highly anxious."

The exciting news is that you can train your HRV. I often recommend HRV trainers, such as those found at www.heartmath.com. They have an Inner Balance iOS app, as well as a stand-alone device (emWave2) and a computer program that both kids and adults love (emWave Pro).

B—Consider Basal Ganglia Supplements or Medications from the Amen Clinics Method Algorithm

At Amen Clinics we use the following algorithm when we see high basal ganglia (BG) activity plus symptom clusters of anxiety.

Supplements for high BG + anxiety—many supplements have antianxiety properties. Some of my favorites include magnesium (80 percent of the population is low in it), theanine from green tea, the calming amino acid GABA, ashwagandha, Relora, and valerian root. B vitamins, especially vitamin B6 in doses of 25 to 100 mg, have also been found by some to be helpful. If you take B6 at these doses, it is important to take a B complex supplement as well. My patients have also found the scents from essential oils of chamomile and lavender to be calming.

Medications for high BG + anxiety—antianxiety medications can be very helpful for more severe anxiety problems. I tend to stay away from medications such as diazepam (Valium), alprazolam (Xanax), clonazepam (Klonopin), and lorazepam (Ativan); typical benzodiazepines such as these suppress brain activity, make the brains of many look toxic (shriveled or low in activity), and have been recently associated with an increased risk of dementia (16, 40). BuSpar (buspirone) is a non-benzodiazepine medication that can be helpful in treating long-term anxiety. It also has the benefit of not being addictive, but may take a few weeks to be effective. Certain antidepressants, such as imipramine (Tofranil) and the MAO inhibitor phenelzine (Nardil) are especially helpful for people who have panic disorders. The anticonvulsants gabapentin (Neurontin) and lamotrigine (Lamictal) can be useful for resistant anxiety, especially when there is excessive basal ganglia activity.

See chapter 16 to learn more about the seven types of anxiety and depression.

B—Nutritional Interventions

The food you eat has an important effect on how you feel and your levels of stress and anxiety. In my experience, people with high anxiety do better eating small meals throughout the day so they do not get hungry. Hypoglycemia (low blood sugar) is a major cause of anxiety disorders, and includes the following symptoms: periods of feeling confused, dizzy, light-headed, irritable, anxious, panicky, or shaky; sweating; or feeling faint. If you have three or more of the above nine symptoms, it is a good idea to have a two-hour glucose tolerance test to see if hypoglycemia is an issue for you.

If you have low basal ganglia activity and low motivation, you will likely do better with a high protein, low carbohydrate diet that gives you more energy during the day. It is also often helpful to eliminate caffeine, as it may worsen anxiety. Eliminating alcohol is often a good idea as well. Even though alcohol decreases anxiety in the short term, withdrawal from alcohol causes anxiety and places a person with anxiety at more risk for alcohol addiction.

PSYCHOLOGICAL BASAL GANGLIA PRESCRIPTIONS

P—ANT Therapy, Especially for Fortune-Telling ANTs

As you read in my story at the beginning of the chapter, people who struggle with anxiety or panic are often experts at predicting the worst. We have an abundance of fortune-telling ANTs. Learning to overcome the tendency toward pessimistic predictions is essential to bringing peace to your life. Through the years, I have met many people who tell me that they're pessimists. They say that if they expect the worst to happen in a situation, they will never be disappointed. While this may be true, it's also true that they're likely to die earlier. The constant stress from negative predictions lowers immune system effectiveness and increases the risk of becoming ill. Your thoughts affect every cell in your body.

Learning how to kill the fortune-telling ANTs that go through your mind is essential to effectively dealing with the anxiety generated in this part of the brain. Whenever you feel anxious or tense, try the following steps.

Write down the event that is causing you anxiety—for example, having to get up in front of people to give a speech.

Notice and write down the automatic thoughts that come into your mind. Odds are, when you are anxious, your thoughts are predicting a negative outcome to a situation. Common anxiety-provoking thoughts include "They will think I'm stupid. Others will laugh at me. I will stumble on my words. I will shake and look nervous."

Label or identify the thought as a fortune-telling ANT if it's appropriate. Often, just naming the thought can help take away its power.

Talk back to the automatic negative thought and "kill the ANT." Write down a response to defuse the negative thought. In this example, write something like "Odds are they won't laugh and I'll do a good job. If they do laugh, I'll laugh with them. I know that speaking in public is nerve-racking for many people, and probably some people will feel empathy for me if I'm nervous."

Do not accept every thought that comes into your mind. Thoughts are just thoughts, not facts. You can learn to change this pattern.

P—Use Self-Hypnosis and Guided Imagery

Self-hypnosis taps into your body's natural soothing power source that most people don't even know exists. It is found within you—within your ability to focus your attention. Hypnosis is a natural phenomenon. It is an altered state we frequently go into and out of. Some natural examples of hypnosis include "highway hypnosis," in which our sense of time and consciousness becomes altered. Have you ever taken a long trip and not remembered a town you drove through? Or has a period of a couple of hours passed in what seemed like only twenty or thirty minutes? Time distortion is a common trait of hypnotic states. Have you ever become so engrossed in a good book or a good movie that two hours rushed by in what seemed like minutes? We become so focused that we enter a hypnotic state.

As you might imagine, because I have naturally overactive basal ganglia with a tendency toward anxiety, my medical internship year produced only more anxiety. When I worked on the cardiac intensive care unit, I had a lot of trouble getting to sleep at night because I was so anxious over the condition of the patients under my care. Being tired the next day didn't help matters much. I had learned hypnosis as a medical student, and even used it with the nursing staff to help them stop smoking and lose weight. I hadn't thought of using it on myself. Besides, I rationalized, I wasn't really very hypnotizable. Late one evening, one of my patients had problems getting to sleep. He requested a sleeping pill. I thought it might be a better idea to use hypnosis to help him sleep. He was agreeable, and it worked quickly. When I made rounds the next morning, the patient asked me what he was going to do that night when I wasn't on call. I taught him self-hypnosis and came up with several sleep prescriptions. It then dawned on me to use self-hypnosis on myself. I learned that self-hypnosis, like most things, is a skill that gets better with practice. I got to the point where I could put myself to sleep in less than one minute through a simple self-hypnotic technique. Good sleep also helps calm anxiety. Sleep deprivation makes everything worse.

Here are the simple self-hypnotic steps I use personally to help me sleep.

Lie on your back with your hands at your sides.

Pick a spot on a wall that is a little bit above your eye level. Stare at the spot. As you do, count slowly to twenty. Notice that in a short while your eyelids begin to feel heavy. Let your eyes close. In fact, even if they don't feel as if they want to close, slowly close them anyway as you get to twenty.

Next, take a deep breath, as deep as you can, and very slowly exhale. Repeat the deep inhale and slow exhale 3 times. With each breath in, feel your chest and belly rise and imagine breathing in peace and calmness. With each breath out, feel your chest and belly relax and blow out all the tension, all the things getting in the way of your relaxation. By this time, you'll notice a calm come over you.

Next, tightly squeeze the muscles in your eyelids. Close your eyes as tightly as you can. Then slowly let the muscles in your eyelids relax. Notice how much more they have relaxed. Then imagine that relaxation spreading from the muscles in your eyelids to the muscles in your face, down your neck into your shoulders and arms, into your chest, and throughout the rest of your body. The muscles will take the relaxation cue from your eyelids and relax progressively all the way down to the bottom of your feet.

After your whole body feels relaxed, imagine yourself at the top of an escalator. Step on the escalator and ride down, slowly counting backward from 20. By the time you reach the bottom, you're likely to feel very relaxed.

Then add relaxation imagery. In your mind choose a haven that promotes sleep. I like to go to a mountain cabin where there is snow outside and a crackling fire in the fireplace. Your haven can be a real or imagined place, as long as it makes you feel relaxed. If sleep does not come right away, keep the imagery in your mind and start counting slowly from 1 to 1,000. In my experience, most people will fall asleep around 300.

To make these steps easy to remember, think of the following words:

FOCUS (focus on the spot)
BREATHE (slow, deep breaths)
RELAX (progressive muscle relaxation)
DOWN (ride down the escalator)
IMAGERY (experience your haven with all of your senses)
COUNT (until you are asleep)

This technique can also be used to help you relax during waking hours. After the "imagery" stage, instead of letting your mind drift off to sleep, get back on the escalator, riding up. Count to ten. When you get to ten, open your eyes, feel relaxed, refreshed, and wide awake.

When you do this the first several times, allow yourself plenty of time. Some people become so relaxed that they fall asleep for several minutes. If that happens, don't worry. It's actually a good sign—you're really relaxed!

If you want to have me as a personal guide in this process, you can join our brain warrior community (www.mybrainfitlife.com), where you'll have access to a number of different hypnosis audios.

P—Meditation

Decades of research have shown that meditation can calm stress and enhance brain function. At the Amen Clinics, we published a brain SPECT study on a simple twelve-minute Kundalini yoga form of meditation called Kirtan Kriya (KK), in which we scanned eleven people on one day when they didn't meditate and then the next day at the end of a meditation session (128).

12-MINUTE MEDITATION INSTRUCTIONS

This twelve-minute meditation involves chanting the simple sounds "saa," "taa," "naa," and "maa" while doing repetitive finger movements with both hands. You should be saying the sound once as you touch the corresponding fingers and then moving to the next.

Touch thumbs to index fingers while chanting "saa."
Touch thumbs to middle fingers while chanting "taa."
Touch thumbs to ring fingers while chanting "naa."
Touch thumbs to pinkie fingers while chanting "maa."
Repeat the sounds for 2 minutes aloud.
Repeat the sounds for 2 minutes in a whisper.
Repeat the sounds for 4 minutes silently.
Repeat the sounds for 2 minutes in a whisper.
Repeat the sounds for 2 minutes aloud.

When you finish, sit quietly for 1 to 2 minutes. Try to hold on to your calmed mind and body throughout the day.

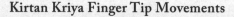

Kirtan Kriya Finger Tip Movements

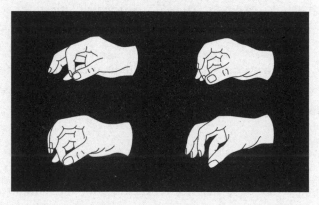

In our study, the scans taken after the meditation showed marked decreases in activity in the left parietal lobes, demonstrating a decreasing awareness of time and space. They also showed significant increases in activity in the prefrontal cortex, which showed that meditation helped to tune people in, not out. We also observed increased activity in the right temporal lobe, an area that has been associated with spirituality.

My colleagues eventually published other studies on this technique. One, which appeared in the journal *Consciousness and Cognition*, found that this technique enhances blood flow to the front parts of the brain, including those involved in attention and emotion (129). The other study, published in the *Journal of Alzheimer's Disease*, used brain SPECT imaging to evaluate the effects of meditation on memory in fifteen people with memory problems due to normal aging or Alzheimer's disease. The results showed that after meditating every day for eight weeks, the group's cerebral blood flow had increased in areas involved in retrieving memories. They also performed better on standardized tests that evaluate memory, cognition, and attention (130).

My friend Dr. Andy Newberg at Thomas Jefferson University has also used brain SPECT imaging to study the neurobiology of meditation. He scanned nine Buddhist monks before and during prolonged meditation. The scans revealed distinctive changes in brain activity as the mind went into a meditative state, just like in the KK study above. Another functional brain-imaging study of Transcendental Meditation (TM) showed calming in the anterior cingulate and basal ganglia, diminishing anxiety and worries and fostering relaxation (131).

The benefits of meditation go far beyond stress relief. Studies have shown that it also improves attention and planning, reduces depression and anxiety, decreases sleepiness, and protects the brain from cognitive decline associated with normal aging. In a study from researchers at UCLA, the hippocampus and frontal cortex were found to be significantly larger in people who meditate regularly. Meditation has also been found to aid in weight loss, reduce muscle tension, and even tighten the skin.

A lot of people think it takes years to learn how to meditate. It doesn't. A fascinating Chinese study by the neuroscientist Dr. Yi-Yuan Tang showed that people who received just twenty minutes of daily meditation training for five days showed a significant decrease in stress-related cortisol (132). You don't need to devote big chunks of time to the practice of meditation either. In my clinical practice, I often recommend meditation as an integral part of a treatment plan. Many of my patients have reported back that they feel calmer and less stressed after dedicating just a few minutes to daily meditation.

You don't have to sit cross-legged on the floor or burn incense or do any of those things you might associate with meditation—it can be done anywhere, at any time. If you are at work, simply close the door to your office, sit in your chair, close your eyes, and relax for a few moments. At home, you can sit on the edge of your bed after you wake up and spend a couple minutes calming your mind. Try the following technique for a simple introduction to meditation.

THE RELAXATION RESPONSE

One of the simplest ways to meditate and reduce stress is a technique called the Relaxation Response, developed by Herbert Benson, MD, at Harvard Medical School, which he outlines in his book *The Relaxation Response* (133).

Sit quietly in a comfortable position.

Close your eyes.

Deeply relax all your muscles, beginning at your feet and progressing up to your face. Keep them relaxed. Breathe through your nose. Become aware of your breathing. As you breathe out, say the word "one" (or some other relaxing word you choose) silently to yourself. For example, breathe in . . . out, "one," in . . . out, "one," etc.

Continue for 10 to 20 minutes. You may open your eyes to check the time, but do not use an alarm. When you finish, sit quietly for several minutes, at first with your eyes closed and later with your eyes open. Do not stand up for a few minutes after finishing.

Do not worry about whether you are successful in achieving a deep level of relaxation. Maintain a passive attitude and permit relaxation to occur at its own pace. When distracting thoughts occur, try to ignore them by not dwelling upon them and return to repeating "one." With practice, the response should come with little effort. Practice the technique once or twice daily, but not within two hours after any meal, since the digestive processes seem to interfere with the elicitation of the Relaxation Response.

P—Eye Movement Desensitization and Reprocessing (EMDR)

As I mentioned in the last chapter, EMDR can be a very powerful treatment for people who have been emotionally traumatized. EMDR uses eye movements or other alternate-hemisphere stimulation to remove the emotional charges of traumatic memories. In 2004, CBS producer Angeline Chew called and asked if I would be interested in doing a story about EMDR, using the following case as an example.

Steven and the Farmers' Market Disaster

Steven, a thirty-three-year-old bicycle repair mechanic working in Santa Monica, California, took an early lunch on July 16, 2003. He was not sure why he needed to go to the downtown farmers' market, but felt drawn to it. While he was walking, eighty-seven-year-old George Russell Weller lost control of his 1992 Buick LeSabre and barreled through the three-block-long farmers' market. Bodies were flying, people were screaming, and Weller's car was headed straight for Steven, who later told me, "I thought he was going to run over my legs . . . I thought I would lose my legs." At the last possible moment, he was able to jump out of the way, but ten people were killed and more than fifty were injured. Steven, who had been a military tank commander in the first Gulf War, used the medical skills he learned to help save others. A woman died in his arms.

Traumatized, Steven went back to work. But for months, he couldn't sleep and he shook constantly. By chance, or fate, if you believe in such things, Linda Alvarez, an anchor at CBS News in Los Angeles, took her bicycle to Steven's shop shortly after the disaster. Linda and Steven chatted about what had happened, and Linda noticed that Steven was shaking. "It started that day," Steven said, showing her his trembling hands, "and it won't stop." The image of Steven's hands stayed with Linda. A month later, while working on another story, Linda learned about the work I was doing with EMDR.

After talking to Steven, who was a willing participant, I recruited a colleague of mine who was an EMDR expert to help. As in the case of most people who develop PTSD, the Santa Monica Farmers' Market disaster was not Steven's only trauma. He grew up in a severely abusive alcoholic home. One of his earliest memories is of his father burning down the family house. His father also once dangled him over a four-hundred-foot bridge. At the age of eleven, his favorite uncle, a firefighter, died in a fire set by an arsonist. As a young adult, Steven faced death as a tank commander during the Gulf War. Clearly, Steven had many layers of trauma.

As part of his evaluation, we scanned Steven three times: before treatment, during his first EMDR session, and after eight hours of EMDR treatments. Initially, his brain showed the classic PTSD pattern, with an extremely active limbic area, basal ganglia, and anterior cingulate. We then went to work with Steven, cleaning out the traumas—one by one—using EMDR. His brain actually showed benefit during the first treatment and was markedly improved after only eight hours of treatment. Steven's shaking had subsided and he felt significantly better. One of the most touching things that happened during the process was that Steven was able to forgive his father. He had held deep and understandable resentment toward his father, but the work with brain science gave him a new perspective. When we helped Steven balance and change his brain, his life improved as well. You can learn more about EMDR at www.emdria.org.

SOCIAL BASAL GANGLIA PRESCRIPTIONS

S—Learn How to Deal with Conflict

As with relationships between countries, relationships between people are often devastated by peace at any price. Many people are so afraid of conflict that they do everything they can to avoid any turmoil. This "conflict phobia" actually sets up relationships for more trouble rather than less. Here are four typical scenarios of people who fear conflict:

1. In an attempt to be a "loving parent," Sara finds herself always giving in to her four-year-old son's temper tantrums. She is frustrated by how much the tantrums have increased in frequency over the past year. She now feels powerless and gives in just to keep the peace.

2. Billy, a ten-year-old boy, was bullied by a bigger ten-year-old named Ryan. Ryan threatened to hurt Billy if he didn't give him his lunch money. To avoid being hurt, Billy gave in and spent the year terrified of Ryan.

3. Kelly found herself feeling very distant from her husband, Carl. She felt that he always tried to control her and treated her like a child. He would complain about how much money she spent, what she wore, and who her friends were. Even though this really bothered Kelly, she said little because she didn't want to fight. However, she found that her interest in sex was nonexistent, she often felt tired and irritable, and she preferred to spend her free time with her friends rather than with Carl.

4. Bruce had worked as the foreman for Chet's company for six years, but for the past four years, Chet had become increasingly critical of Bruce and belittled him in front of others. For fear of losing his job, Bruce said nothing, but he became more depressed, started drinking more at home, and lost interest in his job.

Whenever we give in to the temper tantrums of a child or allow someone to bully or control us, we feel terrible about ourselves. Our self-esteem suffers, and the relationship with that other person is damaged. In many ways we teach other people how to treat us by what we tolerate and what we refuse to tolerate. "Conflict phobics" teach other people that it is okay to walk all over them, that there will be no consequences for misbehavior.

In order to have any personal power in a relationship, we must be willing to stand up for ourselves and for what we know is right. This does not mean we have to be mean or nasty; there are rational and kind ways to be firm. But firmness is essential.

Let's look at how the people in each of the four examples could handle their situations in more productive ways that would give them more power and more say in their lives.

1. Sara needs to make a rule that whenever her son throws a tantrum to get his way, he will not get what he wants ever, *period. No exceptions.* By giving in to his tantrums, Sara has taught her son to throw them, which not only hurts his relationship with his mother but will also teach him to be demanding with others and will hurt his ability to relate socially to others. If Sara can be firm, kind, and consistent, she'll notice remarkable changes in a short time.

2. By giving in to the bully, Billy taught Ryan that his intimidating behavior was okay. Standing up to him early, even if it meant getting beaten up, would have been better than spending a whole year in anguish. Almost all bullies pick on people who won't fight back. They use intimidation and are rarely interested in real conflict.

3. Kelly made a strategic mistake by avoiding conflict early in her relationship with Carl. By giving in to his demands early on, she taught him that it was okay for him to control her. Standing up to him after years of giving in is very difficult but essential to saving the relationship. I see many, many people who even after years of giving in learn to stand up for themselves and change their relationship. Sometimes it takes a separation to convince the other person of your resolve, but the consequences of being controlled in a marriage are often depression and a lack of sexual desire. Standing up for oneself in a firm yet kind way is often marriage-saving.

4. Bruce gave up his power when he allowed Chet to belittle him in front of others. No job is worth being tormented by your boss. Yet most people find that if they respectfully stand up to their boss, he or she is less likely to walk over them in the future. If, after standing up for yourself in a reasonable way, the boss continues to belittle you, it's time to look for a new job. Being in a job you hate will take years off your life.

Assertiveness means expressing your feelings in a firm yet reasonable way. Assertiveness does not mean becoming mean or aggressive. Here are five rules to help you assert yourself in a healthy manner:

1. Don't give in to the anger of others just because it makes you uncomfortable.
2. Don't allow the opinions of others to control how you feel about yourself. Your opinion, within reason, needs to be the one that counts.
3. Say what you mean and stick up for what you believe is right.
4. Maintain self-control.
5. Be kind, if possible, but above all be firm in your stance.

Remember that we teach others how to treat us. When we give in to their temper tantrums, we teach them that that is how to control us. When we assert ourselves in a firm yet kind way, others have more respect for us and treat us accordingly. If you have allowed others to run over you emotionally for a long time, they'll be a little resistant to your newfound assertiveness. But stick to it, and you'll help them learn a new way of relating. You'll also help cool down your basal ganglia.

SPIRITUAL BASAL GANGLIA PRESCRIPTIONS

Sp—Purpose and Passion

Having a deep sense of passion and purpose can lead to a sense of calm. Feeling aimless or purposeless has been associated with free-floating anxiety. When you're feeling anxious, focus on meaningful and goal-directed activities. Not only will the activities distract you from your angst, they will connect you with a higher sense of purpose, which can also help you feel better. The worst thing you can do is anxiously sit around obsessing about how bad you feel.

Sp—Consider Going to Spiritual Services

A strong correlation exists between people who attend religious services and personal happiness, according to a recent study by the Austin Institute for the Study of Family and Culture (134). The study found that people who attend services on a weekly basis are nearly twice as likely to describe themselves as "very happy" (45 percent) than people who never attend (28 percent). Conversely, those who never worship are twice as likely to say they are "very unhappy" (4 percent) compared with those who attend services weekly (2 percent). Research has suggested that deep spiritual beliefs may offer significance and meaning to life. Many different religions teach coping mechanisms that can improve physical and emotional health. My work with the Daniel Plan—the program at Saddleback Church I referenced in the introduction—is a large-scale example. Faith can be a powerful motivating force, plus parishioners often receive emotional support from others.

Sp—Consider Whether the Anxiety
Is from Another Generation

In fascinating but disturbing new research, fear has been shown to be passed down through generations. Perhaps you're afraid of something and have absolutely no idea why. The researchers Brian Dias and Kerry Ressler from Emory University (135) made mice afraid of a cherry blossom scent by shocking them whenever the smell was in the air. This is called classical fear conditioning. Even more startling, the researchers also found that the children and grandchildren of the mice were also afraid of the scent of cherry blossoms, even though they were never exposed to the shocks. The fear was actually transmitted generationally, through a concept called epigenetics. The implications of this finding are wide-reaching. Emotions like fear, anxiety, and maybe even hatred may have ancestral origins. If you are afraid of something and have no idea why, go back through your genealogy and look for any clues that might explain the fear (which may actually have nothing to do with your experience). Prior-generation stress has also been associated with depression, antisocial behaviors, and memory impairment. Fortunately, it seems that stress in your ancestors can go both ways. Another study published in the journal *Nature Communications* suggested prior-generation stress can help animals learn to better cope with stress (136).

10

Looking into Inattention and Impulsivity

The Prefrontal Cortex

FUNCTIONS OF THE PREFRONTAL CORTEX (PFC)

focus
forethought
judgment
impulse control
organization
planning
problem-solving
learning from experience
ability to feel and express emotions
empathy

The prefrontal cortex (PFC) is the most evolved part of the brain. It occupies the front third of the brain, behind the forehead. It is often divided into three sections: the dorsal lateral section (on the outside surface of the PFC), the inferior orbital section (on the front undersurface of the brain), and the anterior cingulate gyrus (which runs through the middle of the frontal lobes). The anterior cingulate gyrus, usually considered to be part of the limbic system, will be covered in its own chapter. The dorsal lateral and inferior orbital gyrus are often termed the "executive control center" of the brain and will be discussed together in this chapter. When necessary, I'll distinguish what is known about their functions.

Overall, the PFC is the part of the brain that watches, supervises, guides, directs, and focuses your behavior. It supervises "executive functions," governing abilities such as time management, judgment, impulse control, planning, organization, and critical thinking. Our ability as a species to think, plan ahead, use time wisely, and communicate with others is heavily influenced by this part of the brain. The PFC is responsible for behaviors that are necessary for you to be goal-directed, socially responsible, and effective.

The North Carolina neuropsychiatrist C. Thomas Gualtieri succinctly summarized the human functions of the PFC as "the capacity to formulate goals, to make plans for their execution, to carry them out in an effective way, and to change course and improvise in the face of obstacles or failure, *and to do so successfully, in the absence of external direction or structure* [italics mine]. The capacity of the individual to generate goals and to achieve them is considered to be an essential aspect of a mature and effective personality. It is not a social convention or an artifact of culture. It is hard wired in the construction of the prefrontal cortex and its connections."

The PFC (especially the inferior orbital PFC) helps you think about what you say or do before you say or do it. For example, if you are having a disagreement with your spouse and you have good PFC function, you are more likely to give a thoughtful response that helps the situation. If you have poor PFC function, you are more likely to do or say something that will make the situation worse. The PFC helps you problem-solve, see ahead of a situation, and, through experience, choose among the most helpful alternatives. Playing a game such as chess effectively requires good PFC function.

This is also the part of the brain that helps you learn from mistakes. Good PFC function doesn't mean that you won't make mistakes. Rather, it generally means that you won't make the same mistake over and over. You are able to learn from the past and apply its lessons. For example, a student with good PFC function is likely to learn that if he or she starts a long-term project early, there is more time for research and less anxiety over getting it done. A student with decreased PFC function doesn't learn from past frustrations and may tend to put everything off until the last minute. Poor PFC function tends to appear in people who have trouble learning from

The Prefrontal Cortex

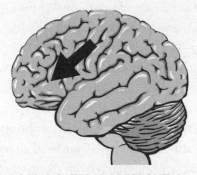

DORSAL LATERAL PREFRONTAL
CORTEX, OUTSIDE VIEW

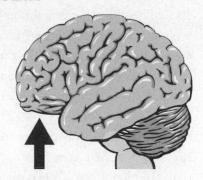

INFERIOR ORBITAL PREFRONTAL
CORTEX, OUTSIDE VIEW

experience. They tend to make repetitive mistakes. Their actions are based not on experience, but rather on the moment, and on their immediate wants and needs.

The PFC (especially the dorsolateral PFC) is also involved with sustaining attention span. It helps you focus on important information while filtering out less significant thoughts and sensations. Attention span is required for short-term memory and learning. The PFC, through its many connections within the brain, helps you stay on task and allows you to follow through on a project until it is finished. The PFC actually sends quieting signals to the limbic and sensory parts of the brain when you need to focus, and decreases the distracting input from other brain areas. When the PFC is underactive, you become more distractible (this will be discussed in detail under attention deficit disorder, below).

The PFC (especially the dorsolateral PFC) is also the part of the brain that allows you to feel and express emotions, to feel happiness, sadness, joy, and love. It is different from the more primitive limbic system. Even though the limbic system controls mood and libido, the PFC is able to translate the workings of the limbic system into recognizable feelings, emotions, and words, such as love, passion, or hate. Underactivity or damage in this part of the brain often leads to a decreased ability to express thoughts and feelings.

Thoughtfulness and impulse control are heavily influenced by the PFC. The ability to think through the consequences of behavior—choosing a good mate, interacting with customers, dealing with difficult children, spending money, driving on the freeway—is essential for effective living in nearly every aspect of human life. Without proper PFC function, it is difficult to act in consistent, thoughtful ways, and impulses can take over.

The PFC has many connections to the limbic system. It sends inhibitory messages that help keep it under control. It helps you "use your head along with your emotions." When there is damage or underactivity in this part of the brain, especially on the left side, the PFC cannot appropriately inhibit the limbic system, causing an increased vulnerability to depression if the limbic system becomes overactive. A classic example of this problem occurs in people who have had left frontal lobe strokes. Sixty percent of patients with these strokes develop major depression within a year.

When scientists scan the prefrontal cortex with neuroimaging studies like SPECT, they often do two studies, one in a resting state and a second during a concentration task. In evaluating brain function, it is important to look at a working brain. When a normal brain is challenged by a concentration task, such as math problems or sorting cards, the PFC activity increases. In certain brain conditions, such as attention deficit disorder and schizophrenia, prefrontal cortex activity decreases in response to an intellectual challenge.

PROBLEMS IN THE PREFRONTAL CORTEX

short attention span
distractibility
lack of perseverance
reduced impulse control
hyperactivity
chronic lateness, poor time management
disorganization
procrastination

unavailability of emotions

misperceptions

poor judgment

trouble learning from experience

short-term memory problems

social and test-taking anxiety

Problems in the dorsal lateral prefrontal cortex often lead to decreased attention span, distractibility, impaired short-term memory, decreased mental speed, apathy, and decreased verbal expression. Problems in the inferior orbital cortex often lead to poor impulse control, mood control problems (due to its connections with the limbic system), decreased social skills, and decreased control over behavior. People with PFC problems often do things they later regret.

Test anxiety and social anxiety may be hallmarks of problems in the PFC. Tests require concentration and the retrieval of information. Many people with PFC problems experience difficulties in test situations because they have trouble activating this part of the brain under stress, even if they have adequately prepared for the test. In a similar way, social situations require concentration, impulse control, and dealing with uncertainty. PFC deactivation often causes a person's mind to "go blank" in conversation, which naturally causes discomfort in social situations.

When men have problems in this part of the brain, their emotions are often unavailable to them and their partners complain that they do not share their feelings. This can cause serious problems in a relationship. Many women, for example, blame their male partners for being cold or unfeeling, when it is really a problem in the PFC that causes a lack of being "tuned in" to the feelings of the moment.

ATTENTION DEFICIT DISORDER (ADD)

ADD, also called ADHD (attention deficit hyperactivity disorder), typically occurs as a result of neurological dysfunction in the prefrontal cortex. As I've mentioned, when people with ADD try to concentrate, PFC activity decreases rather than increases as it does in the normal brains of control group subjects. As such, people with ADD show many of the symptoms discussed in this chapter, such as poor internal supervision, short attention span, distractibility, disorganization, hyperactivity (although only half the people with ADD are hyperactive), impulse control problems, difficulty learning from past errors, lack of forethought, and procrastination.

ADD used to be thought of as a disorder of hyperactive boys who would outgrow it before puberty. We now know that most people with ADD do not outgrow the symptoms of this disorder and that it frequently occurs in girls and women (20 percent of those diagnosed with ADD). It is estimated that ADD affects seventeen million Americans.

ADD has been a particular interest of mine over the past thirty years. Of note, three of my four children have this disorder. I tell people I know more about ADD than I want to. Through the SPECT research done in our clinics, along with the brain-imaging and genetic work done by others (137–140), we have found that ADD is basically a genetically inherited disorder of the PFC, due in part to a deficiency of the neurotransmitter dopamine. ADD is not one simple disorder, but rather has seven different types. You can read a more in-depth discussion in my book *Healing ADD: The Breakthrough Program that Allows You to See and Heal the 7 Types of ADD* and in chapter 16.

Here are some of the common characteristics of ADD that clearly connect this disorder to the PFC.

The Harder You Try, the Worse It Gets

Research has shown that the more people with ADD try to concentrate, the worse things get for them. Instead of increasing as it should, the activity in the PFC will actually decrease (141). This means that when a parent, teacher, supervisor, or manager puts more pressure on a person with ADD to perform, he or she often becomes less effective. Too frequently when this happens, the parent, teacher, or boss interprets this decreased performance as willful misconduct, and serious problems arise. One man with ADD whom I treat told me that whenever his boss puts intense pressure on him to do a better job, his performance becomes much worse, even though he really tries to do better. While it is true that almost all of us perform better with praise, I've found that it is essential for people with ADD. When the boss encourages him to do better in a positive way, he becomes more productive. In parenting, teaching, supervising, or managing someone with ADD, it is much more effective to use praise and encouragement, rather than pressure. People with ADD do best in environments that are highly interesting or stimulating and relatively relaxed.

Short Attention Span

A short attention span is the hallmark of this disorder. People with ADD have trouble sustaining attention and effort over prolonged periods of time. Their attention tends to wander and they are frequently off task, thinking about or doing things other than the task at hand. Yet one of the things that often fools inexperienced clinicians assessing this disorder is that people with ADD do not have a short attention span for everything. Often, people with ADD can pay attention just fine to things that are new, novel, highly stimulating, interesting, or frightening. These things provide enough intrinsic stimulation that they activate the PFC so the person can focus and concentrate. A child with ADD might do very well in a one-on-one situation and completely fall apart in a classroom of thirty children. My son with ADD, for example, used to take four hours to do a half hour's worth of homework, frequently getting off task. Yet if you gave him a car stereo magazine, he would quickly read it from cover to cover and remember every little detail in it. People with ADD have long-standing problems paying attention to regular, routine everyday matters such as homework, schoolwork, chores, or paperwork. The mundane is terrible for them, and it is *not* a choice. They need excitement and interest to kick in their PFC function.

Many adult couples tell me that in the beginning of their relationship, the partner with adult ADD could pay attention to the other person for hours. The stimulation of new love helped him or her focus. But as the "newness" and excitement of the relationship began to fade (as it does in nearly all relationships), the person with ADD had a much harder time paying attention, and his or her ability to listen faltered.

Distractibility

As mentioned above, the PFC sends inhibitory signals to other areas of the brain, quieting stimulation from the environment so that you can concentrate. When the PFC is underactive, it doesn't adequately dampen the sensory parts of the brain, and too many stimuli bombard the brain as a result. Distractibility is evident in many different settings for the person with ADD. In class, during meetings, or while listening to a partner, the person with ADD tends to notice other things going on and has trouble staying focused on the issue at hand. People with ADD tend to look around the room, drift off, appear bored, forget where the conversation is going, and interrupt with extraneous information. Their distractibility and short attention span may also cause them to take much longer to complete their work.

Impulsivity

Lack of impulse control gets many ADD people into hot water. They may say inappropriate things to parents, friends, teachers, supervisors, colleagues, or customers. I once had a patient who had been fired from thirteen jobs because he had trouble controlling what he said. He would just blurt out what he was thinking before he had a chance to process the thought. Poorly thought-out decisions also relate to impulsivity. Rather than thinking a problem through, many ADD people want an immediate solution and act without the necessary forethought. In a similar vein, impulsivity causes these people to have trouble going through the established channels at work. They often go right to the top to solve problems, rather than working through the system. This may cause resentment from coworkers and immediate supervisors. Impulsivity may also lead to such problem behaviors as lying (saying the first thing that comes into your mind), stealing, having affairs, and excessive spending. I have treated many ADD people who have suffered with the shame and guilt of these behaviors.

In my lectures I often ask the audience, "How many people here are married?" A large percentage of the audience raises their hands. I then ask, "Is it helpful for you to say everything you think in your marriage?" The audience laughs, because they know the answer. "Of course not," I continue. "Relationships require tact. Yet because of impulsivity and a lack of forethought, many people with ADD say the first thing that comes to mind. And instead of apologizing for saying something hurtful, many ADD people will justify why they said the hurtful remark, only making the situation worse. An impulsive comment can ruin a nice evening, a weekend, even a whole marriage."

Conflict Seeking

Many people with ADD unconsciously seek conflict as a way to stimulate their own PFC. They do not know they are doing it. They do not plan to do it. They deny that they do it. And yet they do it just the same. The relative lack of activity and stimulation to the PFC craves more activity. Hyperactivity, restlessness, and humming are common forms of self-stimulation. Another way I have seen people with ADD "try to turn on their brains" is by causing turmoil. If they can get their parents or spouses to be emotionally intense or yell at them, that might increase activity in their frontal lobes and help them to feel more tuned in. Again, this is not a conscious phenomenon. But it seems that many ADD people become addicted to the turmoil.

I once treated a man who would quietly stand behind a corner in his house and jump out and scare his wife when she walked by. He liked the charge he got out of her screams. Unfortunately for his wife, she developed an irregular heart rhythm because of the repetitive scares. I have also treated many adults and children with ADD who seemed driven to get their pets upset by playing roughly or teasing them.

The parents of children with ADD commonly report that the kids are experts at upsetting them. One mother told me that when she wakes up in the morning, she promises herself that she won't yell at or get upset with her eight-year-old son. Yet invariably by the time he is off to school, there have been at least three fights and both of them feel terrible. When I explained the child's unconscious need for stimulation to the mother, she stopped yelling at him. When parents stop providing the negative stimulation (yelling, spanking, lecturing, etc.), these children decrease the negative behaviors. Whenever you feel like screaming at one of these kids, stop yourself and instead talk as softly as you can. At least in that way you're helping to break their addiction to turmoil and lowering your own blood pressure.

Another self-stimulating behavior common in people with ADD is worrying or focusing on problems. The emotional turmoil generated by worrying or being upset produces stress chemicals that keep the brain active. I once treated a woman that had depression and ADD. She started each session by telling me she was going to kill herself. She recognized that this would make me anxious and seemed to enjoy telling me the gruesome details of how she would do it. After about a year of listening to her, I finally figured out that she wasn't really going to kill herself, she was using my reaction as a source of stimulation for her. After getting to know her well, I told her, "Stop talking about suicide. I do not believe you'll kill yourself. You love your four children, and I can't believe you would ever abandon them. I think you use this talk as a way to keep things stirred up. Without knowing, your ADD causes you to play the game of 'Let's have a problem.' This ruins any joy you could have in your life." Initially, she was very upset with me (another source of conflict, I told her), but she trusted me enough to at least look at the behavior. Decreasing her need for turmoil became the major focus of psychotherapy.

A significant problem with using anger, emotional turmoil, and negative emotion for self-stimulation is damage to the immune system (142, 143). The high levels of adrenaline produced by conflict-driven behavior decrease the immune system's effectiveness and increase vulnerability to illness. I have seen evidence of this over and over with the connection between ADD and chronic infections, and in the increased incidence of fibromyalgia— chronic muscle pain thought to be associated with immune deficiency.

As noted, many folks with ADD tend to be in constant turmoil with one or more people—at home, work, or school. They seem to unconsciously choose people who are vulnerable and pick verbal battles with them. Many mothers of children with ADD have told me that they feel like running away from home. They cannot stand the constant turmoil in their relationship with the child with ADD. Many children and adults with ADD have a tendency to embarrass others for little or no good reason, which consequently distances their "victims" from them and can result in social isolation. They may be the class clowns in school or the wisecrackers at work. *Witzelsucht* is a term in the neuropsychiatric literature that characterizes "an addiction to making bad jokes." It was first described in patients who had frontal lobe brain tumors, especially on the right side.

Disorganization

Disorganization is another hallmark of ADD. It includes disorganization of physical space, such as rooms, desks, book bags, filing cabinets, and closets, as well as disorganization of time. Often when you look at work areas of people with ADD, it is a wonder they can work there at all. They tend to have many piles of "stuff." Paperwork is often hard for them to keep straight; and they seem to have a filing system that only they can figure out (and then only on good days). Many people with ADD are chronically late or put things off until the last possible minute. I've had several patients who have bought sirens from alarm companies to help them wake up. Imagine what their neighbors thought! They also tend to lose track of time, which contributes to lateness.

Start Many Projects, but Finish Few

The energy and enthusiasm of people with ADD often push them to start many projects. Unfortunately, their distractibility and short attention span impair their ability to complete them. One radio station manager told me that he had started over thirty special projects the year before but completed only a handful. He told me, "I'm always going to get back to them, but I get new ideas that get in the way." I also treat a college professor who told me that the year before he saw me he had started three hundred different projects. His wife finished the thought by telling me he had completed only three.

Moodiness and Negative Thinking

Many people with ADD tend to be moody, irritable, and negative. Since the PFC is underactive, it cannot fully temper the limbic system, which becomes overactive, leading to mood control issues. In another subtle way, as mentioned, many people with ADD worry or become overfocused on negative thoughts as a form of self-stimulation. If they cannot seek turmoil from others in the environment, they seek it within themselves. They often have a "sky is falling" attitude that distances them from others.

Kent

Kent was twenty-four years old when he first came to see me. He came for help because he had gone to junior college for six straight semesters, but hadn't been able to finish a single class. He wanted to go to medical school. Everybody told him he was nuts! How could he go to medical school if he couldn't even finish a junior college semester? Then his mother read my book *Healing ADD*. She wondered if Kent didn't have attention deficit disorder. After I took Kent's history, it was clear he had suffered from an undiagnosed lifelong case of ADD. From the time he had been in kindergarten, he had had problems staying in his seat; he had been restless, distractible, disorganized, and labeled as an underachiever.

Kent's father requested that we do a SPECT study to look at his brain. He wanted to make sure Kent wasn't just looking for another excuse as to

Images 10.1 and 10.2: Kent's ADD-Affected Brain,
at Rest and Concentration

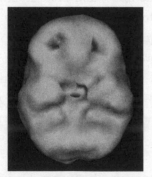

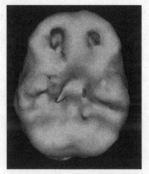

At rest; note overall
good activity.

During concentration;
note markedly decreased
PFC activity.

why he was failing in life. Kent's SPECT study at rest was normal. When Kent tried to concentrate, however, the prefrontal cortex of his brain turned off.

After the results of the clinical examination and SPECT studies, we created Kent's four-circles interventions: B—Adderall, a stimulant medication that is used to treat symptoms of ADD; physical exercise; a higher protein, lower carbohydrate diet; omega-3 fatty acids with a higher EPA ratio; P—meditation to help with focus; S—school accommodations to help with test taking and organization; Sp—encourage Kent to take classes in subjects for which he had a passion.

Kent completed all of his classes at school the next semester. In eighteen months he got his associate's degree, and three years later he finished his bachelor's degree in biology and was accepted to medical school!

It's amazing how much his father's attitude toward him changed. Kent's dad told me, "I thought he was just lazy. It makes me sad to think that all those years he had a medical problem—and I just hassled him for being lazy. I wish I could have those years back."

When the brain is underactive, it's uncomfortable. Unconsciously, people learn how to turn it on, by conflict; coffee or cigarettes (both mild stimulants); anger; highly stimulating physical activities, such as bungee jumping (bungee jumpers need to be screened for ADD!); or by living a fast-paced life. There's one man in my practice who has ten businesses, because that's what he needs in order to keep himself stimulated.

PSYCHOTIC DISORDERS

Psychotic disorders, such as schizophrenia, affect a person's ability to distinguish reality from fantasy. These disorders are complex and involve several brain areas, but at least in part, the neurotransmitter abnormalities cause decreased prefrontal cortex activity. Schizophrenia is a chronic, long-standing disorder characterized by delusions, hallucinations, and distorted thinking. When I first started ordering SPECT studies on schizophrenic patients, I began to understand why they distorted incoming information. The following cases are good examples.

Julie

Julie was forty-eight years old when we met. She had a history of hospital-
izations for paranoid thinking, hearing voices, and delusional thinking.
Her main delusion centered around being assaulted by someone who put
an electrical probe inside her head that "blasted her with electricity." She
had been on multiple medication trials without success. Because of her
lack of responsiveness to standard treatments, I ordered a brain SPECT
study.

In a sense, Julie was right. She *was* being blasted with electricity. She had
multiple focal areas of increased activity in her brain, but because she had
such poor prefrontal cortex activity, she was unable to process the physiological nature of her illness and developed delusions to explain the pain she
experienced. Based on the information from the SPECT study, Julie was
placed on a high therapeutic dose of Depakote, an antiseizure medication,
which lessened her pain and anxiety. For the first time, she was willing to
entertain the possibility that her symptoms were the result of abnormal
brain activity rather than an outside attack. A repeat SPECT study eight
months later showed a marked decrease in the hot spots in her brain along
with subsequent increased activity in her prefrontal cortex.

Derrick

Derrick, a thirteen-year-old boy, was brought to see me because he was severely anxious. He was displaying psychotic symptoms, feeling that other
children were talking about him behind his back and that they were out to
embarrass him in front of his whole school. He started to avoid all contact
with his peer group. If he saw people he knew at the mall, he would hide in
the middle of clothes racks for fear that they might laugh at him or talk
about him to others. He was petrified by his thoughts and stopped going to
school. He even seriously entertained the idea of suicide. He had crying
spells, sleeplessness, and intense anxiety. He wasn't able to rationally discuss
any of these feelings. I saw him for months in psychotherapy and tried him
on several antidepressant and antipsychotic medications without success.
Once he was weaned off all medication, we did a SPECT scan to help us
understand what was going on.

Derrick's SPECT study showed marked decreased activity in his prefrontal cortex at rest, a common finding in psychotic disorders. It is also a finding in some psychotic depressions. The study led me to try the stimulating antidepressant bupropion (Wellbutrin), although I feared it could make him worse, based on his clinical symptoms. However, within two months there was a dramatic clinical improvement in his condition. His mood was better, he had no suicidal thoughts, he was less sensitive to others, and he was more able to entertain alternatives to his distorted thoughts. Seven months later, he was much more like a normal teenager. A second SPECT study performed six months later showed normalization of his prefrontal cortex activity. Six years later, I still see Derrick every six months. He is an honors student at a highly prestigious university.

The SPECT study was very important in the treatment process. It clearly showed Derrick's parents that his problems were based on brain abnormalities and that he couldn't help what he thought or felt. They were able to respond in a more understanding and helpful manner, lowering the level of stress at home.

HEAD INJURIES

Due to its location, the PFC is especially susceptible to head injury. Research suggests the PFC is involved in 91 percent of brain injuries. Many people do not fully understand how head injuries, sometimes even "minor" ones in which no loss of consciousness occurs, can alter a person's character and ability to learn. This is particularly true when the head injury occurs in the brain's "executive director" (the PFC). Unfortunately for the PFC, the inferior orbital cortex sits on top of several sharp, bony ridges inside the skull, and the dorsal lateral prefrontal cortex lies just beneath the place where many blows to the head occur.

It is important to note that many people forget they've had a significant head injury in their lifetime. At Amen Clinics, we ask patients several times whether or not they have had a significant head injury. Our intake paperwork asks the question "Have you ever had a head injury?" The historian, who gathers patients' histories before they see the physician, asks them again about head injuries. The computer testing we have patients complete asks a third time. If I see *no, no,* and *no* to the question of head injuries, I'll ask again. If I get a fourth *no,* I will then say, "Are you sure? Have you ever fallen out of a tree, fallen off a fence, or dove into a shallow pool?" I am constantly amazed at how many people remember head injuries that they'd long forgotten or felt were too insignificant to remember. When asked the question for the fifth time, one patient put his hand on his forehead and said, "Oh yeah! When I was five years old, I fell out of a second-story window." Similarly, I have had other patients forget they went through windshields, fell out of moving vehicles, or were knocked unconscious when they fell off their bicycles.

Phineas Gage provided scientists with an extreme example of PFC dysfunction secondary to a head injury. This was one of the first cases in the medical literature about the outcome of prefrontal cortex damage. In 1848, at the age of twenty-five, Gage was an up-and-coming railroad construction foreman in Vermont working for the Rutland & Burlington Railroad. His job involved using a long tamping iron to ignite explosives to forge a path for the railroad. One day a horrible accident occurred; the explosion sent the tamping iron, which was 1.25 inches in diameter, 3.5 feet long, and weighed 13.5 pounds, through the front part of Gage's skull. It went through his left eye, through the left prefrontal cortex, and out the top front part of his skull, leaving a circular 3.5-inch opening, destroying his left prefrontal cortex and surrounding areas of the brain. Initially the interest in the case was due to Gage's survival, which was called "unprecedented in surgical history." Years later, in 1868, his physician turned his attention to the personality changes in Gage. Before the accident, Gage had been an honest, reliable, deliberate person and a good worker. After the accident, even though he did not appear to suffer any intellectual impairment, he was described as childish, capricious, and obstinate, showed poor judgment, used profane language, and was inconsiderate of others. In short, his physician concluded that "Gage was no longer Gage."

In many ways, the PFC contains our ability to be ourselves.

Zachary

Zachary is a modern-day example similar to that of Gage. At age six, Zachary was a fun-loving, active boy who was affectionate, sweet, and eager to please. He did well in kindergarten and was liked by the other children. One summer, between kindergarten and first grade, Zachary was riding in the front seat of a car with his mother on a trip to his grandparents' house. All of a sudden a drunk driver swerved into their lane, causing Zachary's mother to quickly jerk the car to the side of the road. She lost control, and the car hit a tree. Zachary's mother's leg was broken in the accident, and Zachary, thankfully restrained by a seat belt, hit his head against the side window. He was unconscious for about ten minutes and was diagnosed with a "mild" traumatic brain injury.

About six weeks later, Zachary began to change. He exhibited aggressive behavior, breaking his own toys and hurting his younger brother. He began swearing, blurted out statements at inappropriate times, and interrupted frequently. He became rude, contrary, argumentative, and conflict seeking. He lost his friends at school the next year because he said things that hurt their feelings. He started to tease the two cats at home, so much so that they started to avoid him whenever he came into the house. Six months after the accident, his mother knew that something was seriously wrong. She took him to a counselor, who thought the problem was psychological, a result of the accident. The counselor thought that Zachary and his mother were too close and developed strategies to help Zachary become more independent. That only seemed to make things worse. After two years of counseling, which didn't seem to help much, the mother consulted Zachary's pediatrician. He diagnosed Zachary with ADD and put him on Ritalin. But that didn't help very much either. In fact, it only seemed to make him more aggressive. Zachary was age nine when he was brought to see me, and I thought he might have a chronic postconcussive syndrome, secondary to the accident. His brain SPECT study revealed marked decreased activity in the left PFC and decreased activity in the left occipital cortex, indicating both a front and back injury (common in head injuries). In addition, there was decreased activity in his left temporal lobe. Given the history and scan findings, Zachary's four-circles plan was as follows: **B**—I put Zachary on a combination of medication (an anticonvulsant, to stabilize his aggressiveness and help his temporal lobe function, and amantadine [Symmetrel] to help with focus, concentration, and impulse control), cognitive retraining exercises, a higher protein, lower carbohydrate diet, and omega-3 fatty acids with a higher EPA ratio; **P**—I taught him to ask himself, "Then what?" before he did or said anything, which was a critical exercise; **S**—Zachary was placed in a special class at school with appropriate accommodations; **Sp**—His mother started a local traumatic brain injury support group to help others. Over the next several months Zachary's behavior significantly improved.

Image 10.3: Zachary's Trauma-Affected Brain

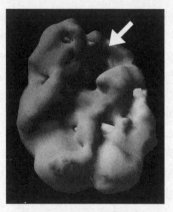

*Note markedly decreased
activity in the left PFC.*

Understanding the functions and problems of this part of the brain is often essential to the healing process of people who suffer.

PREFRONTAL CORTEX CHECKLIST

Here is the prefrontal cortex checklist. Please read this list of behaviors and rate yourself (or the person you are evaluating) on each behavior listed. Use the following scale and place the appropriate number next to the item. Five or more symptoms marked 3 or 4 indicate a high likelihood of prefrontal cortex problems.

0 = never
1 = rarely
2 = occasionally
3 = frequently
4 = very frequently

__ 1. Inability to give close attention to details or avoid careless mistakes

__ 2. Trouble sustaining attention in routine situations (homework, chores, paperwork, etc.)

__ 3. Trouble listening

__ 4. Inability to finish things, poor follow-through

__ 5. Poor organization of time or space

__ 6. Distractibility

__ 7. Poor planning skills

__ 8. Difficulty expressing feelings and emotions

__ 9. Difficulty expressing empathy for others

__ 10. Excessive daydreaming

__ 11. Boredom

__ 12. Conflict seeking

__ 13. Difficulty awaiting turn

__ 14. Impulsivity (saying or doing things without thinking first)

__ 15. Frequent traffic violations

Achieving Total Focus

Prefrontal Cortex Prescriptions

The prefrontal cortex is the most evolved part of the brain. As such, it is essential in helping you reach your goals. To review, the prefrontal cortex is involved with concentration, attention span, judgment, impulse control, and critical thinking. It controls your ability to look at situations, organize your thoughts, plan what you want to do, and carry out your plans.

The following four-circles PFC Prescriptions will help you optimize this part of your brain.

B—Supplements and medications; neurofeedback training; nutritional interventions; Mozart for focus; and exercise

P—One-Page Miracle exercise; "Then what?" exercise; meditation

S—Focusing on the positive; getting organized; learning to ask for help; learning how to not be conflict seeking or another person's stimulant

Sp—Finding meaning, purpose, excitement, and stimulation in your life

BIOLOGICAL PFC PRESCRIPTIONS

B—Consider PFC Supplements or Medications from the Amen Clinics Method Algorithm

At Amen Clinics we use the following algorithm when we see low PFC activity plus symptom clusters of ADD, depression, or psychosis.

Supplements for low PFC + ADD symptoms—consider fish oil, zinc, green tea, rhodiola, ginseng, and ashwagandha. There is growing scientific literature that supports the use of EPA omega-3 fatty acids to enhance focus (144). DHA omega-3 supplements have not been successful in helping with focus, but EPA has shown to benefit some in studies (145, 146). Other studies show that taking 15 to 30 mgs of zinc can also be helpful (147, 148). I particularly like using a combination of green tea—as it has been shown to boost dopamine—with the herbs rhodiola, ginseng, and ashwagandha. Taken together, we have found that they help to boost blood flow in the brain.

Medications for low PFC + ADD symptoms—psychostimulants, such as a combination of amphetamine salts (Adderall, Vyvanse), or methylphenidate (Ritalin, Concerta, Metadate, etc.). I have also used modafinil (Provigil) and armodafinil (Nuvigil) with success, although these tend to be expensive alternatives.

Supplements for low PFC + depressive symptoms—S-adenosylmethionine (SAMe).

Medication for low PFC + depressive symptom—bupropion (Wellbutrin) if the finding is in isolation or together with increased limbic system perfusion.

Supplements for low PFC + psychosis symptoms—omega-3 fatty acids, with antipsychotic medication (not alone). These have been found to have protective effects on young people who are at risk for psychosis (149, 150).

Medication for low PFC + psychosis symptoms—aripiprazole (Abilify).

For a year, I kept a log of what my ADD adult patients told me about the effectiveness of their medication. The following are some of their comments.

"I experienced an increased awareness of the world around me. I saw the hills for the first time when driving to work. I saw the bay when I crossed over the bridge. I actually noticed the color of the sky!"

"I experienced a hundred-and-eighty-degree difference in my attitude."

"I look at my children and say, 'Aren't they cute?' rather than complaining about them."

"I could sit and watch a movie for the first time in my life."

"I am able to handle situations where I used to be hysterical. I am able to see when I'm starting to overreact."

"The lens on my life is much clearer."

"It amazes me that a little yellow pill [5 mg of Ritalin] can take me from wanting to jump off the bridge to loving my husband and enjoying my children."

"I'm not running at train wreck speed."

"For the first time I felt in charge of my life."

"I used to think I was stupid. It seemed everyone else could do more things than me. I'm starting to believe that there may be intelligent life in my body."

"I sleep much better. Can you believe I'm taking a stimulant and it calms me down?"

"I used to be the kind of person who would go walking by myself in downtown Detroit at two a.m. Now on the medication I would never do something so stupid. Before, I just wouldn't think about the consequences."

"Now I can give talks in front of groups. Before, my mind would always go blank. I organized my life around not speaking in public. Now my brain feels calmer, clearer."

"I'm not as intimidated by others as I used to be."

"My husband may not be as happy as before I was on medication. Now I can think, and he doesn't win all of the arguments. I'm going to have to retrain him to not always expect to get his way."

"I feel in control of my life."

"I can't stand useless confrontation, when I used to thrive on it!"

Certainly not everyone with ADD experiences a dramatically positive response to stimulant medication, but many do. When they gain access to their prefrontal cortex, it is often amazing how much more effective they can be.

B—Consider Neurofeedback Training

I've discussed ADD as primarily a problem in the prefrontal cortex. Medication is the cornerstone of the "biological" treatments for ADD, but it is not the only biological treatment. Over the past thirty years, researchers, including Joel Lubar, PhD, of the University of Tennessee, have demonstrated the effectiveness of a powerful adjunctive tool in the treatment of ADD and other prefrontal cortex problems: neurofeedback, or EEG biofeedback (151, 152).

Biofeedback in general is a treatment technique that utilizes instruments to measure physiological responses in a person's body (such as hand temperature, sweat gland activity, breathing rates, heart rates, blood pressure, and brain-wave patterns). The instruments feed the information on these body systems to the patient, who can then learn how to change them. In brain-wave biofeedback, we measure the level of brain-wave activity throughout the brain.

There are five types of brain-wave patterns:

- delta brain waves (1 to 4 cycles per second): very slow brain waves, occurring mostly during sleep;
- theta brain waves (5 to 7 cycles per second): slow brain waves, occurring during daydreaming, relaxation, and twilight states;
- alpha brain waves (8 to 12 cycles per second): brain waves occurring during relaxed states;
- SMR (sensorimotor rhythm) brain waves (12 to 15 cycles per second): brain waves occurring during states of focused relaxation;
- beta brain waves (13 to 24 cycles per second): fast brain waves occurring during concentration or mental work states.

In evaluating more than six thousand children with ADD, Dr. Lubar found that the basic problem with these children is that they lack the ability to maintain "beta" concentration states for sustained periods of time. He also found that these children have excessive "theta" daydreaming brain-wave activity. Dr. Lubar found that through the use of EEG biofeedback, children could be taught to increase the amount of "beta" brain waves and decrease the amount of "theta," or daydreaming, brain waves.

The basic biofeedback technique teaches people to play games using their minds. The more they can concentrate and produce "beta" states, the more rewards they can accrue. With my clinic's neurofeedback equipment, for example, a child or adult sits in front of a computer monitor with a biofeedback game. If he increases the "beta" activity or decreases the "theta" activity, the game continues. The game stops, however, when the player is unable to maintain the desired brain-wave state. People find the activity fun, and we gradually shape their brain-wave pattern to a more normal one. From our and others' research, we know that this treatment technique is not an overnight cure. People often have to practice this form of biofeedback for between forty and sixty sessions. But the results are worth it.

Recently, the American Academy of Pediatrics gave neurofeedback a high scientific evidence rating for ADD/ADHD treatment (153). In my own experience with neurofeedback and ADD, many people are able to improve their reading skills and significantly decrease or eliminate their need for medication. Neurofeedback has also been shown to help decrease impulsivity and aggressiveness. It is a powerful tool, in part because the patient becomes part of the treatment process by taking more control over his or her own physiological processes.

Neurofeedback training can also be used for limbic system (mood), basal ganglia (anxiety), anterior cingulate (overfocusing), and temporal lobe (mood instability, learning, and memory) issues.

B—Nutritional Interventions

Nutritional intervention can be especially helpful in this part of the brain. For years I have recommended a high protein, low carbohydrate diet that is relatively high in fat to my patients with ADD. This diet has a stabilizing effect on blood sugar levels and helps both with energy level and concentration. Unfortunately, the Standard American Diet is filled with refined carbohydrates, which have a negative impact on dopamine levels in the brain and concentration. The breakfasts of today typically consist of foods that are high in simple carbohydrates, such as frozen waffles or pancakes, Pop-

Tarts, muffins, pastry, or cereal. Bacon and eggs have gone by the wayside in many homes because of the lack of time and the perception that fat is bad for us. However, the breakfast of old is not such a bad idea for people with ADD or other dopamine-deficient states.

The major sources of protein I recommend include clean meats (hormone-free, antibiotic-free, grass-fed, free-range), eggs, nuts, and legumes. These are best mixed with a healthy portion of vegetables. An ideal breakfast is an omelet with meat, such as chicken, and veggies. Lunch should consist of protein with vegetables. An ideal dinner contains complex carbohydrates for balance with protein and vegetables. Eliminating foods with simple sugars (such as cakes, candy, ice cream, pastries) and simple carbohydrates that are readily broken down to sugar (such as bread, pasta, rice, and potatoes) will have a positive impact on energy level and cognition. This diet is helpful in raising dopamine levels in the brain. It is important to note, however, that this diet is not ideal for people with anterior cingulate or overfocusing issues, which usually stem from a relative deficiency of serotonin. Serotonin and dopamine levels tend to counterbalance each other; whenever serotonin is raised, dopamine tends to be lowered, and vice versa.

B—Mozart for Focus

One controlled study found that listening to Mozart was helpful for children with ADD. Rosalie Rebollo Pratt and colleagues studied nineteen children, ages seven to seventeen, with ADD. They played recordings of Mozart for them three times a week during neurofeedback sessions. They used *100 Masterpieces,* vol. 3, which included Piano Concerto No. 21 in C, *The Marriage of Figaro*, Flute Concerto No. 2 in D, *Don Giovanni*, and other concertos and sonatas. The group that listened to Mozart reduced their theta brain-wave activity (slow brain waves that are often excessive in ADD) in exact rhythm to the underlying beat of the music, and displayed better focus and mood control, diminished impulsivity, and improved social skill. Among the subjects who improved, 70 percent maintained that improvement six months after the end of the study without further training (154).

PSYCHOLOGICAL PFC PRESCRIPTIONS

P—The One-Page Miracle

Developing an ability to stay totally focused will help guide your thoughts and behavior and give you an "auxiliary prefrontal cortex." It will help strengthen the conscious part of your mind.

In order to be successful in the world, we need to have clearly defined goals. Specifically, we need to know who we are and what we want to accomplish in our relationships, at work, and within ourselves. When we know what we want, we are more likely to change our behavior to get it; being goal-directed helps keep our behavior and choices on track.

When I first mention goal setting to my patients, they generally look at me with blank stares or mutter something vague about a career or money. Goal setting is not for some far-off dream. It is for now, and it is very specific. Making goals that you can focus on daily will make a big difference in your life.

I have my patients—whether they are five or seventy-five years old—do a goal-setting exercise I developed called the One-Page Miracle (OPM). In studying successful children and adults, I have found that the one thing they have in common is a sense of personal responsibility and clear goals. The One-Page Miracle will help guide nearly all of your thoughts, words, and actions. I've seen this exercise quickly focus and change many people.

Here's how to develop your own OPM. Take one sheet of paper and clearly write the following main headings and subheadings:

RELATIONSHIPS

Spouse/lover
Children
Extended family
Friends

WORK

MONEY

Short-term goals
Long-term goals

SELF

Body
Mind
Spirit

Next to each subheading, write down what's important to you in that area; write what you *want*, not what you don't want. Be positive and write in the first person. Keep a copy with you for several days so you can work on it over time. After you finish the initial draft (you'll want to update it frequently), place this piece of paper where you can see it every day, such as in your briefcase, on your refrigerator, by your bed, or on the bathroom mirror. In that way, every day you can focus your eyes on what's important to you. This makes it easier for you to supervise yourself and match your behavior to get what you want. Your life will become more conscious, and you will spend your energy on goals that are important to you.

I separate the areas of relationships, work, money, and self in order to encourage a more balanced approach to life. We burn out when our lives become unbalanced and overextended in one area at the expense of others.

Here is an actual example of an OPM I did with one of my patients who had a prefrontal cortex injury. Jarred was married with three children, and he was an attorney in private practice. Since the injury, he had had significant impulse-control problems and spent excessive time at work, which were the reasons he came to see me.

After you look at the example, work on your own OPM. Remember to put it somewhere you can see and read it every day. It is a great idea to start your morning by reading your OPM to help you get focused for the day ahead.

Jarred's One-Page Miracle
What Do I Want for My Life?

RELATIONSHIPS

Spouse: A close, kind, caring, loving partnership with my wife.

Children: To be a firm, kind, positive force in my children's lives. To be continually present in their lives in a way that enhances their development as responsible, happy people.

Extended Family: To continue to keep close contact with my parents and siblings, to provide support and love.

Friends: To take time to maintain and nurture my friendships.

WORK (To be the best attorney I can be.)

To have the best business possible, while maintaining a balanced life: specifically, my work activities focus on spending time taking care of my current clients, doing activities to obtain new clients, and giving back by doing some pro bono work each month. I will focus on my goals at work and not get distracted by things not directly related to my goals.

MONEY (Money is for needs, wants, and security.)

Short term: To be thoughtful of how our money is spent, to ensure it is directly related to my family's and my needs and goals.

Long term: To save 10 percent of everything I earn. I pay myself and my family before other things. I'll put away $2,500 each month in a pension plan, giving me the desired result of $5,000 per month after the age of sixty-five.

SELF (To be the healthiest person I can be.)

Body: To take care of my body on a daily basis.

Mind: To feel stable, positive, and grateful, to live in a way that makes me feel proud.

Spirit: To live close to God and be the kind of person He would want me to be.

Teach yourself to be focused on what's important to you. This auxiliary prefrontal cortex will help you keep your life on track.

P—"Then what?"

I have my patients remember the two most important words in the English language when it comes to their health: "Then what?" If I do this, "Then what" will happen? If I say this, "Then what" will happen? Does eating the third piece of pizza, skipping a workout, staying up late, or being a jerk to my wife help me with any of my goals? Of course not. According to research, the people who live longest and achieve great success are the most conscientious (120). They know what they want and then they act in consistent ways over time to get it. This is a PFC function. Always protect the health of your brain and put these two words up where you can see them every day: Then what?

In my work with Jose (a sex addict I first met on *Dr. Phil*), I asked him to plant these two words in his head to help boost his PFC by thinking about the future consequences of his behavior. Over time, Jose got in the habit of using a "Then what?" mind-set and has remained sober, which allowed him to keep his family.

P—Meditation

As mentioned in the BG Prescriptions chapter, meditation can help calm the anxious brain, but it also activates the PFC. Make a meditation practice part of your life.

SOCIAL PFC PRESCRIPTIONS

S—Focus on What You Like a Lot
More Than What You Don't Like

The prefrontal cortex is intimately involved with focus, concentration, and attention span. What we attend to and focus on has a very significant impact on how we feel and act day to day. As I mentioned, many people with PFC challenges, especially people with ADD, tend to be conflict-driven as a way to "turn on" prefrontal cortex activity. Unfortunately, this behavior has many negative side effects, especially on relationships and immune system functioning. Focusing on what you like about your life and on what you like about others is a powerful way to keep your prefrontal cortex healthy.

I collect penguins. I have six hundred of them in my office, everything that you could imagine, including a penguin weather vane, penguin clocks, pens, pencils, puppets, dolls, watches, ties, a penguin sewing kit, a penguin vacuum cleaner, and even a pair of penguin boxer shorts given to me by a nine-year-old patient. I know my penguin collection might sound a bit odd, but I tell people that I'm allowed to be a bit odd because I'm a psychiatrist. My friends and family have an easy time buying for me at Christmas. Let me tell you why I collect penguins and how they relate to the prefrontal cortex.

While I was doing my fellowship in child and adolescent psychiatry, my family and I lived in Hawaii. When my son was seven years old, I took him to a marine life educational and entertainment park for the day. We went to the orca show, the dolphin show, and finally, the penguin show. The featured penguin's name was Fat Freddie. He did amazing things: he jumped off a twenty-foot diving board; he bowled with his nose; he counted with his flippers; he even jumped through a hoop of fire. I had my arm around my son, enjoying the show, when the trainer asked Freddie to get something. Freddie went and got it, and he brought it right back. I thought, "Whoa, I ask this kid to get something for me, and he wants to have a discussion with me for twenty minutes, and then he doesn't want to do it!" I knew my son was smarter than this penguin.

I went up to the trainer afterward and asked, "How did you get Freddie to do all these really neat things?" The trainer looked at my son, and then she looked at me and said, "Unlike parents, whenever Freddie does anything like what I want him to do, I notice him! I give him a hug, and I give him a fish." The light went on in my head. Whenever my son *did* what I wanted him to do, I paid little attention to him, because I was a busy guy, like my own father. However, when he *didn't* do what I wanted him to do, I gave him a lot of attention because I didn't want to raise a bad kid! I was inadvertently teaching him to be a little monster in order to get my attention. Since that day, I have tried hard to notice my son's good acts and fair attempts (although I don't toss him a fish, since he doesn't care for them) and to downplay his mistakes. We're both better people for it.

I collect penguins as a way to remind myself to notice the *good* things about the people in my life a lot more than the bad things. This has been so helpful for me as well as for many of my patients. It is often necessary to have something that reminds us of this prescription. It's not natural for most of us to notice what we like about our life or what we like about others', especially if we unconsciously use turmoil to stimulate our prefrontal cortex.

Focusing on the negative aspects of others or of your own life makes you more vulnerable to depression and can damage your relationships.

Jesse

Let me give you a clear example of how powerfully this prescription can work. Seven years ago I met Jesse, a fourteen-year-old teenager who was admitted to the hospital after a suicide attempt. She had tried to kill herself because she was doing so poorly in school and couldn't keep up academically with her friends. On the night of her suicide attempt, she had a terrible fight with her mother, who had berated her poor performance in school. Jesse had a family history of depression on her father's side, and her mother had many ADD symptoms (although she refused to be evaluated and treated for it). Jesse felt sad and had a tendency to look at the negative side of things. She was also disorganized, had lifelong trouble focusing on her schoolwork, and was impulsive. She was diagnosed with depression and ADD. Jesse's SPECT study showed decreased PFC activity and increased

limbic activity. I started her on medication and began seeing her in psychotherapy. Over several months, Jesse's condition significantly improved. Her
mood was better. School was easier for her. She had better frustration tolerance and impulse control. Our initial weekly visits after she left the hospital
turned into every two weeks and then monthly by the end of the first year.
She maintained good stability, except for one area of her life: she continued
to fight with her mother.

Two years after I began seeing Jesse, she came into my office and burst
into tears. "I just can't stand my mother," she started the session. "All she
does is pick on me and try to get me upset. I know you've told me not to
react to her, but I can't help it. She knows every button on my body." As she
finished telling me about her latest fight with her mother, she looked
around my office and asked, "Dr. Amen, how come a grown man collects
penguins?" A bit amazed, I asked, "You've just noticed the penguins? After
two years?" I then told her the story about Fat Freddie. Then I taught her
about the concept of *behavioral shaping*, what the trainer had done to get
Fat Freddie to be a star performer. I told her, "Let me teach you how to
shape the behavior of your mother. Every time your mother is inappropriate with you, conflict seeking toward you, rude, or mean to you, I want you
to keep quiet and not react."

"Oh, Dr. Amen," she said, "I don't know if I can do that. I've tried."

I replied, "I know, but I want you to try with this new understanding.
And every time your mother is appropriate with you, listens to you, and is
helpful to you, I want you to put your arms around her and tell her how
much you love and appreciate her." Jesse said she would try her best.

When she came back a month later, she told me that she had had the
best month she had ever had with her mother. Her mother had yelled at her
only once, and she hadn't reacted. And she had given her mother a lot of
hugs. "I think I get what you're teaching me, Dr. Amen," she said with a
smile. "I have power to help things or make things worse. Even though I'm
not responsible for how my mom acts, I have a big influence on the situation." I was proud of Jesse. She had learned that by focusing on what she
liked about her mother a lot more than on what she didn't like, she could
have a positive impact on a negative situation. I taught her not to be a victim of her mother, but to use her own positive power in the situation.

S—Get Organized; Get Help When You Need It

People who have PFC difficulties often have problems with organization. Learning organizational skills can be very helpful. Day planners and computer organizational programs can be lifesaving. It is also important to know your limitations and, when possible, surround yourself with people who can help organize you. These people can be intimately involved with your life, such as a spouse or friend, or they can be people who work for you. The most successful people I have seen who have ADD or other prefrontal cortex problems are those people who have others help them with organization. Don't be embarrassed to ask for help.

Here are some tips to help with organization:

Set clear goals (as mentioned in Psychological PFC Prescription) in the following areas: relationships (spouse/lover, children, family, and friends), work, money, physical health, emotional health, and spirituality. Then ask yourself every day, "Is my behavior getting me what I want?" This critical exercise will help you stay on track in your life. Manage your time in a way that is consistent with the goals you have for your life.

Take the extra time to organize your work area on a regularly scheduled basis. Devote some time each week to organization—otherwise procrastination will take over.

Keep up with paperwork or have someone do it for you.

Prioritize your projects.

Make deadlines for yourself.

Keep to-do lists, and revise them on a regular basis.

Use your mobile device to help you remember appointments and ideas throughout the day.

Break down overwhelming tasks into small tasks. This happens on assembly lines every day. Remember, "A journey of a thousand miles begins with a single step."

Do unpleasant tasks first. That way, you'll have the more pleasurable ones to look forward to. If you save the unpleasant tasks for last, you'll have little incentive to get to them.

Use file folders, desk organizers, and labeled storage boxes to organize your paperwork.

Hire a professional organizer to help you get and stay organized. When my son with ADD was sixteen years old, I hired a professional organizer to help him. He didn't want to listen to me (what did I know—I was only his dad). She was a gifted woman who helped him immensely. She organized his room with him, as well as his book bag for school, his assignment book, and his study schedule. She helped him set up systems, and then she came back once a month to work with him and help him maintain what he learned. Today he is good with organization. Like many people with ADD, it's not natural for him, but he has the basics down and he is not a victim of his tendencies toward disorganization.

S—Don't Be Another Person's Stimulant

As mentioned, many people with prefrontal cortex problems tend to be conflict seeking to stimulate their brain. It is critical for those around them not to feed the turmoil, but rather to starve it. The more someone with this pattern unknowingly tries to upset or anger you, the more you need to be quiet, calm, and steady, which is easier said than done without the right tools. Whether the person seeking conflict is a child, spouse, sibling, or someone else, this applies. Reacting with yelling or anger only reinforces the need to seek turmoil. The harder the person with ADD tries to escalate the situation, the less intense the respondent should be.

It is fascinating how this prescription works. In general, the conflict-seeking people are used to being able to get you upset. They have mastered all your emotional buttons, and they push them with regularity. When you begin to deny them the drama and adrenaline rush (by being less reactive and calmer in stressful situations), they initially react very negatively, almost as if they are going through a drug withdrawal. In fact, when you first become calmer they may even get worse in the short term. Stick with it, and they'll improve in the long run.

Here are some strategies for dealing with a person who has a tendency toward conflict-seeking behavior:

Don't yell. The more their voice goes up, the more your voice should go down.
If you feel the situation starting to get out of control, take a break. Saying you have to go to the bathroom may be a good prescription. Likely, the person won't try to stop you. It may be a good idea to have a thick book ready if he or she is really upset and you need to stay away for a long time.
Use humor (but not sarcasm or angry humor) to defuse the situation.
Be a good listener.
Say you want to understand and work on the situation, but you can do this only when things are calm.

SPIRITUAL PFC PRESCRIPTIONS

Sp—Have Meaning, Purpose, Stimulation, and Excitement in Your Life

Meaning, purpose, stimulation, and excitement in your life help prevent shutdown and encourage you to focus by activating your prefrontal cortex. As I mentioned, in my clinical practice I treat many patients with ADD. One of the most interesting parts of the disorder is that there is often an inconsistency of symptoms. People with ADD typically struggle with routine, mundane activities. However, when they are engaged in interesting, exciting, or stimulating tasks, they often excel. A very important prescription I give my patients is to ensure that they have positive meaning and stimulation in their lives—whether it is in their work, their relationships, or their spirituality. It can make all the difference between success and chronic failure. A person with ADD in a boring job he dislikes is likely to need more medication to be effective. If he is in a job that excites and motivates him, he is likely to need less medication. The situation will provide the stimulation. Let me give you an example.

Seth

Seth, a very successful owner of several convenience stores in the Bay Area, came into my office feeling very frustrated. He had had a nice response to treatment for his ADD, so I wondered what had gone wrong. "Doc," he started, "I just feel like I have a bad character. I must be a bad person. I try to get my paperwork done, but I just can't bring myself to do it. It bores me literally to tears. Even with the medication and therapy, I still can't get it done." I asked for more information. "I sit down to do it," he continued, "when the meds are fully effective, and I just stare at the paperwork. I don't know what holds me back." "Seth," I replied, "it may have nothing to do with your character. You are a loving husband and father, you have a successful business that gives jobs to lots of people, and you care about others. Maybe what you have is a paperwork disability. Many people with ADD excel at things they like to do and are terrible at things that provide little motivation, like paperwork. Maybe you need to hire someone to do the paperwork. That will leave you more time to grow the business further."

What Seth said next hit the mark. "That makes perfect sense to me. When I was a teenager, I loved to sail. But I never wanted to go out when the water was calm. I waited for the storm warnings to come up before I went out. During the storm I would be scared to death and wondered why I would do such a crazy thing. But when the storm was over and I got back to shore, I couldn't wait to go out again. It was the excitement and stimulation that motivated me."

Seth hired someone to do his paperwork, and his business grew as he spent more time on the things he did best.

12

Looking into Worry
and Obsessiveness

The Anterior Cingulate Gyrus (ACG)

FUNCTIONS OF THE ACG

ability to shift attention
cognitive flexibility
adaptability
movement from idea to idea
ability to see options
ability to "go with the flow"
ability to cooperate
error detection

Inside View of the Brain

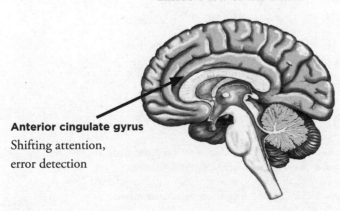

Anterior cingulate gyrus
Shifting attention,
error detection

Deep in the middle of the frontal lobes is a fascinating area of the brain called the anterior cingulate gyrus. I know it is a mouthful, so let's just call it the ACG. In 1991, Allan Mirsky, PhD, and colleagues from the National Institute of Mental Health published a paper on the various forms of attention in the brain and reported that the ACG and surrounding areas of the frontal lobes were involved in shifting attention (Image 12.1) (155). This work was published at the time I started using brain SPECT imaging and was highly influential to my thinking. Concurrently, researchers were mapping serotonin receptors in the brain and found that the ACG contained many of them (Image 12.2). Then, Rudolph Hoehn-Saric, MD, and colleagues from Johns Hopkins published a study that reported fluoxetine (Prozac), a selective serotonin reuptake inhibitor (SSRI), boosted serotonin and calmed activity in the ACG on the SPECT studies of patients with obsessive-compulsive disorder (44). These three findings taken together gave me many aha moments that had very practical clinical relevance. They

Image 12.1: Allan Mirsky's Model of Attention

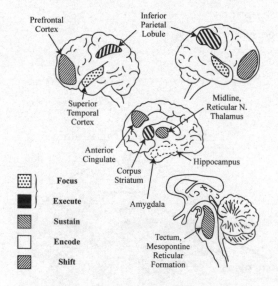

Semischematic representation of the proposed brain attention asystem, with tentative attributions of functional specialization to distinct brain regions. Adapted from Mirsky (1987). Reproduced with permission.

suggested that when the ACG was overactive and when there may be low availability of serotonin in people struggling to shift their attention, they ended up stuck on certain thoughts or behaviors. This symptom crossed many different diagnoses where SSRIs have been found to be somewhat helpful, such as obsessive-compulsive disorder (stuck on obsessive thoughts or compulsive behaviors), eating disorders (stuck on food issues or poor body image), certain addictions (obsessively drinking or doing drugs), chronic pain (stuck on the hurt), oppositional defiant disorder (stuck on saying no), and some with chronic anxiety conditions (stuck on worries).

Image 12.2: Location of Serotonin Receptors

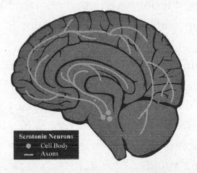

Images 12.3 and 12.4: Anterior Cingulate Gyrus

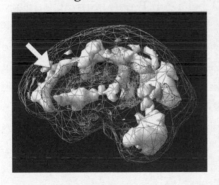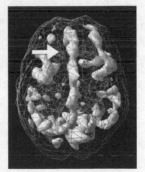

LEFT SIDE VIEW   TOP DOWN VIEW

Through the years, other researchers have also written extensively about the ACG (156). Multiple lines of evidence have linked it to shifting attention, feelings of safety and security, and error detection or knowing when something is wrong or out of place. In my experience, the term that best relates to the ACG is *cognitive flexibility*.

Cognitive flexibility defines a person's ability to go with the flow, adapt to change, and deal successfully with new problems. Many situations in life demand cognitive flexibility. For example, when you start a new job, you need to learn a new system of doing things. Even if you did something another way at a previous job, learning how to shift to please a new boss or adapt to a new system is critical to job success. Junior high school students need cognitive flexibility in order to be successful in school. In seventh grade, many students begin having various teachers throughout the day. It is necessary to shift learning styles in order to adapt to the different styles of the teachers. Flexibility is also important in friendships. What works in a friendship with one person may not be at all effective with someone else.

Effectively managing change and transitions is an essential ingredient in personal, interpersonal, and professional growth. The ACG can be of great help or hindrance to this process. When it is working properly, we are more able to roll with the circumstances of the day. When it is impaired or overactive, cognitive flexibility is diminished.

Along with shifting attention, we have seen that cooperation is also influenced by this part of the brain. When the ACG works effectively, it's easy to shift into cooperative modes of behavior. People with ACG issues have difficulty shifting attention and get stuck in ineffective behavior patterns.

The ACG has also been implicated (along with the other aspects of the PFC) in "future-oriented thinking," such as planning and goal setting. When this part of the brain works well, it is easier to plan and set reasonable goals. Conversely, difficulties in this part of the brain can cause a person to perceive a situation as frightening when it is not, predict negative events, and feel very unsafe in the world.

The capacity to see options and new ideas is crucial to adaptable behavior and prevents stagnation. In many fields, adaptable professionals readily utilize new ideas and technology (after a scientific basis is developed), and they are open to giving their clients and customers the latest information on what is new and exciting. When the ACG works too hard, we have seen it associated with finding too many errors (being overly critical), inflexibility, and focusing too much on the things that bother you. These individuals are often autocratic ("Do it my way if you want me to help you").

Low ACG activity has been associated with apathy and a condition called *akinetic mutism*, which means decreased movement and fewer words in speech (157). It has also been associated with inattention and trouble detecting errors.

PROBLEMS WHEN THE ACG WORKS TOO HARD

worrying
holding on to hurts from the past
getting stuck on thoughts (obsessions)
getting stuck on behaviors (compulsions)
oppositional behavior
argumentativeness
uncooperativeness; tendency to say no automatically
addictive behaviors (alcohol or drug abuse, eating disorders)
chronic pain
cognitive inflexibility
obsessive-compulsive disorder (OCD)
OCD spectrum disorders
road rage

One patient who had difficulties in this part of the brain described this phenomenon as "like being on a rat's exercise wheel, where the thoughts just go over and over and over." Another patient told me, "It's like having a reset button that is always on. Even though I don't want to have the thought anymore, it just keeps coming back."

We'll discuss the clinical problems associated with the ACG shortly. First, I want to talk about a number of what I call "subclinical patterns" associated with abnormalities in this part of the brain. Subclinical problems are those that don't reach the intensity or cause the dysfunction of a full-fledged disorder, but can nonetheless erode our quality of life. Worrying, holding on to hurts from the past, cognitive inflexibility, and rigidity may not send you to the therapist, but they can make your life unnecessarily gloomy and interfere with your relationships.

WORRYING

Even though we all worry at times (and some worry is necessary to keep us working or studying in school), people with an overactive ACG may have integrated chronic worrying into their personality. They may worry to the point of causing emotional and physical harm to themselves. Whenever repetitive negative concerns circle through the mind, they can cause tension, stress, stomachaches, headaches, and irritability. Chronically expressing worries often irritates others and makes a person seem less powerful and perhaps even less mature.

At a dinner party, an old friend of mine, who is also a physician, complained that his wife worried all the time. "She worries for the whole family," he told me. "It upsets me and the children. Her constant worry seems to be associated with her chronic headaches and irritability. How do I help her relax so that she won't get so upset about the little things in life?" he asked. I had known my friend's wife for many years. Even though she had never been clinically depressed and wouldn't fit the diagnostic criteria for panic disorder or OCD (obsessive-compulsive disorder), I knew that it was in her personality to worry. Members of her family, whom she had discussed with me on several occasions, did have clinical problems (such as alcoholism, drug abuse, and compulsive behaviors) associated with the ACG.

HOLDING ON TO HURTS

Holding tightly on to hurts from the past can cause serious problems in a person's life. I once treated a woman who was very angry with her husband. On a trip to Hawaii, he had allowed his eyes to wander toward some of the scantily dressed women on the beach at Waikiki. The wife became irate. She felt he had been unfaithful to her with his eyes. Her anger had ruined the whole trip, and she continued to bring up the incident years later.

Another ACG example occurred in a newly blended family. Dirk married Laura, who had a three-year-old son, Aaron. Laura and Aaron had been living with her parents. Shortly after the wedding Dirk, Laura, and Aaron went to visit Laura's parents. During the visit, Aaron asked for a second bowl of ice cream. Dirk told him no because it might ruin his dinner. Laura's parents undermined Dirk's new authority in front of the little boy by saying he could have the second helping of ice cream. Frustrated, Dirk tried to discuss the issue. The grandparents told him he was being silly. "What does he know?" they thought. "He's new to fatherhood." When Dirk tried further to talk to them, they just dismissed him. The grandparents, unable to let go of the incident, refused to even speak to Dirk or Laura for the next eighteen months. Many family cutoffs are due to excessive ACG activity.

COGNITIVE INFLEXIBILITY

Cognitive inflexibility, the inability to roll with the ups and downs of everyday life, is at the root of most ACG problems. A friend's six-year-old daughter, Kimmy, provides a perfect example of cognitive inflexibility. Her older sister was instructed by her mother to get Kimmy ready to go out for the day. The older sister picked out a shirt and pair of pants for Kimmy. Kimmy complained that the shirt and pants looked stupid. She had the same complaint for the next three outfits that her sister chose for her. Kimmy wanted to wear a sundress (it was February and cold outside). She cried and cried to get her way. Nothing else would do. Once she got the idea of the sundress in her head, she couldn't shift away from it.

In counseling couples through the years, I have frequently heard another example of cognitive inflexibility: the need to do something *now*. Not five minutes from now, but *now*! Here's a fairly common scenario: A wife asks her husband to get some clothes out of the dryer and put the clothes from the washer into the dryer. He asks her to wait a few minutes because he's watching the end of a basketball game. She becomes irate and says that it needs to be done *now*. They get into a fight. She doesn't feel comfortable until the chore is finished. He feels intruded upon, pushed around, and generally degraded. The need to *do it now* can cause some serious relational problems. Of course, if the husband said he would help, then didn't, we could understand her need to have it done *now*.

There are many more everyday examples of trouble shifting attention or cognitive inflexibility. Here's a short list:

- Eating only specific foods; being unwilling to try new tastes
- Having to keep a room a certain way
- Having to make love the same way every time (or avoiding lovemaking because of feeling uncomfortable about the mess that is involved with it)
- Becoming upset if plans for an evening change at the last minute
- Having to do things a certain way at work, even if it's not in the business's best interest (e.g., not being flexible enough to meet a customer's needs)
- Making other family members do chores, such as the dishes, in a certain way (this often alienates others and they become less willing to help)

Cognitive inflexibility can insidiously destroy happiness, joy, and intimacy.

THE AUTOMATIC *NO*

Because they have problems shifting attention, many people with ACG overactivity become stuck on the word *no*. *No* seems to be the first word they say, without ever really thinking about whether or not *no* is even in their best interest. One of my patients told me about his father. Whenever my patient would ask his father for something, such as permission to borrow the car, the father would automatically say no. The children in the family all knew that if they wanted something from their father, he would first say no to them, and then a week or two later he would think about the request and sometimes change his mind. *No* was always his first response.

When partners have ACG problems, they often get the opposite of what they want. One man told me that whenever he wanted to make love with his wife, he had to act as if he really didn't want to make love. He said, "If I would ask her directly, she would say no ninety-nine times out of a hundred. If I would lock our bedroom door at night (a sign that he wanted to be intimate with her), she would automatically become tense and say she wasn't interested. If I acted uninterested, just rubbed her back for a long time, then maybe I would have a chance. The amount of work and planning it took to make it happen often wasn't worth the effort." The "automatic *no*" puts a great strain on many different types of relationships. One of the strongest statistical associations in our database with high ACG activity is being oppositional or argumentative.

ROAD RAGE

Something happens to many people when they get behind the wheel of a car; a territorial animal comes growling to the surface. ACG people tend to struggle in this area. The problem again is trouble shifting attention. For example, if you are driving on a highway and someone accidentally cuts you off, most people would think to themselves, "You bastard," and then leave the situation alone. People with ACG issues say to themselves, "You bastard, you bastard, you bastard, you bastard . . ." and they cannot get the thought out of their head. I have known many ACG people who have acted

Images 12.5: Road-Rage-Affected Brain

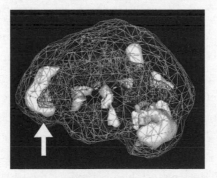

LEFT SIDE ACTIVE VIEW
*Notice markedly increased ACG
activity (arrow).*

out their frustrations by doing crazy things on the road, such as swearing, gesturing, chasing, or harassing the other driver. I have one patient, a very bright, successful professional, who on several occasions chased other drivers who had cut him off and on two occasions got out of the car and bashed their windows in with a baseball bat he kept in the car. After the second incident, he came to see me. He said, "If I don't get help for this, I'm sure I'll end up in jail." His ACG was markedly overactive, causing him to get locked into the negative thoughts and subsequently be less able to control his frustration.

OBSESSIVE-COMPULSIVE DISORDER

Gail

On the outside, Gail seemed normal. She went to work every day, she was married to her high school sweetheart, and she had two small children. On the inside, she felt like a mess. Her husband was ready to leave her, and her children were often withdrawn and upset. She was distant from her family and locked in the private hell of obsessive-compulsive disorder (OCD). She cleaned her house for hours every night after work. She screamed at her husband and children when anything was out of place. She would become especially hysterical if she saw a piece of hair on the floor, and she was often at the sink washing her hands. She also made her husband and children wash their hands more than ten times a day. She stopped making love to her husband because she couldn't stand the feeling of being messy.

On the verge of divorce, Gail and her husband came to see me. At first, her husband was very skeptical about the biological nature of her illness. Gail's brain SPECT study showed marked increased activity in her frontal lobes and ACG, demonstrating that she really did have trouble shifting her attention. With this information I developed a four-circles treatment plan for Gail: B—sertraline (Zoloft) to boost serotonin, a smart carbohydrate diet, and exercise; P—thought-stopping techniques; S—couples therapy to help her husband understand her behavior; Sp—help Gail get back in touch with her purpose in life.

Image 12.6: Gail's OCD-Affected Brain

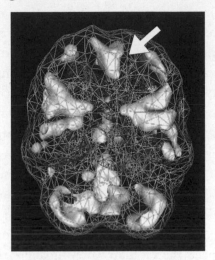

UNDERSIDE ACTIVE VIEW
Note increased ACG activity (arrow).

Within six weeks, she had significantly relaxed, her ritualistic behavior had diminished, and she stopped making her kids wash their hands every time they turned around. Her husband couldn't believe the change. Gail was more like the woman he had married. Today, I would have likely started Gail on a natural supplement to boost serotonin, such as 5-HTP, but if that didn't work I would certainly use the medication.

Obsessive-compulsive disorder (OCD) affects somewhere between two and four million people in the United States. This disorder—almost without exception—dramatically impairs a person's functioning and often affects the whole family. OCD is often unnoticed by people in the outside world, but not by those who live with the obsessive-compulsive person. The hallmarks of this disorder are obsessions (recurrent disgusting or frightening thoughts) or compulsions (behaviors that a person knows make no sense but feels compelled to do anyway). The obsessive thoughts are usually senseless and repugnant. They may involve repetitive thoughts of violence (such as killing one's child), contamination (such as becoming infected by shaking hands), or doubt (such as having hurt someone in a traffic accident, even though no such accident occurred). The more a person tries to control the thoughts, the more powerful they become.

The most common compulsions involve hand washing, counting, checking, and touching. These behaviors are often performed according to certain rules in a very strict or rigid manner. For example, a person with a counting compulsion may feel the need to count every crack on the pavement on the way to work or school. What would be a five-minute walk for most people could turn into a three- or four-hour trip for a person with obsessive-compulsive disorder. A part of the individual generally recognizes the senselessness of the behavior and doesn't get pleasure from carrying it out, although doing it often provides a release of tension.

The intensity of OCD varies widely. Some people have mild versions, where, for example, they have to make the house perfect before they go on vacation or they spend the vacation worrying about the condition of the house. The more serious forms can cause a person to be housebound for years. I once treated an eighty-three-year-old woman who had obsessive sexual thoughts that made her feel dirty inside. It got to the point where she would lock all her doors, draw the shades, turn off the lights, take the phone off the hook, and sit in the middle of a dark room, trying to stop the abhorrent sexual thoughts as they came into her mind. Her life became paralyzed by this behavior, and she needed to be hospitalized.

Research has shown a biological pattern associated with OCD (158–160). Brain SPECT studies have shown increased blood flow in the ACG, along with increased activity in the basal ganglia. There are currently a number of medications that have shown some effectiveness with OCD, including clomipramine (Anafranil), fluoxetine (Prozac), sertraline (Zoloft), paroxetine (Paxil), fluvoxamine (Luvox), citalopram (Celexa), and escitalopram (Lexapro). I often try serotonin supplements, such as 5-HTP.

In addition, behavior therapy is often helpful, especially exposure therapy, where a patient is gradually exposed to the situations most likely to bring out the rituals and habits. The therapist teaches the patient thought-stopping techniques and strongly encourages him or her to face his or her worst fear (for example, by persuading a patient with a fear of dirt or contamination to play in the mud).

OCD SPECTRUM DISORDERS

There is a group of disorders that has been recently labeled obsessive-compulsive spectrum disorders. People with these disorders get stuck on unwanted, repetitive thoughts and cannot get them out of their minds unless they act in a specific manner. According to the psychiatrist Ronald Pies, postulated OCD spectrum disorders include: trichotillomania (pulling out one's own hair), onychophagia (nail biting), Tourette's syndrome (involuntary motor and vocal tics), kleptomania, body dysmorphic disorder (feeling that a part of the body is excessively ugly), hypochondria, autism, compulsive shopping, pathological gambling, chronic pain, addictive disorders, and eating disorders. I would also add oppositional defiant disorder. A sample of repetitive thoughts that significantly interfere with behavior might include:

- Chronic pain: "I hurt! I hurt! I hurt!"
- Eating disorders, such as anorexia and bulimia: "I'm too fat! I'm too fat! I'm too fat!" despite rational evidence to the contrary.
- Addictive disorders: "I need a drink! I need a drink!"
- Pathological gambling: "Next time I'll win! Next time I'll win! Next time I'll win!"
- Compulsive shopping: "I need to buy this one thing! I need to buy this one thing! I need to buy this one thing!"
- Oppositional defiant disorder: "No I won't! No I won't! You can't make me!"

In 1991, Susan Swedo, MD, at the National Institute of Mental Health in Bethesda, Maryland, hypothesized that patients with trichotillomania would exhibit the same brain imaging as those with OCD (161). At rest, these patients exhibited a different brain pattern. Yet when these patients were treated with the antiobsessive antidepressant clomipramine (Anafranil), there was decreased activity in the cingulate aspect of the frontal lobes, which has also been found with successful treatment of OCD.

Dr. Swedo was also the first person to describe PANDAS (pediatric autoimmune neuropsychiatric disorder associated with strep) syndrome (162), an OCD-like pattern associated with bacterial strep infections that also causes increased anterior cingulate and basal ganglia activity.

Jason, age ten, was a happy boy. One day after he'd had a sore throat for a week, he suddenly developed tics and compulsive behaviors. He checked locks repeatedly and started washing his hands. These were brand-new behaviors. Very concerned, his parents had taken him to see several therapists and psychiatrists before coming to Amen Clinics. His SPECT scan showed marked increased ACG and basal ganglia activity. Knowing about Dr. Swedo's work, I ordered a blood test to look for strep titers, and his were very high. Once on an antibiotic and probiotic, his behavior went back to his pre-infectious state.

Here are several other examples from my own practice to illustrate OCD spectrum disorders.

CHRONIC PAIN

Sam

I met Sam, thirty-eight, after a suicide attempt. He was a police officer who had been in chronic pain after three car accidents. Desperate for relief, he had endured six back surgeries to little avail. Sam was essentially bedridden and about to lose his family, because all he could think about was the pain. His SPECT revealed marked overactivity in the ACG, which to me indicated very low serotonin levels. His four-circles plan included: **B**—200 mg of 5-HTP, as well as inositol, a natural supplement found to be helpful for some cases of OCD and anxiety. He also began acupuncture, which has been shown to be helpful for pain. **P**—hypnosis to help with pain; **S**—family therapy to help Sam get reconnected with his loved ones; **Sp**—focus on a deep sense of purpose for his life. After a month, Sam reported that his back still hurt, but he was much less focused on the pain. He was able to get out of bed and start back to school to train for a different line of work.

EATING DISORDERS

Leslie

Twenty-year-old Leslie suffered from bulimia for three years. She had gotten to the point where she was using laxatives several times a day in increasing doses, along with exercising for two to three hours daily. Her binges were also becoming more frequent. By the time she sought treatment, she felt totally out of control. During her initial evaluation, she said she knew her behavior was abnormal and she hated it. However, when she got the urge to eat, she felt she had to give in to it, and afterward she could not get the thoughts of being overweight out of her head. She had a maternal aunt who had been diagnosed with obsessive-compulsive disorder. Leslie's brain SPECT study revealed increased activity in the ACG along with increased activity in her right basal ganglia. With this information, I developed a four-circles treatment plan for her: B—fluoxetine (Prozac) to boost serotonin, a smart carbohydrate diet (this would help her blood sugar remain steady; low blood sugar in bulimics often triggers relapse), and exercise limited to thirty minutes a day; P—ANT therapy to decrease self-loathing; S—group therapy for social support; Sp—help Leslie develop a deep sense of meaning and purpose. Over the next three months, she improved markedly, to the point where she was eating normally, not taking any laxatives at all, and exercising less than an hour a day. Today, I would have started her on 5-HTP and inositol. If that didn't work, I would consider an SSRI like fluoxetine.

DRUG OR ALCOHOL ADDICTION

The Stoned Mouse Story

Recently I saw a twenty-one-year-old man named Jeff who smoked a lot of pot. Jeff suffered with anxiety, depression (had a suicide attempt last year), obesity, and was failing in college. He came into my office hoping I would write him a prescription for medical marijuana.

His brain SPECT scan showed dramatic overactivity in the ACG. I told him it was like he had a little mouse on an exercise wheel in his brain and the mouse could never get off. The mouse was tired and couldn't sleep, and so he yelled and screamed at Jeff so that he couldn't sleep either. Jeff's thoughts were constantly running, like the mouse. In fact, Jeff had to get the mouse stoned in order to calm down the little guy.

As I talked to Jeff about the mouse, he nodded his head, understanding. Jeff was always worrying, overthinking, and holding grudges; he used marijuana to calm his worry and help him sleep. I told Jeff there was a better way. He didn't have to kill the mouse, as he tried to do with the suicide attempt the year before; we could work together to help him and his mouse be strong, calmer, and happy with a four-circles plan: B—5-HTP to boost serotonin and calm Jeff's worries, exercise, and smart carbohydrates; P—ANT therapy to correct his negative thinking patterns; S—family therapy to rally family support; Sp—a deep discussion about his sense of meaning and purpose, which had been lacking to that point.

After getting this new understanding of his brain Jeff left my office— without a prescription for medical marijuana—and a plan to follow this new treatment approach. When I saw him three weeks later he told me he

Image 12.7: Jeff's Stoned Mouse Brain

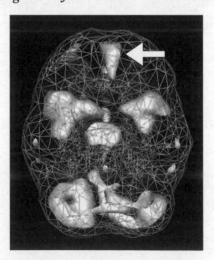

UNDERSIDE ACTIVE VIEW
Note increased ACG activity (arrow).

had stopped using marijuana and that the supplements were working to calm his internal mouse.

PATHOLOGICAL GAMBLING

Many people enjoy gambling. They feel happy when they win, but discouraged when they lose. And they realize that gambling is a game of chance—like many things in life. Some people, however, become addicted to gambling and it can ruin every aspect of their lives. Pathological gambling is defined by the American Psychiatric Association as persistent and recurrent maladaptive gambling behavior that disrupts personal, family, or vocational pursuits. Pathological gambling usually starts with an important "big win." The high from the win gets "stuck" in a gambler's head, and he or she begins to chase it, even to the point of self-destruction.

Adam

Adam came to our office out of desperation. His wife had just left him, and he had seen an attorney to discuss filing for bankruptcy. His gambling had gotten out of control. He was a successful entrepreneur who had worked hard at starting his own business, but in the few years before he came to see me he had begun neglecting his business to spend more of his time at the racetrack and driving back and forth to Reno and Lake Tahoe, Nevada. In our first session he told me, "I feel compelled to gamble. I know it is ruining my life, but it seems I have to place a bet or the tension just builds and builds. Before I started losing everything, I knew I could win. It was all I thought about!" Adam came from an alcoholic home; both his father and paternal grandfather were alcoholics. Even though Adam himself had never had a problem with alcohol, he clearly had an addiction. Explaining the ACG system to Adam was helpful. He could identify many people in his family who had problems shifting attention. "You should see our family gatherings," he told me. "Someone is always mad at someone else. People in my family can hold grudges for years and years." The goal of his treatment plan was to help him be strong, calmer, and happy: **B**—200 mg of 5-HTP to boost serotonin and n-acetyl-cysteine 1,200 mg twice a day, which has been found to be helpful in addictions such as gambling (163); exercise; and smart carbohydrates; **P**—psychotherapy and meditation; **S**—joining Gamblers Anonymous for a supportive and understanding environment; **Sp**—a deep discussion about his sense of meaning and purpose. Eventually Adam was able to reconnect with his wife and rebuild his business.

COMPULSIVE SPENDING

Compulsive shopping is another manifestation of problems in the ACG. Compulsive shoppers get a high from the pursuit and purchase of goods. They spend inordinate amounts of time thinking about shopping activities. This addiction can ruin their financial status and their relationships and have a negative impact on their work.

Jill

Jill worked as the office manager for a big law firm in San Francisco. Before work, during her lunch hour, and after work she found herself drawn to the stores at Union Square, near her office. She felt a rush of internal excitement as she picked out clothes for herself and her family members. She also enjoyed buying presents for others, even if they were just acquaintances. It was the act of shopping that was important. Even though she knew she shouldn't be spending the money, it felt too good to stop. She and her husband had many fights over the money she spent during her shopping sprees. She began embezzling money from work. Jill took care of the company checkbook and began to write and cash checks to fictitious vendors in order to cover her personal debt. When a business audit almost found her out, she stopped. But her addiction didn't. Her husband finally divorced her when he uncovered credit card debt in the amount of thirty thousand dollars. Ashamed, scared, and depressed, Jill entered treatment. All her life she had been a worrier. In her teens she had had an eating disorder, and she had a cousin who had obsessive-compulsive disorder. Her SPECT study revealed a markedly overactive ACG. When she got locked into a train of thought or behavior (spending) she had real problems shifting away from it. A four-circles treatment geared to boost serotonin and calm her ACG was helpful for her as part of the healing process.

OPPOSITIONAL DEFIANT DISORDER

One of the strongest findings in our research database is increased ACG activity in people who report being oppositional or argumentative. Oppositional defiant disorder (ODD) is considered a behavioral disorder of children and teenagers who are negativistic, hostile, defiant, and contrary. They tend to be argumentative, are easily annoyed, and lose their temper often—especially when they do not get their way. These children are chronically uncooperative. They tend to say no even when saying yes is clearly in their own best interest. The question I ask parents to help me diagnose this disorder is "How many times out of ten when you ask this child to do something will he (or she) do it the first time without arguing or fighting?" Most children will comply seven to eight times out of ten without a problem. For most ODD children, the answer is usually three or fewer; for many of them it is zero.

David

I first met David when he was seven years old. He came into my office with his mother. He was wearing typically dirty shoes, and the minute he sat down, he put his feet up on my navy-blue leather couch. His mother, embarrassed by his rudeness, took his feet off the couch. He put them back on the couch. She took them off. He put them back on again. Looking angry, she took them off again. Right away, he put them back on and she took them off. I was watching the cingulate of the mother/son pair in action. David had to have his feet on the couch, mostly because his mother didn't want them on the couch (he also probably wanted to see what would happen if he irritated me). His mother couldn't stand the fact that he wouldn't listen to her, and she had to have his feet off the couch. I knew that many of these problems probably stemmed from an inability to shift attention and the need to hold their own positions. To confirm my suspicions about David, I said ten innocuous things, such as "The weather is good today. . . .

Don't you think California is nice? [he was from out of state] . . . I like your outfit," and so on. David argued with eight of the ten things I said. "The weather is awful. . . . I hate California. . . . My mother made me wear this stupid outfit." With an incredulous look on her face, David's mother argued with him: "This is beautiful weather. . . . Yesterday you said you wanted to live in California. . . . This is your favorite outfit." Further conversation with his mother suggested we had a generational cingulate problem.

When I first suggested a connection between ACG overactivity and oppositional defiant disorder, many of my colleagues did not take me seriously. How could ODD, which is an externalizing behavior disorder, be related to OCD, an internal anxiety disorder? After seeing this pattern over the years it makes perfect sense to me. These children cannot shift their attention. They get stuck on *No. No way. Never. You can't make me do it.* They often have "cingulate parents," and many of them have a family history of OCD and other cingulate problems.

One of the most interesting findings among the patients we studied was that mothers or fathers who had obsessive thoughts, compulsive behaviors, or inflexible personality styles tended to have children with ODD. We studied eleven cases that exhibited this parent-child pattern and obtained brain SPECT studies on both the parent and the child. In nine out of the eleven, the parent's and the child's brain SPECT study revealed increased ACG activity. Both a biological explanation and behavioral etiology can be entertained for this finding. One can postulate that the finding of increased ACG activity (biological component) can cause parents to have problems shifting attention and become stuck on thoughts or behaviors that cause them to be inflexible, while the child's inability to shift attention causes his behavior to appear oppositional. It is also possible that the parent's rigid style causes the child to react in an oppositional way (the behavioral part) as a way to gain independence and autonomy, which induces the subsequent SPECT finding of overactivity in the ACG.

As mentioned above, it has been observed that the brain SPECT abnormalities in the ACG normalize with effective treatment. This does not appear to be merely variability from test to test, because researchers have shown that without intervening in some way, the brain SPECT patterns change very little. In the following case of ODD, follow-up data were obtained.

Jeremy

Jeremy, age nine, was evaluated for significant oppositional behavior. He had been suspended from school five times in second grade for refusing to do what he was told and being openly defiant with his teacher. His parents were told not to bring him back to school until they sought professional help. His clinical evaluation was consistent with a diagnosis of oppositional defiant disorder. His brain SPECT study revealed marked increased anterior cingulate activity. When he improved only minimally with behavioral interventions, he was placed on treatments to calm his ACG. Within two weeks, he showed marked clinical improvement. After two months, his brain SPECT study was repeated and revealed essentially normal anterior cingulate activity. The following year, Jeremy did well in school; in fact, his teacher that year could not understand why his former teachers had warned her about him.

STRESS OFTEN INCREASES ACTIVITY IN THE ACG

For many children and teenagers with ODD, I obtain both rest and concentration SPECT studies. Interestingly, in about half of the cases, I see a further increase in the ACG when these patients try to concentrate. Clinically, I find that this correlates with those oppositional children and teens who get worse ("more stuck") under pressure or when they are pushed to comply with certain requests. I have seen this occur frequently on an adolescent treatment unit. Some of these teens would become so "stuck" that they refused to comply with the staff requests and ended up on restriction because they could not shift their attention in order to behave more appropriately. It can be particularly bad if an ACG teen meets up with an ACG nurse who cannot back off a little to let the situation defuse.

Ken and Lily

Ken's family illustrates the problems an overactive cingulate can cause. His wife and two daughters came to his office to pick him up and go out to dinner. His youngest daughter, Lily, smiled when she saw him and gave him a big hug. As they were going to drive in two separate cars, Ken said to her, "Come on, Lily, ride with me in my car." Lily had been diagnosed with attention deficit disorder and she was often oppositional with Ken. He wanted to spend some extra time with her on the way to the restaurant. As soon as he said, "Come with me," she said, "No. I don't want to." Ken's feelings were a little hurt. He replied, "Come on, Lily, I want to be with you." She said, "*No!* I'm going with Mommy." Not one to give up easily, Ken physically picked her up and put her in the car. She yelled, screamed, and cried halfway to the restaurant (real quality time). All of a sudden she stopped crying, dried her eyes, and said, "I'm sorry, Daddy. I really wanted to go with you." When he had pushed Lily to go with him, her brain locked. She got stuck on her first reaction and became unable to think about what she actually wanted to do.

Lily's SPECT study showed increased activity in the ACG. All of Ken's children are grandchildren of alcoholics. I have seen a significant connection between a family history of alcoholism and increased activity in the ACG.

Given that children and teens with ODD tend to "lock up" cognitively when they are pushed to comply, I have found that behavioral techniques such as distractions and giving options are more effective in obtaining compliance. When you give oppositional children, teens, or even adults an option as to *when* they might do something, they tend to be less likely to get stuck on "No, I won't do it." When they are stuck on a negative thought or behavior, I have found it helpful to distract them for a bit and then come back to the issue at hand later. Ken would have been better at getting Lily to go with him in the car if he had given her a choice rather than just telling her she was going to go with him.

THERAPY FOR A FAMILY WITH SIMILAR BRAIN SPECT FINDINGS

The following family case study demonstrates how the same brain finding can present itself clinically in different ways. Brain SPECT studies were obtained on a mother and two of her children.

Celina, Samuel, and Lisa

Celina is a thirty-six-year-old woman who had experienced depressive feelings after the birth of her first child ten years prior to her evaluation. She suffered from significant irritability, crying spells, sleeplessness, lack of appetite and weight loss, problems concentrating, and difficulty in managing her children. Her condition was brought to a crisis with suicidal behavior when she separated from her husband. She was initially seen by another psychiatrist and started on an antidepressant, which had little effect. After I evaluated her, I started our four-circles plan, including: **B**—medication to boost serotonin; **P**—psychotherapy; **S**—couples counseling; **Sp**—a discussion about meaning and purpose. The plan started to work, but after several months, she decided that she "should be stronger than the depression" and took herself off the medication. Within several weeks her depression worsened, but she remained resistant to restarting the antidepressant.

In an effort to demonstrate to her that her depression existed—at least in part—on a biological level, I ordered a brain SPECT study, which revealed increased activity in her limbic system (consistent with the underlying depressive disorder) and markedly increased ACG activity. I asked her more pointed questions to see if she had obsessive-compulsive tendencies. Although she denied them in the initial evaluation, she was, in fact, perfectionistic at home and had repetitive negative thoughts. She tearfully remarked, "You mean my husband was right when he thought it was strange that I had to have all the shirts in the drawer buttoned a certain way and put just so in the drawer or I would become very upset?"

Celina then reported rituals that her eight-year-old daughter, Lisa, would perform before entering a new room, such as running a finger under her nose and licking her lips. Lisa also had a locking compulsion. Every time someone left the house, she would be right behind, locking the door. Imagine how irritated her brother and sister were because they could never go out of the house to play without being locked out!

I was also seeing Celina's ten-year-old son, Samuel, for attention deficit disorder and oppositional defiant disorder. Samuel's ADD symptoms did not respond to the typical ADD medications; in fact, they made him worse. Celina reported that once Samuel got a thought in his mind, he was unable to let it go. He would follow her around the house for hours asking her the same questions she had already answered. Samuel was also one of the most negative, hostile children I had ever met. Even though his mother was depressed, he defied her, yelled at his sisters, and seemed to do whatever he could to make the turmoil in the home worse.

We did SPECT studies on both children to see if there might be a genetic component to their problems and/or a similar response to treatment. Interestingly, both of them also showed increased ACG activity. Neither of the children had limbic system findings nor showed evidence of clinical depression.

Based on the SPECT and clinical information, I put all three of them on treatments to calm the ACG. Celina had a dramatically positive response and reported that she was no longer bothered when things weren't "just so." The scan had convinced her that her condition was at least, in part, biological and not her fault or the result of a weak will, which encouraged her to stick with treatment for a longer period of time. Samuel had a similarly positive response. His behavior became much less oppositional and his school performance dramatically improved. He made the honor roll for the first time in his life and was placed in the gifted-and-talented program the following year. Initially Lisa refused to comply with treatment, and her ritualistic behaviors continued. Approximately eight months later, she agreed to start treatment and her compulsive behaviors diminished. The family dynamics improved significantly after Celina, Samuel, and Lisa were treated with supplements, medication, and psychotherapy.

It was clear that the dynamics in this family operated and interacted on many levels. The mother's depression and obsessive thinking contributed to the anxiety and behavior problems in her children, and the cerebral blood flow abnormalities in the children probably added to their difficult behavior, which further stressed the mother.

ANTERIOR CINGULATE SYSTEM CHECKLIST

Here is the anterior cingulate system checklist. Please read this list of behaviors and rate yourself (or the person you are evaluating) on each behavior listed. Use the following scale and place the appropriate number next to the item. Five or more symptoms marked 3 or 4 indicate a high likelihood of ACG problems.

0 = never
1 = rarely
2 = occasionally
3 = frequently
4 = very frequently

___ 1. Excessive or senseless worrying
___ 2. Being upset when things do not go your way
___ 3. Being upset when things are out of place
___ 4. Tendency to be oppositional or argumentative
___ 5. Tendency to have repetitive negative thoughts
___ 6. Tendency toward compulsive behaviors
___ 7. Intense dislike of change
___ 8. Tendency to hold grudges
___ 9. Trouble shifting attention from subject to subject
___ 10. Trouble shifting behavior from task to task
___ 11. Difficulties seeing options in situations
___ 12. Tendency to hold on to own opinion and not listen to others
___ 13. Being very upset unless things are done a certain way
___ 14. Perception by others that you worry too much
___ 15. Tendency to say no without first thinking about question
___ 16. Unhealthy perfectionism

13

Getting Unstuck

Anterior Cingulate Gyrus Prescriptions

The ACG allows us to shift our attention from thing to thing, idea to idea, and issue to issue. When this part of the brain works too hard—often due to low serotonin levels in the brain—we have a tendency to get locked into negative thoughts or behaviors; we have trouble seeing the options in situations. Optimizing this part of the mind involves training the brain to become more flexible and see options and new ideas.

Throughout this book I have written about the use of supplements and medications in healing the brain. I will do so in this chapter as well. It is important to remember, however, that your day-to-day thoughts and behaviors also have a powerful effect on your brain chemistry. UCLA psychiatrist Jeffrey Schwartz demonstrated through his award-winning research (164) a powerful mind–body lesson. He and other researchers at UCLA used PET scans (similar to SPECT) to study people with OCD and reported findings similar to those presented in this book. Interestingly, when these patients were treated with antiobsessive medication, the overactive parts of their brains tended to calm down. This was a revolutionary finding: medications help heal the dysfunctional patterns of the brain. What was more striking, however, was that those patients who were treated without medication, through the use of behavior therapy alone, also showed normalization in the ACG and basal ganglia. Changing behavior can also change brain patterns. With this in mind, the following four-circles ACG Prescriptions will help you optimize this part of the brain.

B—Supplements and medications, nutritional interventions, and exercise

P—Thought stopping: notice when you are stuck, distract yourself, and come back to the problem later; thinking through answers before automatically saying no; writing out options and solutions when you feel stuck

S—Seeking the counsel of others when you feel stuck; refraining from trying to convince someone else who is stuck—take a break and come back later; making paradoxical requests when dealing with oppositional children

Sp—Finding meaning and purpose in your life

BIOLOGICAL ACG PRESCRIPTIONS

B—Consider ACG Supplements or Medications from the Amen Clinics Method Algorithm

At Amen Clinics we use the following algorithm when we see high ACG activity plus symptom clusters of worry, obsession, compulsive behaviors, anxiety, and mood issues.

> Supplements for high ACG + getting stuck on negative thoughts (worry, obsession, compulsive behaviors, anxiety, oppositional or argumentative, and mood)—in our experience, 5-HTP, saffron, inositol, tryptophan, St. John's wort, or omega-3 fatty acids higher in DHA are the most helpful supplements to raise serotonin and calm this part of the brain.
>
> Medications for high ACG + getting stuck on negative thoughts—most helpful are medications known to increase serotonin in the brain, which include clomipramine (Anafranil), fluoxetine (Prozac), sertraline (Zoloft), paroxetine (Paxil), fluvoxamine (Luvox), citalopram (Celexa), and escitalopram (Lexapro).
>
> Medications for high ACG + psychotic symptoms—risperidone (Risperdal) and olanzapine (Zyprexa).

Linda

Linda was twenty-six years old when she first came to see me. She had been raped violently twice, had been in a physically abusive intimate relationship, and had experienced the deaths of a great many friends while still a teenager. Her symptoms were depression, anxiety, worrying, and drug use. Her baseline SPECT study showed marked overactivity in the cingulate (problems shifting attention), basal ganglia (anxiety), and limbic areas (depression and mood dysregulation). After four psychotherapy sessions with EMDR (eye movement desensitization and reprocessing, a specific treatment technique for traumatic events) and one month of St. John's wort (900 mg a day), Linda felt significantly better. When we repeated her SPECT study, there was marked normalization of activity in all three areas.

Even though St. John's wort can be effective, it is not completely without side effects. One of my patients experienced a seriously slowed heart rate. Another patient who had gotten worse on Prozac found that St. John's wort made her worse as well. If you have significant struggles with mood or behavior, I recommend you work closely with a psychiatrist and discuss any herbal treatments with him or her.

B—Nutritional Interventions

There are two ways that food can increase serotonin levels. Foods high in simple carbohydrates, such as pastas, potatoes, bread, pastries, pretzels, and popcorn, increase insulin levels and allow more tryptophan (the natural amino acid building block for serotonin) to enter the brain, where it is converted to serotonin. The calming effect of serotonin can often be felt in thirty minutes or less by eating these foods. This may be one of the reasons simple carbohydrates are so addictive. They can be used to make you feel happy, but also cause high blood sugar levels that over time are associated with brain atrophy and dementia. I particularly like complex carbohydrates, such as sweet potatoes and garbanzo beans, as a healthier way to boost serotonin.

Brain serotonin levels can also be raised by eating foods rich in L-tryptophan, such as chicken, turkey, salmon, beef, nut butter, eggs, and green peas. Many people unknowingly trigger cognitive inflexibility or mood problems by eating diets that are low in L-tryptophan. For example, the high protein, low carbohydrate diets that I recommend for low-dopamine states (related to prefrontal cortex underactivity) would generally make ACG problems worse. L-tryptophan is a relatively small amino acid. When you eat a high protein diet, the larger amino acids compete more successfully to get into the brain, causing lower levels of brain serotonin and more negative emotional reactiveness.

B—Exercise

Exercise can also be very helpful in calming worries and increasing cognitive flexibility. Exercise works by increasing brain levels of L-tryptophan. As mentioned above, L-tryptophan is a relatively small amino acid and has trouble competing against the larger amino acids to enter the brain. During exercise, more of the large amino acids are utilized to replenish muscle strength, which causes a decrease in the availability of these larger amino acids in the bloodstream. As such, L-tryptophan can compete more effectively to enter the brain and raise brain serotonin levels. In addition, exercise increases your energy levels and may distract you from the bad thoughts that tend to loop around in your mind. I often recommend exercise for oppositional children as a way to improve their L-tryptophan levels and increase cooperation.

Many people, especially elite athletes, unknowingly use intense exercise as a way to manage low serotonin levels. It just makes them feel normal and clears the low moods and cobwebs from their brains. When someone who does this gets hurt and cannot exercise, they can experience a significant depression, associated with worry and negativity. At those times I find it really helpful to then work on their diet and supplementation to help rebalance their brains and moods.

PSYCHOLOGICAL ACG PRESCRIPTIONS

P—Thought Stopping

Whenever you notice thoughts looping or getting stuck in your head, imagine seeing a traffic stop sign in your head and silently say to yourself, "STOP. THIS IS MY ACG GETTING STUCK!" For some people, the more they actively stop these thoughts, the more control they develop over them.

Some of my patients have had success by wearing a rubber band around their wrist and snapping it when they notice thoughts starting to loop.

P—Notice When You're Stuck, Distract Yourself, and Come Back to the Problem Later

A primary way to overcome a busy ACG is to notice when you're stuck on a thought and do something to distract yourself. Becoming aware of circular or looping thoughts is essential to gaining control over them. Get up and do something else. Distraction is often a very helpful technique. Here's an example.

Maurie

Maurie, age thirty-two, came to see me for chronic tension. He incessantly worried about his job. Despite getting good performance reviews, he felt that his boss didn't like him. The constant worry frequently upset him. He couldn't get these thoughts out of his head—over and over they went. He complained of headaches, tension, and irritability at home. No amount of rational discussion helped. I gave him the task of writing down the times he was stuck on these negative thoughts about work. They occurred every several hours. Learning the ANT therapy exercises was helpful for him, but didn't completely prevent these thoughts from circling around in his head. His homework was to have a distraction. Every time one of these thoughts came into his mind, I told him he had to sing a song. He picked out several songs he liked and rotated through them whenever the thoughts started to bother him. This worked for him. He liked the music, and he felt that it gave him a measure of control over his bothersome thoughts.

Some of my ACG patients find it helpful to make a list of all the things they can do to distract themselves when they get harassing thoughts. Here are some examples:

- Sing a favorite song.
- Listen to music that makes you feel positive.

- Take a walk.
- Do a chore.
- Play with a pet.
- Do structured meditation.
- Focus on a word and do not allow any other thoughts to enter your mind (imagine a broom that sweeps out all other thoughts).

If you actively distract yourself from repetitive thoughts or block them, over time they will lose their control over you.

P—Think Through Answers Before Automatically Saying No

As mentioned, many ACG people have an automatic tendency to say no. Fight the tendency. Before answering questions or responding to requests in a negative way, take a breath and think first whether or not it is best to say no. Often it is helpful to take a deep breath, hold it for three seconds, and then take five seconds to exhale, just to get extra time before responding. For example, if your spouse asks you to come to bed and make love, take a deep breath before responding that you're tired, sick, too busy, or not in the mood. During the deep breath, ask yourself whether you really want to deny your partner. Is it in your best interest to say no and continue doing what you're doing? Or, is it in your best interest to get close to your partner? The automatic *no* has ruined many relationships. Take enough time to ask yourself if saying no is really what you want to say.

P—Write Out Options and Solutions When You Feel Stuck

When you are stuck on a thought, it is often helpful to write it down. Writing it down helps to get it out of your head. Seeing a thought on paper makes it easier to deal with it in a rational way. When repetitive thoughts interfere with sleep, keep a pen and paper near your bed to write them out. After you write out a thought that has "gotten stuck," generate a list of things you can do about it and things you can't do about it. For example, if you are worried about a situation at work, such as whether you'll get a promotion, do the following:

1. Write out the thought:
   "I'm worried about whether or not I'll get the promotion at work."
2. Make a list of the things you can do to offset the worry:
   "I will do the best job I can at work."
   "I will continue to be reliable, hardworking, and creative."
   "I will make sure the boss knows I desire the promotion."
   "In a confident (not bragging) way, I will make sure the boss knows about my contributions to the company."
3. Make a list of the things you cannot do about the worry:
   "I cannot make the decision for the boss."
   "I cannot want the promotion any more than I do."
   "I cannot will the promotion to happen. Worrying will not help."
   "I cannot make the promotion happen (although I do have lots of influence on the process by my attitude and performance)."

Use this simple exercise to unlock the thoughts that keep you up at night.

SOCIAL ACG PRESCRIPTIONS

S—Seek the Counsel of Others When You Feel Stuck

When all of your efforts to get rid of repetitive thoughts are unsuccessful, it is often helpful to seek the counsel of others. Finding someone to discuss the worries, fears, or repetitive behaviors with can be very helpful. Often just talking about feeling stuck will open new options. Through the years, I have used mentors to help me through some of the problems I've had to face. Others can be a "sounding board," helping you to see options and offering reality checks.

Several years after I started performing SPECT studies on my patients, I was professionally attacked by some of the researchers in the field, which caused me a lot of anxiety and sleepless nights.

I sought the advice of a close friend who had seen the development of my work and who had referred to me many patients who had benefited from this technology. When I told him about the attack on my work, he smiled. He wondered why I had expected anything different. He said, "People who say things that differ from the norm used to get burned at the stake. The more controversial an issue is, the more of a nerve you're striking in the established community." When he said "What else would you expect?" it suggested a new way to interpret what had happened. I could look differently at the behavior of these other researchers. In fact, one of the most vocal detractors of my work, who told *20/20* I should be arrested, published research findings recently about how using brain imaging alone can help clinicians make psychiatric diagnoses. When you're stuck, allow others to help you with the unsticking process.

S—Don't Try to Convince Someone Else Who Is Stuck; Take a Break and Come Back Later

If you're locked in the middle of an argument with someone who's stuck, take a break! Take ten minutes, take ten hours, take ten days! If you distract yourself from a lose-lose situation, you're often able to come back later and work it out.

I learned long ago not to try to argue with people who have ACG issues. When another person is "stuck" on a thought or behavior, logical reasoning usually won't work. One of the best techniques I've found to deal with those who get stuck is as follows: I will briefly make the point I want to make. If I can tell the other person is getting locked into his or her position, I try to change the subject and distract him or her from the topic. Distraction allows time for the other person's subconscious mind to process what I said without having to lock in on it or fight it. Often, when we come back to the issue, the other person has a more open mind to the situation.

Here's an example. Jackie came to see me about marital problems. Her husband traveled and was unable to attend many of the sessions. In the individual sessions, I saw that Jackie frequently became locked into her position and left little room for alternative explanations of behavior. Her husband said that she would go on and on for hours and not listen to anything he said. As I realized this was her pattern, I used the brief "attack and retreat" model I described. When she complained about her husband not paying attention to her, I wondered aloud if it wasn't because he felt she didn't listen to his opinion. Immediately she said I was wrong. She said that she was a very good listener. I didn't argue with her, but went on to something else for a while. The next session, Jackie talked about listening more to her husband. Her subconscious was able to hear what I said, as long as I didn't activate her getting locked into opposing me.

This is often a very helpful technique to use with teenagers. Many teens argue and oppose their parents as part of the natural individuation and separation process. I teach parents to get out of struggles with their teenagers by briefly making their points and moving on to other topics. For important issues, come back to them at later times.

One of the best marital suggestions I give couples is to "go to the bathroom" when things start to get upsetting. When you can see that your partner is beginning to get into ACG mode and is starting to go over the same point again and again, excuse yourself and say you have to go to the bathroom. Few people will argue with you when nature calls, and it is often helpful just to take a break. If the ACG issue in the other person seems particularly strong, take a big book with you and settle in for a lengthier stay.

S—Paradoxical Requests

Have you heard of "reverse psychology"? It works with ACG folks. But you need to be sly about it. As you probably know, in reverse psychology, you basically ask for the opposite of what you want. When you want a kiss from a naturally oppositional two-year-old, say, "I don't want a kiss." The next moment the child is begging to give you a kiss. When you want someone to help you with a chore, say, "You probably wouldn't want to help me with this chore." Family therapists have developed whole paradoxical treatment prescriptions to deal with resistant couples. The therapists bet on the couple's resistance to suggestions. For example, if the couple is having problems spending time together and finding time for sex, the therapist would tell them not to spend any time together and definitely not to have sex. Many couples find that after the paradoxical suggestions they start to spend more time together and make love more regularly and passionately than they have in years.

Paradoxical suggestions and interventions have been used as therapeutic prescriptions by psychotherapists for many years. These interventions have gone under many names, such as *antisuggestion, negative practice, paradoxical intention, confusion technique, declaring hopelessness, restraining change, prescribing a relapse*, and *therapeutic double blind*. Basically, they all involve suggesting the opposite of the desired response. A common paradoxical suggestion is given to people who have trouble sleeping: "Stay awake as long as possible when going to bed." In treating male patients who could not urinate in public restrooms because of anxiety, psychologist L. M. Ascher (165) told them they should go to public restrooms and go through the entire procedure of urinating (stand in front of the urinal, unzip their pants, and take out their penis), but refrain from urinating. With repeated trials, the men were able to overcome their fear of urinating in public. It is my contention that these tactics probably work best on ACG clients.

Whenever you want a cingulate person to do something for you, it is best to make it look as if it is his or her idea. If you ask for many things directly, you are likely to be disappointed. Ask for the person's input. Get his or her feedback. Here are some examples:

- If you want someone to meet you for dinner, it is often best to ask what time is good for him or her as opposed to telling him or her to meet you at a certain time.
- If you want a hug, it is often best to say something like "You probably wouldn't want to give me a hug."
- If you want him or her to go to the store with you, say something like "You probably wouldn't want to go with me."
- If you want someone to finish a report by next Thursday, say, "You probably can't finish the report by next Thursday."
- If you want a child to comply with a request without giving you a problem, say, "You probably wouldn't be able to do this without getting upset, would you?"

S—Dealing with Oppositional Children

There are two prescriptions I find essential in dealing with oppositional children. Remember, oppositional children often become rigid or stuck in negative behavior patterns. Effectively intervening with them can make a significant difference in their lives. The first prescription is to know when to distract their attention in order to break the loops of thoughts or behaviors that cause them to be oppositional. Distraction, as mentioned above, is a very powerful technique in helping ACG thinkers get unstuck. Distract the child away from the pattern by changing the subject, getting him or her to do something physical (such as taking a walk or playing a game), or working with a predetermined distraction prescription.

Josh

One prescription I use is having the parent read from a favorite book when the child begins to get stuck or locked into a negative thought or behavior. For example, eight-year-old Josh got stuck on being afraid of going to school. Before school he would complain of headaches, stomachaches, and anything else he thought his mother would accept to keep him home. When she caught on to his ploy, she would try to make him go to school anyway. When that happened, the little boy would scream, cry, throw tantrums, and threaten to run away from home. As the problem escalated, she brought Josh to see me. Not only was he anxious about school, his behavior was typically oppositional. The first intervention was to tell Josh in no uncertain terms that he was going to school! It was the law. It was good for him. And if we allowed him to stay home from school, he would become more afraid of it and would actually become "frozen by his fears." To help him on the mornings when he felt as if he couldn't go to school or he was worried about school, his mom or dad would distract him from his bad thoughts. Josh was very interested in insects and had many beloved books on the topic. When Josh became upset, his parents would read to him about a new insect and try to make it as interesting as possible. If Josh still gave his parents a problem about going to school, then he had to spend the day sitting on his bed without watching television or being able to go out to play. If he was too sick to go to school, then he was too sick to do anything else. Before this intervention Josh had problems on eight mornings out of ten. After the first month, Josh's problems in the morning diminished to two mornings out of ten. By the third month, the problem was eliminated. Both parts of the intervention were crucial to its success. His parents had to let Josh know clearly that his fearful, oppositional behavior would not get him anything positive; the parents would not be bullied. He was going to school or he would have to sit on his bed all day long (no secondary gain by being sick). Second, the parents used distraction to help Josh shift his attention away from the fears that got him stuck.

It is essential that parents lovingly assert their ultimate authority over ACG children. Parents cannot allow oppositional behavior to prevail. If they do, it only reinforces the oppositional behavior, which could ruin a child's life. Permissive parents don't teach their children to deal with authority, and those kids have trouble socially and in school. Authoritative, firm parents tend to raise the most effective children. Just as when people who have OCD give in to their obsessive thoughts or compulsive behaviors, those behaviors become stronger and harder to fight. When you give in to oppositional children and allow them to oppose you and disobey, their oppositional behavior only becomes worse. The earlier you train oppositional children out of this behavior, the better off everyone will be. To that end, I have developed a set of parenting rules that are the first step in dealing with these children. It is important to clearly spell out the rules and make sure the child knows you are going to stick to them. Here are two of the rules that deal with oppositional behavior:

Do what Mom and Dad say the first time.
No arguing with parents.

These rules spell out that you have authority as parents and will not allow your child to argue with you. If you make it a rule for children to comply the first time, then they know that is what is expected of them. You must also quickly intervene if they do not comply the first time. Do not tell a child to do something eight times. Your chance of abusing the child verbally or physically goes up dramatically if you do. For example, if you tell a child to do something and he or she refuses to do it or doesn't do it within a reasonable period of time, very quickly and calmly say, "You have a choice. You can do it now, or you can take a time-out and then you can do it. I don't care, it's up to you." If the child doesn't move quickly to do what you asked, then put him or her in time-out. Repeat as necessary. Deal with misbehavior quickly, firmly, and unemotionally. The more emotional you get, the more these kids tend to misbehave. Consistency is essential here.

The second rule, "No arguing with parents," is very important for oppositional children. If you allow the child to argue with you, then you are only reinforcing and strengthening his or her ACG resistance. Of course, you want to hear your child's opinion, but draw the line between stating one's opinion and arguing. You might want to tell your child, "As your parents, we want to hear your opinion, but arguing means you have made your point more than two times."

These parenting interventions are always more effective when you do them in the context of a good relationship with your child. Parents who become "limbically bonded" to their children by spending time and listening to them have fewer problems with oppositional behavior.

In summary, use distraction when necessary but also be firm and authoritative with oppositional children. Pick your battles and do not fight over every issue. Unfortunately, oppositional children often have one or two cingulate parents, which only feeds the negative family dynamics. Flexibility on the parents' part is often very helpful.

SPIRITUAL ACG PRESCRIPTIONS

Sp—Positive Rituals

One of the most interesting trends related to our imaging work is that it seems people tend to choose their religious affiliations based, in part, on brain function. This is a personal area of interest for me; as I've mentioned, I grew up Roman Catholic and have maintained my connection to my faith. I was an altar boy for many years, and went to a Christian university—Vanguard University in Southern California—and to a Christian medical school, Oral Roberts University. I have given lectures on the connection between mental health and spirituality. After I started our imaging work, I noticed that people who had low PFC activity tended to choose religious services that were more exciting and unpredictable, such as a Pentecostal healing service (they needed stimulation in order to focus), while people who had high ACG activity tended to choose religious practices that had more predictability and ritual. Of course, we often choose the religious faiths in which we were raised. But when people go outside of their family tradition, the brain plays a role in their selection process. People who have high ACG activity find comfort in "sameness" and predictability. If that is true for you, find practices that are both positive and potentially healing, such as prayer and meditation.

PUTTING ACG PRESCRIPTIONS TOGETHER

A doctor once approached me at a seminar and said, "Dr. Amen, I am so grateful for everything you have taught me, especially about the anterior cingulate gyrus. I'm married to a woman who has the ACG from hell. No matter what I say, she says the opposite. It has been so frustrating.

"For years I just thought that she didn't love me. Now I know it has to do with how her brain works. If I asked her to go to the store with me she would always say, 'I am too busy to go. It is so insensitive of you to ask me; don't you see everything I am doing.' Feeling bad, I stopped asking her to do things. Since I have listened to you about the ACG I realize that her brain gets stuck and I need to ask for the opposite of what I really want. For example, if I want her to go to the store with me, I'll say, 'I am going to the store. You probably do not want to go with me.' Incensed, she says, 'Of course I want to go with you. What would ever give you that idea?' We are doing much better now because of your work. But I still have one problem. It's the sex thing. It doesn't sound right to say, 'I am going to have sex. You probably do not want to come with me?' Do you have any ideas for me?"

I loved his question. Brain science can be so practical. "I have several ideas," I said. "First, take her for a long walk. Exercise boosts blood flow to the brain and also increases serotonin levels as well. It works like natural Prozac. Next, when you get home together, give her a small piece of dark chocolate to boost a chemical in her brain called phenylethylamine, which increases the brain's alerting response that something fun is about to happen. Then go in the bathroom and put a little bit of baby powder behind your ears. The scent of baby powder is a natural aphrodisiac for women. Rub her shoulders and never ask for anything directly. Odds are you will be more likely to get lucky."

Several weeks later I received an e-mail from this doctor with a string of thank-yous. Knowing about the brain helps you bring more love into your life.

14

Looking into Memory, Temper, and Mysticism

The Temporal Lobes

Ninety-four-year-old father to his sixty-eight-year-old son: "One day you wake up and realize that you're not eighty-one anymore. You begin to count the minutes, not the days, and you realize that you're not going to be around. All you have left is the experiences. That's all there is."

—FROM THE MOVIE *GRUMPY OLD MEN*

FUNCTIONS OF THE TEMPORAL LOBES

DOMINANT SIDE (USUALLY THE LEFT)

understanding and processing language
intermediate-term memory
long-term memory
auditory learning
retrieval of words
complex memories
visual and auditory processing
emotional stability

NONDOMINANT SIDE (USUALLY THE RIGHT)

recognizing facial expressions
decoding vocal intonation
rhythm

music
visual learning
spiritual experience

Outside View of the Brain

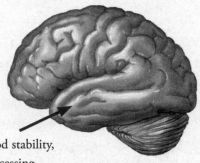

Temporal lobe
Memory, learning, mood stability,
visual and auditory processing

The most precious treasures we have in life are the images we store in the memory banks of our brains. The sum of these stored experiences is responsible for our sense of personal identity and our sense of connectedness to those around us. Our experiences are enormously significant in making us who we are. The temporal lobes, on either side of the brain behind the eyes and underneath the temples, store the memories and images and help us define our sense of ourselves.

On the dominant side of the brain (the left side for most people), the temporal lobes are intimately involved with understanding and processing language, intermediate- and long-term memory, complex memories, the retrieval of language or words, emotional stability, and visual and auditory processing.

Language is one of the keys to being human. It allows us to communicate with other human beings and to leave a legacy of our thoughts and actions for future generations. Receptive language, being able to receive and understand speech and written words, requires temporal lobe stability. The ability to accurately hear your child say "I love you," or to listen and be frightened by a scary story, is housed in this part of the brain. The dominant temporal lobe helps to process sounds and written words into meaningful information. Being able to read in an efficient manner, remember what you read, and integrate the new information relies heavily on the dominant temporal lobe. Problems here contribute to language struggles, miscommunication, and reading disabilities.

I often tell my patients that it is their memories that give them both their greatest joys and their greatest sorrows. Memories can make us strong and self-confident (remember the times you felt most competent), or they can bring us to our knees (remember your biggest mistakes). Memories influence every action and pattern of action you undertake. Essential components of memory are integrated and stored in the temporal lobes. When this part of the brain is damaged or dysfunctional, memory is often impaired.

Memories can sabotage our chances for success and effectiveness. I once treated a couple with severe marital problems. The husband had problems with depression and attention deficit disorder. His wife tended to be rigid and unforgiving. Shortly after they began therapy, the husband's problems were diagnosed and treated with medication. He got significant relief from his symptoms. Everyone except his wife noticed the improvement. Because his more positive behavior was inconsistent with her experience, she could not see his progress and remained in old patterns of behavior. She was stuck on blaming him. She was unwilling to get help for herself, and eventually the marriage died. It was her memories, rather than the new reality, that killed it.

Through our research, we have also found that emotional stability is heavily influenced by the dominant temporal lobe. The ability to consistently feel stable and positive—despite the ups and downs of everyday life—is important for the development and maintenance of consistent character and personality. Optimum activity in the temporal lobes enhances mood stability, while increased or decreased activity in this part of the brain leads to fluctuating, inconsistent, or unpredictable moods and behaviors.

The nondominant temporal lobe (usually the right) is involved with reading facial expressions, processing verbal tones and intonations from others, hearing rhythms, appreciating music, visual learning, and spiritual experiences.

Recognizing familiar faces and facial expressions, and being able to accurately perceive voice tones and intonations and give them appropriate meaning, are critical social skills. Being able to tell when someone is happy to see you, scared of you, bored, or in a hurry is essential for effectively interacting with others. In 1867, Antonio Quaglino, an Italian ophthalmologist, reported on a patient who, after a stroke, was unable to recognize familiar faces despite being able to read very small type (166). Since the 1940s, more than one hundred cases of prosopagnosia (the inability to recognize familiar faces) have been reported in the medical literature. Patients who have this disorder are often unaware of it (right-hemisphere problems are often associated with neglect or denial of illnesses), or they may be ashamed at being unable to recognize close family members or friends. Most commonly, these problems have been associated with deficits of the right temporal and parietal lobes. Results of current research suggest that knowledge of emotional facial expressions is inborn, not learned (infants can recognize their mother's emotional faces) (167). Yet when there are problems in this part of the brain, social skills can be impaired (168–170).

The temporal lobes help us process the world of sight and sound, and give us the language of life. This part of the brain allows us to be stimulated, relaxed, or brought to ecstasy by the experience of great music. The temporal lobes have been called the "interpretive cortex," as they interpret what we hear and integrate it with stored memories to give meaning to the incoming information. Strong feelings of conviction, great insight, and knowing the truth have also been attributed to the temporal lobes.

PROBLEMS WITH THE DOMINANT (USUALLY LEFT) TEMPORAL LOBE

aggression—internally or externally directed
dark or violent thoughts
sensitivity to slights; mild paranoia
word-finding problems
auditory processing problems
reading difficulties
emotional instability

PROBLEMS WITH THE NONDOMINANT (USUALLY RIGHT) TEMPORAL LOBE

difficulty recognizing facial expression
difficulty decoding vocal intonation
implicated in social-skill struggles

PROBLEMS WITH EITHER OR BOTH TEMPORAL LOBES

memory problems, amnesia
headaches or abdominal pain without a clear explanation
anxiety or fear for no particular reason
abnormal sensory perceptions, visual or auditory distortions
feelings of déjà vu or jamais vu
periods of spaciness or confusion
religious or moral preoccupation
hypergraphia (excessive writing)
seizures

Temporal lobe abnormalities occur much more frequently than previously recognized. You'll note that many of the above symptoms are often thought of as psychological, when, in reality, for many they are biological. The temporal lobes sit in a vulnerable area of the skull in the temporal fossa (or cavity), behind the eye sockets and underneath the temples. The front wall of the cavity includes a sharp bony ridge (the lesser wing of the sphenoid bone), which frequently damages the front part of the temporal lobes in even minor head injuries. (God would have done better to put bumper guards on that ridge.) Since the temporal lobes sit in a cavity surrounded by bone on five sides (front, back, right side, left side, and underside) they can be damaged by a blow to the head from almost any angle.

Temporal lobe problems can come from many different sources, the most common being genetics, head injuries, and toxic or infectious exposure. The temporal lobes, prefrontal cortex, and anterior cingulate gyrus are the parts of the brain most vulnerable to damage by virtue of their

Image 14.1: Inside View of the Skull

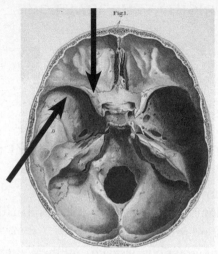

*Model showing the base of the skull. Lower arrow points
to temporal fossa where the temporal lobe sits; top arrow points
to sharp wing of lesser sphenoid bone.*

placement within the skull. They are also the most heavily involved in thinking and behavior.

Blaine

Blaine, age sixty, came to see me because his wife heard me speak at a national conference and she was sure he had a temporal lobe problem. He had memory lapses. He was moody and he was often aggressive. He also frequently saw shadows out of the corner of his eyes and heard an annoying "buzzing" sound, for which his doctor could not find a cause. His temper flare-ups just seemed to come out of the blue. "The littlest things set me off. Then I feel terribly guilty," he said. When Blaine was five years old, he had fallen off a porch, headfirst into a pile of bricks. As a schoolboy, he had had a terrible time learning to read and had frequently gotten into fights. His brain SPECT study showed significantly low activity in his PFC and left temporal lobe. Seeing these abnormalities, it was clear to me that many of Blaine's problems came from these areas, likely a result of his childhood accident.

Blaine's four-circles plan included: **B**—an antiseizure medication, valproate (Depakote), known to stabilize temporal lobe activity, and then a stimulant to enhance PFC activity; **P**—ANT therapy, especially working with the ANTs that give guilt beatings; **S**—working with his wife to enlist her support; **Sp**—a discussion about meaning and purpose. When I spoke to him three weeks after starting his plan, he was elated. The buzzing and shadows had gone away, and he had not lost his temper since he had started the treatment. He said, "That was the first time in my life I can remember going three weeks and not screaming at someone." Four years later his temper remains under control.

Image 14.2: Blaine's Brain

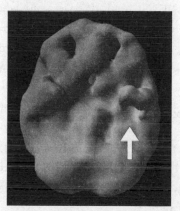

Decreased PFC and left
temporal lobe activity (arrow)

Common problems associated with left temporal lobe abnormalities include aggression (internally or externally directed), dark or violent thoughts, sensitivity to slights, mild paranoia, word-finding problems, auditory processing problems, reading difficulties, and emotional instability. Let's look at each of these in detail.

The aggressiveness often seen with left temporal lobe abnormalities can be expressed either externally toward others or internally in aggressive thoughts about oneself. Aggressive behavior is complex, but in a large study performed in my clinic on people who had assaulted another person or damaged property, more than 70 percent had left temporal lobe abnormalities (171). It seems that temporal lobe damage or dysfunction makes a person more prone to irritable, angry, or violent thoughts.

One patient of mine with temporal lobe dysfunction (probably inherited, as his father was a "rageaholic") complains of frequent, intense violent thoughts. He feels shame over having these thoughts. "I can be walking down the street," he told me, "and someone accidentally brushes against me, and I get the thought of wanting to shoot him or club him to death. These thoughts frighten me." Thankfully, even though his SPECT study confirmed left temporal lobe dysfunction, he had good prefrontal cortex function, so he is able to supervise his behavior and maintain impulse control over his terrible thoughts.

In a similar case, Misty, a forty-five-year-old woman, came to see me about her angry outbursts. One day, someone had accidentally bumped into her in the grocery store and she had started screaming at the woman. "I just don't understand where my anger comes from," she said. "I've had sixteen years of therapy, and it is still there. Out of the blue, I'll go off. I get the most horrid thoughts. You'd hate me if you knew." She had fallen off the top of a bunk bed when she was four years old and had been unconscious for only a minute or two. The front and back parts of her left temporal lobe were clearly damaged. A small daily dose of an antiseizure medication, together with other four-circles strategies, was very helpful in calming the "monster" within.

I often see internal aggressiveness with left temporal lobe abnormalities expressed in suicidal behavior. In a study from our clinic, we saw left temporal lobe abnormalities in 62 percent of our patients who had serious suicidal thoughts or actions. After I gave a lecture about the brain in Oakland, California, a woman came up to me in tears. "Oh, Dr. Amen," she said, "I know my whole family has temporal lobe problems. My paternal great-grandfather killed himself. My father's mother and father killed themselves. My father and two of my three uncles killed themselves, and last year my son tried to kill himself. Is there help for us?" I had the opportunity to evaluate and scan three members of her family. Two had left temporal lobe abnormalities. Anticonvulsants to stabilize this area of the brain were helpful in their treatment.

In terms of suicidal behavior, one very sad case highlights the involvement of the left temporal lobes. For years I wrote a column in my local newspaper about the brain and behavior. One column was about temporal lobe dysfunction and suicidal behavior. A week or so after it appeared, a woman came to see me. She told me that her twenty-year-old daughter had killed herself several months earlier and she was grief-stricken over the unbelievable turn of events in her life. "She was the most ideal child a mother could have," she said. "She did great in school. She was polite, cooperative, and a joy to have around. Then it all changed. Two years ago she had a bicycle accident. She accidentally hit a branch in the street and was flipped over the handlebars, landing on the left side of her face. She was unconscious when an onlooker got to her, but shortly thereafter she came to. Nothing was the same after that. She was moody, angry, easily set off. She started to complain of 'bad thoughts' in her head. I took her to see a therapist, but it didn't seem to help. One evening, I heard a loud noise out front. She had shot and killed herself on our front lawn."

Her tears made me cry. I knew that her daughter might well have been helped if someone had recognized her "minor head injury," which had likely caused temporal lobe damage. Proper treatment may have prevented her suicide. Of interest, in the past thirty years psychiatrists have been using anticonvulsants to treat many psychiatric problems. My suspicion is that we are frequently treating underlying physiological brain problems that we label as psychiatric.

People with left temporal lobe abnormalities are often more sensitive to slights and even appear mildly paranoid. This sensitivity can cause serious relational and work problems.

Reading and language-processing problems are also common when there is dysfunction in the left temporal lobe. Being able to read in an efficient manner, remember what you read, and integrate the new information relies heavily on the dominant temporal lobe. It is currently estimated that nearly 20 percent of the U.S. population has difficulty reading. Our SPECT studies of people with dyslexia (a reading disorder) often show underactivity in the back half of the left temporal lobe. Dyslexia can be inherited, or it can be brought about after a head injury damaging this part of the brain. Here are two illustrative cases.

Denise

Thirteen-year-old Denise came to see me because she was having problems with her temper. She had pulled a knife on her mother; this had precipitated the referral. She also had school problems, especially in the area of reading, and was in special classes. Due to the seriousness of her aggression and learning problems I decided to order a SPECT study at rest and during concentration. At rest her brain showed mild decreased activity in the back half of her left temporal lobe. When she tried to concentrate, the activity in her left temporal lobe completely shut down. As I showed Denise and her mother the scans, I told Denise that it was clear that the more she tried to read, the harder reading would become. As I said this, Denise burst into tears. She cried, "When I read I am so mean to myself. I tell myself, 'Try harder. If you try harder then you won't be so stupid.' But trying harder doesn't seem to help." I told her it was essential for her to talk nicely to herself and that she would do better reading in an interesting, fun, and relaxed setting. I sent Denise to see the educational therapist who works in my office. She taught her a specialized reading program that showed her how to visualize words and use a different part of the brain to process reading.

Carrie

Carrie, a forty-year-old psychologist, came to see me two years after she sustained a head injury in a car accident. Before the accident, she had had a remarkable memory and had been a fast, efficient reader. She said reading had been one of her academic strengths. After the accident, she had memory problems, struggled with irritability, and reading became difficult. She said that she had to read passages over and over to retain any information and that she had trouble remembering what she read for more than a few moments. Again, her SPECT study showed damage to the front and back of her left temporal lobe (the pattern typically seen in trauma). I had her see my biofeedback technician to enhance activity in her left temporal lobe. Over the course of four months she was able to regain her reading skills and improve her memory and control over her temper.

In our experience, left temporal lobe abnormalities are more frequently associated with externally directed discomfort (such as anger, irritability, aggressiveness), while right temporal lobe abnormalities are more often associated with internal discomfort (anxiety and fearfulness). The left-right dichotomy has been particularly striking in our clinical population. One possible explanation is that the left hemisphere of the brain is involved with understanding and expressing language, and perhaps when the left hemisphere is dysfunctional, people express their discomfort inappropriately. When the nondominant hemisphere is involved, the discomfort is more likely to be expressed nonverbally.

Mike

Nondominant (usually right) temporal lobe problems more often involve difficulty with social skills, especially in the area of recognizing facial expressions and voice intonations. Mike, age thirty, illustrates the difficulties we have seen when there is dysfunction in this part of the brain. Mike came to see me because he wanted a date. He had never had a date in his life and was very frustrated by his inability to successfully ask a woman out. During the evaluation Mike said he was at a loss as to what his problem was. His mother, who accompanied him to the session, had her own ideas. "Mike," she said, "misreads situations. He has always done that. Sometimes he comes on too strong and sometimes he is withdrawn when another person is interested. He doesn't read the sound of my voice right either. I can be really mad at him, and he doesn't take me seriously. Or he can think I'm mad when I'm nowhere near mad. When he was a little boy Mike tried to play with other children, but he could never hold on to friends. It was so painful to see him get discouraged." Mike's SPECT study showed marked decreased activity in his right temporal lobe. His left temporal lobe was fine. The intervention that was most effective for Mike was intensive social skills training. He worked with a psychologist who coached him on facial expressions, voice tones, and proper social etiquette. He had his first date six months after coming to the clinic.

Abnormal activity in either or both temporal lobes can cause a wide variety of other symptoms, including abnormal perceptions (sensory illusions), memory problems, feelings of déjà vu (that you have previously experienced something even though you haven't), jamais vu (not recognizing familiar places or people), periods of panic or fear for no particular reason, periods of spaciness or confusion, and preoccupation with religious or moral issues. Illusions are very common temporal lobe symptoms. Common illusions include:

- seeing shadows or bugs out of the corner of the eyes
- seeing objects change size or shape (one patient would see lampposts turn into animals and run away; another would see figures in a painting move)
- hearing bees buzzing or static from a radio not there
- smelling odors or getting odd tastes in the mouth
- feeling bugs crawling on the skin or other skin sensations

Unexplained headaches and stomachaches are also common in temporal lobe dysfunction. Several anticonvulsants, including valproate (Depakote) and topiramate (Topamax) are clinically indicated for migraine headaches. Often when headaches or stomachaches are due to temporal lobe problems, anticonvulsants seem to be helpful. Many of the patients who experience sudden feelings of anxiety, nervousness, or panic make secondary associations to the panic and develop fears or phobias. For example, if you are in a park the first time you experience a feeling of panic or dread, you may then develop anxiety every time you go into a park.

Moral or religious preoccupation is a common symptom with temporal lobe dysfunction. I have a little boy in my practice who, at age six, made himself physically sick by worrying about all of the people who were going to hell. Another patient spent seven days a week in church, praying for the souls of his family. He came to see me because of his temper problems, frequently directed at his family, which were often seen in response to some perceived moral misgiving or outrage. Another patient came to see me because he spent so many hours focused on the "mysteries of life" that he could not get any work done and was about to lose his job.

Hypergraphia, a tendency toward compulsive and extensive writing, has also been reported in temporal lobe disorders. One wonders whether Ted Kaczynski, the Unabomber, didn't have temporal lobe problems, given the lengthy, rambling manifesto he wrote, his proclivity toward violent behavior, and his social withdrawal. (His loathing of high technology would make submitting to a SPECT scan out of the question for him.) Some of my temporal lobe patients spend hours and hours writing. One patient used to write me twenty- and thirty-page letters, detailing all the aspects of her life. As I learned about temporal lobe hypergraphia and had her treated with anticonvulsant medication, her letters became more coherent and were shortened to two or three pages giving the same information. Of note, many people with temporal lobe problems have the opposite of hypergraphia; they are unable to get words out of their heads and onto the page. I know a therapist who's a wonderful public speaker but cannot get the thoughts out of his head to write his book. On his scan there was decreased activity in both temporal lobes. On a very small daily dose of valproate (Depakote), his ideas were unlocked and he could write for hours at a time.

Harriet

Memory problems have long been one of the hallmarks of temporal lobe dysfunction. Amnesia after a head injury is frequently due to damage to the inside aspect of the temporal lobes. Brain infections can also cause severe memory problems. Harriet was a very gracious eighty-three-year-old woman who had lost her memory fifteen years earlier during a bout of encephalitis. Even though she remembered events before the infection, she could remember only bits and pieces afterward. An hour after she ate, she would feel full but couldn't remember what she had eaten. Harriet said, "I left my brain to the local medical school, hoping my problems would help someone else, but I don't think they'll do anything with my brain except give it to medical students to cut up. Plus I want to know what the problem is. And write it down. I won't remember what you tell me!" Harriet's brain showed marked damage in both temporal lobes, especially on the left side, as if the virus had gone to that part of her brain and chewed it away.

Image 14.3: Harriet's Encephalitis-Affected Brain

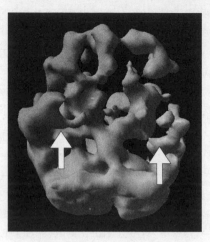

3-D UNDERSIDE SURFACE VIEW
*Note markedly decreased activity in
both temporal lobes.*

Alzheimer's disease, a devastating progressive form of senile dementia, is the cause of one of the most common memory problems in the elderly. Unfortunately, it robs many people of their retirement years and can leave families physically, emotionally, and financially exhausted. SPECT is an important tool in diagnosing this disorder. Before functional studies were available, the only way to diagnose Alzheimer's was through autopsy. SPECT studies show a typical Alzheimer's pattern of decreased activity in both temporal lobes, the parietal lobes, and often in the posterior cingulate. This pattern is seen on SPECT years before the onset of symptoms, when interventions are more likely to work.

Fyodor Dostoyevsky was reported to have had bouts of "temporal lobe seizures." He felt his affliction was a "holy experience." One of his biographers, René Fueloep-Miller (172), quotes Dostoyevsky as saying that his epilepsy "rouses in me hitherto unsuspected emotions, gives me feelings of magnificence, abundance and eternity." In *The Idiot*, Dostoyevsky writes:

There was always one instant just before the epileptic fit . . . when suddenly in the midst of sadness, spiritual darkness and oppression, his brain seemed momentarily to catch fire, and in an extraordinary rush, all his vital forces were at their highest tension. The sense of life, the consciousness of self, were multiplied almost ten times at these moments which lasted no longer than a flash of lightning. His mind and his heart were flooded with extraordinary light; all his uneasiness, all his doubts, all his anxieties were relieved at once; they were all resolved in a lofty calm, full of serene, harmonious joy and hope, full of reason and ultimate meaning. But these moments, these flashes, were only a premonition of that final second (it was never more than a second) with which the fit began. That second was, of course, unendurable. Thinking of that moment later, when he was well again, he often said to himself that all these gleams and flashes of supreme sensation and consciousness of self, and therefore, also of the highest form of being, were nothing but disease, the violation of the normal state; and if so, it was not at all the highest form of being, but on the contrary must be reckoned the lowest. Yet he came at last to an extreme paradoxical conclusion. "What if it is disease?" he decided at last. "What does it matter that it is an abnormal intensity, if the result, if the sensation, remembered and analyzed afterward in health, turns out to be the acme of harmony and beauty, and gives a feeling, unknown and undefined till then, of completeness, of proportion, of reconciliation, and of startled prayerful merging with the highest synthesis of life?"(173)

Bryce

Lewis Carroll is reported to have had "temporal lobe experiences," which were described in the visual distortions of Alice in *Alice's Adventures in Wonderland*. Seven-year-old Bryce became very upset when his mother read *Alice's Adventures in Wonderland* to him. He said that he felt like Alice. "I have weird things happen to me," he told her. "I see things." During the day he saw objects change shapes, often getting smaller. He also saw green, shadowy ghosts at night. Bryce also had a lot of anxiety symptoms. Frightened that Bryce was losing his mind (a cousin had been diagnosed with a "schizophrenic-like" illness), his mother brought him to see me. On hearing of these symptoms, I suspected that one or both of his temporal lobes were acting up. His brain SPECT study confirmed a focal area of increased activity in his right temporal lobe. His treatment included an antiseizure medication to stabilize his temporal lobe and psychotherapy. Within two weeks, Bryce's strange experiences disappeared, and over the next six months his anxiety lessened.

Images 14.4 and 14.5: Bryce's Brain, Affected by Temporal Lobe Epilepsy

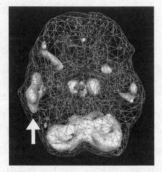 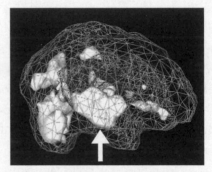

3-D UNDERSIDE ACTIVE VIEW   3-D RIGHT SIDE VIEW
Notice area of increased activity in the right temporal lobe (up arrow).

Ellen and Jack

Ellen and Jack had similar histories: both had been somewhat reclusive, both had periods of spaciness, and both had periods of panic for no particular reason. Both had religious experiences that occupied a good deal of their lives. Ellen, age thirty-two, was nearly paralyzed by her deep religious feelings, unable to work and socially isolated. Jack took great interest in her periods of "deep spiritual awakening," but was never able to make out what they meant. Ellen was brought to my office by her parents, who were concerned about her social isolation. Jack wanted an evaluation for his panic attacks. The couple's SPECT studies revealed marked increased activity in the deep aspects of their temporal lobes. The majority of their symptoms went away on antiseizure medications. Even taking them, both remained deeply religious people, but they were no longer constantly preoccupied with their thoughts.

Jim

Like Ellen and Jack, Jim was bothered by periods of spaciness and panic. He also had periods of "religious thoughts," in which he felt the "presence of the devil" and was unsure and afraid. His fear of the devil haunted him, made him reclusive, and made him seem paranoid to his family. There was an interesting difference between Jim's SPECT study and Ellen's and Jack's studies: Jim's study revealed abnormal activity in the left temporal lobe, not the right. In my experience, left temporal lobe problems are often associated with very negative or "dark" thoughts. After Jim was placed on an antiseizure medication the "presence of the devil" was gone.

TEMPORAL LOBE CHECKLIST

Here is the temporal lobe checklist. Please read this list of behaviors and rate yourself (or the person you are evaluating) on each behavior listed. Use the following scale and place the appropriate number next to the item. Five or more symptoms marked 3 or 4 indicate a high likelihood of temporal lobe problems.

0 = never
1 = rarely
2 = occasionally
3 = frequently
4 = very frequently

___ 1. Short fuse or periods of extreme irritability

___ 2. Periods of rage with little provocation

___ 3. Frequent misinterpretation of comments as negative when they are not

___ 4. Irritability that tends to build, then explodes, then recedes; a person often feels tired after a rage

___ 5. Periods of spaciness or confusion

___ 6. Periods of panic and/or fear for no specific reason

___ 7. Visual or auditory changes, such as seeing shadows or hearing muffled sounds

___ 8. Frequent periods of déjà vu (feelings of having been somewhere you have never been) or jamais vu (not recalling a familiar place or person)

___ 9. Sensitivity or mild paranoia

___ 10. Headaches or abdominal pain of uncertain origin

___ 11. Dark thoughts, such as suicidal or homicidal thoughts

___ 12. Periods of forgetfulness

___ 13. Memory problems

___ 14. Reading comprehension problems

___ 15. Preoccupation with moral or religious ideas

15

Boosting Memory, Learning, and Temper Control

Temporal Lobe Prescriptions

The following prescriptions are geared toward optimizing and healing the temporal lobes (TL). They are based on what we have learned about the temporal lobes, as well as on clinical experience with my patients. Remember that the temporal lobes are involved with mood stability, understanding and processing language, memory, reading social cues (facial expression and voice intonation), rhythm, and music.

The following four-circles TL Prescriptions will help you optimize this part of your brain.

B—Supplements and medications, nutritional interventions, rhythmic movement, listening to classical music, humming or toning to tune up the brain, EEG biofeedback

P—Creating a library of wonderful experiences

S—Conflict resolution

Sp—Singing whenever you can

BIOLOGICAL TL PRESCRIPTIONS

B—Consider TL Supplements or Medications from the Amen Clinics Method Algorithm

At Amen Clinics we use the following algorithm when we see abnormal (low or high) TL activity plus symptom clusters of mood instability, anxiety, irritability, and memory and learning challenges.

Supplements for low or high TL + mood instability, anxiety, or irritability—at Amen Clinics we have found GABA, magnesium, theanine, and taurine helpful for these issues.

Medications for low or high TL + mood instability, anxiety, or irritability—we specifically use gabapentin (Neurontin) for anxiety and irritability; and lamotrigine (Lamictal) and valproate (Depakote) for mood instability and resistant depression.

Supplements for low TL + memory or learning challenges—we often use a combination of gingko biloba, vinpocetine, huperzine A, acetyl-l-carnitine, alpha lipoic acid, phosphatidylserine, B vitamins, including B6, B12, methyltetrahydrofolate, and omega-3 fatty acids.

Medications for low TL + memory or learning challenges—we use medications that boost the learning neurotransmitter acetylcholine, such as donepezil (Aricept), or those that modulate the neurotransmitter glutamate (which also helps with learning) with memantine (Namenda). Sometimes, stimulant medications can help boost temporal lobe activity, but it is important to use them carefully, as they can also increase irritability.

B—Nutritional Interventions

Nutritional support can be very helpful in temporal lobe problems. Many people with aggressive behavior become much worse after a high sugar load. If aggressiveness is present without features of depression or obsessive thoughts (more similar to an explosive or short-fuse form of aggressiveness), then a higher protein, lower simple carbohydrate diet is likely to be very helpful. If the aggressiveness is associated with ruminations, moodiness, and depression, then a balanced diet of equal amounts of carbohydrates and protein is likely to be best. Ketogenic (very low carbohydrate) diets have been found to be particularly helpful for people with seizure disorders.

B—Rhythmic Movement

The temporal lobes are involved with processing and producing rhythms. Chanting, dancing, and other forms of rhythmic movement can be healing.

Many Americans never learn about the concept of rhythm and how important it can be to healing and health.

Chanting is commonly used in Eastern religions and orthodox Western religions as a way to focus and open one's mind. Chanting has a special rhythm that induces a trancelike state, bringing peace and tranquility and opening the mind to new experiences and learning. Dancing and body movement can be very therapeutic. Like song and music, they can change a person's mood and provide positive experiences to treasure throughout the day, week—or even longer. Look for opportunities to move in rhythm.

B—Listen to Healing Music

Listen to a lot of great music. Music, from country to jazz, from rock to classical, is one of the true joys of life. Music has healing properties. Listening to it can activate and stimulate the temporal lobes and bring peace or excitement to your mind.

Music therapy has been a part of psychiatric treatment for decades. Fast-tempo, upbeat music can stimulate depressed patients in a positive way, while certain music has a calming effect on patients. For example, music by composer Barry Goldstein is used for therapeutic purposes in hospitals, hospices, and other healing centers because it helps to facilitate relaxation and improve sleep, reduce stress and anxiety, and provide other supportive benefits for the brain. You can find some of Barry's healing music on our online community www.mybrainfitlife.com.

In highly publicized work, researchers at the University of California, Irvine, demonstrated that listening to Mozart's Sonata for Two Pianos (K448) enhanced visual-spatial learning skills (174). Frances H. Rauscher, PhD, and her colleagues conducted a study with thirty-six undergraduates from the department of psychology who scored eight to nine points higher on a spatial IQ test (part of the Stanford-Binet Intelligence Scale) after listening to ten minutes of Mozart. Gordon Shaw, one of the researchers, suggested that Mozart's music may "warm up" the brain: "We suspect that complex music facilitates certain complex neuronal patterns involved in high brain activities like math and chess. By contrast, simple and repetitive music could have the opposite effect." In a follow-up study, the researchers tested spatial skills by projecting sixteen abstract figures similar to folded pieces of paper on an overhead screen for one minute each. The test looked at the ability of participants to tell how the items would look unfolded. Over a five-day period, one group listened to Mozart's Sonata for Two Pianos, another to silence, and a third to mixed sounds, including music by Philip Glass, an audiotaped story, and a dance piece. The researchers reported that all three groups improved their scores from day one to day two, but the group that listened to Mozart improved their pattern recognition scores 62 percent, compared with 14 percent for the silence group and 11 percent for the mixed group. On subsequent days the Mozart group achieved yet higher scores, but the other groups did not show continued improvement. The researchers proposed that Mozart's music strengthened the creative right-brain processing center associated with spatial reasoning. "Listening to music," they concluded, "acts as an exercise for facilitating symmetry operations associated with higher brain function." Don Campbell, founder of the Institute of Music, Health and Education, gives a nice summary of this work in *The Mozart Effect* (175). He writes that in his experience, Mozart's violin concertos, especially nos. 3 and 4, produce even stronger positive effects on learning.

In the context of the temporal lobes, this research makes perfect sense, since the temporal lobes are involved in processing music and memory. Certain types of music may activate the temporal lobes and help them learn, process, and remember information more efficiently. It is likely that certain types of music open new pathways into the mind.

Certain music may also be very destructive. I believe it is no coincidence that the majority of teenagers who end up being sent to residential treatment facilities or group homes listen to more rap and heavy metal music than do other teens. Music that is filled with lyrics of hate and despair may encourage those same mind states in developing teens. What your children listen to may hurt them. Teach them to love classical music when they are young.

Music is influential from a very early age. Dr. Thomas Verny, in his book *The Secret Life of the Unborn Child* (176), cites scientific experiments showing that fetuses preferred Mozart and Vivaldi to other composers in early as well as later stages of pregnancy. He reported that fetal heart rates steadied and kicking decreased, while other music, especially rock, "drove most fe-tuses to distraction," and they "kicked violently" when it was played to their mothers.

Classical and other beautiful, soothing music can positively stimulate your brain.

B—Use Toning and Humming to Tune Up Your Brain

In *The Mozart Effect,* Don Campbell also lists the benefits of using your voice to enhance mood and memory. He says that all forms of vocalization, including singing, chanting, yodeling, humming, reciting poetry, and sim-ply talking can be therapeutic. But "nothing rivals toning," he concludes. The word *toning* goes back to the fourteenth century and means to make sounds with elongated vowels for extended periods of time. *Ah, ou* (as in *soup*), *ee, ay, oh*, and *om* are examples of toning sounds. Campbell writes that when people tone on a regular basis for five minutes a day, "I have witnessed thousands of people relax into their voices, become more cen-tered in their bodies, release fear and other emotions, and free themselves from physical pain. . . . I have seen many people apply toning in practical ways, from relaxing before a dreaded test to eliminating symptoms of tin-nitus or migraine headaches. . . . Toning has been effective in relieving in-somnia and other sleep disorders. . . . Toning balances brain waves, deepens the breath, reduces the heart rate, and imparts a general sense of well-being." Campbell reports that in his experience certain sounds tend to have certain effects on the body and emotions:

Ahhh—immediately evokes a relaxation response
Ee or **ay**—is the most stimulating of vowel sounds; helps with
    concentration, releasing pain and anger
Oh or **om**—considered the richest of sounds; can warm skin
    temperature and relax muscle tension

Try toning for five minutes a day for two weeks to see if it will help you.

In a similar way, humming can also make a positive difference in mood and memory. Mozart hummed as he composed. Children hum when they are happy. Adults often hum tunes that go through their minds, lifting their spirits and tuning their mind. Consciously focus on humming during the day. As the sound activates your brain, you will feel more alive and your brain will feel more tuned in to the moment.

B—EEG Biofeedback (Also Known as Neurofeedback)

Given what we have learned from SPECT, my clinics often use EEG biofeedback to enhance temporal lobe functioning. When we see over- or underactive areas on SPECT, we put sensors over those areas, measure the activity, and train healthier brain-wave rhythms in that part of the brain. This can be very helpful for brain injury patients. One older man had a fall from a ladder and subsequently had memory problems, anger outbursts, and illusions after the accident. On SPECT, he had decreased activity in the left temporal lobe. After two dozen EEG biofeedback sessions over his left temporal lobe, he reported marked improvement in memory, was less irritable, and the illusions vanished.

PSYCHOLOGICAL TL PRESCRIPTIONS

P—Create a Library of Wonderful Experiences

Strive for a series of experiences that keep you motivated, healthy, and excited about your life. As the temporal lobes store the experiences of your life, keeping them stimulated with positive ones will help keep you healthy. As mentioned earlier, experiencing a sense of awe can even boost your immune system (95). Celebrate your life on a regular basis; make your experiences count.

Record the memorable experiences of your life with pictures, videos, diary entries, and so on. Develop a library of wonderful experiences. Reexperience them whenever you can. Experiences are your link to life itself. Can it be possible that home movies really are therapeutic? Perhaps not for family and friends, but they certainly are for you.

SOCIAL TL PRESCRIPTIONS

S—Anger Management

Since temporal lobe problems are often associated with anger management issues, learning how to deal with negative feelings and impulses is especially important for those vulnerable to them. Through the years I have found the following five steps to be helpful for my patients.

1. **Know and focus on your goals.** If you want to have a kind, caring, loving relationship with your spouse or children, write it down and look at it every day. Then always ask yourself, "Does my behavior get me what I want?"

2. **Keep track of when you get angry.** Write them down and learn as much about those times as possible. Know when you tend to be vulnerable, so you can learn from those experiences and avoid them in the future.

3. **5 x 2 = 10.** Whenever you start to react in an angry or irritated way, get control of your breathing. Even before we are consciously aware of being upset, our breathing starts to become faster and shallower, making it more likely we'll lose control of our behavior. Whenever you start feeling irritated, take a deep breath: 5 seconds in, hold it for 2 seconds, then slowly breathe out for 5 seconds. Repeat that pattern 10 times. This will give you plenty of oxygen for your brain to make a thoughtful decision.

4. **Make a list.** Write and keep handy a list of ten things you can do when you get upset in order to distract yourself. Distraction is a powerful anger management technique. Common distractions include taking a walk, calling a friend, saying a prayer, doing a simple meditation, reading your One-Page Miracle.

5. **Play it out.** Ask yourself: if you react in an angry way to the situation at hand, what will happen to your relationships, to your goals, to those you love? Think about immediate and long-term effects. Fore-

thought is a strength of the human brain. Use it to keep yours under control.

SPIRITUAL TL PRESCRIPTIONS

Sp—Singing

Song is often associated with spiritual experience. When I was in college, I attended Calvary Chapel, a large church in Southern California. The music was magical. Listening to the choir was not just pleasant, it was a wondrous experience that resonated through every cell in my body. The music uplifted both the soul and mood of the congregation. The pastor said the music was "blessed by God Himself." Several of my friends were choir members. They were often transformed when they started to sing. Shy people would become more extroverted, more alive. People in the congregation became more involved in the service during congregational singing. The church community glistened with the contagious joy of the music.

Preschool and kindergarten teachers have known for a long time that children learn best through songs. They remember the material better, and it is easier to keep them engaged in the activity. So why do we stop singing in the second or third grade? Perhaps we should continue singing into the later grades.

Interestingly, when I was in basic training in the military, we often sang when we marched. I still have those songs in my head. When we sang as a group, morale went up, and the tasks that we were doing (like twenty-mile road marches) didn't seem quite as bad.

Sing whenever and wherever you can. You may have to sing softly if your voice is like mine (my children were often embarrassed when I sang in church). It will have a healing effect on your temporal lobes, and probably your limbic system as well.

Sp—Drumming

Likewise, drumming can also enhance brain function and spiritual experience. It has been shown to induce a sense of relaxation and calming brain wave synchronization (177). Drumming produces pleasurable experiences, enhanced self-awareness, and may help release emotional trauma. In groups, drumming connects people to others and creates a sense of connectedness. A fascinating experiment performed during open brain surgery showed that listening to drumming activated the temporal lobes in 74 percent of participants, which was significantly higher than listening to classical music alone (178). Consider drumming lessons as a way to activate your temporal lobes.

16

Know Your Brain Type

7 Types of ADD, 7 Types of Anxiety and Depression,
6 Types of Addicts, 5 Types of Overeaters

One of the first lessons we learned from our brain-imaging work was that issues like ADD/ADHD, anxiety, depression, addictions, and obesity—in fact, any psychiatric illness—are not single or simple disorders in the brain. They each have multiple types. Knowing this changed the whole game of diagnosis and treatment at Amen Clinics. No longer could I just go by a checklist of symptoms and hope to obtain a good outcome for my patients. I needed more information or I could inadvertently hurt them—and I certainly wouldn't be helping them. Here's an example.

Cody was diagnosed with ADD at the age of eight. He struggled in school, homework took hours to do with lots of tears and fighting, and he had trouble getting along with peers. His pediatrician tried him on Adderall, but within a few days he was worse. He couldn't sleep, started obsessively picking his skin, and had explosive outbursts for the first time along with suicidal thoughts. When we saw Cody, it was clear he did not have a pattern associated with a good response to stimulants. He had the opposite pattern, which I have called the Ring of Fire, with excessive activity in his brain. On the right treatments he was calmer and more effective at school and in every area of his life.

I have written books about "typing" different issues in the brain, including: *Healing ADD*, *Unchain Your Brain*, and *Change Your Brain, Change Your Body*. In this chapter, I will briefly discuss the different types of ADD, anxiety, depression, addicts, and overeaters. You will see that they mostly follow the brain systems we have already discussed.

HEALING ADD: 7 TYPES

Over the years, we've seen seven clinically relevant types of ADD:

1. Classic (what most people today call ADHD)
2. Inattentive
3. Overfocused
4. Temporal lobe
5. Limbic
6. Ring of Fire
7. Anxious

Relevant to these types are three common neurotransmitters:

Dopamine, which helps with focus, motivation, and getting things done
Serotonin, the "don't worry, be happy" chemical that helps with mood, sleep, and being flexible, and
GABA, which helps to calm the brain.

Type 1: Classic ADD

Classic ADD is thought to be caused by low dopamine levels and low activity in the PFC and cerebellum. Here people have the hallmark symptoms of ADD, such as a short attention span, distractibility, disorganization, procrastination, and poor impulse control. They also tend to be impulsive, restless, and hyperactive, having trouble sitting still, even as adults. Classic ADD tends to respond to PFC Prescriptions, especially stimulating supplements or medications, exercise, a higher protein, lower carbohydrate diet, and a specific type of omega-3 fatty acid called EPA. The good news is that with the right treatment we can calm the restlessness you feel and improve your focus.

Type 2: Inattentive ADD

This person has trouble focusing, but isn't hyperactive or terribly impulsive. In fact, they tend to be more introverted. Inattentive ADD is more common in girls and is often missed because it lacks the classic behavior problems. Their SPECT scans also show low activity overall, especially in the PFC. Inattentive ADD tends to respond best to PFC Prescriptions and the same kind of lifestyle interventions as classic ADD. One of my daughters has inattentive ADD and until I figured it out she really struggled. With proper treatment, she went on to get straight A's and got into one of the best veterinary schools in the world.

Type 3: Overfocused ADD

Overfocused ADD is found in people who have most of the ADD features, but rather than not being able to pay attention, they have trouble shifting their attention and tend to get stuck in loops of thinking, such as worrying. In order to focus properly on tasks you have to continually shift your attention. If you get stuck on a thought, it's impossible to follow what others are saying. For example: your husband says something that irritates you; you think about it *over* and *over* and you can't hear anything else that's being said. The underlying brain pattern here is different from Classic or Inattentive ADD. Both serotonin and dopamine are likely to be low, and there is generally too much activity in the anterior cingulate gyrus (ACG) and too little activity in the PFC and cerebellum. Remember, the ACG is the brain's gear shifter. It helps you move from task to task and idea to idea, be flexible, and go with the flow. This is the part of the brain that is also involved in error detection or knowing when something isn't right. When the ACG is working too hard, people tend to get stuck. They worry and hold grudges, and if things don't go their way they can get very upset and sometimes even explode. People with Overfocused ADD also tend to be argumentative, oppositional, and very critical, which can be really irritating to others. On the surface these individuals can appear selfish, but they really aren't: their brains are inflexible.

People with Overfocused ADD do best on a combination of ACG and

PFC Prescriptions, including supplements or medications that boost both serotonin and dopamine. Unlike the other types, they do not do well on a higher protein diet. It can actually make them mean, because it makes them focus on things that upset them. They need more healthy carbohydrates in their diet (see chapter 20 on nutrition).

Type 4: Temporal Lobe ADD

These people have the hallmark features of Classic ADD, plus symptoms associated with temporal lobe dysfunction, such as issues with learning, memory, and temper outbursts.

Kris had a long history of being hyperactive, impulsive, and aggressive. At six, he was put on a stimulant medication, but it made him even more aggressive and he started to hallucinate. At eight, another doctor tried him on an antidepressant, which also didn't work. By the time I saw him he had been in family therapy for years, but the therapist blamed the mother for being a big part of Kris's problem. His mother was very frustrated, because she had no idea how to help her son. I finally saw Kris after he attacked a boy at school with a knife when he was twelve. His SPECT study showed a dangerous combination of low activity in Kris's left temporal lobe, an area often associated with violence, and low activity in his prefrontal cortex, which would explain the decrease in his impulse control.

The ideal treatments for Temporal Lobe ADD are supplements or medications that boost GABA to stabilize the temporal lobes, in addition to something like green tea to boost dopamine, which will help with focus—*in that order*. If you get the order wrong, you can do harm, because the brain will not be properly balanced. This is part of the reason why knowing your type is so important. A higher protein and healthy fat diet can also help, along with other TL Prescriptions.

Within a few weeks of treatment, Kris was a dramatically different child. He was happier and was doing better in school, and the aggressive outbursts had stopped. Six years later, I gave a lecture at Kris's high school. When he saw me on campus he ran up to me, gave me a big hug, and introduced me to his friends. What do you think would have happened to Kris if I hadn't figured out he had Temporal Lobe ADD? It's likely that he would have been in jail, in one of a string of psychiatric facilities, or dead. His mother would have continued to feel shame, as if she was the cause of his problems.

SUMMARY CHART OF THE AMEN CLINICS 7 TYPES OF ADD

TYPE	SYMPTOMS	BRAIN FINDINGS/NEURO-TRANSMITTER ISSUE
1. Classic ADD	Inattentive, distracted, disorganized, impulsive, hyperactive	Low PFC and cerebellum, low dopamine (DA)
2. Inattentive ADD	Inattentive, distracted, disorganized, *not* very impulsive or hyperactive	Low PFC and cerebellum, low DA
3. Overfocused ADD	Inattentive plus overfocused, worrying, oppositional, holds grudges	Low PFC and increased ACG, low serotonin (S)
4. Temporal Lobe ADD	Temper problems, mood instability, irritability, memory problems, learning disabilities	Abnormal TLs/low GABA
5. Limbic ADD	Inattentive plus chronic low-level sadness	Low PFC plus high limbic activity
6. Ring of Fire ADD	Inattentive plus hyperactive, impulsive, mood instability, sensitive to noise and touch	Excessive brain activity/ Low DA and GABA levels
7. Anxious ADD	Inattentive plus anxious, tense, nervous, predicts the worst, self-medicates to calm	Low PFC and high basal ganglia/low DA and GABA levels

Type 5: Limbic ADD

In addition to having the hallmark ADD symptoms, people with Limbic ADD tend to be sad and negative and see the glass as half-empty. They often struggle with their appetite and feel socially isolated. In this type, we often see that the limbic brain works too hard. This is the part of the brain that is involved with setting your emotional tone (how happy or sad you are) and being connected to others. Limbic ADD tends to do well with a

SUPPLEMENTS	MEDICATIONS	DIET AND OTHER INTERVENTIONS
Green tea, rhodiola, or L-tyrosine plus EPA fish oil	Stimulants such as Adderall or Ritalin	Higher protein, lower carb diet, exercise
Green tea, rhodiola, or L-tyrosine PLUS EPA fish oil	Stimulants such as Adderall or Ritalin	Higher protein, lower carb diet, exercise
Green tea, rhodiola, or L-tyrosine plus 5-HTP and saffron plus EPA/DHA fish oil	SSRIs, such as Prozac, Zoloft, or Lexapro	Higher carb, lower protein diet, exercise
GABA, B6, magnesium for calming, or huperzine A, acetyl l-carnitine, vinpocetine, ginkgo for memory PLUS EPA fish oil	Anticonvulsants, such as Lamictal for mood stability, Aricept or Namenda for memory enhancement	Higher protein, lower carb diet
SAMe plus EPA fish oil	Wellbutrin	Higher protein, lower carb diet, exercise
GABA, 5-HTP, and L-tyrosine PLUS EPA/DHA fish oil	Anticonvulsants plus SSRI	Balanced diet between protein and carbs
Green tea, rhodiola, or L-tyrosine plus GABA, B6, magnesium plus EPA/DHA fish oil	Anticonvulsants, such as Neurontin plus stimulant	Balanced diet between protein and carbs, meditation and hypnosis

combination of Limbic System and PFC Prescriptions, including supplements or medications that both stimulate the PFC and calm the limbic brain, such as SAMe or bupropion (Wellbutrin) and higher ratio EPA omega-3 fatty acids.

Type 6: Ring of Fire ADD

This type is associated with people who tend to be moody, easily distracted, overwhelmed by too many thoughts, and really sensitive to lights and sounds. It's as if the world comes at them too fast. Its name comes from the excessive activity in the brain, which looks like a ring pattern on the scans. Stimulants, the typical ADD medication, prescribed alone usually make this type worse. Here's the problem: patients with Ring of Fire ADD really need strategies to calm their brains. Stimulants, unsurprisingly, won't help with this. In fact, our published research shows this pattern is made worse by stimulants 80 percent of the time (179).

Jarrett was diagnosed with ADD in preschool. His mother said he was "driven by a motor that was revved way too high." He was hyperactive, hyperverbal, restless, and impulsive, and couldn't focus. He also didn't sleep and interrupted everyone all the time. His third grade teacher said he would never do well in school and his parents should lower their expectations. He had seen five doctors and was prescribed five different medications for ADD. All of them made Jarrett worse, triggering mood swings and terrible rages. He put holes in walls and scared his siblings. He had become so bad that his last doctor wanted to put him on an antipsychotic medication. That is when his mother brought him to see us.

Jarrett's brain scan clearly showed the Ring of Fire pattern with dramatic overactivity. No wonder stimulants didn't work; it was like pouring gasoline on a fire. On a group of natural supplements to calm his brain Jarrett did so much better. His grades improved, the rages stopped, and he was able to make friends. He has now been on the honor roll for two straight years. His parents are grateful to have finally found the correct treatment plan for him, which has completely altered the course of his life. There is no telling what the future held for Jarrett if he had stayed on the previous course.

It's possible that Ring of Fire ADD can be related to bipolar disorder (what used to be called manic-depressive illness), or some form of allergy or inflammation in the brain. We treat this type with a special diet and supplements or medications to calm the brain by boosting both GABA and serotonin—in that order—so people feel less frazzled and more settled.

Type 7: Anxious ADD

These people have most of the hallmark ADD symptoms, plus they tend to get anxious, nervous, and tense, and predict the worst. They generally don't like to speak in public, freeze on timed tests, and often have lots of physical symptoms, such as headaches or stomachaches. Generally, there is too much activity in the areas of the brain involved with anxiety. This type tends to do well with a combination of Basal Ganglia and PFC Prescriptions, including deep relaxation techniques, such as meditation or hypnosis, and supplements or medicines that balance the brain and boost both GABA and dopamine. Our work involves helping them learn how to achieve a relaxed and focused state. Stimulants alone usually make these people more anxious.

My wife, Tana, says she has a combination of Overfocused and Anxious ADD. As a child, she struggled in school and had to work really hard to keep up. Her anxiety kept her doing well, but made her chronically stressed. When she was in her twenties, a doctor put her on medication to lower her anxiety, but he completely missed the ADD. As a result, the medication made her impulsive and careless about consequences, a potentially dangerous combination.

Clearly, ADD is *not* just one thing. Knowing someone's type or types of ADD can make a critical difference in helping them (or yourself). Think of:

- Classic ADD as the hyperactive child or adult who can't sit still and is always on the go.
- Inattentive ADD as someone who is shy and more reserved, yet still can't focus.
- Overfocused ADD as someone who has ADD symptoms plus gets stuck on bad thoughts.
- Temporal lobe ADD as someone who may be more temperamental and struggles with learning.

- Limbic ADD as sad.
- Ring of Fire ADD where way too much is going on in their brains, and
- Anxious ADD where someone has both anxiety and trouble focusing.

HEALING ANXIETY AND DEPRESSION: 7 TYPES

Over the years, we've seen seven clinically relevant types of anxiety and depression. Just like ADD, this is the reason why one treatment for anxiety or depression—whether it is any particular supplement, medication, form of psychotherapy, transcranial magnetic stimulation, neurofeedback, or whatever—will never work for everyone. Here are the types:

1. Pure anxiety
2. Pure depression
3. Mixed anxiety and depression
4. Overfocused anxiety and depression
5. Temporal lobe anxiety and depression
6. Cyclic anxiety and depression
7. Unfocused anxiety and depression

Type 1: Pure Anxiety

Pure anxiety is the first type and is thought to be caused by low levels of GABA and high activity in the basal ganglia, insular cortex, and amygdala. People who struggle with pure anxiety tend to feel anxious, tense, and nervous. They often feel uncomfortable in their own skin. They can be plagued by feelings of panic and self-doubt, and suffer the physical symptoms of anxiety, such as muscle tension, nail biting, headaches, abdominal pain, racing heart, and shortness of breath. Irrational fears or phobias are also common. People with pure anxiety tend to avoid anything that makes them anxious or uncomfortable, such as places or people that might trigger panic attacks or any conflict in relationships. People with this type tend to predict the worst and look to the future with fear.

This type totally used to fit me. I hated conflict, bit my nails, and often predicted the worst. I remember if I narrowly avoided an accident, I didn't say to myself, "Thank God," and go on with my day. My mind would repeatedly play out what might have been—I would see the car being hit and exploding in flames, and me being burned all over. I knew the ambulance driver would get lost because he had ADD and I would have to spend months in the hospital having my bandages ripped off repeatedly. Until I used the Basal Ganglia Prescriptions to help myself, it was just exhausting.

Pure anxiety tends to respond to Basal Ganglia Prescriptions, such as deep relaxation exercises. This is probably why I gravitated toward using hypnosis as a young psychiatrist, and killing the fortune-telling ANTs that drive anxiety. Exercise—especially calming ones like yoga and tai chi—and supplements or medications that boost GABA are also very effective.

One of the reasons I became so interested in supplements and natural ways to heal the brain was that I didn't like how certain medications, especially antianxiety medications like benzodiazepines, affected the brain. Below is the scan of someone who was hooked on benzodiazepines that had been prescribed for anxiety. The bumpy, scalloped appearance is the same result as what we see in brain toxicity and alcoholism. This made me search for a better way.

16.1: Benzodiazepine Image

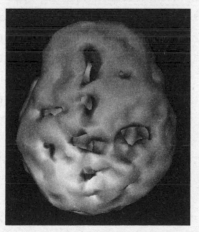

Overall decreased activity

The supplements I like for this type include: GABA, magnesium, the-anine from green tea, ashwagandha, Relora, vitamin B6, probiotics, and DHA omega-3 fatty acids. If the supplements aren't effective, I may use the following medications: anticonvulsants like gabapentin (Neurontin); bus-pirone (Buspar); or certain blood pressure medications like propranolol, which helps block the physical symptoms of anxiety, such as hand tremors. Through the years I have commonly prescribed propranolol to musicians so their hands wouldn't shake when they're performing. The good news is that with the right treatment you can feel calmer and much more relaxed.

Type 2: Pure Depression

The hallmark symptoms of pure depression are persistent sadness, negativ-ity, and a loss of interest in things that are usually pleasurable. There may be periods of crying for little or no reason, along with feelings of isolation or loneliness. This person may have sleep or appetite changes, low energy, low self-esteem, and even suicidal thoughts. In this type we often see low dopamine levels and a limbic or emotional brain that works too hard. This is the part of the brain that is involved with setting your emotional tone and being connected to others. We also usually see low activity in the front part of the brain at rest that becomes more active when they try to concen-trate. This is very important, because this type tends to do better when they are up and engaged in activities. Staying in bed all day actually makes de-pression worse, even though it's the depressed person's first instinct.

Pure depression tends to do well with Limbic Prescriptions, such as: in-tense exercise; ANT therapy; an anti-inflammatory diet; scents such as lav-ender; and supplements or medications that improve mood. The supplements I like for this type include SAMe, curcumin to help with inflammation, vi-tamin D, probiotics, and EPA omega-3 fatty acids. I sometimes prescribe bupropion (Wellbutrin) if the supplements don't work.

Type 3: Mixed Anxiety and Depression

This type is a combination of both pure anxiety and pure depression symp-toms. One type may predominate at any point in time, but both symptom clusters are present on a regular basis. Actually, pure anxiety and pure depression are pretty rare by themselves; in our experience, mixed anxiety and depression is very common, as anxiety and depression run together 75 percent of the time. In this type, usually both GABA and dopamine are low. On scans we often see increases in the limbic and anxiety centers of the brain. This type is treated with a combination of Limbic and Basal Ganglia Prescriptions, including intense exercise alternating with calming ones like tai chi and yoga, deep relaxation techniques to help with the anxiety, ANT therapy, using Byron Katie's four questions (180), an anti-inflammatory diet to help with mood, and certain scents like lavender. The supplements I like for this type include SAMe plus GABA, magnesium, curcumin to help with inflammation, vitamin D, probiotics, and a combination of DHA and EPA omega-3s. I may use a combination of medications such as bupropion (Wellbutrin) and gabapentin (Neurontin) if the supplements don't work. I also like the medications imipramine (Tofranil) or desipramine (Norpramin), which work well for both anxiety and depression. Of course, you should always talk to your health care professional before making any changes to your treatment plan.

Type 4: Overfocused Anxiety and Depression

This type is usually associated with low serotonin levels. Here you might see features of anxiety and depression, plus a tendency to get stuck on negative thoughts or negative behaviors. This results from too much activity in the ACG. Many people with this type get stuck on both anxious and depressing thoughts. They can have obsessive-compulsive disorder (OCD), where they get stuck on negative thoughts or compulsive behaviors (like constantly checking locks); posttraumatic stress disorder (PTSD), where they get stuck on past traumas; or certain types of eating disorders and addictions, where they just can't let go of compulsive behaviors. This type is also associated with people who worry, hold grudges, have problems with being oppositional or argumentative, and they tend to notice what's wrong way before they notice what's right. I have also noticed that this type tends to occur more frequently in children or grandchildren of alcoholics.

Overfocused anxiety and depression responds best to ACG (anterior cingulate gyrus) Prescriptions to boost serotonin. Aerobic exercise can be helpful, and a diet high in complex carbohydrates like garbanzo beans and sweet potatoes can help. ANT therapy can keep the ANTs from spinning in your head. The supplements I like for this type include 5-HTP, saffron, St. John's wort, vitamin D, probiotics, and a combination of the omega-3s DHA and EPA. If I need to prescribe medication I usually start with the SSRIs. They are the most commonly prescribed antidepressants, and they

SUMMARY CHART OF THE AMEN CLINICS 7 TYPES
OF ANXIETY AND DEPRESSION

TYPE	SYMPTOMS	BRAIN FINDINGS/NEURO-TRANSMITTER ISSUE
1. Pure Anxiety	Anxious, tense, nervous, predicts the worst, self-medicates to calm	High basal ganglia/low GABA levels
2. Pure Depression	Depression, feeling hopeless, low energy, poor appetite, insomnia	Low PFC plus high limbic activity/low dopamine (DA)
3. Mixed Anxiety and Depression	Combination of symptoms from Types 1 and 2	High basal ganglia and limbic activity/low GABA and DA
4. Overfocused Anxiety and Depression	Overfocused, worrying, oppositional, holds grudges	Increased ACG/low serotonin (S)
5. Temporal Lobe Anxiety and Depression	Temper problems, mood instability, irritability, memory problems, learning disabilities	Abnormal TLs/low GABA
6. Cyclic Anxiety and Depression	mood cycles (Bipolar, cyclothymia, severe PMS)	High focal limbic activity/ low GABA
7. Unfocused Anxiety and Depression	Sadness, anxiety, low energy, cognitive problems	Overall low activity, brain may look toxic

are very good for this type; however, they can actually make the other types worse, which is why they have a bad reputation. It might be worth noting that 60 percent of people who take them have sexual side effects.

Type 5: Temporal Lobe Anxiety and Depression

This type is often associated with low GABA levels and could be the result of a head injury or associated with seizures. The temporal lobes are very important for memory, moods, and emotions. When there are problems in this part of the brain people tend to struggle with mood instability; irritability; mem-

SUPPLEMENTS	MEDICATIONS	DIET AND OTHER INTERVENTIONS
GABA, B6, magnesium, DHA fish oil	Anticonvulsants, such as Neurontin	Meditation, hypnosis
SAMe, EPA fish oil	Wellbutrin	Exercise
GABA, B6, magnesium, SAMe, EPA/DHA fish oil	Neurontin PLUS Wellbutrin	Meditation, hypnosis, and exercise
5-HTP, saffron, or St. John's wort	SSRIs, such as Prozac, Zoloft, or Lexapro	Higher carb, lower protein diet, exercise
GABA, B6, magnesium for calming, or huperzine A, acetyl-l-carnitine, vinpocetine, ginkgo for memory	Anticonvulsants, such as Lamictal for mood stability, Aricept or Namenda for memory enhancement	Higher protein, lower carb diet, exercise
GABA, B6, magnesium	Anticonvulsants, such as Lamictal for mood stability	Higher protein, lower carb diet
Green tea, rhodiola, or L-tyrosine	Wellbutrin or stimulant	Medical workup of potential causes of toxicity

ory problems; and dark, frightening, or evil thoughts. These individuals might misinterpret comments as negative when they are not, have trouble reading social cues, and experience frequent déjà vu. The SPECT findings typically show low activity in the temporal lobes. My experience has taught me that when temporal lobe abnormalities exist, we should treat those first.

I use Temporal Lobe Prescriptions to treat this type and include a diet higher in protein and fat, and lower in carbohydrates. Researchers have known for decades that a ketogenic diet can help with seizures (181). In fact, my granddaughter Emmy was cured of her seizures on that diet. Neurofeedback may help some people. The supplements I like for this type include GABA, magnesium, taurine, and DHA plus EPA. If the supplements don't work, I will likely use an antiseizure medication, such as gabapentin (Neurontin) or lamotrigine (Lamictal), rather than typical antidepressants, which often cause bad reactions in the type.

Randy was one of my earliest cases where a SPECT scan taught me to really pay attention to the temporal lobes. He was hospitalized for suicidal behavior after he had an explosive fight with his wife. He hated himself because his temper often got the best of him and he struggled with cocaine abuse, anxiety, and depression. He had failed drug treatment and multiple antidepressants. His scan showed clear temporal lobe problems, which caused me to ask about any head injuries. Randy told me about a time when he was six years old and fell off a balcony onto his head and lost consciousness. His temper had been a problem for him ever since, but no one had ever connected it to that fall. Once he was on a medicine to balance his temporal lobes, both he and his marriage fared much better.

Type 6: Cyclic Anxiety and Depression

Likely the issue with this type is also low levels of GABA, but it might also be too much of an excitatory chemical called glutamate. As the name implies, this type is associated with cycles of anxiety and depression. It includes bipolar disorder, cyclothymia (milder mood swings), seasonal mood changes, and severe PMS, called premenstrual dysphoric disorder (PMDD). Times of stress can also trigger a cycle.

On scans we often see discrete areas of increased activity in the brain's emotional centers, similar to seizure activity. As with most seizures, patients have little or no control over these episodes. The scan findings tend to vary with the phase of the illness. For example, when someone is in a manic phase of bipolar illness there is overall increased activity throughout the brain; when this same person is depressed there is less activity overall. Similarly, a woman with PMDD may show problems in her brain during the worst time of her cycle but not at other times. Cyclic anxiety and depression can also get worse around other times of significant hormonal shifts, such as after having a baby or during menopause.

Like the other types, cyclic anxiety and depression is a spectrum disorder, which means that one can have a very mild form or a very severe form, or anything in between. The more severe forms need to be monitored closely, especially when medication is first started, because typical antidepressants can make this type worse and may even trigger mania. Even some supplements, such as St. John's wort or SAMe, can trigger problems. I once treated a boy who was given St. John's wort after his mother saw a show about it on TV. He then started to have dreams of decomposing bodies. It turned out he had cyclic anxiety and depression.

We treat this type using all the strategies necessary to help the anxiety and depression issues, including diet, exercise, deep relaxation, ANT therapy, and supplements or medications that boost GABA and lower glutamate. The supplements I like for this type include GABA, magnesium, taurine, zinc, vitamin B6, and DHA and EPA Omega-3s. If the supplements don't work I will likely consider lithium or antiseizure medications, such as gabapentin (Neurontin), lamotrigine (Lamictal), or valproic acid (Depakote).

Type 7: Unfocused Anxiety and Depression

This type results from too little activity in the brain, especially in the PFC. Remember, this part acts as the brain's supervisor. It helps with executive functions, such as attention span, forethought, impulse control, organization, motivation, and planning. When the PFC is underactive, people complain of low energy, brain fog, being inattentive, bored, and impulsive, and exhibiting poor judgment.

The decreased brain activity may be a result of an injury, toxic exposure (such as mold from a flood or living near the beach), near-drowning, infection, medications, an underlying attention deficit disorder, or other medical illnesses. The treatment for unfocused anxiety and depression starts with finding and remedying the cause of the low activity, then rehabilitating the brain with a healthy diet, exercise, and some simple supplements or medications. From a supplement standpoint, for this type I generally want to stimulate and repair the brain, so I like gingko, L-tyrosine, rhodiola, and EPA fish oil. For medications, I'd consider stimulants or a medicine called modafinil (Provigil).

UNCHAIN YOUR BRAIN: 6 TYPES OF ADDICTS

Just as with the other issues we discuss in this book, one treatment will never work for all types of addicts. As with ADD and anxiety and depression, addicts also have different brain types. Here are the six types I first described in *Unchain Your Brain*.

Type 1: Compulsive Addicts

People with this type have trouble shifting their attention and tend to get stuck on thoughts of gambling, Internet porn, food, or some other substance or behavior. Regardless of what these people are addicted to, the thinking pattern and basic mechanism are the same. They tend to get stuck or locked into one course of action and have trouble seeing options.

The most common brain SPECT finding in this type is increased ACG, which is most often caused by low brain serotonin levels. High protein diets and stimulants usually make this type worse. ACG Prescriptions to boost serotonin, such as SSRIs, are generally the most beneficial. From a supplement standpoint, 5-HTP, inositol, saffron, L-tryptophan, or St. John's wort are helpful.

Type 2: Impulsive Addicts

People with this type have trouble with impulse control, even though they may start each day with the intention of refraining from their risky behaviors. The most common SPECT finding for this type is low activity in the PFC, likely due to low levels of dopamine. The PFC acts as the brain's supervisor and is involved in judgment, impulse control, planning, and follow-through. When it is underactive, people can be easily distracted, bored, inattentive, and impulsive. This type is often seen in conjunction with ADD and is more common in males. PFC Prescriptions are most helpful for this type. From a supplement standpoint, green tea, rhodiola, and L-tyrosine are helpful, as are stimulant medications, like those commonly used to treat ADD.

Type 3: Impulsive-Compulsive Addicts

People with this type have a combination of both impulsive and compulsive features. This type is common in people with bulimia. The brain SPECT scans tend to show low activity in the PFC and too much activity in the ACG. A combination of PFC and ACG Prescriptions are most helpful, while treatments that boost either serotonin or dopamine alone usually makes the problem worse. For example, using supplements or medications that increase serotonin calms the compulsions but makes the impulsivity worse. Taking supplements or medications that raise dopamine levels improves impulse control, but increases the compulsive behaviors. In my experience, I have found that people with this type do best with treatments that raise both serotonin and dopamine; for example, combining green tea (for dopamine) and 5-HTP (for serotonin).

Type 4: Sad or Emotional Addicts

People with this type often use alcohol, marijuana, painkillers, or food to medicate underlying feelings of depression, boredom, or loneliness. This type is more commonly seen in women. For some people, these feelings come and go with the seasons and tend to worsen in winter. Others experience mild feelings of chronic sadness, called dysthymia. Still others suffer from more serious depressions. The typical SPECT findings associated with this type are hyperactivity in the limbic system and low activity in the PFC.

I use Limbic Prescriptions for this type of addict. When depression is mild, it can often be treated with natural supplements like SAMe, in addition to exercise, dietary changes, and ANT therapy. For more serious cases, antidepressant medication and transcranial magnetic stimulation may be needed. Taking vitamin D can also be beneficial to support people with mood issues, especially for people whose behaviors worsen or are triggered during the winter months, a condition called seasonal affective disorder (SAD). Probiotics can also help.

Type 5: Anxious Addicts

People with this type tend to use alcohol, marijuana, painkillers, sleeping pills, or food to medicate underlying feelings of anxiety, tension, nervousness, and fear. More commonly seen in women, this type tends to suffer physical symptoms of anxiety, such as muscle tension, headaches, stomachaches, nail biting, heart palpitations, and shortness of breath. People with this type tend to predict the worst and may be excessively shy or easily startled. The SPECT finding that correlates to this type is too much activity in the basal ganglia, likely due to low levels of GABA.

Basal Ganglia Prescriptions are most helpful here, including interventions that boost GABA. Relaxation therapies can also be helpful to calm this area of the brain.

Type 6: Temporal Lobe Addicts

People with this type tend to have problems with temper, mood swings, learning problems, and memory problems. Abnormal activity in the temporal lobes is commonly due to head injuries, infections, a lack of oxygen, or exposure to environmental toxins, or it may be genetic. The typical SPECT findings are decreased activity in the temporal lobes, although we also see excessive increased activity.

Temporal Lobe Prescriptions are used to stabilize activity in the temporal lobes, including boosting the calming neurotransmitter GABA or the memory and learning neurotransmitter acetylcholine, a higher protein diet, and eliminating sugar. Ways to boost GABA include using the supplements

GABA and magnesium or anticonvulsant (antiseizure) medications, like gabapentin (Neurontin) or lamotrigine (Lamictal). Boosting acetylcholine in the brain to help with memory and learning can include using supplements like huperzine A and choline. Together, these strategies can help with temper control, mood stability, learning, and memory.

CHANGE YOUR BRAIN, CHANGE YOUR BODY: 5 TYPES OF OVEREATERS

I became interested in weight loss when I discovered that as your weight goes up the size and function of your brain goes down. That's when it hit me: it's your brain that pushes you away from the table or your brain that gives you permission to have the third bowl of ice cream. If you want a better body, the first place to start is your brain. Like ADD, anxiety, depression, and addictions, the brains of our overweight and obese patients clearly do not show one pattern in the brain. We discovered five different types that parallel the addict types and have the same basic interventions.

TYPES OF OVEREATERS

1. Compulsive overeaters—always think about food (low serotonin)
2. Impulsive overeaters—poor impulse control (low dopamine)
3. Impulsive-compulsive overeaters (low serotonin and dopamine)
4. Sad overeaters—associated with mood issues (low dopamine)
5. Anxious overeaters—associated with anxiety (low GABA)

DO YOU HAVE MORE THAN ONE TYPE OF ADD, ANXIETY, DEPRESSION, ADDICTION, OR OVEREATING?

Having more than one type is common, and it just means that you may need a combination of interventions. In general, we treat temporal lobe or Ring of Fire types first, and then it just depends on the primary symptoms.

SUMMARY CHART OF THE AMEN CLINICS 6 TYPES OF ADDICTS

TYPE	SYMPTOMS	BRAIN FINDINGS/ NEURO-TRANSMIT-TER ISSUE	SUPPLE-MENTS	MEDICA-TIONS
1. Compulsive Addicts	Overfocused, worrying, trouble letting go of hurts	Increased ACG/low serotonin (S)	5-HTP, inositol, saffron, or St. John's wort	SSRIs, such as Prozac, Zoloft, or Lexapro
2. Impulsive Addicts	Inattentive, impulsive, easily distracted	Low PFC/low dopamine (DA)	Green tea, rhodiola, or L-tyrosine	Stimulants such as Adderall or Ritalin
3. Impulsive-Compulsive Addicts	Combination of types 1 and 2	High ACG plus low PFC/ low S and DA	5-HTP plus green tea and rhodiola	SSRI plus stimulant
4. Sad or Emotional Addicts	Sad or depressed mood, winter blues, carbohy-drate cravings, loss of interest, sleeps a lot, low energy, self-medicates to improve mood	High limbic activity, low PFC/check vitamin D and DHEA levels	SAMe, vitamin D, or DHEA if needed	Wellbutrin
5. Anxious Addicts	Anxious, tense, nervous, predicts the worst, self-medicates to calm	High basal ganglia/low GABA levels	GABA, B6, magnesium	Anticonvul-sants, such as Topamax, Neurontin
6. Temporal Lobe Addicts	Temper problems, mood instability, memory problems, learning disabilities	Abnormal TL	GABA, B6, magnesium for calming, or huperzine A, acetyl-l-carni-tine, vinpo-cetine, ginkgo for memory	Anticonvul-sants, such as Lamictal for mood stability, Aricept or Namenda for memory enhancement

17

Imaging Changes Everything in Relationships

Understanding the Brain Patterns That
Interfere with Intimacy

One of the consequences of being a doctor who specializes in brain-imaging work was that I absolutely wanted to know the brain health of the people who dated my children. In fact, if you dated one of my kids for a while, I would subtly make the offer of coming into the clinic for a scan. Fortunately, all of the potential mates who ended up marrying one of my kids were in favor of knowing more about their own brain health. In fact, my son-in-law Dr. Jesse Payne wrote about the experience in the introduction of his book, *Change Your Brain, Change Your Life for Under 25* (182).

I was twenty-one years old, sitting in the office of Dr. Daniel Amen . . . father of my girlfriend. Even though I am more than a foot taller than he is, I felt intimidated as he reviewed the scans he had just taken of my brain. I had been dating his daughter for a little more than a year and, apparently, agreeing to have a detailed scan of the brain was a requirement for anyone who had dated one of his daughters for any significant amount of time. He said it was to make sure that everything "looked okay." Riiiiight.

It was like a twisted version of the scene in *Meet the Parents* when Robert De Niro sweats out Ben Stiller—except this was very real. Plus, this wasn't a lie detector test. This man could actually peer straight into the inner workings of my brain.

As he gazed down at the images and data from my scans, I saw his forehead wrinkle as he frowned ever so slightly. "Hmmm," he said. This was not a good start.

"I see that you can be pretty stubborn and argumentative at times. Does this sound about right?" he asked.

I knew that my response would shape the rest of this conversation, and possibly the future of my relationship with the girl I had fallen in love with. Instinctively, before I realized I was doing it, my arms folded across my chest. "No. I wouldn't say that I'm stubborn at all." My reply had an undeniable tone of defensiveness.

A hint of a smirk appeared at the corners of his mouth. "Are you sure about that?" he asked.

Crap. My brain had betrayed me.

It was the first time I saw a connection between my brain and how it was related to my thoughts, feelings, actions, and behaviors. More importantly, it occurred to me in that moment that if my brain determined my behavioral tendencies, perhaps the power went both ways and I could have some control over how my brain worked. The prospect gave me hope for my future.

Some of you might think wanting to know about the brain health of the people in my life is shallow. I actually got hate mail after the *New York Times Magazine* did an article on me. The author related the story about getting scanned if you dated my kids. People said I was discriminating against those with mental illness, which couldn't be further from the truth. Jesse's mother has paranoid schizophrenia and his father committed suicide, both of which stories are chronicled in his book. As with anyone who walks into my clinic, an unhealthy brain scan never meant banishment, but rather a quest on my part to help them make it better. If they were not open to the idea of brain health, that was a bad sign.

Over the past twenty-four years I have scanned hundreds of couples who've had serious marital difficulties. I have been fascinated, saddened, and enlightened by this research. I now look at marriages and marital conflict in a whole new way, as involving compatible and incompatible brain patterns. I have come to realize that many marriages do not work because of brain misfires that have nothing to do with character, free will, or desire. Many relationships are sabotaged by factors beyond conscious or even unconscious control. Sometimes a little intervention can make all the difference between love and hate, staying together and divorce, effective problem-solving and prolonged litigation. I realize that many people, especially some marital therapists, will see the ideas in this chapter as radical, premature, and heretical. Frankly, I know of no marital therapy system or school of thought that seriously looks at the brain function of couples who struggle. But I wonder how you can develop paradigms and "schools of thought" about how couples function (or don't function) without taking into account the organ that drives behavior. Seasoned therapists who see couples day to day in their offices will recognize the truths in this chapter, and I hope they will gain new insights into their most difficult cases through the lens of the brain.

Is He Just an Asshole or Is He Being Poisoned?

Let's start with a couple who failed marital therapy. After spending three years and over $25,000, the therapist told them to get divorced. This made the couple very upset, because they wanted to be married. When they protested, the therapist got nervous and told them that she knew a doctor

Image 17.1: Chuck's Brain

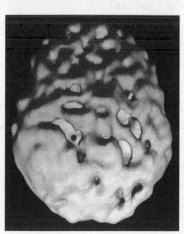

Overall low activity

who takes care of really difficult people and sent them to see me. As part of their evaluations, I ordered brain SPECT scans on both of them. The wife's brain looked healthy. The husband's brain looked awful, with serious low overall activity, the same pattern we often see in our drug or alcohol abusers.

But the scan didn't fit the husband's history, because he said he didn't drink and had never used drugs. Now, I know that drug and alcohol abusers often lie, so in front of his wife, I asked the husband again if he drank much alcohol or used drugs. He said, "Dr. Amen, I have many problems, but that is not it."

So, I turned to the wife and asked if that was true. "Yes, Dr. Amen, he doesn't drink and he has never done drugs. He is just an asshole."

I chuckled at her comment. But in my mind, I wondered why his scan looked so awful. I went through the list in my head of potential causes: brain infections, a near-drowning episode, severely low thyroid, or environmental toxins. My next question to the husband was, "Where do you work?"

"I work in a furniture factory," he said.

"What do you do?" I asked.

"I finish furniture all day long."

He *was* doing drugs. In fact, he was doing one of the worst drugs for the brain: inhaling organic solvents. My next question was to the wife. "When did he become an asshole?"

"What do you mean?" she replied.

"Did you marry him that way?" I asked. "Do you have father issues that you are trying to work out?"

"No," she said. "When we first got married he was great. It wasn't until about five years ago that we started having trouble." Then she put her hand over her mouth and said, "Oh my God, that was about the time he started this job. Do you think his personality change can be from his job?"

"Yes," I answered. "Something is damaging his brain, making it hard for him to be a good husband."

In that moment, her husband went from being an asshole whom everyone was telling her to divorce to someone who was being poisoned while he was trying to provide for his family—and he needed help.

The first intervention was to stop the toxic fume exposure. We worked to get him transferred to another place in the company where he was not exposed to solvents, and put him on a brain rehabilitation program, which will be discussed in the next part of the book. With the right treatment, his behavior got better, as did their marriage.

I wonder how many marriages are suffering because one partner has a brain problem that no one is aware of. How could you ever be successful doing marital therapy with a broken brain? It will never work until you change the brain.

Brain Systems and Love

In my work I have seen all of the five brain systems discussed in this book at play within couples. I have found that properly diagnosing which pattern or patterns are present leads to more effective strategies to help couples. As far as I know, this is the first time any psychiatrist has presented a model of marital discord based on brain misfires. You might want to share this book with your therapist and see if he or she is open to new ideas.

Let's start by looking at the relational traits of each brain system, both when they work right and when they misfire.

LIMBIC RELATIONAL TRAITS

When the limbic system functions properly, people tend to be more positive and better able to connect with others. They're inclined to filter information in an accurate light and give others the benefit of the doubt. They are able to be playful and sensual, and tend to maintain and have easy access to positive emotional memories. They tend to draw people toward them with their positive attitude.

Positive Limbic Relational Statements

"We have a lot of good memories."
"Let's have friends over."
"I accept your apology. I know you were just having a bad day."

"Let's have fun."
"I feel sexy. Let's make love."

When the limbic system is overactive, people tend toward depression, negativity, and distancing themselves from others. They are likely to focus on the most negative aspects of others and see the glass as half-empty, and are less likely to give others the benefit of the doubt. They tend not to be playful. They do not feel sexy, and often shy away from sexual activity due to a lack of interest. Most of their memories are negative, and it is hard for them to access positive emotional memories or feelings. They tend to push people away with their negativity.

NEGATIVE LIMBIC RELATIONAL STATEMENTS

"Don't look at me that way."
"All I can remember is the bad times."
"I'm too tired."
"Leave me alone. I'm not interested in sex."
"You go to bed. I can't sleep."
"I don't feel like being around other people."
"I don't want to hear you're sorry. You meant to
    hurt me."
"I'm not interested in doing anything."

STATEMENTS FROM THE PARTNERS OF PEOPLE WITH LIMBIC PROBLEMS

"She's negative."
"He's often depressed."
"He doesn't want to be around other people."
"She tends to take things the wrong way."
"He's not interested in sex."
"She can't sleep."
"There's little playfulness in our relationship."

Sheila and Joe

Sheila and Joe had been married for five years. They both worked and did not have any children. At the end of the day, Sheila was frequently very tired. Most often she liked to be on her own and didn't want to do anything after work. She usually wasn't interested in sex, except for one or two days after she started her menstrual cycle. Sheila also tended to look at the negative side of any situation. Joe complained about the lack of companionship in their relationship. He was very upset by her lack of interest in sex and her nonchalant attitude toward it. He felt she was too negative, and their lack of connectedness made him feel lonely. Joe tried to talk to Sheila, but she said she didn't have any problems and he just expected too much from her. Joe made an appointment with me. He said, "I wanted to see if there was anything I could do before I saw a divorce attorney." I encouraged him to bring Sheila with him to see me. I first got Sheila's reading on the situation. She admitted to feeling chronically tired, overwhelmed, and negative. She just figured she had a low libido and was destined to live with it. Sheila had experienced a major depression when she was a teenager. Her mother also had a history of depression, and her parents had divorced when she was five years old.

Sheila's SPECT scan showed a very active limbic system, and while her lab tests were in the normal range, they weren't optimal. Together we developed the following four-circles plan: **B**—Sheila's thyroid, testosterone, and vitamin D levels were all on the low end of normal. Working together with one of our integrative medicine physicians, we optimized those numbers for her. I also added omega-3 fatty acids in a higher EPA ratio. I also started her on a low dose of bupropion (Wellbutrin) to calm her limbic system. It also boosts sexual function and interest. **P**—Sheila began ANT therapy to help with her automatic negative thoughts; **S**—We added marital counseling for better communication with her husband; **Sp**—We sat down and had an extended discussion on Sheila's and Joe's deepest sense of meaning and purpose.

Over the course of two months, Sheila began to feel much better. She had better energy and focus, and she also felt more social. In addition, her libido increased and she was more sexually receptive to Joe.

BASAL GANGLIA RELATIONAL TRAITS

When the basal ganglia system functions properly, people tend to be calm and relaxed. They tend to predict the best and, in general, see a positive future. Their bodies usually feel good, and they are relaxed enough to be playful, sexy, and sexual. They are not plagued by multiple physical complaints. They are able to deal with conflict in an effective way.

When the basal ganglia are overactive, people have a tendency toward anxiety, panic, fear, and tension. They tend to focus on negative future events and what can go wrong in a situation. They filter information through fear and seldom give others the benefit of the doubt. They tend to have headaches, backaches, and a variety of other physical complaints. They have lowered sexual interest because their bodies tend to be wrapped in tension. They often do not have the physical or emotional energy to feel sexy or sexual, and they tend to shy away from sexual activity. Most of their memories are filled with anxiety or fear. They tend to wear out people by the constant fear they project.

Positive Basal Ganglia Relational Statements

"I know things will work out."
"I can speak out when I have a problem. I don't let problems fester."
"I usually feel physically relaxed."
"I'm usually calm in new situations."

Negative Basal Ganglia Relational Statements

"I know this isn't going to work out."
"I'm too tense."
"I'm scared."
"I'm too afraid to bring up problems. I tend to avoid them."
"I can't breathe. I feel really anxious in this situation."
"I can't make love—I have a headache (chest pain, backaches, muscle aches, etc.)."
"You're going to do something to hurt me."

Statements from the Partners of People with Basal Ganglia Problems

"She's anxious."

"He's nervous."

"She's uptight."

"He cares too much about what others think."

"He predicts the worst possible outcomes to situations."

"She complains of feeling bad a lot (has headaches, stomachaches)."

"He won't deal with conflict."

"She won't deal with problems head-on."

Ryan and Betsy

Ryan was a nervous wreck. He tended to see the worst in situations and often predicted failure. He was anxious, nervous, and sickly (frequently complaining of headaches, backaches, and muscle tension). He had been married to Betsy for fifteen years. When they were first married, Betsy mothered him, taking care of his aches and pains and soothing his fears and negativity. She liked to feel needed. After years of this, however, she had gotten tired of Ryan's whining and his tendency to be afraid in even the most benign situations. Ryan's anxiety and medical problems were taking over their relationship. She felt isolated and alone. She became irritable, less understanding, and distant from him. Seeing the love go out of their relationship, she made an appointment for me to see them both. Ryan was angry with her about the appointment. He complained that they didn't have the money, counseling wouldn't help, his problems were physical and not psychological (actually, he was right; this was his brain torturing him), and all psychiatrists were crazy anyway (I wouldn't say all of us are crazy, just a bit odd). When I first saw Ryan and Betsy, it was clear to me that Ryan's basal ganglia were overactive. The basal ganglia hyperactivity was interfering with their relationship. When I explained his behavior in medical/brain-physiology terms to Ryan, he relaxed. I helped the couple with communication and goal setting and then engaged Ryan in his own therapy. I taught him how to kill fortune-telling ANTs (his were very strong). I worked with him using biofeedback (teaching him how to warm his hands, relax his muscles, and breathe diaphragmatically). And I taught him self-hypnosis. Ryan was a very fast learner and quickly soaked up the Basal Ganglia Prescriptions. He no longer used Betsy as his doctor; he began to work with his physician to address his physical issues and started to predict positive things rather than fear in his conversations with his wife. Once we treated Ryan's basal ganglia problems, the marital therapy became more effective and the marriage improved.

PREFRONTAL CORTEX RELATIONAL TRAITS

When the PFC functions properly, people can engage in goal-directed behavior and effectively supervise their words and deeds. They are able to think before they say things and tend to say things that affect their goals in a positive way. They also tend to think before they do things, and their actions are consistent with their goals. They tend to learn from mistakes and don't make the same ones over and over. In addition, they are able to focus and attend to conversations, follow through on commitments and chores, and organize their actions. They are able to be settled and sit still, and express what they feel. And, they tend to dislike conflict, tension, and turmoil.

When the PFC is underactive, people tend to be impulsive in what they say or do, often causing serious problems in relationships (such as saying hurtful things without forethought). They tend to live in the moment and have trouble delaying gratification ("I want it now"). They tend not to learn from their mistakes and to make repetitive mistakes. They also have trouble listening and are easily distracted. They often have difficulty expressing thoughts and feelings, and their partners frequently complain of a lack of communication in the relationship. It is often hard for people with low PFC activity to sit still; they tend to be restless and fidgety. In addition, they can be especially sensitive to noise, smells, light, and touch. They have difficulty staying on task and finishing projects, commitments, and chores. They are often late. Many people with low PFC have an unconscious urge to seek conflict or to look for problems when none exist. I call this tendency the game of "Let's have a problem." They also like to seek stimulation or indulge in highly stimulating behaviors that upset or frighten their partner (driving too fast, bungee jumping, getting into the middle of a fight between strangers).

POSITIVE PREFRONTAL CORTEX RELATIONAL STATEMENTS

"You're important to me. Let's do something tonight."

"I love you. I'm glad we're together."

"I love to listen to you."

"I'll be on time for our date."

"Let's get these chores done so that we'll have more time together."

"I don't want to fight. Let's take a break and come back in ten minutes and work this out."

"I made that mistake before. I'm not making it again."

NEGATIVE PREFRONTAL CORTEX RELATIONAL STATEMENTS

"I'm only a half hour late. Why are you so uptight about it?"

"If you want the checkbook balanced, do it yourself."

"I'll do it later."

"I find it hard to listen to you."

"Go ahead and talk to me. I can listen to you while I'm watching TV and reading this book."

"I can't express myself."

"My mind goes blank when I try to express my feelings."

"I didn't mean to have the affair (overspend, embarrass you at the party, make hurtful comments, etc.)."

"I just can't sit still."

"The noise bothers me."

"I get so distracted (while listening, during sex, when playing a game, etc.)."

"I need the answer now."

"I want it now."

"I'm so mad at myself. I've made that mistake too many times."

STATEMENTS FROM THE PARTNERS OF PEOPLE WITH PREFRONTAL CORTEX PROBLEMS

"He's impulsive."

"She blurts out and interrupts."

"He doesn't pay attention to me."

"She won't let me finish a comment. She says she has to say whatever thought comes into her head or she'll forget it."

"He has to have the fan on at night to sleep. It drives me crazy."

"She often seems to start a problem for no particular reason."

"He loves to challenge everything I say."

"She gets so distracted during sex."

"He teases the animals, and it makes me furious."

"She can't sit still."

"He puts things off and tends not to finish things."

"She's always late, rushing around at the last minute."

Ray and Linda

Ray and Linda came to see me on the advice of their marital counselor. Two of their three children had been diagnosed with ADD, and the counselor felt that Ray had it as well. Even though Ray owned a very successful restaurant, he was restless, impulsive, and very easily distracted. He spent excessive time at work due to inefficiency, and he had frequent employee problems (often because he hired impulsively without adequate screening). Marital counseling was Ray's idea, because he saw his wife turning away from him. He told the counselor that his wife was chronically stressed, tired, and angry. "She's not the woman I married," he said to their counselor. In my first session with this couple, Linda clearly explained that it was true; she had changed. It was an all-too-familiar story to me. She had married Ray because he was fun, spontaneous, thrill seeking (she was actually a bit reserved), and hardworking. She now felt her life had been taken from her. Her ADD children were a handful, and she felt she had no support from Ray. She said, "When he's home, he's not with me. He's always working on projects that don't get finished. He stirs up the kids after I get them settled down. And I can't get him to pay attention to me. He's so restless. When I try to talk with him, I have to follow him around the house." In addition, Ray had made several bad financial business decisions and the family was struggling with debt, despite Ray's successful business. He had had an affair several years before they entered counseling, and Linda didn't believe she could trust him. She felt isolated, alone, and angry.

There was no question in my mind that Ray had ADD. As a child and teenager he had been restless, impulsive, hyperactive, and disorganized. He had underachieved in school and barely finished high school, despite obviously being very bright. The chronic stress of living in an ADD home was beginning to change Linda's personality. She had gone from being a relaxed, happy person to being depressed, angry, and withdrawn. Something had to change.

The couple's four-circles plan included: **B**—I put Ray on Adderall, a stimulant medication, and omega-3 fatty acids higher in EPA, which helped him be more thoughtful, more attentive, and more efficient at work. I encouraged Linda to try 5HTP and saffron to help calm her anterior cingulate and limbic system that had been triggered by all the stress. **P**—We worked on Ray's and Linda's ANTs to start looking forward, rather than at the past with regret; **S**—They continued in marital counseling, which was more effective now that Ray could focus. I also got involved with the children's treatment to make sure they were on the optimal treatment for their ADD, and that Ray and Linda used effective parenting strategies (many of Ray and Linda's fights were over disciplining the children); **Sp**—The couple identified their sense of purpose as improving their marriage so they could love each other and effectively parent together to help the next generation not have as many struggles. Over the next four months, this couple dramatically improved; even the kids noticed a big difference.

ANTERIOR CINGULATE RELATIONAL TRAITS

When the anterior cingulate gyrus (ACG) functions properly, people are able to shift their attention easily. They tend to be flexible and adaptable. They are likely to see options in tough situations. They are usually able to forgive the mistakes of others and tend not to hold on to hurts from the past. They do not rigidly try to control situations. They usually have a positive outlook and see a hopeful future. They are able to roll with the ups and downs of relationships.

When the ACG is overactive, people can get locked into thoughts— thinking them over and over. They're known to hold grudges, hold on to hurts from the past, and be unforgiving of perceived wrongs. They tend to be inflexible, rigid, and unbending. They often want things done a certain way (their way), and they may get very upset when things do not go their way. They have difficulty dealing with change. They tend to be argumentative and oppositional.

Positive ACG Relational Statements

"It's okay."
"I can roll with this situation."
"How would you like to do this?"
"Let's collaborate."
"What would you like to do?"
"I'm not upset, it's in the past."

Negative ACG Relational Statements

"You hurt me years ago."
"I won't forgive you."
"It'll never be the same."
"I'm always worried."
"I get stuck on these bad thoughts."
"Do it my way."
"I can't change."
"It's your fault."
"I don't agree with you."
"No. No. No."
"I won't do it."
"I don't want to do it."

"I have a lot of complaints about you."

"I've never hated anyone more than you."

"This will never change."

STATEMENTS FROM PARTNERS OF PEOPLE WITH ACG ISSUES

"Nothing gets forgiven or let go."

"She brings up issues from years and years ago."

"Everything has to be the way he wants it."

"He can't say he's sorry."

"He holds on to grudges forever."

"She never throws anything away."

"She's rigid."

"If things aren't perfect, he thinks they are no good at all."

"I don't help her because I have to do it exactly her way or she goes ballistic."

"He argues with everything I say."

"She tends to be oppositional."

"He doesn't like to try new things."

Rose and Larry

Rose and Larry had been married for twenty-two years. They had been unhappy for twenty-one of them. I was the sixth marriage counselor they had seen. They were a very persistent couple. Larry had heard me speak in San Francisco at a local conference on children of alcoholics. He said when I talked about problems associated with the ACG, it seemed like I was talking about him and his wife. He bought one of my DVDs and took it home for Rose to see. Rose was stunned when she recognized herself as I talked about working with couples who had incompatible brains. She had grown up in an alcoholic home. As a teenager, she had problems with alcohol and marijuana, and as an adult, she had periodic bouts of depression. More damaging to the marriage was her inflexibility: She had to have things a certain way or she'd explode. She was "the world's worst worrier," according to her husband. Her house looked perfect. "The president could visit any time of the day or night," her husband said. "I don't know why she cleans so much. It's not like we're dirty people." She also held grudges. Things would get brought up multiple times over the years. If she liked someone, she was a wonderful friend. If someone rubbed her the wrong way, she would write that person off and never let go of her anger. She hadn't talked to her own mother for eighteen years because of a trivial fight one Christmas. Rose never said she was sorry. She tended to oppose whatever Larry wanted to do, and their arguments were frequently over nothing. Larry said, "We argue just to argue." Sex was often an ordeal. The setting had to be just right in order for anything to happen. "God help me if I ask for it directly," Larry said.

When I asked Larry what kept him in the relationship, he said he didn't know. He had grown up Catholic and felt it was his obligation to stay. He found gratification at work and just spent more and more time away. Plus, he felt Rose really tried. She always set up the counseling appointments, and she was committed to staying with him. I was very surprised that no one had sent Rose to see a psychiatrist. None of her previous therapists had considered the brain to be an important factor in this couple's struggles. They wanted to help this couple with their problems but never wondered if the hardware that drove their behavior was working properly.

Before I tackled this couple, I wanted to see how Rose's brain functioned. I was betting there were brain patterns interfering with intimacy. As I suspected, Rose had one of the most active ACGs I had ever seen. No wonder she had so many problems shifting her attention! Her brain's gear shifter was stuck, unable to move into new and different modes of thinking.

They desperately needed a four-circles plan: **B**—I put Rose on the serotonin-enhancing medication sertraline (Zoloft) to help her mood and flexibility and calm her ACG, along with omega-3 fatty acids high in DHA. I taught the couple about how the brain works and how it can interfere with intimacy. **P**—We worked on the ACG Prescriptions mentioned in chapter 13, including distraction and thought stopping. I also worked with them on developing a new perspective about their past behavior and healing the memories of pain. **S**—I continued to see Rose and Larry as a couple to help them get beyond the past and support each other in the present.

Sp—They appreciated the discussion on meaning and purpose to make their family and the world a better place.

After four months of working the plan they were much better. They were able to have fun together. Larry was able to ask for sex without fear of rejection. He no longer had to play "ACG games." He spent more time at home because the atmosphere was so much more relaxed. Rose called her mother and reconnected with her. Ultimately, Rose stayed on her medication for three years and then slowly tapered off. When some of her problems resurfaced, she tried 5-HTP, which she liked better because it didn't affect her sexuality like the Zoloft did.

TEMPORAL LOBE RELATIONAL TRAITS

When the temporal lobes function properly, people tend to be emotionally stable. They are able to process and understand what others say in a clear way. They can retrieve words for conversations. They tend to read the emotional state of others accurately. They have good control over their temper. They have access to accurate memories. Because of their memory, they have a sense of personal history and identity.

When the temporal lobes do not function properly, people tend to have memory struggles. They don't have clear access to their own personal history and identity. They are often emotionally labile (up and down). They tend to be temperamental and have problems with anger. They often have violent thoughts and express their frustration with aggressive talk. They often take things the wrong way and appear to be a little paranoid. They may have periods of spaciness or confusion and misinterpret what is said to them.

Positive Temporal Lobe Relational Statements

"I remember what you asked me to do."
"I have a clear memory of the history of our relationship."
"I feel stable and even."
"I can find the words to express my feelings."
"I can usually tell when another person is happy, sad, mad, or bored."

"I have good control over my temper."

"My memory is good."

NEGATIVE TEMPORAL LOBE RELATIONAL STATEMENTS

"I struggle with memory."

"I blow things way out of proportion."

"I get angry easily. I have a bad temper."

"My moods tend to be volatile."

"I tend to get scary, violent thoughts in my head."

"It's hard for me to read."

"I often misinterpret what others say."

"I tend to be too sensitive to others or feel others are talking about me."

"I tend to misread the facial expressions of others."

"I frequently have trouble finding the right words in a conversation."

STATEMENTS FROM PARTNERS OF PEOPLE WITH TEMPORAL LOBE PROBLEMS

"He can be physically or verbally very aggressive."

"She's volatile."

"His memory is very poor."

"She misreads situations."

"He's very moody."

"She takes things the wrong way."

"He spaces out easily."

"She doesn't seem to learn by reading something or hearing directions. You have to show her what to do."

Don and Shelley

Don and Shelley had been married for four years when they sought therapy. Don had a terrible problem with his temper. He had physically abused Shelley on three occasions and had been charged with felony assault against her. During one of those times he had been drunk, but during the other two he had not been drinking at all. Shelley's family and friends thought she was crazy for staying with him. Shelley said she loved Don and wanted the marriage to work. She was afraid when she thought about staying and sad when she thought about leaving, but she knew the violence had to stop. Don was always so sorry after the attacks. He always cried for a long time and seemed truly sorry. When the therapist learned that Don had had a significant head injury from a motorcycle accident at the age of seventeen, he suggested that Don see me as part of his evaluation. Don and Shelley seemed to truly love each other. Don did not have a good explanation for his problems, and he denied that he ever wanted to hurt Shelley. "I just get out of control," he said. I found out that Don saw shadows. He had many periods of feeling spacy and had difficulties finding the right words. He was very forgetful. He was moody, volatile, and temperamental, and he had odd sensations of déjà vu. Don often took things the wrong way, and he thought many other people were out to hurt him. In Don's motorcycle accident, he had swerved to avoid a deer and skidded on the left side of his helmet for approximately eighty feet. I suspected he had temporal lobe problems (probably on the left), which was confirmed by his SPECT scan.

I knew Don and Shelley would both benefit from each circle of his plan. **B**—I placed Don on carbamazepine (Tegretol), an antiseizure medication, to stabilize the activity in his left temporal lobe. We also worked with his diet to make sure he never allowed himself to get into a low blood sugar state. **P**—I helped Don make sense of the past by understanding his brain; **S**—The therapist continued to see the couple and taught them about forgiveness and understanding based on this new information; **Sp**—We discussed Don and Shelley's sense of meaning and purpose, and why they wanted to stay together, despite the challenges. Within three weeks, Don reported feeling calmer, less angry, and less easily agitated. "It takes much more to get me upset," he said. Shelley had also noticed an almost immediate difference. "He is more relaxed. He's calmer, and he's much mellower. Things don't upset him like before."

IT IS IMPORTANT to remember that there's no rule that says people get only one problem. Some of the toughest couples have multiple system problems in both partners. It is always important to consider the brain when thinking about couples who struggle.

BETTER RELATIONSHIPS THROUGH BIOCHEMISTRY?

One of the underlying messages of this chapter is that many couples struggle because one or both partners have underlying brain patterns that interfere with intimacy. As we've discussed throughout the book, natural supplements and medications often help alleviate these problems. I have seen many relationships literally saved by balancing brain function. While you can refer back to the individual brain system prescriptions in other chapters, here are several additional tips about the use of supplements and medication in couples:

1. Some supplements or medications, such as stimulants, work for defined periods of time. Be aware of this and try to be especially cautious about conflict at those times. If a medication's effectiveness wears off around 8:00 p.m., do not bring up emotionally loaded topics at 10:30 p.m.

2. Be sensitive to the sexual side effects of medication. Medications that enhance serotonin production in the brain, such as fluoxetine (Prozac), paroxetine (Paxil), sertraline (Zoloft), citalopram (Celexa), escitalopram (Lexapro), and venlafaxine (Effexor), often decrease libido or delay the ability to achieve orgasm. If this occurs, there are strategies your doctor can use to counteract these problems, such as adding gingko biloba or the antidepressant bupropion (Wellbutrin). Talk these problems over with your doctor. Also, let your partner know that there may be these kinds of medication side effects.

3. Be persistent with supplements or medications. Too often people will try them for a few days and then abandon them if they aren't immediately effective. Be persistent.

RELATIONAL THERAPY BRAIN PRESCRIPTIONS

Just as with brain system issues overall, it's clear that using supplements or medications are only part of the solution to relationship issues. Based on my brain-imaging work, I have developed a number of effective non-medication brain system prescriptions to help couples, which I've broken up into the different systems we've discussed. Of course, there is overlap between systems, but I think this is a useful way to think about helping couples. The "Self" prescriptions here are for those affected by these problems, and the "Partner" prescriptions are for the partners of those affected.

Limbic Relational Prescriptions for Self

1. Spend time together: Bonding is essential to all human relationships. You need to spend physical time with your partner. The less you are around each other, the less bonded or limbically connected you become.

2. Smell good: Choose scents your partner likes and wear them. The limbic system directly processes the sense of smell, and it can have a positive or negative effect on your relationship.

3. Focus on the times you have enjoyed with each other. The limbic system stores highly charged emotional memories. When you focus on the negative in a relationship, you feel more distant from each other. When you focus on the positive in your relationship, you feel more connected.

4. Touch each other: Touch is healing, and couples need to have their hands on each other. Sexual and nonsexual touching is essential to intimacy. It is likely that touch cools the limbic system and is involved with the stabilization of mood.

5. Kill the ANTs: Automatic negative thoughts (ANTs) infest and destroy relationships (see chapter 7). Do not believe every thought you have. Focus on positive, uplifting, and nurturing thoughts about your partner. It makes a difference to your brain function and subsequently affects your relationship.

Limbic Relational Prescriptions for Partner

1. Don't let your partner isolate him- or herself. Even though isolation is a natural tendency in depression, it makes the situation worse. Encourage activity and togetherness.

2. Touch your partner. Back rubs or a touch on the shoulder or hand can be very reassuring to someone who feels alone. Connectedness is very important.

3. If your partner has a loss of sexual interest, do not take it personally. Often depression is accompanied by sexual problems. Work on getting him or her help.

4. Help your partner around the house—with the children, chores, and so on. Often limbic problems are associated with low energy and poor concentration. Your partner may feel overwhelmed and need your help. Many partners, not properly understanding the reality of conditions like depression, become critical and make the situation much worse. Your partner needs understanding, love, and support—not criticism.

5. Help get your partner to the doctor if the limbic problems interfere with functioning. Limbic problems are often very treatable.

6. Take care of yourself. It is stressful to be married to someone who is depressed. Take time to replenish yourself.

Basal Ganglia Relational Prescriptions for Self

1. Kill the fortune-telling ANTs: Predicting failure, pain, or an unhappy outcome often causes erosion in relationships. Clear thinking is essential in relationships. Do not believe every thought you have.

2. Predict the best: looking to the future in a positive manner is a key to happiness. Your mind helps to make happen what it sees. People with basal ganglia issues have a natural tendency to predict the worst, which can sometimes become a self-fulfilling prophecy. Fight that tendency. When you see good things happening in your relationship, act in ways to make them even more likely to happen. Hope for the best.

3. Get control of your breathing: Anxiety, tension, and out-of-control behavior are often preceded by shallow, rapid breathing. Before responding to your partner in an anxious or tense situation, take a deep breath, hold it for 2 seconds, and then very slowly exhale (taking 5 seconds to exhale). After three or four deep breaths of this type, your brain will be filled with oxygen, you will feel more relaxed, and you will be much more likely to make better decisions.

4. Deal with conflict: Effectively dealing with conflict is one of the keys to relationship health. Whenever couples bury their differences or put off dealing with their conflicts, anxiety, tension, and subversive behavior result. It is important to develop both negotiation and conflict resolution skills in relationships (see the Basal Ganglia Prescription chapter). It is also important to deal with conflict in a kind, respectful manner.

Basal Ganglia Relational Prescriptions for Partner

1. Help your partner look at the positive side of things. Help him or her predict good things rather than bad things. Join forces to kill the fortune-telling ANTs.

2. Do not get irritated with your partner's anxiety or negative predictions. Soothe him or her with gentle words or a touch.

3. Pace your breathing to help your partner's breathing. Often people unconsciously mirror their partner. When you breathe slowly and

deeply, your partner is likely to pick up a more relaxed breathing pattern, automatically calming his or her anxiety.

4. Encourage your partner to face conflict in an effective way.

Prefrontal Cortex Relational Prescriptions for Self

1. Focus on what you want: clear focus is essential to relationships. I have many of my couples develop a "two-minute focus statement." In this statement, they write down, on one piece of paper, the major goals they have for their relationship in the areas of communication, time together, money, work, parenting, and sexuality. Then they post this statement where they will see and read it every day.

2. Focus on what you like about your partner more than what you don't like: many people with low PFC activity seek conflict as a way to stimulate themselves, even inadvertently. The problem with focusing on negative behavior is that you drive the other person away. The negativity kills the relationship.

3. Positive stimulation is helpful: Look for new, exciting ways to stimulate the relationship. The prefrontal cortex seeks stimulation. It is important to have new, exciting, stimulating experiences to keep the relationship fresh and alive. Look for ways to do new things together, such as sharing a hobby, going to new places, or spicing up your sex life.

4. Learn to say "I'm sorry": admitting mistakes and saying you're sorry is essential to relational health. When the prefrontal cortex doesn't work hard enough, people don't have access to good internal supervision, and they may say or do things impulsively. When that happens, it is important to apologize and let your partner know you're sorry. Unfortunately, many people aren't good at saying they are sorry, and they try to justify why they did or said hurtful things. Learn to apologize and take responsibility for your mistakes.

5. Then what? Think about what you say or do before you say or do it: Thoughtfulness and forethought are essential to effective relationships. Before you say or do something in a relationship, ask yourself if what you say or do fits with the goals you have for the relationship. Will your behavior help or hurt the relationship? Supervising your thoughts and actions is essential to relational health.

Prefrontal Cortex Relational Prescriptions for Partner

1. Do not be your partner's stimulant: because the prefrontal cortex seeks stimulation, many partners unconsciously seek stimulation in a negative way. Without knowing it, they unconsciously try to upset you. They try to get you to yell. They try to make you angry. It is very important to have a calm demeanor when you notice this is happening. Do whatever you can to not yell or become emotionally intense. When you feel as if you are going to blow, take a deep breath or a break until you can get yourself under control.

2. Notice the positive. You change behavior by focusing on what you like a lot more than what you don't like. Often people with prefrontal cortex problems have low self-esteem and need encouragement and positive input from those they love.

3. Help your partner with organization. Disorganization is often a hallmark of prefrontal cortex problems. Rather than complain about the disorganization, it is generally much more effective to help your partner become more organized—if he or she will allow you to.

4. Make the appointment and drive your partner to the doctor. Often forgetfulness, procrastination, and denial accompany prefrontal cortex problems. Help may be put off for many years, even when it is obviously needed. Professional help can make a big difference in these problems, and I often see partners bring their loved ones in for evalua-

tion and treatment. Don't wait for your partner to have the desire, will, or commitment to change; you may wait too long.

5. If medication is necessary, help your partner remember to take it. Do not do this in a condescending way, such as "Did you take your medicine? Your behavior is way off." Instead, help your partner with a gentle (non-sarcastic) reminder, or help your partner come up with a reminder system, such as weekly pill organizers or calendars.

Anterior Cingulate Relational Prescriptions for Self

1. Notice when you are stuck: the first step in breaking negative cycles is for you to notice when you are in them. Being aware of repetitive negative patterns of behavior allows you to do something different. Notice these patterns when you have the same argument over and over and find the courage to do something differently than you normally would. If you usually just go on and on trying to make your point, stop and say, "I'm finished. What is your perspective?" Then be quiet long enough to really hear what your partner is saying.

2. Take a break when things get heated: When you notice things are getting into a negative "cingulate" loop, take a break. When you notice tension in your voice, your body, or your conversation, find a way to distract yourself or take a break from the situation.

3. Stop nagging: nagging erodes a relationship and needs to stop. Nagging—complaining about something over and over—is very common in cingulate people. It often has a seriously negative impact on a relationship. When you find yourself going over the same material again and again, stop it. Beating someone over the head who is not listening to you is ineffective and irritating. Try to find new ways to deal with your frustrations.

4. Use good problem-solving techniques: when you are stuck at an impasse, writing down the issues that bother the relationship can often be very helpful. Use the following model: Write out the issue (such as

spending too much money), write out the options and solutions to the problem (spending less, budgeting, cutting up credit cards), and then choose among the options. Writing problems down often helps to get them out of your head and out of repetitive relational arguments.

5. Exercise together: exercise enhances serotonin production in the brain and often helps a person (maybe even a couple) to become more flexible and less stuck on unhelpful behavior.

6. Have a smart carbohydrate snack. Smart carbs, such as sweet potatoes or hummus, often improve moods and help anterior cingulate people be more flexible. Low blood sugar often correlates with anger and irritability.

Blood Sugar Voodoo

In one of the most fascinating studies, researchers measured the blood sugar levels of 107 married couples right before bedtime. Then they gave each spouse voodoo dolls and asked them to express their feelings about their partners by putting the pins in the dolls. The people who had the lowest blood sugar scores stuck more than twice the number of pins in their dolls (183). Protect your blood sugar levels; your marriage and maybe even your life could depend on it.

Anterior Cingulate Relational Prescriptions for Partner

1. Notice when your partner is stuck: the first step to breaking negative cycles is for couples to notice when they are in them. Being aware of repetitive negative patterns in your partner allows you to be helpful in the situation rather than inflame it. For example, if you notice your partner is not listening to you but holding firmly on to his or her own position, take a breath and really try to listen to your partner. Do something different to break the negative cycle.

2. Take a break when things get heated: when you notice your partner is getting into a negative "anterior cingulate" loop, change the pace. If you see your partner going over and over the same territory, or when his or her anger is escalating, find a way to distract your partner or take a break from the situation. As I've said, one of the most helpful things I tell people to do is learn how to go into the bathroom when things get heated.

3. Deal effectively with nagging. Nagging may be caused by an overactive anterior cingulate, or it may arise because you're not listening to your partner. When someone has repetitive complaints about you, let him or her know you hear what they are saying. Ask your partner what steps you can take to make the situation better. Also, make it clear that you have heard about the issue and would appreciate not hearing about it again. In a kind way, ask what you can do to make that happen.

4. Exercise together: Exercise enhances serotonin production in the brain and often helps people be happier and more flexible.

Temporal Lobe Relational Prescriptions for Self

1. Use memory helpers to keep the relationship fresh: reminders can make all the difference between your partner knowing you care and feeling he or she is not important to you. Given the busy pace of our lives, we often forget to notice the people who are most special to us. Use notes, signs, computer reminder systems, ticklers, and so on to keep your attention focused on making the person you love feel loved. Flowers (limbic scents), cards, CDs, and loving notes help your partner remember you love and care for him or her. Temporal lobe partners need constant reminders to keep you lovingly in their memory banks.

2. Listen to beautiful music together: music is healing and often has a positive impact on relationships. As we have seen, music can enhance

moods and sharpen learning and memory. Use beautiful music to enhance your connection to your partner.

3. Engage in rhythmic movement together: dancing and walking hand in
   hand help maintain connection and promote bonding in a relationship. They provide rhythms that help to solidify memories of togetherness.

4. Remember the best times. Develop a positive sense of the history of
   the relationship. Reread loving cards and letters on a regular basis to
   maintain an overall happy sense of the relationship.

5. Deal effectively with anger. Practice effective anger management strategies, like deep breathing, correcting negative thoughts, and clear communication. In addition, be sure to stay away from alcohol and drugs;
   they can unleash a vulnerable temporal lobe, uncorking anger and
   causing serious problems.

6. Know you have a tendency to be extremely sensitive to the behavior
   of others. Mild paranoia often accompanies a temporal lobe problem. When you feel others are being negative toward you, don't automatically believe your negative thoughts or feelings. Check them
   out.

7. Protein snacks may be helpful. Often, stabilizing blood sugar with a
   protein snack (nuts, lean meat, hard-boiled eggs) helps to settle down
   a situation caused by temporal lobe irregularities.

Temporal Lobe Relational Prescriptions for Partner

1. Do not take this problem personally. Often people with temporal lobe
   problems struggle in relationships because of their negativity, anger,
   and mild paranoia. Help your partner see situations clearly, but do not
   take the negativity personally.

2. Take anger seriously. Sometimes temporal lobe rage can get out of control. If you see your partner escalating, do not worsen the situation further—especially if substance abuse is involved. Talk in a soft voice. Take a break. Actively listen. Offering food may also help. Do not use addictive substances around the temporal lobe partner. The more you use, the more likely your partner will use, and things can really get out of control.

3. Keep protein snacks around.

4. Make sure you help get your partner to the doctor if the temporal lobe problems interfere with functioning. Such problems are often very treatable.

Use these prescriptions to enhance the love in your life. Love makes life worth living.

18

The Missing Links

Drugs, Alcohol, Head Trauma, Toxins,
Infections, and the Brain

When my work with SPECT began in 1991, I was the director of a psychiatric hospital unit that took care of patients with drug and alcohol addictions. Compared to healthy brains, the scans of addicts generally looked awful. They showed significantly low activity and had a Swiss cheese or moth-eaten appearance on the 3-D images. In fact, they looked so bad I brought the pictures home to show my children, effectively inducing anxiety disorders in all of them, as it related to substance abuse. On my children's mother's side there is a significant family history of alcoholism. I told my kids, "If you never drink you'll never have a problem, but if you drink you may have a very big problem, and this may be the brain that awaits you," as I showed them the brain-damaged images. "Which brain do you want?" I would ask. They answered that they wanted the healthy ones, and despite their genetic vulnerability, none of them have ever had a problem.

The pictures were so powerful that my son, Antony, brought them to school, which caused quite a discussion among his friends and teachers. He planted the seed for our poster "Which Brain Do You Want?," which has healthy scans in the center surrounded by drug-affected scans. The poster now hangs in hundreds of thousands of schools, prisons, drug treatment centers, therapists' offices, businesses, and courts around the world. You might recall the "This is your brain on drugs" public service commercial that showed eggs being cracked into a pan. Well, these SPECT pictures

Image 18.1: Poster of Drug Affected Brains Compared to a Healthy One

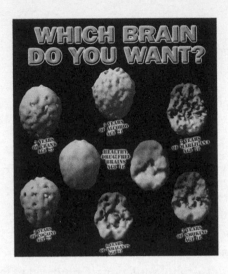

showed the devastation to real brains and were even more powerful. One judge in Cleveland has purchased thousands of posters to give away to addicts who appear in his courtroom. In my work, I've discovered that SPECT scans are an incredibly useful tool in getting addicts to stop substance abuse. The scans gave them brain envy.

Robert

Robert, age thirty-nine, came to see me because he thought he had ADD. He was forgetful, disorganized, and impulsive, and had a very short attention span. However, these problems had come on gradually during his adult life, not during childhood. Most notably, he also had a twenty-year history of heroin abuse and had been in multiple treatment settings without success. It is hard to describe how I felt when I initially saw Robert's SPECT study. This man was about my age, yet his brain looked fifty years older, with a toxic dementia-like appearance. When I showed Robert his SPECT study compared to one of a healthy brain, he was horrified. Even though he had tried unsuccessfully to stop abusing heroin on many occasions, this time he went into treatment and was able to stop. Later he told me, "It was either the heroin or my brain. I wasn't giving any more of my brain to the drug."

THE IMAGES BELOW are real scans from the brains of substance abusers. Notice the holes of activity in all the scans.

Image 18.2: Robert's Heroin-Affected Brain

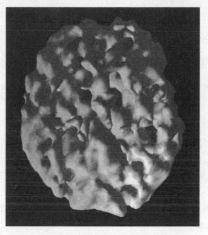

3-D TOP-DOWN SURFACE VIEW
Notice the large holes of activity across the brain surface.

Image 18.3: Alcohol Abuse

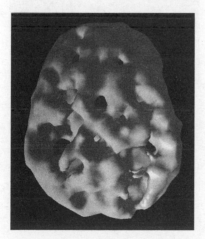

Image 18.4: Cocaine-Affected

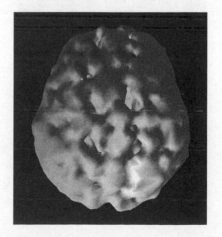

Image 18.5:
Methamphetamine-Affected

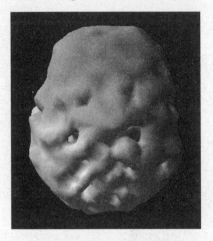

Image 18.6:
Inhalant-Affected

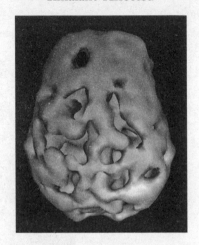

Image 18.7:
Marijuana-Affected

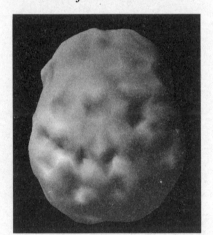

Image 18.8:
Benzodiazepine-Affected

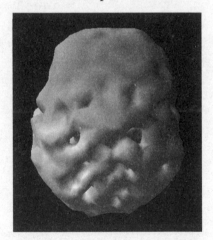

In my experience, inhalants, such as gasoline, paint thinners, nail polish remover, and nitrous oxide (laughing gas) cause the most brain damage. Cocaine and high-dose methamphetamines, which can increase psychosis, agitation, and depression, are not far behind. People with ADD often self-medicate with methamphetamines; of course, because the dosages are unregulated, many people seriously damage their brains and lives. Opiates can depress overall brain function (184, 185), which is why I encourage my patients to try everything else for chronic pain relief, such as acupuncture and hypnosis, before depending on opiate drugs. Benzodiazepines, commonly used for anxiety, decrease brain function (186). Cigarette smoking also damages the brain. A 2015 study found that smoking's association with dementia and cognitive decline is caused by the thinning of the cortex (187). In other words, it causes brain cells to die.

People ask me about all sorts of things on social media, but I've noticed that one of the most common questions I get is about the safety and effects of marijuana. In scanning thousands of marijuana users over the years, it is clear that this plant powerfully impacts the brain. Over time, it clearly gives the brain a toxic appearance in many users. Marijuana significantly lowers brain activity and I've seen it decrease memory, motivation, learning, focus, and coordination. In young people it also increases the risk of psychosis (188). According to the National Institutes of Drug Abuse (189), marijuana can lead to a drop in IQ by eight points, and is linked to lower educational outcomes, with users who are less likely to graduate from high school or college, who have a lower overall satisfaction with life, and who are more likely to earn a lower income or be unemployed. People who come to our clinics report that it makes them feel less socially anxious and sometimes less depressed, which is why they use it, but chronic recreational use clearly takes its toll and outweighs any benefit in the moment. In one study on veterans with posttraumatic stress disorder (PTSD), researchers tested marijuana as a treatment. Results showed that marijuana use was actually significantly associated with higher PTSD symptom severity, as well as higher levels of violent behavior and alcohol and drug use.

Is marijuana worse than alcohol or some legal prescription drugs, such as Xanax or Valium? Not really, in my experience. None of them are good for your brain over the long term. Should we incarcerate pot users? That doesn't seem like a good idea to warehouse people in a chronically stressful environment with terrible nutrition and a peer group that clearly won't elevate them.

Head Trauma and Alcohol Don't Mix: John

John, a seventy-nine-year-old contractor, had a long-standing history of alcohol abuse and violent behavior. He had physically abused his wife over forty years of marriage and had been abusive to their children when they were young. Almost all of the abuse occurred when he was intoxicated. Then John underwent open-heart surgery. After the surgery he had a psychotic episode that lasted ten days. His doctor called me for a consult. I ordered a SPECT study as part of his evaluation, which showed markedly decreased activity in the left prefrontal cortex and left temporal lobe—a clear indication of a past head injury. When I asked John if he had ever had any significant head injuries, John said, "By golly, I did. When I was twenty years old I was driving a milk truck that was missing its side rearview mirror. When I put my head out of the window to look behind me, my head smacked into a pole, knocking me unconscious for several hours." After the head injury he had problems with his temper and memory. There was a family history of alcohol abuse in four of his five brothers, although none of his brothers had problems with aggressive behavior. Given the location of the brain abnormality (left prefrontal cortex and temporal lobe), John was vulnerable to exhibiting violent behavior. Alcohol abuse, which did not elicit violent behavior in his brothers, contributed to John's violence. If John had seen and understood his brain damage earlier, he could have sought help and prevented the devastation to his family.

Father and Son Study

I believe all people in a domestic violence situation could benefit from knowing about their brains. Nine-year-old Phillip was frightened when the police came to his school to talk to him. His teacher had noticed bruises on his arms and legs and called Child Protective Services. Phillip wasn't sure if he should tell them the truth—that his father, Dennis, had beaten him up—or if he should say that he had fallen down a flight of stairs or something like that. Phillip did not want to get his dad into trouble, and he felt responsible for the beatings he received. After all, he thought, his father had told him ten times to clean his room, but for some reason unknown to

Phillip, he hadn't done it. Phillip and his father often fought, but it had never been apparent to people outside the home.

Phillip decided to tell the truth, which led his family to get help. The court ordered counseling for the family and a psychiatric evaluation for Dennis, who was found to be impulsive and explosive in many different situations. He had begun to have problems after sustaining a head injury in a car accident six years earlier. His wife reported that when Phillip was first born, Dennis was loving, patient, and attentive. After the accident, he had become irritable, distant, and angry.

In family counseling sessions, Phillip was very difficult—restless, overactive, impulsive, and defiant. He ignored his parents' request to stop his annoying behaviors. I soon discovered that the interaction between Phillip and his father was the problem and counseling alone would not be helpful. I believed there was some underlying biological or physical "brain problem" that contributed to the abusive interactions. In an effort to further understand the biology of this family's problems, I ordered brain SPECT studies on Phillip and his father.

The studies for both were abnormal. The father's clearly showed an area of decreased activity in his left temporal lobe, probably a result of the car accident. Phillip's revealed decreased activity in the front part of his brain when he tried to concentrate. As we have seen, this finding is often found in children who have ADD and are impulsive and overly active. After taking a history, watching the family interact, and reviewing the SPECT studies, it was clear to me that Phillip's and his father's problems needed to be addressed in all four circles.

B—I put Dennis on medicine to stabilize his temporal lobe, and Phillip on medicine for ADD, plus both on omega-3 fatty acids, exercise—which they did together—and a higher protein, lower carbohydrate diet (good for both of their brain types); **P**—therapy to deal with impulse control and alternatives to anger; **S**—training for Dennis on how to parent a challenging child, based on my book *New Skills for Frazzled Parents*; **Sp**—We discussed their sense of family and their mission for being on earth. After about six months of intensive work, the family began to heal the wounds of abuse. In counseling sessions, Phillip was calmer and more attentive, and his father was better able to learn how to deal with Phillip's difficult behavior in a constructive way. Whenever abuse of a child occurs, it is a severe tragedy. The tragedy is compounded when the underlying brain problems that may be contributing to the abuse are ignored.

Self-Medicating Rusty

Many substance abusers use their drugs as a way to medicate underlying emotional or cognitive problems, such as depression, panic symptoms, posttraumatic stress, anxiety, and even aggressive behavior.

Twenty-eight-year-old Rusty was brought to see me by his parents. He had a severe methamphetamine problem that had wreaked havoc in his life. He was unable to keep steady work; he was involved in a physically abusive relationship with his girlfriend (he had been arrested four times for assault and battery); he was mean to his parents even though they tried to help him; and he had failed five drug treatment programs. In the last program the counselor had recommended a "tough love" approach: he had told the parents to let Rusty "hit bottom" so that he would want help. The parents read about my work and decided to do one more thing before going the "tough love" route.

Rusty's lack of responsiveness to traditional treatments made me suspect an underlying brain problem. We scheduled a SPECT scan with the parents, but Rusty didn't know about it until the morning he was supposed to have it. He showed up at the clinic loaded on high-dose methamphetamine from the night before. Rusty told me about his drug abuse. He said, "I'm sorry for messing up the scan. I'll come back next week. I promise I won't use anything." I had often wanted to do SPECT studies on people intoxicated with illegal substances to see their effects on the brain, but because of ethical concerns I hadn't. But if a person shows up for the scan on drugs there isn't an ethical issue. I decided to scan Rusty that morning with the effects of the methamphetamine still in his system and then a week later off all drugs. It turned out to be a very fortuitous decision. When Rusty was under the influence of high-dose methamphetamine, his brain activity was suppressed. A week later, however, off all drugs, he had a terribly overactive left temporal lobe, probably causing his problems with violent behavior. Likely, Rusty was unconsciously self-medicating an underlying temporal lobe problem with high-dose methamphetamine. As I probed deeper into any history of a head injury (which initially both Rusty and his parents did not remember), Rusty recalled a time when he had been in second grade and had run full speed into a solid metal basketball pole and briefly been knocked unconscious. It's possible that set off a bad chain reaction in his brain.

After the results of the clinical examination and brain SPECT studies, I put Rusty on the following four-circles program: **B**—Given his temporal lobe abnormality, I put him on carbamazepine (Tegretol), an antiseizure medication to stabilize his temporal lobes; omega-3 fatty acids, and nutrients to help support brain repair; exercise; a higher protein, lower carbohydrate diet; **P**—therapy to deal with his impulses; **S**—counseling with his parents and an intensive outpatient program that taught him the importance of a new peer group if he was to stay sober; **Sp**—We discussed what gave Rusty a sense of meaning and purpose, and he decided to work toward being able to mentor others. Within two weeks Rusty felt better than he had in years. He was calmer and his temper was under control. After a year, he was able to remain gainfully employed. An additional benefit of the scan was that I was able to show Rusty the serious damage he had been doing to his brain by abusing the methamphetamines. Even though the drugs helped his temporal lobe problem, they were clearly toxic to his brain. Rusty, like others who abuse drugs, had developed holes in activity across the surface of his brain. Seeing these pictures was even more incentive to stay away from the drugs and get proper treatment for his problems. SPECT worked both as a powerful diagnostic tool to better assess one of the root causes of Rusty's problem and as a therapeutic tool to address his denial. *A picture is worth a thousand denials.* Often, having this type of information is valuable in helping patients make a more positive move toward sobriety. I wondered how many people with severe nonresponsive drug problems are self-medicating an underlying brain problem, yet are labeled by their families and society in general as weak-willed or morally defective. "Tough love" for Rusty wouldn't have solved his problem.

Drugs + Emotional and Physical Trauma
Precipitate a Disaster: Miguel

Miguel, a sixteen-year-old gang member, was arrested and charged with attempted murder after he beat another teenager nearly to death. His gang claimed the color red. One evening, when he was in an intoxicated state (from both alcohol and heavy marijuana usage), he approached a boy who was wearing a red sweater while walking his dog. Miguel asked, "What colors do you bang?" (a reference to his gang affiliation). When the boy said he did not know what he was talking about, Miguel replied, "Wrong answer," and he hit and kicked the boy repeatedly until he was unconscious. Other gang members described pulling Miguel off the boy, because once he had started, he wouldn't stop. They were afraid he would kill the boy.

The public defender ordered psychological testing on Miguel, which found frontal lobe dysfunction and evidence of ADD, depression, and learning disabilities. The psychologist suggested a SPECT series for independent verification. The scans were significantly abnormal. Both studies showed markedly increased activity in the anterior cingulate gyrus, consistent with problems in shifting attention. At rest, Miguel's SPECT study also showed mildly suppressed prefrontal cortex activity. While he was doing a concentration task, there was also marked suppression of the prefrontal cortex and both temporal lobes, consistent with ADHD, learning disabilities, and aggressive tendencies.

Miguel was eight years old when his mother was murdered. He subsequently had periods of depression and panic attacks. He had also suffered three concussions as a child. After these emotional and physical traumas, he started getting stuck on bad thoughts and troubled behaviors. "Once he got a thought in his head," his father said, "he would talk about it over and over." Miguel thought the substance abuse settled him down, but those close to him told me it made him more aggressive. Ultimately, the combination of Miguel's drug abuse, emotional trauma, and past concussions was nearly lethal to the boy whom he assaulted, and it ruined the lives of both the perpetrator and the victim. The saddest part of the case for me was that Miguel had a treatable brain, but no one thought about it until this terrible tragedy occurred.

Images 18.9–11: Miguel's ACG, Temporal Lobe, PFC Affected Brain

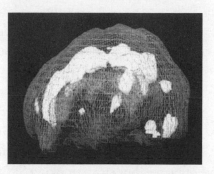

ACTIVE SIDE VIEW
Markedly increased ACG

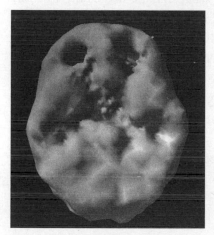

AT REST
Decreased PFC activity

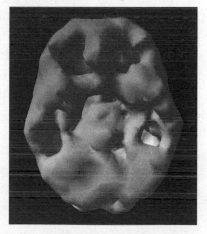

DURING CONCENTRATION
*Markedly decreased PFC and
temporal lobe activity*

What Happens When You Stop Abusing Drugs or Alcohol?

One of the most common questions I get is about what happens to the brain when you stop abusing alcohol or drugs. It depends on many factors: what you used (inhalants seem to be the worst); how long you used it; what your brain reserve was like before you started using drugs; your day-to-day other brain health habits; and your genetic vulnerability. Generally, the longer you abused substances, the more damage will be present. There are rare individuals who can abuse drugs for a long time before stopping with few if any lasting ill effects. Others can incur brain damage after a very short period of time. In either case, the sooner you stop, the better chance your brain has to heal.

If You Are Not Using Drugs, Why Does Your Brain Look So Bad? Another Epiphany

At Amen Clinics, we often see those toxic-looking SPECT scans in patients who have no history of drug or alcohol abuse. The state of these brains has forced me to ask more questions about what may be happening to cause this. We consider things like the possibility of environmental toxins at work, anoxia (a lack of oxygen), infections like Lyme disease, carbon monoxide poisoning, chemotherapy (which poisons cancer and often normal cells), extremely low thyroid, or anemia. And, when some of these factors are combined, watch out; the police might get involved, because an individual's behavior can become very troubled.

SPECT has taught me that there are many important missing links in understanding troubled behavior. Without knowledge of these links, people can be labeled as bad, willful, uncaring, or even possessed in some societies. Before imaging, it was easy for me to give someone a "personality disorder" diagnosis (borderline, antisocial, narcissistic, dependent, etc.), thinking their personality or character was the problem. But as I began to look at my patients' brains, one simple question occurred to me again and again: what is the organ of personality? It's our brain. If someone has a difficult personality, their brain may be the cause, and there is a chance it could be improved, leaving them with a happier and healthier life.

Infectious Disease and the Brain

One very common cause of scans that look toxic is an undiagnosed infectious disease, like Lyme disease or HIV. Untreated, these infections can attack the brain and significantly affect one's ability to learn, love, and behave.

Just like Adrianna's story in chapter 1 (the normal sixteen-year-old who became psychotic after being bitten by a deer tick and got her sanity back after being treated with antibiotics), many people with resistant psychiatric conditions, such as anxiety, depression, bipolar disorder, schizophrenia, and dementia, have been exposed to infectious agents that damaged their brains. In 1994, the *Schizophrenia Bulletin* published an image comparing the areas of the United States with the highest rates of Lyme disease and schizophrenia. They were nearly identical. The image was heralding a new era of infectious disease psychiatry, yet few knew it at the time.

Image 18.12: Schizophrenia vs. Lyme (190)

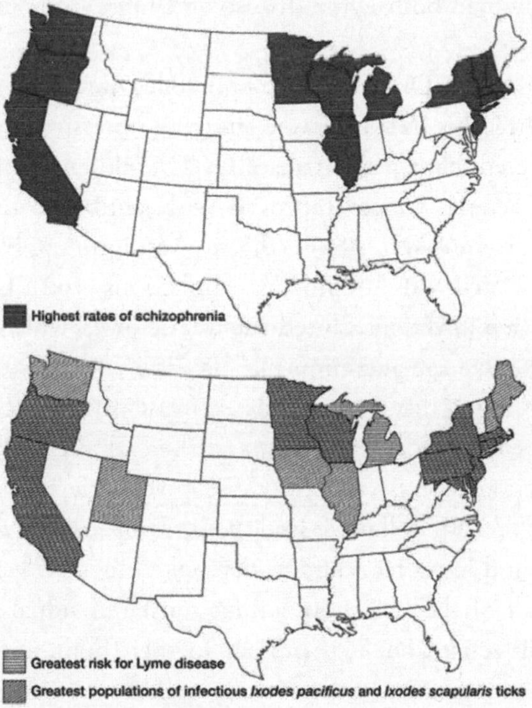

Highest rates of schizophrenia

Greatest risk for Lyme disease

Greatest populations of infectious *Ixodes pacificus* and *Ixodes scapularis* ticks

Reprinted with permission.

At Amen Clinics we've treated hundreds of patients who came to us with resistant psychiatric symptoms, tested positive for Lyme disease, and were helped by treating it. A 2014 study reported that the antibiotic minocycline, used to treat Lyme disease, was found to decrease symptoms of schizophrenia in a twelve-month period.

Erin

Erin was a nine-year-old girl who came to see me for obsessive thoughts, anxiety, depression, tics, and academic problems. She had been treated with antidepressants, stimulants, and play therapy, which all seemed to make her worse. When she started to voice suicidal thoughts, her parents called us. Erin's scan was strikingly overactive, indicating the possibility of inflammation. Something sinister was happening in her brain. Her lab studies showed that she had both Lyme disease and high antibodies to the strep bacteria.

In the early 1990s, Dr. Sue Swedo and colleagues at the National Institute of Mental Health (NIMH) were studying obsessive-compulsive disorder and discovered that a percentage of OCD children had high antibodies to the strep bacteria, which improved with antibiotic treatment. They called this syndrome PANDAS—Pediatric Autoimmune Neuropsychiatric Disorders Associated with Streptococcal Infections (162). Until then, physicians knew strep infections caused rheumatic fever, which was associated with heart valve damage and abnormal physical movements, but Dr. Swedo's discovery showed that strep could also cause psychiatric symptoms. We treated Erin for Lyme and PANDAS, and she had a remarkable recovery.

Other infectious agents can also cause psychiatric illnesses. But if one never looks for them, they'll never find them. *Toxoplasma gondii*, or *T. gondii*, is a parasite found in cat feces and undercooked food. *T. gondii* infects just over 20 percent of the U.S. population; most individuals infected aren't aware of the infection, but it is present in their brain and muscles. This parasite has been associated with psychiatric illnesses, including schizophrenia and suicide (191). Research estimates that approximately one-fifth of schizophrenia cases may be related to it. Gary Smith, MA, DPhil, professor of population biology and epidemiology at the University of Pennsylvania's School of Veterinary Medicine, wrote in *Preventive Veterinary Medicine* (October 2014), "Thus, prevention of *T. gondii* infection during a lifetime may prevent one-fifth of cases of schizophrenia. That, to me, is significant."

I believe infectious disease psychiatry will become a major discipline of psychiatry within the next thirty years.

Think Environmental Toxins

Carolyn moved into a home that had been flooded in the recent past. Shortly after she and her family moved in, they started experiencing health issues. Carolyn began to suffer from skin rashes and numerous bouts of bronchitis, with her symptoms worsening over time. A therapist, she began to have trouble focusing and remembering details of her clients' lives. She often felt anxious and confused and had to quit working. Her oldest son went from being a straight-A student to getting C's and could no longer concentrate well enough to finish projects. A black belt in jujitsu, he lost his coordination and couldn't participate in the sport. Her youngest son kept telling her that he couldn't focus or concentrate well enough to study at home, but when he would head over to a friend's house, he had no problem hitting the books. At home, it was also a struggle for him to get going in the morning, and he started racking up tardies at school. Whenever he spent the night at a friend's house, he popped up out of bed with no problem and easily made it to school on time.

By 2001, Carolyn knew there was something very wrong. One day, she saw a news feature about toxic mold on TV, and suspected that it might be the problem. She immediately set up an appointment with an allergist and she hired a mold inspector to check the house. The inspector's tests came back positive—mold was the culprit. She and her family moved out of the house that year and never went back. Her children have mostly recovered, but it took Carolyn nearly a decade to return to work.

Carolyn's story is very distressing not only because of what happened to her family, but also because it could happen to anyone. Most of us go through life assuming that the products we use, the foods we eat, and the places we live are completely safe. As frightening as it may seem, a number of household items that we use on a regular basis, our favorite foods, and even our schools and workplaces could be poisoning our brains and bodies. Drinking from plastic water bottles, using insecticides in your garden, breathing in fumes as you fill up the gas tank, or working around noxious fumes in a hair or nail salon or as a house painter could be affecting your mental and physical health.

Many occupations are considered high risk for exposure to environmental toxins. In my experience, brain scans of indoor painters show some of the highest levels of brain damage. Grounds maintenance workers work with insecticides, tree trimmers inhale dust, welders breathe in welding fumes, and hairstylists and nail technicians inhale product fumes. The risk to beauty salon workers has been documented in a recent study that showed that hairstylists have a higher than normal risk for Alzheimer's disease (192).

One patient came to me because he was experiencing memory problems. I noticed he looked much older than his stated age. His scan showed scalloping, a sign of toxic exposure. He said he didn't drink or do drugs, so it had to be something else. When asked when his symptoms began, he said about four years ago, right around the time he bought a new car. After some investigation and a few trips to the mechanic, he discovered that the hoses weren't attached correctly to his car's engine. Every time he got into his car, carbon monoxide was pouring into the cabin. He was literally poisoning himself and his brain every time he drove somewhere.

I once gave a lecture to a thousand people at Skyline Church in San Diego. The next year I was invited back. As often happens when I speak at a place for the second time, a number of people approached me as I walked into the lecture hall to show me SPECT scans they'd had done. My lecture motivated them to come to one of our clinics to have their own brain evaluated. On this occasion, a thirty-five-year-old man named Todd came up to me to show me his scan. It looked like Swiss cheese, the same pattern we often see in our drug or alcohol abusers. As I looked at the scan Todd said, "You think I am a drug addict, don't you?"

"The thought had crossed my mind," I replied.

"I have never used drugs," Todd said. "And, I don't drink. Before I came to your clinic I used to paint cars in my garage, without much ventilation. I don't do that anymore."

"That is the sign of intelligent life," I replied. "New information caused you to change your behavior."

He went on to tell me that he and his wife had been in marital therapy for several years without any benefit. After his visit to our clinic in Southern

California he started to live a brain-healthy life. The difference, he said, has been life-changing. After his brain health began to improve, he was able to be a better husband and had more cognitive clarity than he had in years. Being married is hard enough with a good brain. It's really hard with a troubled one.

Image 18.13: Todd's Toxicity

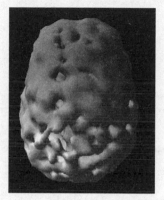

Painting car inside closed garage

Medical Causes of Toxicity

At Amen Clinics, whenever we see a toxic scan in someone who is suffering, we always ask why. Here is a list of common reasons:

Drugs or alcohol
Infections
Cancer chemotherapy
Environmental toxins, such as mold
Carbon monoxide poisoning
Lack of oxygen, such as near-drowning, hanging (strangulation), auto-erotic asphyxiation
Sleep apnea
Infection, such as Lyme, HIV, *T. gondii*
Low thyroid
Severe anemia, low red blood cell count
Liver, kidney, or lung disease

Part Three

The Brain Warrior's Way

AMEN CLINICS METHOD

ASSESS THE **4 CIRCLES OF BRAIN HEALTH**

Biological

Social

Psychological

Spiritual

BRAIN SPECT IMAGING Changes Everything

SPECT measures
cerebral blood flow:

Is it:

Healthy,
Low, or High
in Activity

Rest   Concentration

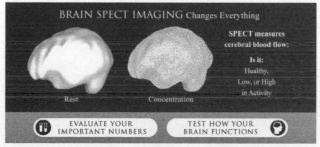

EVALUATE YOUR
IMPORTANT NUMBERS

TEST HOW YOUR
BRAIN FUNCTIONS

TREATMENT TARGETED TO YOUR BRAIN

Least toxic,
most effective
strategies

ALL LEADS TO BETTER OUTCOMES

BOOST BRAIN RESERVE & RESILIENCE

**Brain Envy
Avoid Bad
Do Good**

BETTER BRAIN = HAPPIER LIFE!!!

19

The Amen Clinics Program to Explode Your Potential, Reverse Illness, and Reduce Your Risk for Alzheimer's

As I was writing this chapter, one of my patients, Dr. Steve Arterburn, *New York Times* bestselling author, radio host, and entrepreneur, sent me this note and gave me permission to share it with you.

My rental car confirmation number for Aruba was 63012078US2 and hotel was 55505510931. The reason I know this is that I'm supernaturally able to remember things that I would never even try to before. And they don't go away! My productivity and creativity is off the chart. I would say I am getting 4 X the work done 4 X better than ever and creativity has resulted in book ideas and proposals that I can't wait to publish. I have the ability to focus on tasks and connect with my wife in ways I have never experienced.

Here's what I'm doing consistently:

Exercising in bursts as you suggested vs. 30 minutes continuous running.
No sodas vs. 4 a day
Severely restricted sugar intake while increasing protein and reducing grains and processed carbs
Taking the supplements you recommended
CPAP machine every night vs. never
Brain Warrior's Way exercises, where I have a ways to go on memory and other areas, but in problem-solving I am up to the 99.5 percentile.

WOW!!!! What a difference!!!! And sexual intimacy is another amazing peak performance area!!! I know it sounds a bit difficult to believe all of this.

Steve's experience is exactly why I do what I do. He is a brain warrior. The last step in the Amen Clinics Method is to live "the Brain Warrior's Way." It involves planting the strategies and tools in your daily life to explode your potential, reverse illnesses (such as depression and obesity), and prevent Alzheimer's disease and the untoward effects of aging.

YOU ARE IN A WAR FOR THE HEALTH OF YOUR BRAIN

Make no mistake, you are in a war for the health of your brain. Nearly everywhere you go, someone is trying to make money by offering you bad food that will kill you early. Food companies use neuroscience principles to develop addictive food-like substances that work on the pleasure centers of your brain, making you crave them, and then they use half-naked, beautiful women biting into burgers you know they would never eat to advertise them. If you are not a brain warrior, it is very easy for your weight to balloon out of control, which will shrink your brain. In addition, news channels repeatedly pour negative thoughts and horrific images into our minds, by repeatedly showing us every bad thing that happens anywhere in the world. News corporations know that human beings pay attention to fearful news much more than they do to peaceful news. And electronics companies develop gadgets that hook our attention and decrease the time and intimacy we have with our loved ones.

In addition, **Alzheimer's disease is expected to triple in the next thirty years** and there is no cure on the horizon. Fifty percent of people eighty-five years old and older will be diagnosed with Alzheimer's disease or another form of dementia. To put this into perspective: if you are fortunate to live that long, you have a 50 percent risk of losing your mind as a reward. Frightening new research suggests that Alzheimer's disease actually starts in your brain *decades before* you have *any* symptoms (193–195). This finding means that a patient of mine who was recently diagnosed with Alzheimer's disease at fifty-nine years old likely had noxious changes in her brain in her twenties!

Depression is the most expensive medical illness on the planet and is one of the greatest killers of our time, affecting fifty million Americans at some point in their lives. Nearly all of us have either suffered from depression or know someone who has. My adopted son and my son-in-law had fathers who committed suicide. Depression is a risk factor for Alzheimer's disease, heart disease, cancer, and obesity. An astonishing 23 percent of women between the ages of forty and sixty are now taking antidepressants.

Obesity is a serious national crisis, with two-thirds of Americans overweight and one-third obese (196). Obesity is the third leading cause of death and a risk factor for over thirty medical illnesses, including Alzheimer's disease, depression, and suicide.

The answer in my mind to the epidemic problems of Alzheimer's disease, depression, and obesity is not to look for separate causes or cures for these problems, but rather to think of them as different expressions of the same unhealthy lifestyle that can only be solved by a brain warrior revolution in brain health. To show how these disorders are related, there are dozens of studies now—my team and I published two of them—that report as your weight goes up the actual physical size and function of your brain go down (197–199). That should scare the fat off anyone. The **obesity crisis is the biggest brain drain in our history.** In our own studies at the Amen Clinics, we found that as your weight goes up, your ability to think and reason go down. This means that if someone doesn't get their weight under control, over time it will become harder and harder for them to use their own good judgment to get healthy. The fat on your body is not just a storage place for excess calories; it produces toxic chemicals that promote inflammation and damage your brain. Losing weight is not just about vanity; it is important for your physical and mental health. When I first read these studies I told myself I had to get healthy. I absolutely love being a husband, a father, and a grandfather, but I want to be one who is healthy and energetic, not one who is sad and forgetful. By using the strategies I am teaching you I have not only dropped twenty-five pounds since writing the first edition of this book, but I feel more energetic and more productive than I did thirty years ago.

Another exciting development comes from Dr. Dale Bredesen of UCLA. He put ten patients with Alzheimer's disease (or its precursor, known as mild cognitive impairment) on a comprehensive and personalized treatment program similar to the one you'll find in this chapter. Within six months of completing the program, nine of the ten patients displayed improvements in thinking or memory. Six were able to return to work or continue working with better performance (200). The gains have been sustained for up to four years for some patients, much like Nancy's story in the introduction. A larger study from Finland reported similar findings (201). These studies dovetail with our experience at Amen Clinics.

Bredesen's work centers around four central concepts.

1. Optimize parameters, don't just normalize them. For example, vitamin D, testosterone, and thyroid levels need to be in the optimal or high normal range, not just anywhere in the normal range.

2. Multiple mechanism approach. When we get sick or age, it is never just one biological mechanism, such as blood flow, that fails us, it is generally multiple mechanisms, such as blood flow, toxic buildup, nutrient depletion, and inflammation.

3. Personalize based on individualized parameters. The interventions need to be tailored to your unique situation.

4. Iterative, optimized over time. You can never stop being a brain warrior. Once you stop, the weapons of mass destruction (highly processed, low-fiber, high-glycemic, pesticide-sprayed food, and aging) will overwhelm you.

Basic training for a brain warrior means developing the skills to love and care for your brain to keep it as healthy for as long as possible. In this chapter I'm going to give you our twelve-step program to explode your potential, reverse illness, and significantly reduce your risk for Alzheimer's disease.

Step #1: Develop Brain Envy

Freud was wrong, "penis envy" is not the cause of most of your problems. He was about two and a half feet too low on your body. Falling in love with your brain is the first step to reclaiming, sustaining, and strengthening your brain. Far too many people don't consider the importance of keeping their brain healthy. You can see the wrinkles in your skin or the fat around your belly and do something when you are unhappy with how they look. However, since most people never look at their brains, most have no idea if and when they are headed for trouble. To get truly well, it starts by developing a deep sense of love and care for your brain—what I call brain envy.

Here's one of my favorite stories about brain envy from Jason Garner, former CEO of Global Music for Live Nation and the author of *And I Breathed: My Journey from a Life of Matter to a Life That Matters.*

Five years ago I was at the top of my career and then it all came crashing down. I found myself in the middle of my second divorce, my mom died suddenly from cancer, and I was soon unemployed. Those events were the beginning of a journey that led me to study health, peace of mind, and spiritual awareness with many of the world's leading experts. As part of that journey, I attended a health conference where I saw Dr. Amen speak. As I listened to him talk about the importance of focusing on brain health, I realized that in all my self-exploration and wellness practice I had completely overlooked one of the most important parts of me—my brain. As a family, we went through the Amen Clinics Method and got scanned. The medical staff gave us a plan to change our brains and keep them healthy throughout life. The doctors spoke to my children about the ways they could avoid damaging their brains through contact sports, alcohol, and drugs. We discussed how, as a family, we could better understand our brain function and how that affected our interactions with each other. This has led us to include brain exercises in our daily routine, to take supplements that promote brain health, and to think about the brain when choosing our foods. The best way to sum up our experience is to say that we now have a giant case of "Brain Envy"—a strong desire to have a healthy, vibrant, and fully functioning brain. My life would not be the same without the lessons I learned from Amen Clinics.

Step #2: Regularly Assess Your Brain

As mentioned in chapters 3 through 5, it is critical to assess your brain and important numbers. You cannot change what you do not measure. Periodic brain imaging can help, especially if there are signs of trouble or risk factors. We routinely screen other organs for trouble, but very few people ever screen their brains. When I turned fifty, my doctor wanted me to have a colonoscopy. I asked him why he didn't want to look at my brain. "Isn't the other end of my body just as important?" In the same way, regular screening with brain SPECT or other imaging tools such as quantitative EEG would give real biological data on the physical organ that makes decisions and runs our life.

Other ways to assess the brain include taking our computerized neuropsychological assessment (WebNeuro) at www.mybrainfitlife.com. Based on how you score, we give you targeted brain exercises in the form of fun games to strengthen your vulnerable areas. Knowing the health of your brain is critical to keeping it strong over the long run.

It is also critical to know your important health numbers (BMI, waist-to-height ratio, sleep hours) and baseline screening labs discussed in chapter 5. Work with your health-care professionals to optimize their numbers, not just have them in the normal range. If you cannot find a health-care professional to help you, call one of our clinics.

Step #3: Know and Reduce Your Risk of Alzheimer's and Other Forms of Dementia

Alzheimer's disease is no small problem. It currently affects 5.2 million people in the United States, a number estimated to quadruple by 2050 (202). Everyone in the family is affected by AD. The level of emotional, physical, and financial stress is constant and enormous. Another frightening statistic is that an estimated 15 percent of caregivers of people with AD have it themselves.

When I wrote *Preventing Alzheimer's* with my colleague Dr. William Shankle in 2005, our argument was that the best way to prevent AD was to prevent all the illnesses that put you at risk for it. Research from others has confirmed our original assertion (10, 48, 204–219). If you want to keep your brain healthy with age, it is critical to avoid the following risk factors as much as possible. Except for genetic risk factors and aging itself, most of them are preventable.

Mark the ones that apply to you. At the end, determine your score by adding the numbers in parentheses by the factors you checked off. Those numbers signify the relative increase in risk for Alzheimer's compared with those without that factor.

1. One family member with Alzheimer's or dementia (3.5), more than one family member with Alzheimer's or dementia (7.5)
2. A single head injury with loss of consciousness (2), several head injuries without loss of consciousness (2)
3. Alcohol dependence or drug dependence in past or present (4.4)
4. Major depression or ADD/ADHD diagnosed by a physician in past or present (2 in females, 4 in males)
5. Standard American Diet (2)
6. Being obese (2)
7. History of a stroke (10)
8. Heart disease or heart attack (2.5)
9. Prehypertension or hypertension (2.3)
10. Prediabetes or diabetes (3.4)
11. Cancer chemotherapy (3)
12. Seizures in past or present (1.5)
13. Parkinson's disease (3)
14. Sleep apnea (2)
15. Less than a high school education (2)
16. Limited exercise, less than twice a week (2)
17. Jobs that do not require new learning (2)
18. Periodontal disease (2)
19. Presence of inflammation in the body, such as high homocysteine or C-reactive protein (2)
20. Smoking cigarettes for ten years or longer (2.3)
21. Low estrogen in females (2) or low testosterone in males or females (2)

22. Within the age range 65 to 74 years old (2)
23. Within the age range 75 to 84 years old (2.0)
24. Over 85 years old (38)

____ Total Score

INTERPRETATION:

If your score is 0–4 you likely have low risk factors for developing AD.
If your score is between 4–10 you have a moderate risk and should consider annual screening after age fifty.
If your score is greater than 10, consider annual screening after age forty.

To keep your brain healthy it is critical to eliminate as many of the above risk factors as possible. Here are some very specific strategies.

Risk: Family member with AD or other form of dementia.
Reduce: Be serious. Having AD or dementia in your family doesn't mean you will get it. It means you are at greater risk of getting it. For my patients with AD or dementia in their families I recommend early screening, around the age of forty, with WebNeuro. If your results point to any problems, then consider functional imaging such as SPECT.

Risk: Single head injury with loss of consciousness or multiple ones without a loss of consciousness for more than a few minutes.
Reduce: Prevent further head injuries: Doing all you can to avoid traumatic brain injuries (concussions) should be obvious, but unfortunately, it isn't. Many parents allow their children to do way too many things that are potentially damaging for them, which can then ruin their lives.

One of my close friends, Jeff, had a thirteen-year-old boy who really wanted to play football. "What should I tell him? I was going to help him find a coach to guide him," he asked.

"How about no," I said.

"But he really wants to play," Jeff replied.

"What if he said he really wanted to do cocaine? Would you help him find a drug dealer?" I replied.

"No, of course not," Jeff said, a little irritated.

"Why? What if he really wanted to do it? In my experience, the damage from football is about the same," I said. "A parent's job is to be your child's prefrontal cortex until his or hers develops, which is much later than most anyone thought, typically twenty-five in females and twenty-seven or twenty-eight in males."

Risk: Heavy alcohol use, drug dependence, or smoking in the past or present. Face it, alcohol is not a health food. According to a study from Johns Hopkins, people who drink every day have smaller brains (220), and when it comes to the brain, size matters. Another important lesson we've learned is that heavy alcohol, marijuana, and tobacco use lower blood flow to the brain and make it harder to think over time.

Reduce: If needed, get treatment to stop any addictions. I recommend that my patients completely stop the use of pot and cigarettes, and have no more than two normal-size alcoholic drinks twice a week.

Most carbohydrates have four calories per gram; alcohol has seven and no nutritional value. Alcohol is listed as the seventh leading preventable cause of death. It is associated with a fatty liver, damaged neurons, and lowered blood flow to the cerebellum, which is associated with physical and thought coordination. Alcohol interferes with the absorption of vitamin B1. It disinhibits you, which is why you say and do stupid things when intoxicated. It also causes sleep disturbances and stimulates your appetite. Alcohol affects your pancreas and causes hypoglycemia (remember the voodoo doll study—you don't want your spouse to become hypoglycemic) (221). If you want a better brain, less is more with all of these substances.

Risk: Major depression or ADD in the past or present. Both of these issues are typically associated with low blood flow to the brain. Some people think late-life depression can be a precursor to Alzheimer's disease (206). Untreated ADD is associated with many other listed risk factors, such as TBI

(222), obesity (223), depression (224), alcohol and drug abuse (225), and smoking (226).

Reduce: Get treatment. Start prevention strategies as early as you can. Treatment does not necessarily mean medicine. In head-to-head studies, exercise, taking fish oil, and learning not to believe every stupid thought you have were shown to effectively help depression. Obviously, it is also critical to know your brain type.

Risk: Eating the Standard American Diet (SAD). The SAD, filled with sugar, processed foods, high omega-6 fatty acids, excessive calories, and trans fats, is associated with dementia, depression, ADD, and obesity.

Reduce: Having brain-healthy nutrition is absolutely critical. See chapter 20 for more on how you can change your diet.

Risk: Being overweight or obese.

Reduce: Get to a healthy weight, without fad or quick-fix diets. Follow all twelve steps, especially the physical exercise advice in this chapter and the nutrition advice in the next.

Risk: Stroke, heart disease, high cholesterol, prehypertension or hypertension, prediabetes or diabetes, history of cancer treatment, seizures, Parkinson's, or sleep apnea in past or present.

Reduce: Get treatment and start prevention strategies early. An anti-inflammatory, nutrient-rich diet, and exercise regimen are the mainstays of prevention for vascular and blood sugar issues. As far as sleep apnea, it is critical to have it evaluated and treated. Too often, it goes undiagnosed (symptoms include snoring, periods of apnea or breath holding during sleep, and chronic daytime tiredness). Even when diagnosed, many people have trouble getting used to the CPAP machine and simply stop using it, which is a huge mistake. Your brain is the most energy-hungry organ in the body and any oxygen deprivation can damage it. We see that untreated sleep apnea actually looks like early Alzheimer's disease on SPECT scans. Be serious about getting it diagnosed and treated.

Risk: Less than a high school education or a job that does not require new learning.
Reduce: Engage in lifelong learning, starting now, and follow the advice in Step 5 below.

Risk: Limited or no exercise (less than twice a week or less than thirty minutes per session).
Reduce: See Step 6 below.

Risk: Periodontal disease. This causes inflammation and alterations in your gut flora, which puts you at risk for immune system problems.
Reduce: Floss regularly, see your dentist, and take dental health seriously.

Risk: Chronic inflammation. This is now considered to be a major cause of many diseases of aging, including cancer (227), diabetes (228), heart disease (229), and Alzheimer's (217). Inflammation is promoted by free radical formation, smoking, low levels of vitamin D or omega-3s, high levels of omega-6s, diets high in meat and/or sugar, diabetes, long-term infections, gum disease, and stress.
Reduce: Anti-inflammatory diet (low glycemic, high fiber, omega-3s rich) and nutrients, such as fish oil, curcumin, and vitamin D.

Risk: Estrogen or testosterone deficiency.
Reduce: Natural strategies to boost these hormones and replacement therapy if needed. Engaging in regular brain-healthy habits will help boost both estrogen and testosterone naturally, especially:

- stress management (the stress hormone cortisol steals the building blocks for estrogen and testosterone)
- decreasing sugar, which raises insulin levels and decreases sex hormone production
- getting adequate sleep
- adequate amounts of vitamin D (sunshine) and zinc (oysters, crab, dark meat poultry, beef)

- strength and interval training, and losing your belly (belly fat turns healthy testosterone into unhealthy forms of estrogen).

Risk: Increasing age.

Reduce: Be serious about brain health by using the risk reduction strategies listed here along with regular screening. I turned sixty-one this year. After looking at thousands of seniors' brains, I know that I am in a war for the health of my brain. But I have seen many healthy ninety-two-year-old brains and I'm planning for mine to be one of them.

Know better, do better. I say this a lot. If you have any of these risk factors, now is the time to get very serious about your brain health so that you can remain vibrant and cognitively sharp for as long as possible—and not end up as a burden to your family.

Step #4: Follow the Brain Warrior Diet

See chapter 20 for advice on how to eat a brain-healthy diet.

Step #5: Work Your Brain

Be a lifelong learner. The more you use your brain, the more you can continue using it. New learning creates new connections in the brain, but the absence of learning causes the brain to start disconnecting itself. No matter what your age, mental exercise has a global, positive effect on the brain. Learning has a very real effect on neurons: it keeps them firing and it makes it easier for them to fire. There are approximately a thousand trillion synapses in the brain, and each one of them may wither and die if not actively firing. Like muscles that don't get used, idle nerve cells waste away.

Community-dwelling seniors who took just a few weeks of cognitive training experienced significantly improved reasoning and speed of processing skills, as well as better activities of daily living ten years later, compared with those who didn't get such training (230).

The best mental exercise is acquiring new knowledge and doing things that you have not done before. Even if your routine activities are fairly complicated, such as teaching a college course, reading brain scans, or fixing a crashed computer network, they won't help your brain specifically because they aren't new. Whenever the brain does something over and over, it learns how to do it using less and less energy. New learning, such as learning a new medical technique, a new hobby, or a new game helps establish new connections, thus maintaining and improving the function of other less often used brain areas.

Likewise, just doing crossword puzzles or sudoku is not going to give you the full benefit you want. Just doing crossword puzzles is like going to the gym, doing right bicep curls, and then leaving. Here are some ideas for exercising various parts of the brain:

Prefrontal cortex—language games, such as Scrabble, Boggle, Words with Friends, and crossword puzzles; strategy games, such as chess, Rail Baron, Axis, and Blokus; meditation

Temporal lobes—memory games, learning to play new instruments (also involves PFC and cerebellum)

Parietal lobes—math games like sudoku, juggling (also involves PFC and cerebellum), map reading

Cerebellum—coordination games, like table tennis (also involves PFC), dancing (learn new dance steps), yoga, tai chi

New-Learning Tips

Spend 15 minutes a day learning something new. Einstein said that if anyone spends 15 minutes a day learning something new, in a year he will be an expert; in 5 years a national expert.

Take an online course (we offer courses at www.amenclinics.com).

Cross-train at work. Learn someone else's job. Perhaps you can even look into switching jobs for several weeks. This benefits the business and employees alike, as both workers will develop new skills and better brain function.

Break the routines of your life to stimulate new parts of your brain. Do the opposite of what feels natural to activate the other side of your brain and gain access to both hemispheres. Write with your other hand, shoot basketballs with both hands, hit baseballs left-handed (if you are right-handed), play table tennis with the opposite hand, use the computer mouse with your other hand—make your brain feel uncomfortable.

Mental exercise is as important to your brain as diet and physical exercise is.

Step #6: Move to Think

Physical exercise is the fountain of youth; it's critical to keeping your brain vibrant and young. If you want to attack Alzheimer's, depression, obesity, and aging all at once, move every day. Research has shown that cognitive abilities are best in those who exercise (231–234). Exercise improves the flow of oxygen, blood, and nutrients to the brain and protects the brain against things that hurt it, such as high sugar levels. It reduces stress, improves your mood, and lowers your blood pressure and blood sugar levels. Exercise decreases inflammation, fat cells, weight, and frailty, while at the same time increases metabolism, longevity, bone density, and an overall sense of well-being. Research has also shown that regular exercise helps to turn off the obesity gene (235), positively impacts those at risk for Alzheimer's disease with the Apo E4 gene (236, 237), and has also been shown to reduce cravings. One study even found that exercise helps people choose better foods, seek out more social support, and improves sleep (238).

Best Exercises for Your Brain

I like to keep it simple: four types of exercise are great for your brain: bursting or interval training, strength training, coordination exercises, and mindful exercise (239). Of course, you should check with your physician before starting any new exercise routines.

Burst training involves sixty-second bursts at go-for-broke intensity followed by a few minutes of lower-intensity exertion. I recommend you take a thirty-minute walk every day. During the walk take four or five one-minute periods to "burst" (walking or running as fast as you can), then go back to walking. A 2006 study from researchers at the University of Guelph in Canada found that doing high-intensity burst training burns fat faster than continuous moderately intensive activities. Short-burst training helps raise endorphins, lift your mood, and make you feel more energized.

Strengthen your brain with strength training. The stronger you are as you age, the less likely you are to get Alzheimer's disease. Canadian researchers found that resistance training plays a role in preventing cognitive decline (240). It also helps with weight loss and losing belly fat (241). I recommend two thirty- to forty-five-minute weight lifting sessions a week—one for the lower body (abs, lower back, and legs), the other for the upper body (arms, upper back, and chest). A 2010 study from researchers at the University of Rhode Island compared body composition changes between two groups of dieters (242). Both groups followed the same nutrition plan, but one group did moderate intensity resistance training while the other group did not. At the end of the ten-week trial, the group that participated in resistance training lost nine pounds of body fat compared with less than half a pound for the diet-only group. Plus, the resistance training group's thighs got thinner while the other group's thighs remained the same size.

Boost your brain with coordination activities. Doing coordination activities—like dancing, tennis, or table tennis (the world's best brain sport)—boosts the activity in the cerebellum. While the cerebellum is only 10 percent of the brain's volume, it contains 50 percent of the brain's neurons. It's involved with both physical and thought coordination. A fascinating brain imaging study from Japan found that just ten minutes of table tennis increases activity in the PFC and cerebellum. It's like aerobic chess.

Calm and focus your mind with mindful exercise. Yoga, tai chi, and other mindful exercises have been found to reduce anxiety and depression and increase focus (243–246).

Best Exercises for Your Brain Type

Which exercises are best for your individual brain type? In addition to the general suggestions for all types above, see specific recommendations below.

Overfocused or compulsive types (high ACG activity): Aerobic exercise boosts serotonin in the brain to help you get unstuck when you can't stop thinking about pepperoni pizza, potato chips, or checking your phone. Be sure to vary your workout each time. This will help you learn to be less rigid. When you get stuck on thoughts, get up and move! One study found that as little as five minutes of exercise could help curb cravings (247).

Impulsive types (low PFC activity): Aerobic exercise helps increase blood flow and dopamine in the brain to boost the PFC and improve impulse control. Impulsive types need lots of exercise. At least thirty minutes every day is best, but make sure it is in an activity you love. If you don't love it, you probably won't keep it up. Yoga that includes meditation will sharpen your focus and strengthen your PFC so you can make better decisions and reduce impulsivity.

Limbic or sad types (high limbic activity): Try aerobic coordination activities that are social activities, like dancing. Or join a local tennis club or basketball team. The aerobic activity boosts blood flow and multiple neurotransmitters in the brain. The social-bonding aspect of the activity can help calm hyperactivity in the limbic system and enhance your mood.

Anxious types (high basal ganglia activity): In addition to aerobic coordination workouts, try practicing yoga or tai chi for relaxation. Relaxation exercises can soothe overactive basal ganglia to reduce anxiety.

Step #7: Soothe Your Stress

As we've seen, stress raises cortisol, which can damage cells in your brain, steal your memory, and make you fat. Having a regular stress-management program is critical to keeping your brain healthy for the long run. Without it, you are more likely to treat your anxious and uncomfortable feelings with drugs, alcohol, or poor-quality, addictive food. See chapter 9 for a comprehensive stress-management program.

Step #8: Boost Blood Flow

Blood flow is essential to life. Blood brings nutrients to your cells and takes away toxins. New research suggests that brain cells do not age as fast as we thought. Rather, it is the blood vessels that feed them that age (248).

If you want to keep your brain healthy, it is critical to protect your blood flow. Since the brain uses 20 percent of the blood flow in your body, I used to say, "Whatever is good for your heart is good for your brain, and whatever is bad for your heart is also bad for your brain." In 2007, when I wrote *The Brain in Love*, I realized I was missing a very important part of the puzzle. Now I say, "Whatever is good for your heart is good for your brain is good for your genitals. And, whatever is bad for your heart is bad for your brain is bad for your genitals. It is all about blood flow." As erectile dysfunction is skyrocketing (just turn on the television and you'll be bombarded with commercials for Viagra, Levitra, and Cialis), so are brain problems. According to the Massachusetts Male Aging Study, 40 percent of forty-year-old men have erectile dysfunction, which means 40 percent of forty-year-old men also have brain dysfunction. With age, the rate increases to a frightening level. The same study reported that 70 percent of seventy-year-old men had erectile dysfunction, which means that 70 percent of seventy-year-old men likely also have brain dysfunction (249).

In this context, blood flow envy (the new way to think of penis envy) seems very appropriate. To keep your brain healthy it is critical to focus on strengthening vascular health. To do this takes three strategies:

1. Blood flow envy—you have to care about your blood vessels.
2. Avoid things that hurt your blood vessels, such as stress, caffeine, and nicotine (both constrict blood flow to the brain and other organs), and take measures to reduce your risk of coronary artery disease, heart arrhythmias, prediabetes and diabetes, prehypertension and hypertension, poor sleep, sleep apnea, and drug and alcohol abuse.

3. Do things that promote vascular health, such as stress management, the Brain Warrior Diet, drinking plenty of water, practicing great sleep habits, and taking gingko biloba and omega-3 fatty acids.

Step #9: Decrease Inflammation

Inflammation, from the Latin word *inflamma*, meaning fire, is associated with many illnesses, including depression and dementia. Just as poor blood flow is devastating to brain function, so is chronic inflammation in your body. Acute inflammation is an immune response by our white blood cells to trauma, infections, or toxins where your tissue becomes red, swollen, hard, hot, and painful. It's the body's attempt at self-protection to remove the outside invaders and promote healing. Think about what happens in your body when you stub your toe or cut your arm. However, when inflammation becomes chronic, because of a poor diet, obesity, allergens (such as dairy or gluten in sensitive people), infections, repetitive trauma, environmental toxic exposure, or sleep deprivation, it is associated with the development of cancer, heart disease, arthritis, and diabetes, and can devastate your brain. C-reactive protein is a good way to measure chronic inflammation.

To decrease inflammation, follow the Brain Warrior Diet, making sure you get plenty of omega-3 fatty acids from fish, nuts, cooked broccoli, and avocados. Green tea and cocoa can be helpful, as can certain spices such as curcumin, rosemary, and garlic. Taking care of your gums and avoiding periodontal disease is also critical to decreasing inflammation.

Step #10: Supplement Your Success

Many physicians say that if you eat a balanced diet you do not need supplements. I agree with what Dr. Mark Hyman wrote in his book *The Ultra-Mind Solution: Fix Your Broken Brain by Healing Your Body First:* "If people eat wild, fresh, organic, local, non–genetically modified food grown in virgin mineral- and nutrient-rich soils that has not been transported across vast distances and stored for months before being eaten . . . and work and live outside, breathe only fresh unpolluted air, drink only pure, clean water, sleep nine hours a night, move their bodies every day, and are free from chronic stressors and exposure to environmental toxins, then it is possible that they might not need supplements. Because we live in a fast-paced society where we pick up food on the fly, skip meals, eat sugar-laden treats, buy processed foods, and eat foods that have been chemically treated, we could all use a little help from a multiple vitamin/mineral supplement"(250).

Natural supplements have advantages and disadvantages. They are often effective when targeted properly, usually have dramatically fewer side effects than most prescription medications, and they are significantly less expensive. Plus, you never have to tell an insurance company that you've taken them. As awful as it sounds, taking prescription medications can affect your insurability. I know many people who have been denied or made to pay higher rates for life, long-term, and disability insurance because they have taken certain medications. Natural alternatives are worth considering for many reasons.

Yet, natural supplements also have their own set of problems. Even though they tend to be less expensive than medications in general, they may be more expensive for you because they are usually not covered by insurance. Many people are also unaware that natural supplements can have side effects and need to be thoughtfully used. Just because something is natural does not mean it is innocuous. Both arsenic and cyanide are natural, but that doesn't mean they are good for you. One of the major concerns about natural supplements is the lack of quality control. There is variability and you need to find brands you can trust. Another disadvantage is that many people get their advice about supplements from the clerks at the health food store who may not have the best information. But, even when weighing the problems, the benefits of natural supplements make them worth considering, especially if you can get thoughtful, research-based information. Of course, talk about them with your health-care professional. If he or she doesn't know much about them, which is common, talk to a naturopath or integrative medicine physician.

In the Amen Clinics supplement program we support brain health through multiple mechanisms.

Anti-inflammatory—omega-3 fatty acids
Vitamins—B6, B12, folate (methyltetrahydrofolate), C, D

Blood flow—gingko biloba and omega-3 fatty acids
Acetylcholine (neurotransmitter involved with learning and
    memory)—huperzine A, choline and acetyl-l-carnitine
Antioxidant—N-acetyl-cysteine (NAC)
Blood sugar stabilization—alpha lipoic acid
Energy—acetyl-l-carnitine, CoQ10
Nerve cell membrane fluidity—phosphatidylserine (PS)

You can find products with these ingredients formulated by my team at our website www.brainmdhealth.com.

Step #11: Break Through Your Barriers

In order to be an effective brain warrior you have to be prepared for the inevitable roadblocks and setbacks that will come your way. It is critical to identify your most vulnerable moments and have a plan to overcome them.

I often go to the whiteboard in my office and draw the following diagram.

Image 19.1: Change Occurs in Stages

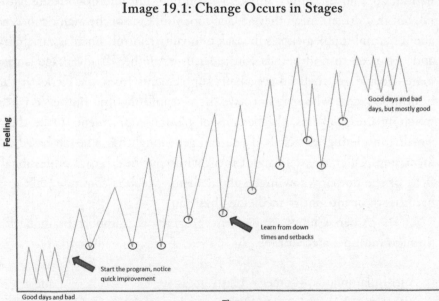

When people come to see me they usually are not doing very well. Over time, if they work the plan we develop, they get better. But no one gets better in a straight line. They get better, then there is a setback, then they get better still, then there may be a setback, then they continue to improve. Over time, they reach a new steady state where they are consistently better. The setbacks are critically important, because if we pay attention to them, they can be the best teachers.

Do you learn from your failures or ignore them? New brain-imaging research suggests that when some people fail their *motivation* centers become more active, making it more likely they will be able to learn from their experience. When others fail the brain's *pain* centers become more active—it literally hurts—making it more likely they will do whatever they can to avoid thinking about the episode, which means they are more likely to repeat the mistake. Learn from your mistakes and use them as a stepping stone to success.

Also, who you spend time with matters. Bad (and good) habits are a team sport. Ask family, friends, or mentors to help you by supporting your positive behaviors. Adding healthy friends improves your chances for success up to 40 percent. Spend less time around accomplices, or people who encourage your negative behaviors. If you want to change your brain, you need to develop a support group of healthy people. Many accomplices can change into friends if you have crucial conversations with them. Explain what these people can start doing to help you, and what they can stop doing, and what they can continue doing.

IMPROVE YOUR DECISIONS

Consistently making great decisions is not hard if you put your brain in a position to help you make them. In order to boost the quality of your decisions, here are the most important strategies:

Start with clear focus. Know your goals and look at them every day.
Make decisions about your brain health ahead of time. It is good to have a few simple rules, such as no bread or drinking alcohol at restaurants before meals, as they both lower prefrontal cortex function and have a negative impact on decisions.

Eat breakfasts with some high-quality protein to balance your blood sugar levels daily. Low blood sugar is associated with lower overall blood flow to the brain. Continue to eat small amounts throughout the day to maintain your blood sugar levels.

Eliminate sugar and artificial sweeteners. These often trigger cravings and poor decisions.

Get at least seven hours of sleep at night. Less than that is associated with lower blood flow to the brain.

Don't put yourself in vulnerable situations. Think ahead. If you know you are going to a party that is likely to serve unhealthy food, eat before you go so you won't feel hungry and lose control. My wife often brings food with her to gatherings, just to have something in case of emergency low blood sugar.

Step #12: Keep Motivation Top of Mind

In order for you to consistently make the right decisions regarding your brain you must have a burning desire to get it healthy, but more important, you have to know *why* you care about it. Write down at least five important reasons to get healthy, such as: I want to live longer, look younger, feel happier, feel calmer and more relaxed, make better decisions, have better energy, increase my mental clarity, be a better role model for my children, have a better relationship with my spouse, reverse diabetes, heart disease, or other health risks, and decrease my risk for Alzheimer's disease and other diseases of aging. Once you write these down, post them where you can see them every day. Knowing your motivation is essential to wanting to do the right things for your brain.

The Fork in the Road

One of my favorite motivational exercises with my patients is called the Fork in the Road. Here, I want you to vividly imagine a fork in the road with two paths. To the left, imagine a future of pain. If you don't care about your brain and just keep doing what you've always done, what will your life be like in a year . . . in five years . . . in ten years . . . in thirty or even fifty years? I want you to imagine your brain continuing to get old and all that goes with that . . . brain fog, tiredness, depression, memory loss, and physical illness. To the right, imagine a future of health. If you care about your brain and do the exercises I recommend, what will your life be like in a few days, in a year . . . in five years . . . in ten years? I want you to imagine your brain getting healthier and younger and all that goes with that . . . mental clarity, better energy, a brighter mood, great memory, a trimmer and healthier body, healthier skin, and a younger brain. Ultimately, with this knowledge you get to choose.

Anchor Images

Fifty percent of the brain is dedicated to vision. Having visual cues and reminders about brain envy is a very effective tool to help you stay on track. I have pictures of my wife, my four children, and my four grandchildren everywhere to remind me why I need and want a great brain. Plus I have special "anchor" images that remind me in an instant why I want a better brain.

My granddaughter Emmy is my primary anchor image. As I write this, she is four years old. Emmy has a very rare genetic deletion syndrome,

Images 19.2 and 19.3: My Anchor Images of Emmy

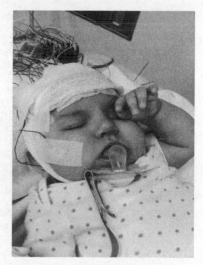

which causes seizures and developmental delay. When her seizures first started, she had 160 a day. I know that I need to be here and be healthy to help Emmy and my daughter Breanne for as long as I can. If I am not healthy, I will never be my best for the people who need me. I never want to be a burden to my children. I want to be the leader of my family, but the only way that is possible is if I have a good brain. I post my anchor images where I can see them every day to remind me why I need to stay healthy. I suggest you do the same.

Putting It All Together: The Amen Clinics NFL Brain Rehabilitation Study

In July 2007, former professional football player Anthony Davis came to see me at the Amen Clinics. He had heard about our work and thought perhaps we could help him. Anthony's fifty-four-year-old brain looked like it was eighty-five. It showed clear evidence of brain trauma to the prefrontal cortex and left temporal lobe. He was also concerned about the cognitive problems he saw in other retired football players. Anthony is a College Football Hall

Image 19.4: Anthony Davis

of Fame running back from the University of Southern California. He is called the "Notre Dame Killer," because in 1972 he scored six touchdowns against the University of Notre Dame. The students at Notre Dame hated Anthony so much that they put his picture on the walkways of the campus so they could walk all over him. In 1974, he scored four more touchdowns against Notre Dame. I put Anthony on the steps discussed in this chapter and within several months he told me that he felt better, more focused, and had better energy and memory.

Through my relationship with Anthony, I met many other active and retired NFL players. Meeting Anthony was also the impetus for our large-scale study of brain injury and brain rehabilitation in professional football players. At the time, the NFL was still saying they did not know if playing football caused long-term brain damage, but had never done any brain-imaging studies on humans to prove it or not. My colleagues and I decided to tackle it. To date, we have scanned and treated more than two hundred active and retired players. Clear evidence of brain damage was seen in almost all of them. The most exciting part of our study was that 80 percent of our players showed significant improvement on their SPECT scans and their neuropsychological testing on our program.

Roy

Roy Williams came to see us at age seventy-three. He is part of a three-generational NFL family. He played for the San Francisco 49ers. His son Eric played for the Dallas Cowboys and his grandson Kyle played for the Seattle Seahawks. Roy's cognitive testing scores for attention, reasoning, and memory were in the normal range, but he was significantly overweight at 334 pounds, which was too much for his six-foot-seven frame. Plus, his brain SPECT scan was not healthy and showed overall decreased activity.

When I told Roy about the research studies that say as your weight goes up the size of your brain goes down, I got his attention. When I added that brain shrinkage is associated with aging, he got the picture and said he wanted to do whatever it took to get a younger brain. Roy runs a highly successful business that helps families transition their wealth to the next generation—so he was not too keen on having a smaller, older brain.

Roy eliminated his bad brain habits and adopted a host of new ones. When he came back for retesting a few months later, he had lost thirty pounds, but more astounding was the fact that his attention, memory, and reasoning scores had improved. His brain was getting younger! Plus, his wife says he had the energy of a forty-year-old, which initially really irritated her. Over time our program ideas rubbed off on her and she has lost weight too.

Marvin

Marvin Fleming is another example of how a severely damaged brain can recover. Marvin is the first player in NFL history to play in five Super Bowls. He played tight end for twelve years for the Green Bay Packers and then the Miami Dolphins, including the Dolphins' perfect season in 1972. He was sixty-seven when he first came to see us and his brain was in trouble. Marvin is one of the nicest people we have had the privilege of helping. He is funny, caring, and always looking for ways to improve himself.

When I asked him if he ever had a brain injury he said no. I thought to myself, "You played tight end for twelve seasons in the NFL, how could you *not* have had a brain injury?" So I pressed him. Marvin seemed so proud of himself because he did not remember ever getting his bell rung, being unconscious, seeing stars, or being confused on the football field—like almost all of our players. But I persisted. I had seen his brain and it showed clear evidence of brain injury. I asked about other potential causes of injuries from childhood, adolescence, and outside of football, such as from motor vehicle accidents, falls, or fights. He persisted in saying no. I have been doing this a long time and had seen thousands of scans like Marvin's and knew better.

"Okay, Marvin, last time, then I will leave you alone, you are telling me you do not *ever* remember a car accident, fight, or fall, or a time when you played football where you hit your head so hard it caused changes in your awareness or thought process?"

What happened next in my office is so common it is a running joke at the Amen Clinics. Ask patients ten times whether or not they had a brain injury and those who initially say no, with brain trauma evidence on scans, may actually end up remembering multiple occasions where they lost consciousness or were in severe car accidents. Our research director, Kristen Willeumier, PhD, was in the interview with Marvin and gave me a knowing look.

Marvin's face changed. The right hemisphere of his brain had an "aha" memory experience and it was all over his face. "I am so sorry I lied to you, Dr. Amen. When I was in college at the University of Utah we were driving from Utah to California in the snow and our car skidded off a mountain road and we fell a hundred and fifty feet to a riverbed below. I was knocked unconscious and my friends had to drag me out of the car so I wouldn't drown."

I wondered how one could forget such an emotionally powerful event. But I have seen it happen so many times in my work. Take all the head hits he had given and received in football, plus the car accident and whatever else he did not remember; no wonder his brain was in trouble.

Images 19.5 and 19.6: Marvin Before and After

Damage to PFC and   *Marked improvement*
temporal lobes

All of our players also undergo extensive cognitive testing. Marvin's general cognitive testing was not good. What Marvin had going for him was a great personality and a willingness to do the things Dr. Willeumier and I asked. We asked Marvin to lose weight (he was a sugar addict who ate frosting right out of the can). We also gave him supplements that worked through multiple mechanisms, hyperbaric oxygen therapy to boost oxygen to his brain, and had him increase his exercise. Two years later, his brain looks dramatically younger (as does he), he has lost twenty pounds, and his cognitive scores have improved by as much as 300 percent.

Typically, the brain becomes less active and less efficient with age. Marvin's brain, like many of the retired NFL players in our study, became more active and more efficient.

Fred

We have dozens of great testimonials and e-mails from our players. One of my favorite ones came from Fred Dryer, the famous Los Angeles Ram defensive tight end who later became an actor and television star of the popular show *Hunter*.

> With the program, supplements, and certainly with the neurofeedback sessions themselves, I have replaced a part of me that over time had slowly slipped away. It is very odd to describe the feeling but it is while going through the program, I noticed mental energy and "speed" of thought and cognition that I "recognized" I had lost!
>
> Playing a contact sport for so many years did so much cumulative damage it actually mesmerized me into not noticing the slow progression of brain function loss. It was only when I began to "feed" my brain with the supplements and at the same time go through the neurofeedback sessions that I began to notice just how far my brain function had slipped. I wish I had knowledge of this science-technology while I was playing professional football. It would have helped prevent all of what had been lost over the years.

Soldiers Too

While deployed in Afghanistan in 2008 Captain Patrick Caffrey, a combat engineer officer, was in the middle of phasing in new, specially armored vehicles. These are the vehicles all of our troops ride in today. "We knew one thing about them," he said. "They could take an enormous blast and you'd be able to walk away unscathed—or so we thought."

One of the many tasks of the Second Battalion, Seventh Marines' (2/7)

Combat Engineer Platoon was to conduct route clearance—the intense mission of taking mine detectors and other special detection equipment on roads laden with mines and improvised explosive devices (IEDs). Captain Caffrey's mission was to find and clear them from the road so that logistics, convoys, and the infantry could move freely.

At the time, he did not know a thing about traumatic brain injuries (TBIs), despite having had five or six concussions in his life from sports and other injuries. In his ignorance he said to one of his sergeants, "So, am I screwed up because I kinda *want* to get blown up? I mean, not get hurt, just blown up then walk away?" The sergeant said he had the same thought on his own—must be a marine thing. Little did they know that they'd be together in the same vehicle for more than one blast. This redefines the saying *Be careful what you wish for.*

Before he left Afghanistan, Captain Caffrey survived three blasts that caused concussions. But he thought he felt okay. After all, he reasoned, many others were much worse off than he was. However, his personality began to change. He became prone to angry outbursts, a new thing for him. Upon arriving home, the changes became more pronounced. In Patrick's words, "I was more irritable than ever, I had intense headaches, trouble focusing and concentrating (particularly listening to what people were saying), trouble with memory, and an inability to sleep. I was rude and nasty to people, and the worst part was that I didn't really know just how much I had changed."

Patrick decided to have SPECT imaging at Amen Clinics. "Boy, did I underestimate the value of actually looking at the brain when you have a brain problem!" Patrick said. We saw the damage to his right temporal lobe, which explained his behavioral and cognitive changes, headaches, decrease in ability to focus and concentrate, and memory issues. We also targeted our rehabilitation program to his specific brain issues. He said, "I felt a dramatic difference right away. I felt more mentally sharp and focused than ever."

What All This Means for You!

So why should you care about the brains of these retired gladiators? If we can improve the brains of retired NFL players who have had tens of thousands of hits to their heads and soldiers exposed to violent blasts, imagine the benefit you can get with a brain-healthy program, even if you have been bad to your brain. Becoming a brain warrior can literally slow down—and in some cases reverse—the aging process.

We have seen people improve from brain damage, infection, strokes, oxygen deprivation, substance abuse, and toxic exposure. SPECT scans give us a sense of how much reserve the brain has and how much improvement is possible.

20

The Brain Warrior Diet

Eat Right to Think Right

Your brain uses 20 to 30 percent of the calories you consume. It is the most expensive real estate in your body. Because of this, one of the most important things you can do for your brain and personal health is to get your nutrition right. There is simply no way around it. You can exercise all you want, think all the right thoughts, meditate, and take dietary supplements, but if you continue to eat highly processed foods laden with sugar, bad fats, and salt, and made from ingredients grown with pesticides, flavored with artificial sweeteners, colored with artificial dyes, and treated with artificial preservatives, there is just no way to keep your brain and body working at their peak. If your food is not the best, you will never be your best. This chapter is about helping you make the best choices to serve your body and brain.

If you start making better food choices today you will quickly notice that you have more energy, better focus, a better memory, better moods, and even a flatter tummy. A number of new studies (251, 252) have reported that a healthy diet is associated with significantly lower risks of Alzheimer's disease and depression. Plus, what really surprises most people is that when they decide to get healthy, their food options get better, not worse. It is the start of a wonderful relationship with food.

When it comes to food, so many people are like how I used to be . . . a yo-yo. Crave bad food . . . overeat it . . . feel lousy . . . and hate yourself in the process. It is way too much drama. When you decide to get healthy and get control of your food you will eat better than ever and it will affect everything in your life in a positive way. In my experience, when you get your diet right, it also has the potential to carry over to help other people in your family, community, place of worship, and workplace. I have seen this happen repeatedly in my own practice and in my work with corporations and churches.

My wife, Tana, has written several amazing cookbooks to help support our patients and readers in their efforts to get healthy, and of course, I get to try everything first. I love her breakfast protein smoothies, lentil soup, rack of lamb, and turkey Bolognese. I feel smarter when I eat fresh wild salmon, and I can't get enough of Tana's stuffed red bell peppers. I don't want fast or poor-quality food anymore because it makes me feel tired and stupid. I want the foods that help me stay sharp, and I want that for you too. Contrary to what most people think, eating in a brain-healthy way is not more expensive; it is less expensive. Your medical bills will be lower and your productivity will go way up. And what price can you put on feeling amazing?

Your mind-set here is critical. Ultimately, eating right is not about deprivation, it is about abundance. You will realize that giving in to bad food cravings is indeed sabotaging your health and is definitely not the sign of a rational mind.

A BIO/PSYCHO/SOCIAL/SPIRITUAL APPROACH TO FEEDING YOUR BRAIN

In this chapter I am going to give you a four-circles approach to feeding your brain.

- Biological
  - Nine rules of brain-healthy eating
  - Fifty-two best brain-healthy superfoods
  - How to manipulate your mind with food
  - Foods to boost mood, focus, motivation, and memory
  - How to heal your gut to boost your brain
- Psychological
  - Ways to make your thoughts around food helpful, instead of hurtful
  - How to break hurtful psychological food patterns from the past

- Social
  - The health of the people with whom you eat significantly influences your longevity
- Spiritual
  - Honoring your food
  - Respecting and replenishing food sources for generations to come

BIOLOGICAL

THE AMEN CLINICS 9 RULES OF BRAIN-HEALTHY EATING

If you are going to eat right to think right, it is critical to make sure your food is loaded with proper nutrients that your body is able to properly digest. Here are the nine rules we have refined over years of experience for our patients at Amen Clinics.

Rule #1: Think "high-quality" calories— and not too many of them.

If you have to choose between quality and quantity, go for the quality calories. The smartest strategy is to be both quality and quantity smart. One cinnamon roll can cost you 720 calories and will drain your brain, while a 400-calorie salad made of spinach, salmon, organic blueberries, apples, walnuts, and red bell peppers with oil and vinegar dressing will supercharge your energy and make you smarter.

I think of calories like money, and I hate wasting money. If you have a high metabolism, like having a lot of money, you don't have to worry much about calories. If you have a low metabolism, like me, which gets worse as we grow older, you have to be very wise in how you spend your calories.

The research about calories is clear: if you eat more calories than you need you'll be fatter, sicker, and less productive. In one study, researchers followed a large group of rhesus monkeys for twenty years. One group ate all the food they wanted; the other group ate 30 percent less. The monkeys who ate as much as they wanted were three times more likely to suffer from cancer, heart disease, and diabetes, plus researchers saw significant shrinkage in the important decision-making areas of their brains. In addition, the calorie-restricted monkeys had smoother skin and healthier fur (253).

Making smart calorie decisions helps you control weight and decreases your risk for heart disease, cancer, and stroke from obesity (a major risk factor for all these illnesses). Even better, calorie restriction triggers certain mechanisms in the body to increase the production of nerve growth factors, which are beneficial to the brain (254).

> *To get the most out of your food, think CROND (Calorie Restriction, Optimally Nutritious, and Delicious). That means making sure that every calorie you consume counts.*

Counting calories is also one of the keys to lasting weight loss. While many diet programs today have discarded this concept, instead insisting that you need to eat a specific ratio of protein, carbohydrates, and fats in order to lose weight, a 2009 study in the *New England Journal of Medicine* found that calorie reduction—regardless of the percentage of fats, carbohydrates, or proteins in a diet—is what leads to weight loss (255). Conducted at the Harvard School of Public Health and Brigham and Women's Hospital, the study enlisted 811 overweight individuals and assigned them to one of the following four diets, all of which had caloric restriction:

1. 20 percent fat, 15 percent protein, 65 percent carbohydrates
2. 20 percent fat, 25 percent protein, 55 percent carbohydrates
3. 40 percent fat, 15 percent protein, 45 percent carbohydrates
4. 40 percent fat, 25 percent protein, 35 percent carbohydrates

At the conclusion of the two-year study, all four groups had achieved a similar weight loss of an average of nearly nine pounds. Regardless of the amount of fat, carbohydrates, or protein in their particular diet, the participants reported experiencing similar feelings of hunger and satiety. These findings reinforce the concept that calorie restriction is essential if you want to lose extra pounds.

If weight is an issue for you, it is a smart idea to know how many calories a day you need to either maintain or lose weight. The average active fifty-year-old woman needs about 1,800 calories a day. Keeping a food journal is an invaluable tool to help you stop lying to yourself and having calorie amnesia. Visit our online community (www.mybrainfitlife.com) for more resources. You'll also find information on how to cut your calories by 30 percent without feeling hungry.

Rule #2: Don't drink your calories.

Your brain is 80 percent water. Anything that dehydrates it, such as too much caffeine or alcohol, decreases your thinking and impairs your judgment. Make sure you drink eight glasses of water a day.

On a trip to New York City I saw a poster that read, "Are You Pouring on the Pounds? . . . Don't Drink Yourself Fat." I thought it was brilliant. A study found that on average Americans drink 450 calories a day, twice as many as we did thirty years ago (256). Most people tend to *not* count the calories they drink, but those extra 225 calories a day will put twenty-three pounds of fat on your body in a year. Did you know that some coffee drinks or some cocktails, such as margaritas, can cost you more than 700 calories? One very simple strategy that can help you lose a lot of weight is to eliminate any of the calories you drink.

My favorite drink is water mixed with a little lemon juice and a little bit of the natural sweetener stevia. It tastes like lemonade, so I feel like I'm spoiling myself . . . and it has virtually no calories. Many of my patients make spa water (water with a few cucumber slices, lemons, or strawberries in it) and really feel like they are spoiling themselves.

Rule #3: Eat clean protein.

Protein helps balance your blood sugar and provides the necessary building blocks for brain health. And it's critically important because it helps maintain lean muscle mass, which is a real issue as we age. As much as possible, make sure your protein sources and the rest of your food are clean, which means organic, hormone-free, antibiotic-free, free-range, and grass-fed. Always think about what was fed to the things you eat, because you are eating those things as well. Great sources of protein include eggs, fish (wild, not farmed), lamb, turkey or chicken, raw nuts, and high-protein vegetables such as broccoli and spinach. I use spinach instead of lettuce in my salads for a huge nutrition boost. Protein powders can also be a good source, but read the labels, because many companies put a lot of sugar and other unhealthy ingredients in their powders. It is important to start each day with protein to boost your focus and concentration skills. More on this in a bit.

Rule #4: Eat smart carbohydrates.

Carbs are divided into two categories: simple (which includes white breads, cake, etc.) and complex (whole plant foods, like green or starchy vegetables, fruits like blueberries and apples, etc.). Simple carbohydrates, which have a high glycemic index, cause your blood sugar to spike, while complex carbohydrates have a lower glycemic index, are digested more slowly, are generally accompanied by other nutrients, and are higher in fiber. Carbohydrates, per se, are not the enemy; they are essential to your life. But carbohydrates that have been stripped of any nutritional value *are* the enemy.

While simple sugars are created in the body from any type of carb, those that come from simple carbs generally don't have any nutritional value attached to them. Sugar, which is addictive, increases inflammation in your body, increases erratic brain cell firing, and has been implicated in aggression. In a new study, children who were given sugar every day had a significantly higher risk for violence later in life (257). I don't agree with the people who say, Everything in moderation. Cocaine, arsenic, or having affairs in moderation is not a good idea. The less sugar in your life, the better your life will be . . . period. I like the old saying *The whiter the bread, the faster you're dead.*

Get to know the glycemic index (GI). The glycemic index rates carbohydrates according to their effects on blood sugar. Foods are ranked on a scale from one to 100+ (glucose is 100), with the lowest glycemic foods at the smaller end of the scale. In general I like to stick to healthy foods that are under 60. Eating a diet that is filled with low-glycemic foods will lower your blood glucose levels, decrease cravings, and help with weight loss. The important concept to remember is that high blood sugar levels are bad for your blood vessels, your brain, and your waistline.

However, you'll want to be careful not to go only by the GI to choose your foods. Some foods that are low-glycemic aren't healthy for you, while others that rank higher on the scale are quite good for you. For example, peanut M&M's have a GI of 33, while steel-cut oatmeal has a GI of about 52. Does this mean that it's better for you to eat peanut M&M's? No! Peanut M&M's are loaded with saturated fat, artificial food coloring, and other things that are not brain-healthy. Steel-cut oatmeal is a high-fiber food that helps regulate your blood sugar for hours. Use your brain when choosing your food.

Similarly, some fruits like watermelon and pineapple have a high-GI ranking. While they are still healthy (and certainly better than M&M's), it's wise to consume more fruits from the low end of the spectrum. Some starches, like potatoes, and some high-fiber products, like whole wheat bread, are also on the high end of the list. My advice is to think of these foods as condiments—eat smaller portions and combine them with proteins and healthy fats to reduce their impact on blood sugar levels.

In general, vegetables, fruits, legumes, and nuts are the best low-GI options. A diet rich in whole, minimally processed low-GI foods not only helps you lose weight, it has also been found to help control diabetes, according to a 2011 review of the scientific literature in the *British Journal of Nutrition* (258).

Choose high-fiber carbohydrates. High-fiber foods are one of your best weight-loss and brain health weapons. Years of research have found that the more fiber you eat, the better for your health and weight. How does dietary fiber fight fat? First, it helps regulate the appetite hormone ghrelin, which tells your brain that you are hungry. Ghrelin levels are often out of balance in people with a high BMI, so you always feel hungry, no matter how much you eat. New research shows that high ghrelin levels not only make you feel hungrier, they also increase the desire for high-calorie foods compared with low-calorie fare, so it's a double whammy. But fiber can help. A 2009 study showed that eating a diet high in fiber helped balance ghrelin levels in overweight and obese people (259). This can turn off the constant hunger and reduce the appeal of high-calorie foods. Second, no matter how much you weigh, eating fiber-rich foods helps you feel full longer so you don't get the munchies an hour after you eat. Third, fiber slows the absorption of food into the bloodstream, which helps balance your blood sugar. This can help you make better food choices and fight cravings later in the day. In fact, fiber takes so long to be digested by your body, a person eating a diet that provides 20 to 35 grams of fiber a day will burn an extra 150 calories a day, or lose sixteen extra pounds a year. These three things alone can go a long way in helping you avoid extra calories. Fiber-friendly foods boast a number of other health benefits as well, including:

- balancing cholesterol
- keeping your digestive tract moving
- reducing high blood pressure, and
- reducing the risk of cancer.

Experts recommend eating 25 to 35 grams of fiber a day, but research shows that most adults fall far short of that. So how can you boost your fiber intake? Eat more brain-healthy foods like vegetables, fruits, and legumes.

Rule #5: Focus on healthy fats.

Fat is not the enemy. Good fats are essential to your health. After all, the solid weight of your brain is 60 percent fat (after the water is removed). When the medical establishment recommended we get fat out of our diets, we got fat, period. You want to eliminate all bad fats, such as trans fats. Did you know that certain fats found in foods like pizza, ice cream, and cheeseburgers fool the brain into ignoring the signals that you should be full? No wonder I used to always eat two bowls of ice cream and eight slices of pizza. Focus your diet on healthy fats, especially those that contain omega-3 fatty acids, found in foods like salmon, avocados, walnuts, and leafy green vegetables.

High cholesterol levels are not good for your brain. A new study reports that people who had high cholesterol levels in their forties had a higher risk of getting Alzheimer's disease in their sixties and seventies (260). There is evidence that the B vitamin niacin helps lower LDL cholesterol and raise HDL cholesterol. Avocados and garlic can help as well. But don't let your cholesterol levels go too low. Cholesterol levels under 160 have been associated with depression, homicide, and suicide. If I am at a party and someone is bragging to me about their low cholesterol levels, I am always *very* nice to that person.

Rule #6: Eat from the rainbow.

Your diet should have natural foods of many different colors, such as blueberries, pomegranates, yellow squash, and red bell peppers. This will boost the antioxidant levels in your body and help keep your brain young. Of course, the key word here is *natural*: Skittles, jelly beans, and M&M's don't qualify.

Rule #7: Cook with brain-healthy herbs and spices to boost your brain.

Here is a little food for thought, literally.

- Turmeric, found in curry, contains a chemical, curcumin, that has been shown to decrease the plaques in the brain thought to be responsible for Alzheimer's disease (261).
- A meta-analysis of five studies found saffron extract to be as effective as antidepressant medication in treating people with major depression (262).
- Scientific evidence shows that rosemary, thyme, and sage help boost memory (263, 264).
- Cinnamon has been shown to help attention and blood sugar. It is high in antioxidants and is a natural aphrodisiac.
- Garlic and oregano boost blood flow to the brain.
- Use ginger, cayenne, and black pepper—the hot, spicy taste comes from gingerols, capsaicin, and piperine, compounds that boost metabolism and have an aphrodisiac effect.

Rule #8: Make sure your food is as clean as possible.

As much as you can, eat organically grown and/or raised foods, because pesticides used in commercial farming can accumulate in your brain and body, even though the levels in each food may be low. Try to eat meat that is hormone-free, antibiotic-free, and that is free-range and grass fed. In addition, eliminate food additives, preservatives, and artificial dyes and sweeteners. This means you must start reading labels. If you do not know what is in something, do not eat it. Would you ever buy something if you did not know the cost of it? Of course not! Now is the time to really get thoughtful and serious about the food you put in your body.

14 Foods with the Highest Levels of Pesticide Residues (Buy Organic) (265)

1. Celery
2. Peaches
3. Strawberries
4. Apples
5. Blueberries
6. Nectarines
7. Cucumbers
8. Sweet Bell Peppers
9. Spinach
10. Cherries
11. Collard Greens/Kale
12. Potatoes
13. Grapes
14. Green Beans

The following foods are okay to buy nonorganic, because they have the least amount of pesticide residue.

17 Foods with the Lowest Levels of Pesticide Residues (265)

1. Onions
2. Avocado
3. Sweet Corn (Frozen)
4. Pineapples

5. Mango
6. Asparagus
7. Sweet Peas (Frozen)
8. Kiwi Fruit
9. Bananas
10. Cabbage
11. Broccoli
12. Papaya
13. Mushrooms
14. Watermelon
15. Grapefruit
16. Eggplant
17. Cantaloupe

Fish is a great source of healthy protein and fat, but it is important to consider the toxicity in some fish. Here are a couple of general rules to guide you: (1) The larger the fish, the more mercury it may contain, so go for the smaller varieties. (2) From the safe fish choices, eat a fairly wide variety of fish, preferably those highest in omega-3s, like wild Alaskan salmon, anchovies, and Pacific halibut. Wild fish is generally safer than farmed fish, but not always. Check out www.seafoodwatch.org for a list of the safest fish to eat.

Rule #9: If you're having trouble with your mood, energy, memory, weight, blood sugar, blood pressure, or skin, make sure to eliminate any foods that might be causing trouble, especially wheat and any other gluten-containing grains or food, as well as dairy, soy, and corn.

Did you know that gluten can literally make some people crazy? There are scientific reports of people having psychotic episodes when they're exposed to gluten; when they eliminate wheat and other gluten sources (such as barley, rye, spelt, imitation meats, soy sauce) from their diets, their stomachs and their brains get better (266). One of my patients lost thirty pounds, and her moodiness, eczema, and irritable bowel symptoms completely went away, when she got wheat out of her diet. Another one of my patients would become violent whenever he ate MSG. When we scanned him on MSG his brain changed into a pattern more consistent with our aggressive patients. ADD/ADHD and autistic children often do better when we put them on elimination diets that get rid of wheat, dairy, processed foods, food dyes, and additives.

Summary of the Amen Clinics 9 Rules of Brain-Healthy Eating

Rule #1: Think "high-quality calories" and not too many of them.

Rule #2: Drink plenty of water and not your calories.

Rule #3: Eat high-quality lean protein throughout the day.

Rule #4: Eat smart carbohydrates (low glycemic, high fiber).

Rule #5: Focus your diet on healthy fats.

Rule #6: Eat from the rainbow

Rule #7: Cook with brain-healthy herbs and spices to boost your brain.

Rule #8: Make sure your food is as clean as possible.

Rule #9: If you're having trouble with your mood, energy, memory, weight, blood sugar, blood pressure, or skin, make sure to eliminate any foods that might be causing trouble, especially wheat and any other gluten-containing grain or food, as well as dairy, soy, and corn.

---

52 Brain Superfoods

Here is my list of the fifty-two best foods for your brain based on the above principles. Again, make sure these foods are organic when you can and, when appropriate, hormone-free, antibiotic-free, free-range, and grass-fed.

NUTS AND SEEDS

1. Almonds, raw—for protein, healthy fats, and fiber
2. Brazil nuts—great source of zinc, magnesium, thiamine, high selenium content, healthy fat, and fiber

3. Cacao, raw—loaded with antioxidants, high in flavonoids (substances shown to increase blood flow), magnesium, iron, chromium, zinc, copper, and fiber. Can help decrease cravings and balance blood sugar, plus it can make you happy by stimulating serotonin, endorphins, and phenylethylamine (PEA). But eat only a small amount of dark chocolate or it will turn into fat on your body. I make two amazing dairy-free, sugar-free dark chocolate bars called Brain in Love and Brain on Joy. You can learn about them at www.brainmdhealth.com.

4. Cashews—rich in phosphorus, magnesium, zinc, and antioxidants

5. Chia seeds—very high in plant-based omega-3 fatty acids, fiber, and antioxidants

6. Coconut—high in fiber, manganese, and iron; low in natural sugars; high in medium chain triglycerides shown to be helpful for brain tissue

7. Hemp seeds—high in protein, contain all essential amino acids and fatty acids, high in omega-3s and healthy 6s, including 6 GLA, which has anti-inflammatory properties; also high in fiber and vitamin E

8. Sesame seeds—high in fiber, help to stabilize blood sugar and lower cholesterol; good source of calcium, phosphorus, and zinc.

9. Walnuts—of all nuts, contain the most omega-3 fatty acids to help lower bad cholesterol; may reduce inflammation; great source of antioxidants, vitamin E, selenium, and magnesium.

LEGUMES (SMALL AMOUNTS)

10. Lentils—high in fiber
11. Chickpeas—high serotonin content

FRUITS

12. Acai berries—for fiber, omega-3s, antioxidants, minerals, vitamins, plant sterols, and phytonutrients; low glycemic index and sugar

13. Apples—rich in antioxidants and fiber, and will help you not overeat

14. Avocados—high in omega-3 fats, high in lutein (for eyesight), potassium, and folate

15. Blackberries—high in antioxidants, phytonutrients, and fiber; low glycemic index
16. Blueberries—loaded with antioxidants. Anthocyanins, the compounds that give blueberries their deep color, may have antidiabetic effects. Labeled brain berries, in some studies they are shown to make you smarter.
17. Cherries—high fiber, low glycemic index
18. Goldenberry—high in fiber, phosphorus, calcium, and vitamins A, C, B1, B2, B6, and B12; very high in protein for fruit (16 percent)
19. Goji berries—rich in antioxidants, fiber, amino acids, iron, and vitamin C; help lower blood pressure, stabilize blood sugar, and fight yeast
20. Grapefruit—for fiber, nutrients, and lower glycemic index
21. Honey, raw, wild (small amounts only)—rich in minerals, antioxidants, probiotics, all twenty-two essential amino acids. Some types from Hawaii (Lehua and Noni) and New Zealand (Manuka) have antifungal, antibacterial, and antiviral properties.
22. Kiwi—for fiber, nutrients, and lower glycemic index
23. Pomegranates—high in fiber and antioxidants; low in calories

VEGETABLES

24. Asparagus—for fiber and antioxidants
25. Bell peppers—for fiber and vitamin C
26. Beets—high in fiber, phytonutrients, folate, and beta-carotene
27. Broccoli—loaded with sulforaphanes; may increase enzymes that lower the incidence of some cancers.
28. Brussels sprouts—high in fiber and sulforaphanes; may increase enzymes that lower the incidence of some cancers.
29. Cabbage—loaded with sulforaphanes; may increase enzymes that lower the incidence of some cancers.
30. Cauliflower—loaded with sulforaphanes; may increase enzymes that lower the incidence of some cancers.
31. Chlorella—a blue-green algae rich in chlorophyll, helps detoxify the body and remove dioxin, lead, and mercury; contains high concentrations of B-group vitamins and helps digestion.
32. Garlic—in the allium family, it can help lower blood pressure and cho-

lesterol; inhibits growth of some cancer; has antibiotic properties; boosts blood flow to the brain.

33. Horseradish—high in calcium, potassium, vitamin C, and helps maintain collagen.
34. Kale—this and other dark leafy greens contain omega-3 fats, iron (especially important for women), and phytonutrients.
35. Leeks—from the allium family; can help lower blood pressure and cholesterol, inhibit growth of some cancer, and have antibiotic properties.
36. Maca root—a South American plant root that is extraordinarily rich in amino acids, minerals, plant sterols, vitamins, and healthy fatty acids
37. Onions—from the allium family; can help lower blood pressure and cholesterol and inhibit growth of some cancer; have antibiotic properties, and boost blood flow to the brain.
38. Seaweed—this is where fish get their omega-3s; high in magnesium.
39. Spinach—and other dark leafy greens contain omega-3 fats, iron, and phytonutrients
40. Spirulina—highest concentration of any protein and a top source of iron (avoid if your iron is too high); rich in antioxidants and can help you have healthy hair and skin
41. Sweet potatoes—loaded with phytonutrients, fiber, and vitamin A
42. Wheatgrass juice—mineral and vitamin dense, this is 70 percent chlorophyll and is a complete protein with thirty enzymes; excellent source of phosphorus, magnesium, zinc, and potassium

OILS

43. Coconut oil—stable at high temperatures
44. Grapeseed oil—stable at high temperatures; high in omega-3s
45. Olive oil—stable only at room temperature

POULTRY/FISH

46. Chicken or turkey
47. Eggs

48. Lamb—high in omega-3s
49. Salmon, wild caught—loaded with brain-boosting omega-3s
50. Sardines, wild caught—low in mercury, high in brain-boosting omega-3s, vitamin D, and calcium; sustainable

TEA

51. Green tea—this is the best kind of tea to drink. It has protective antioxidants, less caffeine than coffee, and metabolism-boosting compound EGCG, and contains theanine, which helps you relax and focus at the same time.

SPECIAL CATEGORY

52. Shirataki noodles—the root of a wild yam plant (goes by the brand name Miracle Noodles). High in fiber and virtually calorie-free, they are Tana's secret weapon as a replacement for pasta noodles.

How to Enhance Your Mind and Mood with Food

Food can help you feel relaxed, happy, and focused, or downright dumb. How we feed ourselves and our children in this country is backward.

Generally, simple carbohydrates such as those found in pancakes, waffles, muffins, bagels, or cereal boost serotonin levels that help us feel relaxed, calm, and less worried and less motivated. Protein, found in meat, nuts, or eggs, boosts dopamine levels and helps us feel more driven, motivated, and focused. Yet, many people eat simple carbs in the morning and have more protein-based meals at night.

For example, it is very common to feed children or ourselves a breakfast of donuts, pancakes, waffles, sugary cereals, muffins, bagels, or toast, along with fruit juices (concentrated sugar). Then we ask ourselves or our children to focus, which can cause real problems and make you or your children look like they have ADD (attention deficit disorder). These simple-carbohydrate-based meals spike insulin, which can often cause low blood sugar levels in a short period of time, causing brain fog. In addition, simple carbohydrates also spike serotonin levels in the brain, so we feel happier after the meal. The problem is that serotonin can also decrease our ability to get things done, and for many people can give them a more "don't worry, be happy" attitude. Not exactly the best mind-set for school or work. Protein-based meals tend to do the opposite. They can boost dopamine levels in the brain, give us energy, and help us focus.

Therefore, it makes sense to eat a protein-rich meal earlier in the day to get started or at dinner if you still need to get work finished in the evening. If you want to relax in the evening and go to bed early, I recommend decreasing the protein and eating more healthy complex-carbohydrate-rich foods.

Often, when kids come home from school, parents give them a few cookies and a soda (a high simple-carbohydrate-based snack). Then they tell them to do their homework. Unfortunately, the parents have unwittingly diminished their children's ability to get their homework finished and it causes a night of stress for everyone.

Foods to Boost Mood, Focus, Motivation, and Memory

As a reminder, serotonin is a neurotransmitter that helps soothe the brain. It is intimately involved in sleep, mood regulation, appetite, and social engagement. It helps decrease our worries and concerns. Based on research at MIT, foods rich in simple carbohydrates have been found to quickly boost serotonin (267). They cause a spike in insulin, which lowers most large amino acids with the exception of tryptophan, the amino acid building block for serotonin, thereby decreasing the competition for tryptophan to get into the brain. This is why many people can become dependent on or even addicted to bread, pasta, potatoes, rice, and sugar. They use these as "mood foods" and feel more relaxed and less worried after they eat them. Unfortunately, because they boost serotonin, they can also lower prefrontal cortex function and diminish a person's internal braking ability. I think this is precisely why restaurants serve bread and alcohol before a meal. If you consume them you are much more likely to order dessert.

Brain-healthy foods that help to boost serotonin include smart carbohydrates such as sweet potatoes, apples, blueberries, carrots, steel-cut oatmeal, and chickpeas. These cause a more gradual increase in serotonin. It is a myth that foods that contain high levels of tryptophan, such as turkey, actually raise serotonin in the brain. This is because tryptophan is transported into the brain by a system that is geared toward larger protein molecules, and tryptophan, being smaller and less abundant, doesn't compete well against the other proteins to get in the brain. This is one of the main reasons why exercise helps people feel better. Exercise pushes the larger amino acids into your muscles and thereby decreases the competition for tryptophan to get into the brain. If you want to feel happier, grab an apple and go for a walk.

Dopamine is the neurotransmitter involved in motivation, emotional significance, relevance, focus, and pleasure. It helps you get things done. Protein generally helps boost dopamine levels, which is why if you need to focus, avoid sugar, bread, pasta, rice, and white potatoes. Foods that tend to increase dopamine include beef, poultry, fish, eggs, seeds (pumpkin and sesame), nuts (almonds and walnuts), cheese, protein powders, and green tea. In addition, avocados and lima beans can help. Tyrosine is the amino acid building block for dopamine and is also essential for thyroid function. Simple carbohydrates tend to deplete dopamine. Acetylcholine is the neurotransmitter involved with learning and memory. Liver, eggs, milk, salmon, and shrimp tend to boost these levels.

Heal Your Gut to Boost Your Brain

The gut is often called the second brain. It is loaded with nervous tissue and is in direct communication with our big brain, which is why we get butterflies when we get excited, or have loose bowels when upset. Anxiety, depression, stress, and grief all express themselves with emotional pain and, quite often, gastrointestinal (GI) distress.

Your gut is one of the most important organs for the health of your brain. It is estimated that the GI tract is loaded with about 100 trillion microorganisms (bacteria, yeast, and others), about ten times the total number of cells in the human body. To be healthy, the relationship of good bugs to bad bugs needs to be positively skewed—around 85 percent good guys to 15 percent bad guys. When it starts heading the other way, all sorts of physical and mental problems can arise. Keeping the good and bad bugs in proper balance is essential to your mental health (268).

There is new evidence that friendly gut bacteria actually deter invading troublemakers, such as *E. coli,* and help us withstand stress. If the friendly bugs are deficient, either from a poor diet that feeds yeast overgrowth (think sugar), or the excessive presence of antibiotics (even as far back as childhood) that killed the good bacteria, we are more likely to feel anxious, stressed, and depressed. In fact, the greatest danger from antibiotics does not come from those prescribed by your doctor, but rather from the foods you eat. The prevalence of antibiotics found in conventionally raised meats and vegetables have the potential to throw off the balance of good to bad bacteria. It is estimated that 70 percent of the total antibiotic use in the United States is for livestock, which is why it is critical to eat antibiotic- and hormone-free, grass-fed, free-range meats.

Disorders ranging from ADD to autism in children, from mental fogginess to depression in adults, have been connected to intestinal bacteria imbalances that cause increased gut permeability. The intestines provide an important barrier to bad bugs from the outside world. If they become too permeable, often called "leaky gut," inflammation and illness can be created throughout the body. Optimizing the "gut-brain axis" is critical to your mental health.

Factors That Decrease Healthy Gut Bacteria

- medications (antibiotics, oral contraceptives, proton pump inhibitors, steroids, NSAIDs)
- refined sugar intake
- artificial sweeteners
- bactericidal chemicals in water
- pesticide residues in food
- alcohol
- stress, including physiological, emotional, and environmental
- radiation
- high-intensity exercise, such as marathons

A Few Good Germs Can Be Good for You

Research shows that animals raised in a germ-free environment display exaggerated responses to psychological stress. We all need the good bugs in our intestinal tract to boost our immune system, so be careful not to go overboard in keeping your children away from the dirt. When researchers gave the animals probiotics, their stress levels normalized.

Stress, all by itself, decreases healthy gut flora (269). Early-abandonment issues can cause increased stress, decreased healthy bacteria, and increased gut permeability (270). When young rats were separated from their mothers, the layer of cells that line the gut became more permeable, allowing bacteria from the intestine to pass through the bowel walls and stimulate immune cells to start attacking other organs (271). "In rats, it's an adaptive response," reports Dr. Emeran Mayer from UCLA. "If they're born into a stressful, hostile environment, nature programs them to be more vigilant and stress responsive in their future life." Dr. Mayer said that up to 70 percent of the patients he treats for chronic gut disorders had experienced early childhood traumas like parents divorcing, chronic illnesses, or parents' deaths. "I think that what happens in early life, along with an individual's genetic background, programs how a person will respond to stress for the rest of his or her life."

Teresa grew up in a single-parent home filled with stress. When she was four, her uncle was murdered, and shortly thereafter her mother was bringing her to the doctor for GI complaints. At age nine she started having panic attacks, especially when her mother came home late from work. As a teenager she developed bulimia, again with serious intestinal consequences. Decreasing her stress, along with giving her probiotics to help boost the friendly bugs in her gut, made a positive difference for her both physically and emotionally.

In a recent study (272), Drs. A. Venket Rao and Alison Bested administered thirty-nine patients with chronic fatigue syndrome either three doses of a probiotic (healthy bugs) a day or a placebo for two months. They found that 73 percent of subjects taking the probiotic experienced an increase in levels of good bacteria in the gut, which corresponded with a significant decrease in anxiety symptoms. The researchers found no significant change in anxiety for the placebo group. The researchers believed that pro-biotics "crowd out" the more toxic gut bacteria linked to depression and other mood disorders. Dr. Bested reported, "The subjects felt less anxious, calmer, better able to cope with their illness, sleeping better, had fewer heart palpitations, and less symptoms of anxiety."

What does this mean for you? Follow the brain-healthy food guidelines in this chapter carefully, especially by eliminating most of the simple sugars from your diet that feed the bad bugs. Focus on eating smart carbohydrates (low glycemic, high fiber), which enhance healthy gut flora. Also, consider taking a daily probiotic to give the good bugs a head start. Be careful with antibiotics, and if you have had a lot of them in the past, a probiotic and a healthy diet become even more important to the health of your brain.

PSYCHOLOGICAL

The Psychology of It All

In order to get your eating habits under control, it is critical to have the right attitude about it. As I've mentioned, getting healthy is about abundance, not deprivation. This is a critical mind shift to make. Being unhealthy or overweight is a thinking disorder as much as it is an eating disorder. While I was consulting for a large organization, the wife of the CEO told me that when we first introduced the brain-healthy program into their organization she told her husband she would rather get cancer than give up sweets. That was when she realized that she had a serious problem with sugar.

Eating in a brain-healthy way is one of the strongest forms of self-love. If you truly love and care for yourself you need to be diligent about only putting healthy fuel inside your body. But it takes the right thoughts and attitudes to make it happen. If you want to unleash your full brain power, you have to be a warrior for the health of your brain, and gain the upper hand against the constant bombardment of bad messages that try to make you shove bad food down your throat. How you think dramatically affects how you feel and **every decision you make.** And the lies you tell yourself are one of the biggest factors that drive illness. Here are some of the most common "little lies" I hear about food:

- "I don't want to deprive myself." Doesn't eating bad food deprive you of your health—your most precious resource? What is worth more—energy, a trim waistline, and good health, or the mountain of fries, sodas, cakes, and cookies that you have consumed over the last decade?
- "I can't eat healthy because I travel." I am always amused by this one, because I travel a lot. It just takes a little forethought and planning.
- "My whole family is overweight—it is in my genes." This is one of the biggest lies. Genes account for only about 20 to 30 percent of your health. The vast majority of health problems are driven by the bad decisions you make. My genes say I'm likely to be fat, but I no longer make the decisions that make this likely to happen.
- "I can't afford to get healthy." Being sick is always more expensive than getting healthy.
- "I can't find the time to work out." With a sharper mind, you will actually save time if you work out.
- "It's Easter, Memorial Day, the Fourth of July, Labor Day, Thanksgiving, Christmas, Monday, Tuesday, Wednesday, Thursday, Friday, Saturday, or Sunday." There is always an excuse to hurt yourself. You have to find the excuse not to.

So what are the lies you are telling yourself about food? Write them down, then talk back to them.

SOCIAL

Getting Social

Preparing meals and feeding our families is an important social activity. Being Lebanese, I know about this firsthand. We are known for delicious Mediterranean food. It can be incredibly healthy: hummus, tabbouleh, and grilled fish or lamb; or incredibly unhealthy: butter cookies and baklava.

Throughout my life it has been common for my mother, my wife, my aunts, my sisters, my daughters, and my nieces to be in the kitchen together cooking great meals. When the matriarch or patriarch leads the brain health charge, she or he has a huge influence on those who follow. The earlier you start, the better.

As you've learned by now, social ties are so strong that they can have an immense effect on our health and habits. Researchers have found that the health of our family and friends is one of the strongest predictors of longevity. In 1921, Stanford psychologist Lewis Terman evaluated 1,548 ten-year-old children (120). He and subsequent researchers then followed this group over the next ninety years, looking for the traits that were associated with success, health, and longevity. One of the main findings of the research was that social relationships had a dramatic impact on health. If your friends and family were unhealthy you were much more likely to be unhealthy too. For people who want to improve their health, associating with other healthy people is usually the strongest and most direct path to change. This does not mean you have to give up all of your friends and family who are struggling with their health; share this program with them and offer to do it together.

Right now, I want you to think of the people you love most in this world. Who do you call when something good happens . . . or when something bad happens? I call my wife, my parents, and my children. For each of these people, ask yourself, "Am I their friend or their accomplice?" A friend is someone who helps their loved ones be successful, while an accomplice is someone who helps them maintain bad habits.

- "Oh, come on, it will be fine, it's just one time."
- "I cooked for you all weekend. Have more."
- "Don't be a party pooper."
- "It's the weekend, you've worked hard, you've earned it."

Are you helping those you love prevent devastating illnesses like Alzheimer's and depression? Or, are you unknowingly encouraging them to be sick? You can lead the change in your family.

SPIRITUAL

Spiritual (SOUL Food)

Your sense of spirituality underlies everything you do. As we have discussed, it is the fuel that provides your life with a deep sense of meaning, passion, and purpose; it is your connection to God, generations past and future, and even the future of our planet. Ask yourself, "What is the underlying meaning and purpose for the food I eat and feed my family? Is it just for basic nutrition? For pleasure? Fellowship? Is it to sustain my life so I can accomplish what I am here on Earth for?" If your life has meaning and purpose, it is best served by a highly nutritious diet that nourishes your brain, body, and soul.

When I was first asked to a be a consultant for the Daniel Plan at Saddleback Church, which I talked about earlier in the book, Pastor Rick Warren talked to me about the biblical directive to honor our bodies. *Do you not know that your body is a temple of the Holy Spirit, who is in you, whom you have received from God? You are not your own; you were bought at a price. Therefore honor God with your body. (1 Cor. 6:19–20).* The way many people eat is definitely not honoring their bodies.

I like to use the acronym SOUL to understand how to eat in a spiritual way. It stands for:

- Sustainable (we can continue to grow the food indefinitely without hurting our planet)
- Organic (raised in a clean environment without toxins)
- Unadulterated (pure, whole foods, without artificial food dyes, sweeteners, or additives)
- Locally grown (gives you a better chance of knowing the food is fresh and supports your local community)

Consider how the food you eat was raised, as I have mentioned. How are the animals treated? Is it humane? Would it make you sick if you knew? This is a question that has concerned me for a long time. Animals, like humans, release different chemicals in their bodies when they feel relaxed or stressed, happy or depressed, approachable or angry. If they are raised and then killed in a confined, toxic environment where they feel stressed, angry, and depressed, then ultimately we are consuming the chemicals the animals released when they were stressed, angry, and depressed. How your food was treated matters to the health of your body for many reasons.

If you think of eating as a spiritual discipline, it will help you not only give thanks for the food you have, but also take a much more thoughtful approach to raising, harvesting, and consuming it.

Therapy for Your Kitchen

Just like therapists will explore the cabinets of your mind and help to clean them of the toxic or unhelpful memories, I want you to take an hour and clean your kitchen of any unhealthy or toxic food. Refer to the nine rules of brain-healthy eating above. If the food doesn't serve your health, get rid of it. Don't donate it to the poor. It will make them sick as well.

21

PLEASE HELP ME!

When and How to Seek Professional Care

This chapter will attempt to answer four questions that I am frequently asked:

- When is it time to see a professional about these problems?
- What should I do when a loved one is in denial about needing help?
- How can I find a competent professional?
- When should I think about getting a functional imaging study, such as SPECT?

WHEN TO SEEK HELP

This is relatively easy to determine. I recommend that people seek professional help when their attitudes, behaviors, feelings, or thoughts interfere with their ability to be successful in the world—whether in their relationships, in their work, or within themselves—and when self-help techniques have not helped them fully understand or alleviate the problem. Let's look at all three situations.

Relationships

As seen in this book, underlying brain problems can truly sabotage relationships. *If you or someone you know has issues that interfere with the quality of relationships, get help.* Often it is necessary to address brain health concerns before working on communication and intimacy issues. I often use a computer analogy: you need to first fix computer hardware before it can effectively run sophisticated software. Let's take another look at how each brain system can interfere with relationships.

Limbic system issues can be associated with depression and cause people to feel distant, irritable, unfocused, tired, negative, and uninterested in sex. Unless the partners understand this disorder, this often causes severe relational problems. People who suffer from depression have a divorce rate six times higher than those who are not depressed.

Basal ganglia issues can be associated with anxiety and cause sufferers to feel tense, uptight, physically ill, and conflict avoidant. Partners often misinterpret the anxiety or physical symptoms as complaining or whining and do not take seriously the level of suffering.

Anterior cingulate issues can lead to obsessive or overfocused tendencies and, as we have seen, cause rigid thinking styles, oppositional or argumentative behavior, holding on to grudges, and chronic stress in relationships. Seeking help is essential to establishing a new ability to relate effectively.

Prefrontal cortex problems, such as ADD, often sabotage relationships because of the impulsive, restless, and distractible behavior involved. Without help there is a high degree of relational and family turmoil.

Temporal lobe problems may be associated with frequent attacks of rage, angry outbursts, mood swings, hearing things incorrectly, and low frustration tolerance. I have seen these problems ruin otherwise good relationships.

Workplace

The workplace is also affected by underlying and often unrecognized brain system problems. *If you or someone you know suffers with these problems and they interfere with work, it is often essential to get professional help.* Addressing these problems can literally change the whole atmosphere at work.

Limbic system issues can cause depression, which can be associated with people being negative, unfocused, tired, and unmotivated, and taking things too personally or the wrong way. Such employees may negatively affect others' morale and unknowingly skew everyone's perceptions at work so they see positive things in a bad light. Depressed people have more sick days than people without depression.

Basal ganglia issues can be associated with feelings of being anxious, tense, physically sick, and conflict avoidant. Their level of anxiety often causes them to be dependent and require too much supervision. Their anxiety tends to be contagious, and those around them may also begin predicting negative outcomes to situations. They can negatively affect a work group and tend to be fearful rather than hopeful.

Anterior cingulate issues can lead to obsessive or overfocused tendencies, causing rigid thinking styles. Employers or employees tend to be more irritable, oppositional, or argumentative. They often hold grudges and can be unforgiving, causing long-term workplace problems.

Prefrontal cortex problems, such as ADD, cause many problems at work, including chronic lateness, inefficiency, missing deadlines, impulsive decision making, and conflict-seeking behavior.

Temporal lobe problems often affect work. Workplace violence may be associated with temporal lobe disorders. More commonly, temporal lobe problems are manifested at work by mood swings or unpredictable behavior, low frustration tolerance, misperceptions, auditory processing problems, and memory problems. The anger, misperceptions, and mild paranoia can wreak havoc in a work group.

Ben

Let me give an example of how brain system problems can affect the workplace. Ben was on the verge of being fired. He was frequently late to work, disorganized, forgetful, late on deadlines, and off task. His boss let his behavior slide because she felt that Ben had a good heart and wanted to do well. His boss's boss, however, wanted Ben fired. He thought Ben was bad for overall discipline and morale. Ben's boss was my patient. I was treating her for ADD. She saw many of her own characteristics in Ben. One day she asked Ben to come into her office. She told him her own story, about her problems in school and with timeliness, organization, distractibility, and procrastination. She told him she had ADD and that her treatment had made a big difference for her. She said that her boss wanted her to fire him, but she had convinced him to give Ben another chance. She suggested that Ben seek professional help if he could relate to her story. Ben started to cry. His history was a carbon copy of hers. He had done poorly in school and had trouble with concentration, organization, completing assignments, and underachievement. He did not expect his boss to care enough about him to try to help. Other employers would just fire him, as the boss's boss wanted to do. Ben came to see me. He had a classic case of ADD. With a four-circles plan that included medication and ANT therapy, his behavior improved dramatically. His boss and those higher up in the company saw a wonderful turnaround in Ben. The company saved money by not having to hire and retrain someone to take Ben's place, and Ben was deeply grateful that he was given another chance, along with the information he needed to heal. The odds are that he will always be a loyal employee of this company.

Internal Life

All of these brain systems can have a significantly negative effect on internal life, self-esteem, emotional health, and physical health.

Depression (limbic system) clouds a sense of accomplishment (even with incredible achievement) and causes intense sadness and internal pain. Depression is not the absence of feeling, but rather the presence of painful feelings. Depression is one of the most common precursors to drug abuse and suicide. Depression often compromises immune system function, leaving people more prone to illness.

The tension and panic associated with anxiety (often a result of basal ganglia problems) can feel like torture. I have known many patients with panic attacks who become suicidal in hope of escaping their fear. Anxiety is often associated with physical tension and an increase in illness. Many anxious people self-medicate by drinking alcohol, taking drugs, overeating, engaging in inappropriate sex, and other potentially addictive behaviors.

Overfocus (cingulate) issues cause repetitive thoughts and worries that are often self-medicated with drugs or alcohol. Internal torture by constant worry is common. When someone says one negative thing, they may hear it in their minds five hundred times. They cannot get away from negative thoughts.

People with prefrontal cortex issues, such as ADD, often feel a tremendous sense of underachievement, repetitive failure, and low self-esteem. People with prefrontal cortex issues may use internal problems for self-stimulation and be chronically upset. The stress associated with these problems is often accompanied by increased illness.

Temporal lobe problems can wreak internal havoc. The internal violent mood swings and thoughts often torment the soul. Unpredictable behavior, low frustration tolerance, misperceptions, and memory problems are often associated with an internal sense of damage. Anger often alienates others, and loneliness is common.

GAINING ACCESS TO YOUR OWN GOOD BRAIN

The internal problems associated with these brain system difficulties can ruin lives, relationships, and careers. It is essential to seek help when necessary. It is also critical for people not to be too proud to get help. Pride often devastates relationships, careers, and even life itself. Too many people feel they are somehow "less than others" if they seek help. I often tell my patients that, in my experience, *it is the successful people who seek help when they need it*. Successful businesspeople hire the best possible outside consultants when they are faced with a problem that they cannot solve or when they need extra help. Unsuccessful people tend to deny they have problems, bury their heads, and blame others for their problems. If your attitude, behavior, thoughts, or feelings sabotage your chances for success in relationships, work, or within yourself, get help. Don't feel ashamed; feel as though you're being good to yourself. In thinking about getting help, it is important to put these brain system problems in perspective.

I Just Want to Be Normal

Recently, Sarah came up to me after a lecture and started to cry. When she composed herself she told me about her son, William, who had bipolar disorder and refused to take his medication, because he just wanted to be "normal." But as his illness worsened, he had been arrested three times, and she had been sick with worry. Then one day she watched one of my public television shows and heard me say it is more normal to have a problem than not to have a problem. "Normal is a myth." She recorded it for her son. When he came to understand he had a brain problem—just like people can have eye problems or heart problems—he took his medicine and began to do so much better. The mother told me that her son often said, "Normal people get help. The smarter they are, the sooner they get it."

I tell my patients to get rid of the concept of "normal versus not normal." Most of us have traits from one or more brain system misfires. Sometimes the problems associated with each section are subclinical (they don't get in your way much), and sometimes they are severe enough that they significantly interfere with your life. One of the most persuasive arguments I give potential patients about seeking help is that I am often able to help them have *more access* to their own good brain. When their brain does not work efficiently, they can't be efficient. When their brain works right, they can work right. I will often show them a number of brain SPECT studies to show them the difference between being on and off medication or supplements or from targeted psychotherapy, as a way to help them understand the concept. As you can imagine after looking at the images in this book, when you see an underactive brain versus one that is healthy, you want the one that is healthy. I actually spoke in Normal, Illinois, at a major university several years ago. I got to meet Normal people, shop at the Normal grocery store, see the Normal police department and fire department. I even met Normal women. They were a very nice group, but really not much different from folks in California. The Normal people seemed to have all of the same problems I mention in this book.

WHAT TO DO WHEN A LOVED ONE IS IN DENIAL ABOUT NEEDING HELP

Unfortunately, the stigma associated with "psychiatric illness" prevents many people from getting help. People do not want to be seen as crazy, stupid, or defective, and they often don't seek help until they (or their loved one) can no longer tolerate the pain (at work, in their relationships, or within themselves).

Jerry and Jenny

When Jerry and Jenny started to have marital problems early in their marriage, Jenny wanted to get help. Jerry refused. He said that he didn't want to air his problems in front of a stranger. It wasn't until Jenny threatened to leave him that he finally agreed to go for counseling. Initially, Jerry listed many reasons why he wouldn't go for help: He didn't see that the problems were that bad; it was too much money; he thought all counselors were "messed up"; and he didn't want to be perceived as crazy by anyone who might find out about the counseling.

Unfortunately, Jerry's attitude is common among men. Many men, when faced with obvious problems in their marriages, their children, or even themselves, refuse to see the issue. Their lack of awareness and strong tendency toward denial prevent them from seeking help until more damage than necessary has been done. In Jerry's case, he had to be threatened with divorce before he would go. Another factor in Jerry's case was that he had ADD. As a child he had been forced to see a counselor for behavioral problems at school. He hated feeling different from the other kids and resented his mom for making him talk to the doctor.

Some people may say it is unfair for me to "pick on" men. And indeed, some men see problems long before some women do. Overall, however, in my experience mothers see problems in children before fathers do, and are more willing to seek help, and many more wives call for marital counseling than husbands. What is it in our society that causes men to overlook obvious problems, to deny problems until it is too late to deal with them effectively or until unnecessary damage is done? Some of the answers may be found in how boys are raised, the societal expectations we place on men, and the overwhelming pace of many men's daily lives.

Boys most often engage in active play (sports, war games, video games, etc.) that involves little dialogue or communication. The games often involve dominance and submission, winning and losing, and little interpersonal communication. Force, strength, or skill is used to handle problems. Girls, on the other hand, often engage in more interpersonal or communicative types of play, such as with dolls and storytelling. Fathers often take their sons out to throw the ball around or shoot hoops, rather than to go for a walk and talk.

Many men retain the childhood notions of competition and that one must be better than others to be any good at all. To admit to a problem is to be less than other men. As a result, many men wait to seek help until their problem is obvious to the whole world. Other men feel totally responsible for all that happens in their families; to admit to a problem is to admit that they have in some way failed.

Clearly, the pace of life prevents some men from being able to take the time to look clearly at the important people in their lives and their relationships with them. When I spend time with fathers and husbands and help them slow down enough to see what is really important to them, more often than not they begin to see the problems and work toward more helpful solutions. The issue is not one of being uncaring or uninterested; it is not seeing what is there.

Many teenagers also resist getting help even when faced with obvious problems. They worry about labels and don't want yet another adult judging their behavior.

Here are several suggestions to help people who are unaware of a problem or unwilling to get the help they need:

1. Try the straightforward approach first (but with a new brain twist). Clearly tell the person what behaviors concern you. Tell him or her that the problems may be due to underlying brain patterns that can be tuned

up. Explain that help may be available—help not to cure a defect but rather help to optimize how the brain functions. Tell the loved one that you know he or she is trying to do his or her best, but unproductive behavior, thoughts, or feelings may be getting in the way of success (at work, in relationships, or within themselves). Emphasize access, not defect.

2. Give the loved one information. Books, websites, and articles on the subjects you are concerned about can be of tremendous help. Many people come to see me because they read a book of mine, saw a video I produced, or read an article I wrote. Good information can be very persuasive, especially if it is presented in a positive, life-enhancing way. One of the most effective tools is to show them my fourteen-minute TEDx talk titled "The Most Important Lesson from 83,000 Brain Scans," which you can find on our website at www.amenclinics.com.

3. When a person remains resistant to help, even after you have been straightforward and given him or her good information—plant seeds. Plant ideas about getting help and then water them regularly. Drop an idea, article, or other information about the topic from time to time. However, if you talk too much about getting help, people become resentful and won't get help, just to spite you. Be careful not to go overboard.

4. Protect your relationship with the other person. People are more receptive to people they trust than to people who nag and belittle them. I do not let anyone tell me something bad about myself unless I trust him or her. Work on gaining the person's trust over the long run. It will make him or her more receptive to your suggestions. Do not make getting help the only thing that you talk about. Make sure you are interested in the person's whole life, not just potential medical appointments.

5. Give new hope. Many people with these problems have tried to get help and it either didn't work or made them worse. Educate them on new brain technology that helps professionals be more focused and more effective in treatment efforts.

6. There comes a time when you have to say, "Enough is enough." If, over time, the other person refuses to get help and his or her behavior has a negative impact on your life, you may have to separate yourself. Staying in a toxic relationship is harmful to your health, and it often enables the other person to remain sick. Actually, I have seen that the threat or act of leaving can motivate people to change, whether it is about drinking, drug use, or treating underlying ADD or bipolar disorder. Threatening to leave is not the first approach I would take, but after time it may be the best approach.

7. Realize that you cannot force people into treatment unless they are dangerous to themselves, dangerous to others, or unable to care for themselves. You can do only what you can do. Fortunately, today there is a lot more we can do than even ten years ago.

FINDING A COMPETENT PROFESSIONAL

At this point in my career, I get many e-mails, social media posts, and calls each week from people all over the world who are looking for competent professionals in their area who think in ways similar to myself and utilize the principles outlined in this book. Because these principles are still on the edge of what is new in brain science, these professionals may be hard to find. Still, finding the right professional for evaluation and treatment is critical to the healing process. The wrong professional can make things worse. There are a number of steps you can take to find the best person to assist you:

1. **Get the best person you can find.** Saving money up front may cost you a lot in the long run. The right help not only is cost-effective but saves unnecessary pain and suffering. Don't rely on a therapist solely because he or she is on your managed care plan. That person may or may not be a good fit for you. Don't settle for someone who isn't a good fit for you. If he or she is on your insurance plan—that's great. Just don't let that be the primary criterion if you can help it.

2. **Use a specialist.** Brain science is expanding at a rapid pace. Specialists keep up with the latest developments in their fields, while generalists (family physicians) have to try to keep up with everything. If I had a heart arrhythmia, I would see a cardiologist rather than a general internist. I want to be treated by someone who has seen hundreds or even thousands of cases like mine.

3. **Get information about referrals from people who are highly knowledgeable about your problem.** Sometimes well-meaning generalists give very bad information. I have known many physicians and teachers who make light of brain system problems, such as ADD, learning disabilities, or depression, and discourage people from getting help. One family physician told one of my recent patients: "Oh, ADD is a fad. You don't need help. Just try harder." In searching for help, contact people who are likely to give you good information, such as specialists in the field, people at major research centers, and people in support groups for your specific problem. Check out Internet medical support groups. Support groups often have members who have visited the professionals in the area, and they can give you important information about the doctor, such as his or her bedside manner, competence, responsiveness, and organization.

4. **Once you get the names of competent professionals, check their credentials.** They should have board certification; to become board certified, physicians have to pass certain written and verbal tests. They have had to discipline themselves to gain specialized skill and knowledge. Don't give excessive weight to the medical school or graduate school the professional attended to the exclusion of other factors. I have worked with some doctors who went to Yale and Harvard who did not have a clue about how to treat patients appropriately, while other doctors from less prestigious schools were outstanding, forward-thinking, and caring.

5. **Set up an interview with the professional to see whether or not you want to work with him or her.** Generally you have to pay for his or her

time, but it is worth spending time getting to know the people you will rely on for help. If you sense the fit isn't good, keep looking.

6. Many professionals write articles or books or speak at meetings or local groups. If possible, read their writings or hear them speak to get a feel for the kind of people they are and their ability to help you.

7. **Look for a person who is open-minded, up to date, and willing to try new things.**

8. **Look for a person who treats you with respect, who listens to your questions, and who responds to your needs.** Look for a relationship that is collaborative and trusting.

I know it is hard to find a professional who meets all of these criteria and who also has the right training in brain physiology, but it is possible. Be persistent. The right caregiver is essential to healing.

WHEN SHOULD I THINK ABOUT GETTING A FUNCTIONAL IMAGING STUDY, SUCH AS SPECT?

We order SPECT studies on most of our patients, because, generally, they come to us after they have failed to get better with other specialists and therapies. Many patients tell us, "You are my last hope." In these cases, we need more detailed information to see if we can identify something that has been overlooked. In general, I think of SPECT like radar. If it is sunny outside, it is easy for pilots to land planes at the airport. If you have a simple case, you don't need a scan. But if it is stormy out, with dark clouds, lightning, and thunder, radar can be lifesaving. Likewise, if your case is complicated and you have not gotten better with other providers or treatments, a scan could be lifesaving.

Here are several common questions and answers about SPECT:

Will the SPECT study give me an accurate diagnosis? No. A SPECT study by itself will not give a diagnosis. SPECT studies help the clinician understand more about the specific function of your brain. Each person's brain is unique, which may lead to unique responses to medicine or therapy. Diagnoses about specific conditions are made through a combination of clinical history, personal interviews, information from families, diagnostic checklists, SPECT studies, and other neuropsychological tests. No imaging study alone is a "doctor in a box" that can give accurate diagnoses on individual patients.

Why are SPECT studies ordered? Some of the common reasons include:

1. Evaluating seizure activity
2. Evaluating cerebral vascular disease such as stokes
3. Evaluating cognitive impairment and dementia
4. Evaluating the effects of mild, moderate, and severe head trauma
5. Suspicion of underlying organic brain condition, such as seizure activity contributing to behavioral disturbance, prenatal trauma, or exposure to toxins
6. Evaluating atypical or unresponsive aggressive behavior
7. Determining the extent of brain impairment caused by drug or alcohol abuse
8. Subtyping ADD, anxiety, depression, addictions, and obesity
9. Evaluating treatment-resistant couples
10. General wellness screenings for people who are interested in optimization

Are there any side effects or risks to the study? The study does not involve a dye, and people do not have allergic reactions to the study. The possibility exists, although in a very small percentage of patients, of a mild rash, facial redness and edema (swelling), fever, and a transient increase in blood pressure. The amount of radiation exposure from one brain SPECT study is approximately the same as from one head CT scan, or one-third of an abdominal CT scan.

How is the SPECT procedure done? The patient is placed in a quiet room, and an intravenous (IV) line is started. The patient remains quiet for approximately ten minutes with eyes open to allow his or her mental state to equilibrate to the environment. The imaging agent is then injected through the IV. After another short period of time, the patient lies on a table and the SPECT camera rotates around his or her head (the patient does not go into a tube). The time on the table is approximately fifteen minutes. If a concentration study is ordered, the patient returns on another day to repeat the process; a concentration test is performed during the injection of the isotope.

Are there alternatives to having a SPECT study? In our opinion, SPECT is the most clinically useful study of brain function. There are other studies, such as quantitative electroencephalograms (qEEGs), positron emission tomography (PET) studies, and functional MRIs (fMRIs). PET studies and fMRIs tend to be more costly, and they are performed mostly in research settings. qEEGs can provide useful information, but often do not give information on the deep areas of the brain.

Does insurance cover the cost of SPECT studies? Reimbursement by insurance companies varies according to your plan. It is a good idea to check with the insurance company ahead of time to see if it is a covered benefit.

Is the use of brain SPECT imaging accepted in the medical community? Brain SPECT studies are widely recognized as an effective tool for evaluating brain function in seizures, strokes, dementia, and head trauma. There are literally thousands of research articles on these topics. In our clinics, based on our experience over twenty-four years, we have developed this technology further to evaluate aggression and nonresponsive psychiatric conditions. Unfortunately, many physicians do not fully understand the application of SPECT imaging and may tell you that the technology is experimental, but over five thousand medical and mental health professionals around the world have referred patients to us for scans.

22

Who Is Andrew Really?

Questions on the Essence of Our Humanity

I n the introduction, I told the story of Andrew, my nephew who became violent because of a brain cyst occupying the space in his left temporal lobe. When the cyst was removed, he returned to being his kind, caring, inquisitive self. In subsequent chapters I also discussed:

- Michelle, a woman who attacked her husband with a knife several days before her period and who, when treated effectively, became her normal nonviolent self.
- Samuel, a negative, oppositional ten-year-old who was failing in school and isolated from friends and who, when given treatment to calm his anterior cingulate gyrus, became successful at school, at home, and with friends.
- Rusty, a man who was arrested four times for assault and failed five drug treatment programs for methamphetamine abuse and who, since his underlying temporal lobe disorder was diagnosed and properly treated, has been able to remain personally more effective as well as gainfully employed.
- Sally, a woman admitted to the hospital as suicidal, depressed, and anxious and who, when properly diagnosed with adult ADD and effectively treated, felt less depressed and more focused, and was able to be the mother and wife she had always wanted to be.
- Willie, a college student who experienced "minor" head injuries in two car accidents and whose whole personality subsequently changed.

He became aggressive and depressed, and nearly killed his roommate. With the proper treatment he was able to return to his funny, happy, effective self.

- Randy, who had an explosive temper, a problem with drug abuse, and became suicidal. On the proper treatment he became pleasant, effective, and someone his family wanted to be around.
- Linda, a woman who had been raped on two occasions and who suffered from anxiety, depression, worry, and drug abuse. With St. John's wort and EMDR psychotherapy, her brain normalized and she was able to be much more effective in her life.
- John, a retired contractor who had been physically and emotionally abusive to his wife during most of their marriage, and emotionally abusive to his children. At the age of seventy-nine, after a psychotic episode following open-heart surgery, it was discovered that he had had a serious head injury at the age of twenty that had damaged his left frontal-temporal region. The head injury likely changed his behavior and affected three generations of his family.

These stories and many others in the book have caused me to question the very essence of who we are. Who are we really? Are we really who we are when our brain works right? Or are we really who we are when our brain misfires?

I believe, after seeing more than one hundred thousand SPECT studies (along with the patients and stories that go with them), that we are really who we are when our brain works right. When our brain works right, we are more thoughtful, more goal-oriented, and more interested in other people. We are kinder, our moods are more stable, and we are more tolerant. When our brains work right, anxiety doesn't rule us, although we have enough anxiety to get out of bed in the morning and go to work. When our brains work right, even though we may have negative thoughts from time to time, they do not rule our internal life. When our brains work right, even though we may have graphic, violent thoughts, they are not common and we do not act them out. When our brain works right and our spouse makes a mistake, we do not hold on to that mistake for twenty or thirty years. When our brains work right, we feel sexual, but we are not ruled by our sexual desires. When our brains work right, our children may still drive us crazy, but we act toward them in a positive, helpful way the vast majority of the time. When our brain works right, we are more able to be who we really want to be.

Other questions that this work has stimulated me to ask are:

- *What choices do we really have about our behavior?* Probably not as many as we think. Free will is not a black or white concept. It is gray.
- *Does our relationship with God depend on brain function?* It is probably easier to see a kind, loving, involved God when our brain works right. And it is probably easier to imagine a harsh, punitive God when we have an overactive cingulate and limbic system coloring the world in a negative way. (Although this will probably get a few people mad at me, I am not trying to be conflict seeking.)
- *Do we make bad choices as a result of bad training, in defiance of God's will, as a result of poverty, or because of a moral or character defect?* Perhaps, but again, we are more likely to make bad choices when our prefrontal cortex is underactive as a result of brain trauma or having ADD. Of course this doesn't mean we cannot make bad choices as a result of bad training, defiance of God, poverty, and the like, but doing so will be more likely when our internal supervisor is less active than necessary.
- *Do we make better choices when our brains work right?* "Of course we do" is the obvious answer from this book.
- *Is our personality a collection of neurons, neurotransmitters, and hormones?* Yes and no. Our personality is intimately connected to brain function, but as we have seen, brain function is also intimately connected to our thoughts and environment. They work in a circle and cannot be separated.
- *What does Mike Tyson's brain look like? Did he bite Evander Holyfield's ear in the heavyweight championship fight in 1997 because he wanted to embarrass himself and seem like an animal? Or did his brain misfire after a head butt and did his anterior cingulate and temporal lobes subsequently go haywire with little prefrontal cortex supervision?* I bet on the latter.

- *What would the brain SPECT scans of mass murderers, such as Sandy Hook killer Adam Lanza or the Batman killer James Holmes, look like? What about Adolf Hitler's brain scan?*
- *Should we scan potential presidential candidates? Don't we want to know about the brain health of the person who runs our country and could ruin life on earth?*
- *Should I scan my son's and daughter's romantic interests?* I think so. My kids were not thrilled about the idea, but both of my sons-in-law were scanned about a year after they started dating my daughters.

The questions could go on and on. The main point is that the brain matters in all we do. The brain is one of the first things we should think about when we try to understand abnormal behavior. Self-help programs need to consider the brain. To prevent relapse from substance abuse, to cut down on violence in our society, and to curtail the alarming rates of divorce and family discord, we need to think about the brain.

Of course, the brain doesn't function in a vacuum—we always need to think about the psychological, social, and spiritual underpinnings of behavior as well—but all behavior starts in the actual physical functioning of the brain. Your brain matters.

GRATITUDE AND APPRECIATION

So many people have been involved in the process of creating this book and helping me create brain warriors. I am grateful for and appreciate:

The tens of thousands of patients and families who have believed in our work, who allowed the staff at Amen Clinics and me to help them have better brains and better lives.

The amazing staff at Amen Clinics. As I write this, we currently serve four thousand patient visits a month, making us one of the most active private mental and brain health centers in the world. Our professionals work hard every day serving our patients. Special appreciation to my colleagues Tiffany Lesko and Jenny Faherty, who read every word of this book to make sure they all made sense and were easy to understand.

Our professional colleagues who believed in us and sent us their patients to evaluate, even when others were critical, especially Earl Henslin, Mark Laaser, Daniel McQuoid, David Jarvis, Linda Pepper, Jane Massengill, Jennifer Lendl, Sheila Krystal, Rick Lavine, David Smith, Rick Gilbert, Mark Kosins, Leon and Linda Webber, Matt Stubblefield, Mark Hyman, Steve Lawrence, Jerry Kartzinel, Marcello Urban, Jack Felton, Peg Kay, Glen Havens, Rick Sponaugle, Charles Parker, Orlando Vargas and our friends at the House of Freedom, the Crosby Center, Terrina Picarello, Russ Talbot and Talbot Recovery, Bruce Rind, Raphael Stricker, Curt Rouanzoin, Steve Eggleston, Darren and Jill CdeBaca, Bart Main, Barry Jay, Thomas Morell, Stephen Cobb, Paula Jo Husack, Heidi Kunzli at Prive Swiss, Jan Hackelman, Connie Hornyak, Michael Sampley, Susie Graff, Rogerio Rita, Begona Quintana, Fabiola Albani, and many others.

The myriad of people at Random House who helped make the book possible, including my publishers Shaye Areheart, Tina Constable, and Aaron Wehner, editors Betsy Rappaport, Kim Meisner, Julia Pastore, Heather Jackson, and Diana Baroni.

My literary agency for this book and many others, Sanford Greenburger Associates, including Faith Hamlin and Stephanie Diaz, our foreign rights agent. If you are reading this outside of the United States, Stephanie made that happen.

My friends and colleagues at public television stations across the country, including my mentors and friends Alan Foster, Lori Sugar, Alicia Steele, Kurt Mendelsohn, Greg Sherwood, Camille Dixon, Stacey Wiggins, Maura Phinney, Henry Broderson, Karen Nowak, Jackie Boyer, Jerry Liwanag, Suzanna Fiske, Stephen Hegg, Babette Davidson, Claire O'Conner-Solomon, Duane Huey, John Bell, and countless others. Public television is a treasure and I am grateful to be able to partner with stations to bring our message of hope and healing to millions.

My family, who have lived through my obsession with everything brain-related, especially my amazing wife, Tana, my children, Antony, Breanne, Kaitlyn, and Chloe, our grandchildren, and extended family. I know that many times you were tired of listening about the brain, but nonetheless loved me and gave me the limbic connectedness necessary to make a difference in the lives of others.

ABOUT DANIEL G. AMEN, M.D.

Daniel Amen believes that brain health is central to all health and success. When your brain works right, he says, you work right; and when your brain is troubled you are much more likely to have trouble in your life. His work is dedicated to helping people have better brains and better lives.

The *Washington Post* wrote that Dr. Amen is the most popular psychiatrist in America and Sharecare named him the Web's number one most influential expert and advocate on mental health.

Dr. Amen is a physician, double-board-certified psychiatrist, and ten-time *New York Times* bestselling author. He is the founder of Amen Clinics in Costa Mesa and San Francisco, California; Bellevue, Washington; Reston, Virginia; Atlanta, Georgia; Chicago, Illinois; and New York, New York. Amen Clinics have the world's largest database of functional brain scans relating to behavior, totaling more than one hundred thousand scans on patients from 111 countries.

He is a Distinguished Fellow of the American Psychiatric Association, the highest award given to members, and is the lead researcher on the world's largest brain-imaging and rehabilitation study on professional football players. His research has not only demonstrated high levels of brain damage in players, but Dr. Amen has also shown the possibility of significant recovery for many with the principles that underlie his work.

Together with Pastor Rick Warren and Dr. Mark Hyman, Dr. Amen is also one of the chief architects of Saddleback Church's "Daniel Plan," a program to get the world healthy through religious organizations.

Dr. Amen has written, produced, and hosted nine popular shows about the brain, which have raised more than $55 million for public television.

Dr. Amen is the author or coauthor of seventy professional articles, seven book chapters, and over thirty books, including the number one *New York Times* bestseller *The Daniel Plan*; *Change Your Brain, Change Your Life*; *Magnificent Mind at Any Age*; *Change Your Brain, Change Your Body*; *Use Your Brain to Change Your Age*; *Unleash the Power of the Female Brain*; and *Healing ADD*.

Dr. Amen's published scientific articles have appeared in the prestigious journals *Molecular Psychiatry, PLOS One, Brain Imaging and Behavior, Nature's Translational Psychiatry, Nature's Obesity, Journal of Neuropsychiatry and Clinical Neuroscience, Minerva Psichiatrica, Journal of Neurotrauma, American Journal of Psychiatry, Nuclear Medicine Communication, Neurological Research, Journal of the American Academy of Child and Adolescent Psychiatry, Primary Psychiatry, Military Medicine*, and *General Hospital Psychiatry*.

Dr. Amen has appeared in movies, including *After the Last Round* and *The Crash Reel*, and has appeared on Emmy-winning shows, such as *The Truth About Drinking* and the *Dr. Oz Show*. He has also spoken for the National Security Agency (NSA), the National Science Foundation (NSF), Harvard's Learning & the Brain Conference, the Department of the Interior, the National Council of Juvenile and Family Court Judges, and the Supreme Courts of Delaware, Ohio, and Wyoming. Dr. Amen's work has been featured in *Newsweek, Time, Huffington Post, ABC World News, 20/20, BBC, London Telegraph, Parade Magazine, New York Times, New York Times Magazine, Washington Post, LA Times, Men's Health, Bottom Line*, and *Cosmopolitan*.

Dr. Amen is married to Tana and is the father of four children, and grandfather to Elias, Emmy, Liam, and Louie. He collects penguins and is an avid table tennis player.

ABOUT AMEN CLINICS, INC.

Amen Clinics, Inc. (ACI), was established in 1989 by Daniel G. Amen, M.D. It specializes in innovative diagnosis and treatment planning for a wide variety of behavioral, learning, emotional, cognitive, and weight issues for children, teenagers, and adults. ACI has an international reputation for evaluating brain–behavior problems, such as ADD, depression, anxiety, school failure, brain trauma, obsessive-compulsive disorder, aggressiveness, marital conflict, cognitive decline, brain toxicity from drugs or alcohol, and obesity. In addition, we work with people to optimize brain function and decrease the risk for Alzheimer's disease and other age-related issues.

Brain SPECT imaging is performed in the clinics. ACI has the world's largest database of brain scans for emotional, cognitive, and behavioral problems. ACI welcomes referrals from physicians, psychologists, social workers, marriage and family therapists, drug and alcohol counselors, and individual patients and families.

Our toll-free number is (888) 564–2700.

Amen Clinics Orange County, California
3150 Bristol St., Suite 400
Costa Mesa, CA 92626

Amen Clinics San Francisco
1000 Marina Blvd., Suite 100
Brisbane, CA 94005

Amen Clinics Northwest
616 120th Ave. NE, Suite C100
Bellevue, WA 98005

Amen Clinics Washington, DC
1875 Campus Commons Dr.
Reston, VA 20191

Amen Clinics New York
16 East 40th St., 9th Floor
New York, NY 10016

Amen Clinics Atlanta
5901-C Peachtree Dunwoody Road, N.E., Suite 65
Atlanta, Georgia 30328

WWW.AMENCLINICS.COM

Amenclinics.com is an educational, interactive website geared toward mental health and medical professionals, educators, students, and the general public. It contains a wealth of information and resources to help you learn about and optimize your brain. The site contains more than three hundred color brain SPECT images, thousands of scientific abstracts on brain SPECT imaging for psychiatry, a free brain health audit, and much, much more.

Based on Dr. Amen's thirty years as a clinical psychiatrist, he has developed a sophisticated online community to help you feel smarter, happier, and younger. It includes:

- Detailed questionnaires, to help you know your BRAIN TYPE and personalize a program to your own needs
- WebNeuro, a sophisticated neuropsychological test, to assess your brain
- Based on WebNeuro results, targeted brain exercises in the form of fun games to strengthen your vulnerable areas
- Exclusive, award-winning 24/7 BRAIN GYM MEMBERSHIP
- Interactive daily journal to track your numbers, calories, and brain-healthy habits
- Hundreds of brain-healthy recipes, tips, shopping lists, and menu plans
- Daily tips that can be sent via text messages to help you remember your supplements and stay on track
- Relaxation room to help you eliminate stress and overcome negative thinking patterns
- Hypnosis audios for sleep, anxiety, overcoming weight issues, pain, and peak performance

REFERENCES

1. Amen DG, Newberg A, Thatcher R, Jin Y, Wu J, Keator D, et al. Impact of playing American professional football on long-term brain function. *The Journal of Neuropsychiatry and Clinical Neurosciences.* 2011;23(1):98–106. doi: 10.1176/appi.neuropsych.23.1.98. PubMed PMID: 21304145.

2. Amen DG, Wu JC, Taylor D, Willeumier K. Reversing brain damage in former NFL players: implications for traumatic brain injury and substance abuse rehabilitation. *Journal of Psychoactive Drugs.* 2011;43(1):1–5. doi: 10.1080/02791072.2011.566489. 10.1080/02791072.2011.602282. PubMed PMID: 21615001.

3. Insel TR. Disruptive insights in psychiatry: transforming a clinical discipline. *The Journal of Clinical Investigation.* 2009;119(4):700–5. doi: 10.1172/JCI38832. PubMed PMID: 19339761; PubMed Central PMCID: PMC2662575.

4. Kirsch I. Review: benefits of antidepressants over placebo limited except in very severe depression. *Evidence-based Mental Health.* 2010;13(2):49. doi: 10.1136/ebmh.13.2.49. PubMed PMID: 21856612.

5. Kempf EJ. An Analytical Biography of a Great Mind. Available from: http://www.lincolnportrait.com/common_sense_fracture.html.

6. Hippocrates. *The Genuine Works of Hippocrates.* California: W. Wood and Company, 1886.

7. Reber P. What Is the Memory Capacity of the Human Brain? 2010. Available from: http://www.scientificamerican.com/article/what-is-the-memory-capacity/.

8. Defense and Veterans Brain Injury Center. DoD Worldwide Numbers for TBI 2014 [cited 2014 September 9]. Available from: http://dvbic.dcoe.mil/dod-worldwide-numbers-tbi.

9. Liu CS, Carvalho AF, McIntyre RS. Towards a "metabolic" subtype of major depressive disorder: shared pathophysiological mechanisms may contribute to cognitive dysfunction. *CNS & Neurological Disorders Drug Targets.* 2014. PubMed PMID: 25470395.

10. Pan W, Kastin AJ. Can sleep apnea cause Alzheimer's disease? *Neuroscience and Biobehavioral Reviews.* 2014;47C:656–69. doi: 10.1016/j.neubiorev.2014.10.019. PubMed PMID: 25451764.

11. Allan CL, Zsoldos E, Filippini N, Sexton CE, Topiwala A, Valkanova V, et al. Lifetime hypertension as a predictor of brain structure in older adults: cohort study with a 28-year follow up. *The British Journal of Psychiatry: The Journal of Mental Science*. 2014. doi: 10.1192/bjp.bp.114.153536. PubMed PMID: 25497301.

12. Windham BG, Simpson BN, Lirette S, Bridges J, Bielak L, Peyser PA, et al. Associations between inflammation and cognitive function in African Americans and European Americans. *Journal of the American Geriatrics Society*. 2014;62(12):2303–10. doi: 10.1111/jgs.13165. PubMed PMID: 25516026; PubMed Central PMCID: PMC4270090.

13. Barbagallo M, Dominguez LJ. Type 2 diabetes mellitus and Alzheimer's disease. *World Journal of Diabetes*. 2014;5(6):889–93. doi: 10.4239/wjd.v5.i6.889. PubMed PMID: 25512792; PubMed Central PMCID: PMC4265876.

14. Salak Djokic B, Spitznagel MB, Pavlovic D, Jankovic N, Parojcic A, Ilic V, et al. Diabetes mellitus and cognitive functioning in a Serbian sample. *Journal of Clinical and Experimental Neuropsychology*. 2014:1–12. doi: 10.1080/13803395.2014.985190. PubMed PMID: 25523209.

15. Dassanayake TL, Michie PT, Jones A, Carter G, Mallard T, Whyte I. Cognitive impairment in patients clinically recovered from central nervous system depressant drug overdose. *Journal of Clinical Psychopharmacology*. 2012;32(4):503–10. doi: 10.1097/JCP.0b013e31825d6ddb. PubMed PMID: 22722510.

16. Sander R. Link between Alzheimer's disease and benzodiazepines suspected. *Nursing Older People*. 2014;26(10):13. doi: 10.7748/nop.26.10.13.s15. PubMed PMID: 25430840.

17. Jiang T, Yu JT, Tian Y, Tan L. Epidemiology and etiology of Alzheimer's disease: from genetic to non-genetic factors. *Current Alzheimer Research*. 2013;10(8):852–67. PubMed PMID: 23919770.

18. Munoz-Quezada MT, Lucero BA, Barr DB, Steenland K, Levy K, Ryan PB, et al. Neurodevelopmental effects in children associated with exposure to organophosphate pesticides: a systematic review. *Neurotoxicology*. 2013;39:158–68. doi: 10.1016/j.neuro.2013.09.003. PubMed PMID: 24121005; PubMed Central PMCID: PMC3899350.

19. Griffin GD, Charron D, Al-Daccak R. Post-traumatic stress disorder: revisiting adrenergics, glucocorticoids, immune system effects and homeostasis. *Clinical & Translational Immunology*. 2014;3(11):e27. doi: 10.1038/cti.2014.26. PubMed PMID: 25505957; PubMed Central PMCID: PMC4255796.

20. Moench KM, Wellman CL. Stress-induced alterations in prefrontal dendritic spines: implications for post-traumatic stress disorder. *Neuroscience Letters*. 2014. doi: 10.1016/j.neulet.2014.12.035. PubMed PMID: 25529195.

21. Christakis NA, Fowler JH. The spread of obesity in a large social network over 32 years. *The New England Journal of Medicine*. 2007;357(4):370–79. doi: 10.1056/NEJMsa066082. PubMed PMID: 17652652.

22. Pembrey ME, Bygren LO, Kaati G, Edvinsson S, Northstone K, Sjostrom M, et al. Sex-specific, male-line transgenerational responses in humans. *European Journal of Human Genetics: EJHG*. 2006;14(2):159–66. doi: 10.1038/sj.ejhg.5201538. PubMed PMID: 16391557.

23. Karsli-Ceppioglu S, Dagdemir A, Judes G, Ngollo M, Penault-Llorca F, Pajon A, et al. Epigenetic mechanisms of breast cancer: an update of the current knowledge. *Epigenomics.* 2014;6(6):651–64. doi: 10.2217/epi.14.59. PubMed PMID: 25531258.

24. Labbe DP, Zadra G, Ebot EM, Mucci LA, Kantoff PW, Loda M, et al. Role of diet in prostate cancer: the epigenetic link. *Oncogene.* 2014. doi: 10.1038/onc.2014.422. PubMed PMID: 25531313.

25. Suva ML. Genetics and epigenetics of gliomas. *Swiss Medical Weekly.* 2014;144:w14018. doi: 10.4414/smw.2014.14018. PubMed PMID: 25356909.

26. Dauncey MJ. Nutrition, the brain and cognitive decline: insights from epigenetics. *European Journal of Clinical Nutrition.* 2014;68(11):1179–85. doi: 10.1038/ejcn.2014.173. PubMed PMID: 25182020.

27. Devall M, Mill J, Lunnon K. The mitochondrial epigenome: a role in Alzheimer's disease? *Epigenomics.* 2014;6(6):665–75. doi: 10.2217/epi.14.50. PubMed PMID: 25531259.

28. Babenko O, Kovalchuk I, Metz GA. Stress-induced perinatal and transgenerational epigenetic programming of brain development and mental health. *Neuroscience and Biobehavioral Reviews.* 2015;48C:70–91. doi: 10.1016/j.neubiorev.2014.11.013. PubMed PMID: 25464029.

29. Debnath M, Venkatasubramanian G, Berk M. Fetal programming of schizophrenia: select mechanisms. *Neuroscience and Biobehavioral Reviews.* 2014. doi: 10.1016/j.neubiorev.2014.12.003. PubMed PMID: 25496904.

30. Lesseur C, Paquette AG, Marsit CJ. Epigenetic regulation of infant neurobehavioral outcomes. *Medical Epigenetics.* 2014;2(2):71–79. doi: 10.1159/000361026. PubMed PMID: 25089125; PubMed Central PMCID: PMC4116357.

31. Zhou D, Pan YX. Pathophysiological basis for compromised health beyond generations: role of maternal high-fat diet and low-grade chronic inflammation. *The Journal of Nutritional Biochemistry.* 2015;26(1):1–8. doi: 10.1016/j.jnutbio.2014.06.011. PubMed PMID: 25440222.

32. Reddy MA, Zhang E, Natarajan R. Epigenetic mechanisms in diabetic complications and metabolic memory. *Diabetologia.* 2014. doi: 10.1007/s00125–014–3462-y. PubMed PMID: 25481708.

33. Yuan W, Xia Y, Bell CG, Yet I, Ferreira T, Ward KJ, et al. An integrated epigenomic analysis for type 2 diabetes susceptibility loci in monozygotic twins. *Nature Communications.* 2014;5:5719. doi: 10.1038/ncomms6719. PubMed PMID: 25502755.

34. Amen DG, Jourdain M, Taylor DV, Pigott HE, Willeumier K. Multi-site six month outcome study of complex psychiatric patients evaluated with addition of brain SPECT imaging. *Advances in Mind-Body Medicine.* 2013;27(2):6–16. PubMed PMID: 23709407.

35. Thornton JF, Schneider H, McLean MK, van Lierop MJ, Tarzwell R. Improved outcomes using brain SPECT-guided treatment versus treatment-as-usual in community psychiatric outpatients: a retrospective case-control study. *The Journal of Neuropsychiatry and Clinical Neurosciences.* 2014;26(1):51–56. doi: 10.1176/appi.neuropsych.12100238. PubMed PMID: 24275845.

36. Hill PL, Turiano NA. Purpose in life as a predictor of mortality across adulthood. *Psy-*

chological Science. 2014;25(7):1482–86. doi: 10.1177/0956797614531799. PubMed PMID: 24815612; PubMed Central PMCID: PMC4224996.

37. Steptoe A, Deaton A, Stone AA. Subjective wellbeing, health, and ageing. *Lancet.* 2014. doi: 10.1016/S0140–6736(13)61489–0. PubMed PMID: 25468152.

38. Cohen R, Bavishi C, Rozanski A. Abstract 52: Purpose in life and its relationship to all-cause mortality and cardiovascular events: a meta analysis. *EPI/LIFESTYLE.* 2015 Scientific Sessions; Baltimore, MD: American Heart Association/Circulation; 2015.

39. Amen DG, Highum D, Licata R, Annibali JA, Somner L, Pigott HE, et al. Specific ways brain SPECT imaging enhances clinical psychiatric practice. *Journal of Psychoactive Drugs.* 2012;44(2):96–106. doi: 10.1080/02791072.2012.684615. PubMed PMID: 22880537.

40. Billioti de Gage S, Moride Y, Ducruet T, Kurth T, Verdoux H, Tournier M, et al. Benzo-diazepine use and risk of Alzheimer's disease: case-control study. *BMJ.* 2014;349:g5205. doi: 10.1136/bmj.g5205. PubMed PMID: 25208536; PubMed Central PMCID: PMC4159609.

41. Gallacher J, Elwood P, Pickering J, Bayer A, Fish M, Ben-Shlomo Y. Benzodiazepine use and risk of dementia: evidence from the Caerphilly Prospective Study (CaPS). *Journal of Epidemiology and Community Health.* 2012;66(10):869–73. doi: 10.1136/jech-2011–200314. PubMed PMID: 22034632.

42. Wu CS, Wang SC, Chang IS, Lin KM. The association between dementia and long-term use of benzodiazepine in the elderly: nested case-control study using claims data. *The American Journal of Geriatric Psychiatry: Official Journal of the American Association for Geriatric Psychiatry.* 2009;17(7):614–20. doi: 10.1097/JGP.0b013e3181a65210. PubMed PMID: 19546656.

43. Kelly JB. Children's adjustment in conflicted marriage and divorce: a decade review of research. *Journal of the American Academy of Child and Adolescent Psychiatry.* 2000;39(8):963–73. doi: 10.1097/00004583–200008000–00007. PubMed PMID: 10939225.

44. Hoehn-Saric R, Pearlson GD, Harris GJ, Machlin SR, Camargo EE. Effects of fluoxetine on regional cerebral blood flow in obsessive-compulsive patients. *American Journal of Psychiatry.* 1991;148(9):1243–45. PubMed PMID: 1883007.

45. GE Reports. No Cure but a Wish to Know: We Want to Know If Brain Disease Will Strike: GE; 2014. Available from: http://www.gereports.com/post/95174800798/no-cure-but-a-wish-to-know-we-want-to-know-if.

46. Kiliaan AJ, Arnoldussen IA, Gustafson DR. Adipokines: a link between obesity and demen-tia? *The Lancet Neurology.* 2014;13(9):913–23. doi: 10.1016/S1474–4422(14)70085–7. PubMed PMID: 25142458; PubMed Central PMCID: PMC4228955.

47. Garcia-Ptacek S, Faxen-Irving G, Cermakova P, Eriksdotter M, Religa D. Body mass index in dementia. *European Journal of Clinical Nutrition.* 2014;68(11):1204–9. doi: 10.1038/ejcn.2014.199. PubMed PMID: 25271014.

48. Deckers K, van Boxtel MP, Schiepers OJ, de Vugt M, Munoz Sanchez JL, Anstey KJ, et al. Target risk factors for dementia prevention: a systematic review and Delphi consensus study on the evidence from observational studies. *International Journal of Geriatric Psy-chiatry.* 2014. doi: 10.1002/gps.4245. PubMed PMID: 25504093.

49. Parthasarathy S, Vasquez MM, Halonen M, Bootzin R, Quan SF, Martinez FD, et al. Persistent insomnia is associated with mortality risk. *The American Journal of Medicine.* 2014. doi: 10.1016/j.amjmed.2014.10.015. PubMed PMID: 25447616.

50. Sivertsen B, Pallesen S, Glozier N, Bjorvatn B, Salo P, Tell GS, et al. Midlife insomnia and subsequent mortality: the Hordaland health study. *BMC Public Health.* 2014;14:720. doi: 10.1186/1471-2458-14-720. PubMed PMID: 25024049; PubMed Central PMCID: PMC4223526.

51. Yaffe K, Falvey CM, Hoang T. Connections between sleep and cognition in older adults. *The Lancet Neurology.* 2014;13(10):1017–28. doi: 10.1016/S1474-4422(14)70172-3. PubMed PMID: 25231524.

52. Pace-Schott EF, Spencer RM. Sleep-dependent memory consolidation in healthy aging and mild cognitive impairment. *Current Topics in Behavioral Neurosciences.* 2014. doi: 10.1007/7854_2014_300. PubMed PMID: 24652608.

53. Winsler A, Deutsch A, Vorona RD, Payne PA, Szklo-Coxe M. Sleepless in Fairfax: the difference one more hour of sleep can make for teen hopelessness, suicidal ideation, and substance use. *Journal of Youth and Adolescence.* 2014. doi: 10.1007/s10964-014-0170-3. PubMed PMID: 25178930.

54. Coughlin JW, Smith MT. Sleep, obesity, and weight loss in adults: is there a rationale for providing sleep interventions in the treatment of obesity? *International Review of Psychiatry.* 2014;26(2):177–88. doi: 10.3109/09540261.2014.911150. PubMed PMID: 24892893.

55. Williamson AM, Feyer AM. Moderate sleep deprivation produces impairments in cognitive and motor performance equivalent to legally prescribed levels of alcohol intoxication. *Occupational and Environmental Medicine.* 2000;57(10):649–55. PubMed PMID: 10984335; PubMed Central PMCID: PMC1739867.

56. Iliff J. One more reason to get a good night's sleep. In TED, editor. 2014.

57. Hajjar I, Marmerelis V, Shin DC, Chui H. Assessment of cerebrovascular reactivity during resting state breathing and its correlation with cognitive function in hypertension. *Cerebrovascular Diseases.* 2014;38(1):10–6. doi: 10.1159/000365349. PubMed PMID: 25171390; PubMed Central PMCID: PMC4216224.

58. Peterson CA, Tosh AK, Belenchia AM. Vitamin D insufficiency and insulin resistance in obese adolescents. *Therapeutic Advances in Endocrinology and Metabolism.* 2014;5(6):166–89. doi: 10.1177/2042018814547205. PubMed PMID: 25489472; PubMed Central PMCID: PMC4257980.

59. Polak MA, Houghton LA, Reeder AI, Harper MJ, Conner TS. Serum 25-hydroxyvitamin D concentrations and depressive symptoms among young adult men and women. *Nutrients.* 2014;6(11):4720–30. doi: 10.3390/nu6114720. PubMed PMID: 25353666; PubMed Central PMCID: PMC4245559.

60. Perna L, Mons U, Kliegel M, Brenner H. Serum 25-hydroxyvitamin D and cognitive decline: a longitudinal study among non-demented older adults. *Dementia and Geriatric Cognitive Disorders.* 2014;38(3–4):254–63. doi: 10.1159/000362870. PubMed PMID: 24969663.

61. Schlogl M, Holick MF. Vitamin D and neurocognitive function. *Clinical Interventions*

in Aging. 2014;9:559–68. doi: 10.2147/CIA.S51785. PubMed PMID: 24729696; PubMed Central PMCID: PMC3979692.

62. Ruwanpathirana T, Reid CM, Owen AJ, Fong DP, Gowda U, Renzaho AM. Assessment of vitamin D and its association with cardiovascular disease risk factors in an adult migrant population: an audit of patient records at a Community Health Centre in Kensington, Melbourne, Australia. *BMC Cardiovascular Disorders.* 2014;14:157. doi: 10.1186/1471–2261–14–157. PubMed PMID: 25387481; PubMed Central PMCID: PMC4233056.

63. Khadanga S, Massey CV. Incidence of vitamin D insufficiency in coastal south-eastern US patient population with cardiovascular disease. *Journal of Clinical Medicine Research.* 2014;6(6):469–75. doi: 10.14740/jocmr1953w. PubMed PMID: 25247022; PubMed Central PMCID: PMC4169090.

64. Hewison M. An update on vitamin D and human immunity. *Clinical Endocrinology.* 2012;76(3):315–25. doi: 10.1111/j.1365–2265.2011.04261.x. PubMed PMID: 21995874.

65. Sahay T, Ananthakrishnan AN. Vitamin D deficiency is associated with community-acquired clostridium difficile infection: a case-control study. *BMC Infectious Diseases.* 2014;14:661. doi: 10.1186/s12879–014–0661–6. PubMed PMID: 25471926; PubMed Central PMCID: PMC4258019.

66. Wranicz J, Szostak-Wegierek D. Health outcomes of vitamin D. Part II. Role in prevention of diseases. *Roczniki Panstwowego Zakladu Higieny.* 2014;65(4):273–79. PubMed PMID: 25526571.

67. Belvederi Murri M, Respino M, Masotti M, Innamorati M, Mondelli V, Pariante C, et al. Vitamin D and psychosis: mini meta-analysis. *Schizophrenia Research.* 2013;150(1):235–39. doi: 10.1016/j.schres.2013.07.017. PubMed PMID: 23906618.

68. Afzal S, Brondum-Jacobsen P, Bojesen SE, Nordestgaard BG. Genetically low vitamin D concentrations and increased mortality: Mendelian randomisation analysis in three large cohorts. *BMJ.* 2014;349:g6330. doi: 10.1136/bmj.g6330. PubMed PMID: 25406188; PubMed Central PMCID: PMC4238742.

69. Bjelakovic G, Gluud LL, Nikolova D, Whitfield K, Wetterslev J, Simonetti RG, et al. Vitamin D supplementation for prevention of mortality in adults. *The Cochrane Database of Systematic Reviews.* 2014;1:CD007470. doi: 10.1002/14651858.CD007470.pub3. PubMed PMID: 24414552.

70. Nowakowski AC. Chronic inflammation and quality of life in older adults: a cross-sectional study using biomarkers to predict emotional and relational outcomes. *Health and Quality of Life Outcomes.* 2014;12:141. doi: 10.1186/s12955–014–0141–0. PubMed PMID: 25260501; PubMed Central PMCID: PMC4189208.

71. O'Doherty MG, Jorgensen T, Borglykke A, Brenner H, Schottker B, Wilsgaard T, et al. Repeated measures of body mass index and C-reactive protein in relation to all-cause mortality and cardiovascular disease: results from the consortium on health and ageing network of cohorts in Europe and the United States (CHANCES). *European Journal of Epidemiology.* 2014. doi: 10.1007/s10654–014–9954–8. PubMed PMID: 25421782.

72. Chen JM, Cui GH, Jiang GX, Xu RF, Tang HD, Wang G, et al. Cognitive impairment among elderly individuals in Shanghai suburb, China: association of C-reactive protein and its interactions with other relevant factors. *American Journal of Alzheimer's Disease and Other Dementias.* 2014;29(8):712–17. doi: 10.1177/1533317514534758. PubMed PMID: 24928820.

73. Purves et al. *Neuroscience,* 2nd Edition. Purves E, Augustine GJ, Fitzpatrick D, et al., editor. Sunderland, MA: Sinauer Associates; 2001.

74. Papez JW. A proposed mechanism of emotion. *Arch Neurol Psychiatry.* 1937;38:725–43.

75. MacLean PD. *The Triune Brain in Evolution: Role in Paleocerebral Functions.* New York: Plenum Press; 1990.

76. Morgane PJ, Galler JR, Mokler DJ. A review of systems and networks of the limbic forebrain/limbic midbrain. *Progress in Neurobiology.* 2005;75(2):143–60. doi: 10.1016/j.pneurobio.2005.01.001. PubMed PMID: 15784304.

77. Hubbard NA, Hutchison JL, Turner M, Montroy J, Bowles RP, Rypma B. Depressive thoughts limit working memory capacity in dysphoria. *Cognition and Emotion.* 2015:1– 17. doi: 10.1080/02699931.2014.991694. PubMed PMID: 25562416.

78. Sublette ME, Ellis SP, Geant AL, Mann JJ. Meta-analysis of the effects of eicosapentaenoic acid (EPA) in clinical trials in depression. *The Journal of Clinical Psychiatry.* 2011;72(12):1577–84. doi: 10.4088/JCP.10m06634. PubMed PMID: 21939614; PubMed Central PMCID: PMC3534764.

79. Martins JG. EPA but not DHA appears to be responsible for the efficacy of omega-3 long chain polyunsaturated fatty acid supplementation in depression: evidence from a meta-analysis of randomized controlled trials. *Journal of the American College of Nutrition.* 2009;28(5):525–42. PubMed PMID: 20439549.

80. Sarris J, Papakostas GI, Vitolo O, Fava M, Mischoulon D. S-adenosyl methionine (SAMe) versus escitalopram and placebo in major depression RCT: efficacy and effects of histamine and carnitine as moderators of response. *Journal of Affective Disorders.* 2014;164:76–81. doi: 10.1016/j.jad.2014.03.041. PubMed PMID: 24856557.

81. Hopton A, Macpherson H, Keding A, Morley S. Acupuncture, counselling or usual care for depression and comorbid pain: secondary analysis of a randomised controlled trial. *BMJ Open.* 2014;4(5):e004964. doi: 10.1136/bmjopen-2014–004964. PubMed PMID: 24793257; PubMed Central PMCID: PMC4024599.

82. MacPherson H, Richmond S, Bland M, Brealey S, Gabe R, Hopton A, et al. Acupuncture and counselling for depression in primary care: a randomised controlled trial. *PLOS Medicine.* 2013;10(9):e1001518. doi: 10.1371/journal.pmed.1001518. PubMed PMID: 24086114; PubMed Central PMCID: PMC3782410.

83. Chang BH, Sommers E. Acupuncture and relaxation response for craving and anxiety reduction among military veterans in recovery from substance use disorder. *The American Journal on Addictions* / American Academy of Psychiatrists in Alcoholism and Addictions. 2014;23(2):129–36. doi: 10.1111/j.1521–0391.2013.12079.x. PubMed PMID: 25187049.

84. Lee I, Wallraven C, Kong J, Chang D, Lee H, Park H, et al. When pain is not only pain: inserting needles into the body evokes distinct reward-related brain responses in

the context of a treatment. *Physiology & Behavior.* 2014;140C:148–55. doi: 10.1016/j.physbeh.2014.12.030. PubMed PMID: 25528104.

85. Chen JR, Li GL, Zhang GF, Huang Y, Wang SX, Lu N. Brain areas involved in acupuncture needling sensation of de qi: a single-photon emission computed tomography (SPECT) study. *Acupuncture in Medicine: Journal of the British Medical Acupuncture Society.* 2012;30(4):316–23. doi: 10.1136/acupmed-2012–010169. PubMed PMID: 23023060.

86. Chae Y, Chang DS, Lee SH, Jung WM, Lee IS, Jackson S, et al. Inserting needles into the body: a meta-analysis of brain activity associated with acupuncture needle stimulation. *The Journal of Pain: Official Journal of the American Pain Society.* 2013;14(3):215–22. doi: 10.1016/j.jpain.2012.11.011. PubMed PMID: 23395475.

87. McGirr A, Van den Eynde F, Tovar-Perdomo S, Fleck MP, Berlim MT. Effectiveness and acceptability of accelerated repetitive transcranial magnetic stimulation (rTMS) for treatment-resistant major depressive disorder: an open label trial. *Journal of Affective Disorders.* 2015;173:216–20. doi: 10.1016/j.jad.2014.10.068. PubMed PMID: 25462419.

88. Barclay TH, Barclay RD. A clinical trial of cranial electrotherapy stimulation for anxiety and comorbid depression. *Journal of Affective Disorders.* 2014;164:171–77. doi: 10.1016/j.jad.2014.04.029. PubMed PMID: 24856571.

89. Feusner JD, Madsen S, Moody TD, Bohon C, Hembacher E, Bookheimer SY, et al. Effects of cranial electrotherapy stimulation on resting state brain activity. *Brain and Behavior.* 2012;2(3):21120. doi: 10.1002/brb3.45. PubMed PMID: 22741094; PubMed Central PMCID: PMC3381625.

90. Kubik A, Biedron A. Neurofeedback therapy in patients with acute and chronic pain syndromes—literature review and own experience. *Przeglad Lekarski.* 2013;70(7):440–42. PubMed PMID: 24167944.

91. Linden DE, Habes I, Johnston SJ, Linden S, Tatineni R, Subramanian L, et al. Real-time self-regulation of emotion networks in patients with depression. *PLOS ONE.* 2012;7(6):e38115. doi: 10.1371/journal.pone.0038115. PubMed PMID: 22675513; PubMed Central PMCID: PMC3366978.

92. Christiansen H, Reh V, Schmidt MH, Rief W. Slow cortical potential neurofeedback and self-management training in outpatient care for children with ADHD: study protocol and first preliminary results of a randomized controlled trial. *Frontiers in Human Neuroscience.* 2014;8:943. doi: 10.3389/fnhum.2014.00943. PubMed PMID: 25505396; PubMed Central PMCID: PMC4244863.

93. Micoulaud-Franchi JA, Geoffroy PA, Fond G, Lopez R, Bioulac S, Philip P. EEG neurofeedback treatments in children with ADHD: an updated meta-analysis of randomized controlled trials. *Frontiers in Human Neuroscience.* 2014;8:906. doi: 10.3389/fnhum.2014.00906. PubMed PMID: 25431555; PubMed Central PMCID: PMC4230047.

94. Blumenthal JA, Babyak MA, Moore KA, Craighead WE, Herman S, Khatri P, et al. Effects of exercise training on older patients with major depression. *Archives of Internal Medicine.* 1999;159(19):2349–56. PubMed PMID: 10547175.

95. Stellar JE, John-Henderson N, Anderson CL, Gordon AM, McNeil GD, Keltner D. Positive affect and markers of inflammation: discrete positive emotions predict lower

levels of inflammatory cytokines. *Emotion.* 2015. doi: 10.1037/emo0000033. PubMed PMID: 25603133.

96. Byron K, Mitchell S. *Loving What Is: Four Questons That Can Change Your Life.* New York: Three Rivers Press, 2002.

97. Resnick MD, Bearman PS, Blum RW, Bauman KE, Harris KM, Jones J, et al. Protecting adolescents from harm. Findings from the National Longitudinal Study on Adolescent Health. *JAMA.* 1997;278(10):823–32. PubMed PMID: 9293990.

98. Shea MT, Elkin I, Imber SD, Sotsky SM, Watkins JT, Collins JF, et al. Course of depressive symptoms over follow-up. Findings from the National Institute of Mental Health Treatment of Depression Collaborative Research Program. *Archives of General Psychiatry.* 1992;49(10):782–87. PubMed PMID: 1417430.

99. Chugani HT, Behen ME, Muzik O, Juhasz C, Nagy F, Chugani DC. Local brain functional activity following early deprivation: a study of postinstitutionalized Romanian orphans. *NeuroImage.* 2001;14(6):1290–301. doi: 10.1006/nimg.2001.0917. PubMed PMID: 11707085.

100. Eapen V, Clarke RA. Autism spectrum disorders: from genotypes to phenotypes. *Frontiers in Human Neuroscience.* 2014;8:914. doi: 10.3389/fnhum.2014.00914. PubMed PMID: 25429265; PubMed Central PMCID: PMC4228832.

101. Kim YS, Leventhal BL. Genetic epidemiology and insights into interactive genetic and environmental effects in autism spectrum disorders. *Biological Psychiatry.* 2015;77(1):66–74. doi: 10.1016/j.biopsych.2014.11.001. PubMed PMID: 25483344; PubMed Central PMCID: PMC4260177.

102. Bush B. Barbara Bush Reflects on Her Life as First Lady. In King L, editor. *Larry King Live Weekend:* CNN, 2001.

103. Sin NL, Lyubomirsky S. Enhancing well-being and alleviating depressive symptoms with positive psychology interventions: a practice-friendly meta-analysis. *Journal of Clinical Psychology.* 2009;65(5):467–87. doi: 10.1002/jclp.20593. PubMed PMID: 19301241.

104. Weng HY, Fox AS, Shackman AJ, Stodola DE, Caldwell JZ, Olson MC, et al. Compassion training alters altruism and neural responses to suffering. *Psychological Science.* 2013;24(7):1171–80. doi: 10.1177/0956797612469537. PubMed PMID: 23696200; PubMed Central PMCID: PMC3713090.

105. Burguiere E, Monteiro P, Mallet L, Feng G, Graybiel AM. Striatal circuits, habits, and implications for obsessive-compulsive disorder. *Current Opinion in Neurobiology.* 2014;30C:59–65. doi: 10.1016/j.conb.2014.08.008. PubMed PMID: 25241072.

106. Da Cunha C, Gomez AA, Blaha CD. The role of the basal ganglia in motivated behavior. *Reviews in the Neurosciences.* 2012;23(5–6):747–67. doi: 10.1515/revneuro-2012–0063. PubMed PMID: 23079510.

107. Langmaid RA, Papadopoulos N, Johnson BP, Phillips JG, Rinehart NJ. Handwriting in children with ADHD. *Journal of Attention Disorders.* 2012;18(6):504–10. doi: 10.1177/1087054711434154. PubMed PMID: 22617862.

108. Stathis P, Panourias IG, Themistocleous MS, Sakas DE. Connections of the basal ganglia with the limbic system: implications for neuromodulation therapies of anxiety and affec-

tive disorders. *Acta Neurochirurgica Supplement.* 2007;97(Pt 2):575–86. PubMed PMID: 17691350.

109. Howe MW, Atallah HE, McCool A, Gibson DJ, Graybiel AM. Habit learning is associated with major shifts in frequencies of oscillatory activity and synchronized spike firing in striatum. *Proceedings of the National Academy of Sciences of the United States of America.* 2011;108(40):16801–6. doi: 10.1073/pnas.1113158108. PubMed PMID: 21949388; PubMed Central PMCID: PMC3189047.

110. Lewis M, Kim SJ. The pathophysiology of restricted repetitive behavior. *Journal of Neurodevelopmental Disorders.* 2009;1(2):114–32. doi: 10.1007/s11689–009–9019–6. PubMed PMID: 21547711; PubMed Central PMCID: PMC3090677.

111. Volkow ND, Tomasi D, Wang GJ, Logan J, Alexoff DL, Jayne M, et al. Stimulant-induced dopamine increases are markedly blunted in active cocaine abusers. *Molecular Psychiatry.* 2014;19(9):1037–43. doi: 10.1038/mp.2014.58. PubMed PMID: 24912491.

112. Atmaca M. What about the neuroimaging findings in social anxiety disorder? *Reviews on Recent Clinical Trials.* 2013;8(2):124–27. PubMed PMID: 24032545.

113. Messerly J, Link J, Hayhurst H, Roberts C, Amen D, Willeumier K, et al. C-19A Preliminary investigation of SPECT differences between individuals with varying levels of anxiety. *Archives of Clinical Neuropsychology: The Official Journal of the National Academy of Neuropsychologists.* 2014;29(6):579. doi: 10.1093/arclin/acu038.200. PubMed PMID: 25176862.

114. Aupperle RL, Melrose AJ, Francisco A, Paulus MP, Stein MB. Neural substrates of approach-avoidance conflict decision-making. *Human Brain Mapping.* 2015;36(2):449–62. doi: 10.1002/hbm.22639. PubMed PMID: 25224633; PubMed Central PMCID: PMC4300249.

115. Herwig U, Bruhl AB, Viebke MC, Scholz RW, Knoch D, Siegrist M. Neural correlates of evaluating hazards of high risk. *Brain Research.* 2011;1400:78–86. doi: 10.1016/j.brainres.2011.05.023. PubMed PMID: 21645880.

116. Robertson MM. The Gilles de la Tourette syndrome: the current status. *Archives of Disease in Childhood Education and Practice Edition.* 2012;97(5):166–75. doi: 10.1136/archdischild-2011–300585. PubMed PMID: 22440810.

117. Silk JS, Siegle GJ, Lee KH, Nelson EE, Stroud LR, Dahl RE. Increased neural response to peer rejection associated with adolescent depression and pubertal development. *Social Cognitive and Affective Neuroscience.* 2014;9(11):1798–807. doi: 10.1093/scan/nst175. PubMed PMID: 24273075; PubMed Central PMCID: PMC4221220.

118. Guyer AE, Choate VR, Detloff A, Benson B, Nelson EE, Perez-Edgar K, et al. Striatal functional alteration during incentive anticipation in pediatric anxiety disorders. *The American Journal of Psychiatry.* 2012;169(2):205–12. PubMed PMID: 22423352; PubMed Central PMCID: PMC3307369.

119. Clauss JA, Seay AL, VanDerKlok RM, Avery SN, Cao A, Cowan RL, et al. Structural and functional bases of inhibited temperament. *Social Cognitive and Affective Neuroscience.* 2014;9(12):2049–58. doi: 10.1093/scan/nsu019. PubMed PMID: 24493850; PubMed Central PMCID: PMC4249486.

120. Terman LM, et al. Terman Life-Cycle Study of Children with High Ability, 1922–1991. In (ICPSR) I-uCfPaSR, editor. Ann Arbor, MI1992.

121. Blanchard EB, Eisele G, Vollmer A, Payne A, Gordon M, Cornish P, et al. Controlled evaluation of thermal biofeedback in treatment of elevated blood pressure in unmedicated mild hypertension. *Biofeedback and Self-Regulation.* 1996;21(2):167–90. PubMed PMID: 8805965.

122. Hahn YB, Ro YJ, Song HH, Kim NC, Kim HS, Yoo YS. The effect of thermal biofeedback and progressive muscle relaxation training in reducing blood pressure of patients with essential hypertension. *Image: The Journal of Nursing Scholarship.* 1993;25(3):204–7. PubMed PMID: 8225352.

123. Bauer A, Kantelhardt JW, Barthel P, Schneider R, Makikallio T, Ulm K, et al. Deceleration capacity of heart rate as a predictor of mortality after myocardial infarction: cohort study. *Lancet.* 2006;367(9523):1674–81. doi: 10.1016/S0140–6736(06)68735–7. PubMed PMID: 16714188.

124. Boskovic A, Belada N, Knezevic B. Prognostic value of heart rate variability in post-infarction patients. *Vojnosanitetski Pregled Military-Medical and Pharmaceutical Review.* 2014;71(10):92530. PubMed PMID: 25518271.

125. Roy A, Kundu D, Mandal T, Bandyopadhyay U, Ghosh E, Ray D. A comparative study of heart rate variability tests and lipid profile in healthy young adult males and females. *Nigerian Journal of Clinical Practice.* 2013;16(4):424–28. doi: 10.4103/1119–3077.116882. PubMed PMID: 23974732.

126. Chalmers JA, Quintana DS, Abbott MJ, Kemp AH. Anxiety disorders are associated with reduced heart rate variability: a meta-analysis. *Frontiers in Psychiatry.* 2014;5:80. doi: 10.3389/fpsyt.2014.00080. PubMed PMID: 25071612; PubMed Central PMCID: PMC4092363.

127. Jones KI, Amawi F, Bhalla A, Peacock O, Williams JP, Lund JN. Assessing surgeon stress when operating using heart rate variability and the State Trait Anxiety Inventory: will surgery be the death of us? *Colorectal Disease: The Official Journal of the Association of Coloproctology of Great Britain and Ireland.* 2014. doi: 10.1111/codi.12844. PubMed PMID: 25406932.

128. Khalsa DS, Amen D, Hanks C, Money N, Newberg A. Cerebral blood flow changes during chanting meditation. *Nuclear Medicine Communications.* 2009;30(12):956–61. doi: 10.1097/MNM.0b013e32832fa26c. PubMed PMID: 19773673.

129. Newberg AB, Wintering N, Waldman MR, Amen D, Khalsa DS, Alavi A. Cerebral blood flow differences between long-term meditators and non-meditators. *Consciousness and Cognition.* 2010;19(4):899–905. doi: 10.1016/j.concog.2010.05.003. PubMed PMID: 20570534.

130. Moss AS, Wintering N, Roggenkamp H, Khalsa DS, Waldman MR, Monti D, et al. Effects of an 8-week meditation program on mood and anxiety in patients with memory loss. *Journal of Alternative and Complementary Medicine.* 2012;18(1):48–53. doi: 10.1089/acm.2011.0051. PubMed PMID: 22268968.

131. Yamamoto S, Kitamura Y, Yamada N, Nakashima Y, Kuroda S. Medial profrontal cortex and anterior cingulate cortex in the generation of alpha activity induced by Tran-

scendental Meditation: a magnetoencephalographic study. *Acta Medica Okayama.* 2006;60(1):51–58. PubMed PMID: 16508689.

132. Tang YY, Ma Y, Wang J, Fan Y, Feng S, Lu Q, et al. Short-term meditation training improves attention and self-regulation. *Proceedings of the National Academy of Sciences of the United States of America.* 2007;104(43):17152–6. doi: 10.1073/pnas.0707678104. PubMed PMID: 17940025; PubMed Central PMCID: PMC2040428.

133. Benson H, Klipper MZ. *The Relaxation Response.* Updated & expanded ed. New York, NY: Quill, 2001. liv, 179 p. p.

134. The Austin Institute for the Study of Family and Culture. 2014. Are religious people happier? Available from: http://relationshipsinamerica.com/religion/are-religious-people-happier-people.

135. Dias BG, Ressler KJ. Parental olfactory experience influences behavior and neural structure in subsequent generations. *Nature Neuroscience.* 2014;17(1):89–96. doi: 10.1038/nn.3594. PubMed PMID: 24292232; PubMed Central PMCID: PMC3923835.

136. Gapp K, Soldado-Magraner S, Alvarez-Sanchez M, Bohacek J, Vernaz G, Shu H, et al. Early life stress in fathers improves behavioural flexibility in their offspring. *Nature Communications.* 2014;5:5466. doi: 10.1038/ncomms6466. PubMed PMID: 25405779.

137. Friedman LA, Rapoport JL. Brain development in ADHD. *Current Opinion in Neurobiology.* 2015;30C:106–11. doi: 10.1016/j.conb.2014.11.007. PubMed PMID: 25500059.

138. Hasler R, Salzmann A, Bolzan T, Zimmermann J, Baud P, Giannakopoulos P, et al. DAT1 and DRD4 genes involved in key dimensions of adult ADHD. *Neurological Sciences: Official Journal of the Italian Neurological Society and of the Italian Society of Clinical Neurophysiology.* 2015. doi: 10.1007/s10072–014–2051-7. PubMed PMID: 25555995.

139. Yassin S, Spengler K, Amen D, Willeumier K, Taylor D, Golden C. B-15 Differences in SPECT Perfusion in Children and Adolescents with ADHD. *Archives of Clinical Neuropsychology: The Official Journal of the National Academy of Neuropsychologists.* 2014;29(6):541–42. doi: 10.1093/arclin/acu038.103. PubMed PMID: 25176765.

140. Zusman M, Amen D, Willeumier K, Taylor D, Golden C. B-16, The effect of inattention on cerebral blood flow perfusion. *Archives of Clinical Neuropsychology: The Official Journal of the National Academy of Neuropsychologists.* 2014;29(6):542. doi: 10.1093/arclin/acu038.104. PubMed PMID: 25176766.

141. Santra A, Kumar R. Brain perfusion single photon emission computed tomography in major psychiatric disorders: From basics to clinical practice. *Indian Journal of Nuclear Medicine.* 2014;29(4):210–21. doi: 10.4103/0972–3919.142622. PubMed PMID: 25400359; PubMed Central PMCID: PMC4228583.

142. Brod S, Rattazzi L, Piras G, D'Acquisto F. "As above, so below" examining the interplay between emotion and the immune system. *Immunology.* 2014;143(3):311–18. doi: 10.1111/imm.12341. PubMed PMID: 24943894; PubMed Central PMCID: PMC4212945.

143. McIntosh RC, Hurwitz BE, Antoni M, Gonzalez A, Seay J, Schneiderman N. The ABCs of trait anger, psychological distress, and disease severity in HIV. *Annals of Behavioral Medicine: A Publication of the Society of Behavioral Medicine.* 2014. doi: 10.1007/s12160–014–9667-y. PubMed PMID: 25385204.

144. Bauer I, Hughes M, Rowsell R, Cockerell R, Pipingas A, Crewther S, et al. Omega-3 supplementation improves cognition and modifies brain activation in young adults. *Human Psychopharmacology.* 2014;29(2):133–44. doi: 10.1002/hup.2379. PubMed PMID: 24470182.

145. Milte CM, Parletta N, Buckley JD, Coates AM, Young RM, Howe PR. Increased erythrocyte eicosapentaenoic acid and docosahexaenoic acid are associated with improved attention and behavior in children with ADHD in a randomized controlled three-way crossover trial. *Journal of Attention Disorders.* 2013. doi: 10.1177/1087054713510562. PubMed PMID: 24214970.

146. Puri BK, Martins JG. Which polyunsaturated fatty acids are active in children with attention-deficit hyperactivity disorder receiving PUFA supplementation? A fatty acid validated meta-regression analysis of randomized controlled trials. *Prostaglandins, Leukotrienes, and Essential Fatty Acids.* 2014;90(5):179–89. doi: 10.1016/j.plefa.2014.01.004. PubMed PMID: 24560325.

147. Akhondzadeh S, Mohammadi MR, Khademi M. Zinc sulfate as an adjunct to methylphenidate for the treatment of attention deficit hyperactivity disorder in children: a double blind and randomized trial [ISRCTN64132371]. *BMC Psychiatry.* 2004;4:9. doi: 10.1186/1471–244X-4–9. PubMed PMID: 15070418; PubMed Central PMCID: PMC400741.

148. Bilici M, Yildirim F, Kandil S, Bekaroglu M, Yildirmis S, Deger O, et al. Double-blind, placebo-controlled study of zinc sulfate in the treatment of attention deficit hyperactivity disorder. *Progress in Neuro-Psychopharmacology & Biological Psychiatry.* 2004;28(1):181–90. doi: 10.1016/j.pnpbp.2003.09.034. PubMed PMID: 14687872.

149. Amminger GP, Chanen AM, Ohmann S, Klier CM, Mossaheb N, Bechdolf A, et al. Omega-3 fatty acid supplementation in adolescents with borderline personality disorder and ultra-high risk criteria for psychosis: a post hoc subgroup analysis of a double-blind, randomized controlled trial. *Canadian Journal of Psychiatry (Revue Canadienne de Psychiatrie).* 2013;58(7):402– 8. PubMed PMID: 23870722.

150. Mossaheb N, Schafer MR, Schlogelhofer M, Klier CM, Cotton SM, McGorry PD, et al. Effect of omega-3 fatty acids for indicated prevention of young patients at risk for psychosis: when do they begin to be effective? *Schizophrenia Research.* 2013;148(1–3):163–67. doi: 10.1016/j.schres.2013.05.027. PubMed PMID: 23778032.

151. Lubar JF, Swartwood MO, Swartwood JN, O'Donnell PH. Evaluation of the effectiveness of EEG neurofeedback training for ADHD in a clinical setting as measured by changes in T.O.V.A. scores, behavioral ratings, and WISC-R performance. *Biofeedback and Self-Regulation.* 1995;20(1):83–99. PubMed PMID: 7786929.

152. Monastra VJ, Lubar JF, Linden M, VanDeusen P, Green G, Wing W, et al. Assessing attention deficit hyperactivity disorder via quantitative electroencephalography: an initial validation study. *Neuropsychology.* 1999;13(3):424–33. PubMed PMID: 10447303.

153. American Academy of Pediatrics. Evidence-based child and adolescent psychosocial interventions. American Academy of Pediatrics, 2010.

154. Pratt RR, Abel HH, Skidmore J. The effects of neurofeedback training with background

music on EEG patterns of ADD and ADHD children. *International Journal of Arts Medicine.* 1995;4(1).

155. Mirsky AF, Anthony BJ, Duncan CC, Ahearn MB, Kellam SG. Analysis of the elements of attention: a neuropsychological approach. *Neuropsychology Review.* 1991;2(2):109–45. PubMed PMID: 1844706.

156. Bissonette GB, Powell EM, Roesch MR. Neural structures underlying set-shifting: roles of medial prefrontal cortex and anterior cingulate cortex. *Behavioural Brain Research.* 2013;250:91–101. doi: 10.1016/j.bbr.2013.04.037. PubMed PMID: 23664821; PubMed Central PMCID: PMC3708542.

157. Posner MI, Di Girolamo GJ. Executive attention: conflict, target detection, and cognitive control. In Parasuraman R, editor. *The Attentive Brain.* Cambridge, MA: MIT Press, 1998.

158. Chang JW, Kim CH, Lee JD, Chung SS. Single photon emission computed tomography imaging in obsessive-compulsive disorder and for stereotactic bilateral anterior cingulotomy. *Neurosurgery Clinics of North America.* 2003;14(2):237–50. PubMed PMID: 12856491.

159. Diler RS, Kibar M, Avci A. Pharmacotherapy and regional cerebral blood flow in children with obsessive compulsive disorder. *Yonsei Medical Journal.* 2004;45(1):90–99. PubMed PMID: 15004874.

160. Carey PD, Warwick J, Niehaus DJ, van der Linden G, van Heerden BB, Harvey BH, et al. Single photon emission computed tomography (SPECT) of anxiety disorders before and after treatment with citalopram. *BMC Psychiatry.* 2004;4:30. doi: 10.1186/1471-244X-4-30. PubMed PMID: 15482603; PubMed Central PMCID: PMC529251.

161. Swedo SE, Rapoport JL, Leonard HL, Schapiro MB, Rapoport SI, Grady CL. Regional cerebral glucose metabolism of women with trichotillomania. *Archives of General Psychiatry.* 1991;48(9):828–33. PubMed PMID: 1929773.

162. Swedo SE. Pediatric autoimmune neuropsychiatric disorders associated with streptococcal infections (PANDAS). *Molecular Psychiatry.* 2002;7 Suppl 2:S24–5. doi: 10.1038/sj.mp.4001170. PubMed PMID: 12142939.

163. Grant JE, Kim SW, Odlaug BL. N-acetyl cysteine, a glutamate-modulating agent, in the treatment of pathological gambling: a pilot study. *Biological Psychiatry.* 2007;62(6):652–7. doi: 10.1016/j.biopsych.2006.11.021. PubMed PMID: 17445781.

164. Brody AL, Saxena S, Schwartz JM, Stoessel PW, Maidment K, Phelps ME, et al. FDG-PET predictors of response to behavioral therapy and pharmacotherapy in obsessive compulsive disorder. *Psychiatry Research.* 1998;84(1):1–6. PubMed PMID: 9870412.

165. Ascher LM. Paradoxical intention in the treatment of urinary retention. *Behaviour Research and Therapy.* 1979;17(3):267–70. PubMed PMID: 526243.

166. Quaglino A, Borelli GB, Della Sala S, Young AW. Quaglino's 1867 case of prosopagnosia. *Cortex; A Journal Devoted to the Study of the Nervous System and Behavior.* 2003;39(3):533–40. PubMed PMID: 12870826.

167. Thomas LA, De Bellis MD, Graham R, LaBar KS. Development of emotional facial recognition in late childhood and adolescence. *Developmental Science.* 2007;10(5):547–58. doi: 10.1111/j.1467–7687.2007.00614.x. PubMed PMID: 17683341.

168. Cohn M, St-Laurent M, Barnett A, McAndrews MP. Social inference deficits in temporal lobe epilepsy and lobectomy: risk factors and neural substrates. *Social Cognitive and Affective Neuroscience.* 2014. doi: 10.1093/scan/nsu101. PubMed PMID: 25062843.

169. Irish M, Hodges JR, Piguet O. Right anterior temporal lobe dysfunction underlies theory of mind impairments in semantic dementia. *Brain: A Journal of Neurology.* 2014;137(Pt 4):1241–53. doi: 10.1093/brain/awu003. PubMed PMID: 24523434.

170. Saitovitch A, Bargiacchi A, Chabane N, Brunelle F, Samson Y, Boddaert N, et al. Social cognition and the superior temporal sulcus: implications in autism. *Revue Neurologique.* 2012;168(10):762–70. doi: 10.1016/j.neurol.2012.07.017. PubMed PMID: 22981269.

171. Amen DG, Stubblefield M, Carmicheal B, Thisted R. Brain SPECT findings and aggressiveness. *Annals of Clinical Psychiatry: Official Journal of the American Academy of Clinical Psychiatrists.* 1996;8(3):129–37. PubMed PMID: 8899131.

172. Fueloep-Miller R. *Fyodor Dostoevsky: Insight, Faith, and Prophecy.* 1st ed. New York: Scribner, 1950.

173. Dostoevsky F. *The Idiot.* Reprint edition: Vintage, 1869; July 8, 2003.

174. Rauscher FH, Shaw GL, Ky KN. Listening to Mozart enhances spatial-temporal reasoning: towards a neurophysiological basis. *Neuroscience Letters.* 1995;185(1):44–47. PubMed PMID: 7731551.

175. Campbell D. *The Mozart Effect: Tapping the Power of Music to Heal the Body, Strengthen the Mind, and Unlock the Creative Spirit.* New York: HarperCollins, 2001.

176. Verny T, Kelly J. *The Secret Life of the Unborn Child: How You Can Prepare Your Baby for a Happy, Healthy Life.* New York: Dell, 1982.

177. Winkelman M. Complementary therapy for addiction: "drumming out drugs." *American Journal of Public Health.* 2003;93(4):647–51. PubMed PMID: 12660212; PubMed Central PMCID: PMC1447805.

178. Creutzfeldt O, Ojemann G. Neuronal activity in the human lateral temporal lobe. III. Activity changes during music. *Experimental Brain Research.* 1989;77(3):490–98. PubMed PMID: 2806443.

179. Amen DG, Hanks C, Prunella J. Predicting positive and negative treatment responses to stimulants with brain SPECT imaging. *Journal of Psychoactive Drugs.* 2008;40(2):131–38. Epub 2008/08/30. PubMed PMID: 18720661.

180. Byron K. *Loving What Is: Four Questions That Can Change Your Life.* New York: Three Rivers Press; 2003.

181. Lima PA, Sampaio LP, Damasceno NR. Neurobiochemical mechanisms of a ketogenic diet in refractory epilepsy. *Clinics.* 2014;69(10):699–705. doi: 10.6061/clinics/2014(10)09. PubMed PMID: 25518023; PubMed Central PMCID: PMC4221309.

182. Payne J. *Change Your Brain, Change Your Life (Before 25): Change Your Developing Mind for Real-World Success.* Ontario: Harlequin, 2014.

183. Bushman BJ, Dewall CN, Pond RS, Jr., Hanus MD. Low glucose relates to greater ag-

gression in married couples. *Proceedings of the National Academy of Sciences of the United States of America.* 2014;111(17):6254–57. doi: 10.1073/pnas.1400619111. PubMed PMID: 24733932; PubMed Central PMCID: PMC4035998.

184. Lagos R, Hogan M, Raghuram K. The face of hillbilly heroin and other images of narcotic abuse. *The West Virginia Medical Journal.* 2010;106(4 Spec No):34–37. PubMed PMID: 21932751.

185. Rose JS, Branchey M, Buydens-Branchey L, Stapleton JM, Chasten K, Werrell A, et al. Cerebral perfusion in early and late opiate withdrawal: a technetium-99m-HMPAO SPECT study. *Psychiatry Research.* 1996;67(1):39–47. PubMed PMID: 8797241.

186. Stewart SA. The effects of benzodiazepines on cognition. *The Journal of Clinical Psychiatry.* 2005;66 Suppl 2:9–13. PubMed PMID: 15762814.

187. Karama S, Ducharme S, Corley J, Chouinard-Decorte F, Starr JM, Wardlaw JM, et al. Cigarette smoking and thinning of the brain's cortex. *Molecular Psychiatry.* 2015. doi: 10.1038/mp.2014.187. PubMed PMID: 25666755.

188. Bhattacharyya S, Atakan Z, Martin-Santos R, Crippa JA, Kambeitz J, Malhi S, et al. Impairment of inhibitory control processing related to acute psychotomimetic effects of cannabis. *European Neuropsychopharmacology: The Journal of the European College of Neuropsychopharmacology.* 2015;25(1):26–37. doi: 10.1016/j.euroneuro.2014.11.018. PubMed PMID: 25532865.

189. National Institute on Drug Abuse. NIDA Notes: Articles that address research on marijuana. Available from: http://archives.drugabuse.gov/pdf/nncollections/nnmarijuana .pdf. 2007. p. 64.

190. Brown JS, Jr. Geographic correlation of schizophrenia to ticks and tick-borne encephalitis. *Schizophrenia Bulletin.* 1994;20(4):755–75. PubMed PMID: 7701281.

191. Smith G. Estimating the population attributable fraction for schizophrenia when Toxoplasma gondii is assumed absent in human populations. *Preventive Veterinary Medicine.* 2014;117(3–4):425–35. doi: 10.1016/j.prevetmed.2014.10.009. PubMed PMID: 25453822.

192. Park RM, Schulte PA, Bowman JD, Walker JT, Bondy SC, Yost MG, et al. Potential occupational risks for neurodegenerative diseases. *American Journal of Industrial Medicine.* 2005;48(1):63–77. doi: 10.1002/ajim.20178. PubMed PMID: 15940722.

193. Ferrari C, Nacmias B, Bagnoli S, Piaceri I, Lombardi G, Pradella S, et al. Imaging and cognitive reserve studies predict dementia in presymptomatic Alzheimer's disease subjects. *Neuro-degenerative Diseases.* 2014;13(2–3):157–9. doi: 10.1159/000353690. PubMed PMID: 23942061.

194. Reiman EM, Quiroz YT, Fleisher AS, Chen K, Velez-Pardo C, Jimenez-Del-Rio M, et al. Brain imaging and fluid biomarker analysis in young adults at genetic risk for autosomal dominant Alzheimer's disease in the presenilin 1 E280A kindred: a case-control study. *The Lancet Neurology.* 2012;11(12):1048–56. doi: 10.1016/S1474-4422(12)70228-4 . PubMed PMID: 23137948; PubMed Central PMCID: PMC4181671.

195. Zamrini E. D. Santi S, Tolar M. Imaging is superior to cognitive testing for early diagnosis of Alzheimer's disease. *Neurobiology of Aging.* 2004;25(5):685–91. doi: 10.1016/j. neurobiolaging.2004.02.009. PubMed PMID: 15172748.

196. Centers for Disease Control and Prevention. Overweight and Obesity. Available from: http://www.cdc.gov/obesity/data/adult.html.

197. Raji CA. Ho AJ, Parikshak NN, Becker JT, Lopez OL, Kuller LH, et al. Brain structure and obesity. *Human Brain Mapping.* 2010;31(3):353–64. doi: 10.1002/hbm.20870. PubMed PMID: 19662657; PubMed Central PMCID: PMC2826530.

198. Willeumier K, Taylor DV, Amen DG. Elevated body mass in National Football League players linked to cognitive impairment and decreased prefrontal cortex and temporal pole activity. *Translational Psychiatry.* 2012;2:e68. doi: 10.1038/tp.2011.67. PubMed PMID: 22832730; PubMed Central PMCID: PMC3309539.

199. Willeumier KC, Taylor DV, Amen DG. Elevated BMI is associated with decreased blood flow in the prefrontal cortex using SPECT imaging in healthy adults. *Obesity.* 2011;19(5):1095–97. doi: 10.1038/oby.2011.16. PubMed PMID: 21311507; PubMed Central PMCID: PMC3125099.

200. Bredesen DE. Reversal of cognitive decline: a novel therapeutic program. *Aging.* 2014; 6(9):707–17. PubMed PMID: 25324467; PubMed Central PMCID: PMC4221920.

201. Kivipelto M, Solomon A, Ahtiluoto S, Ngandu T, Lehtisalo J, Antikainen R, et al. The Finnish Geriatric Intervention Study to Prevent Cognitive Impairment and Disability (FINGER): study design and progress. *Alzheimer's & Dementia: The Journal of the Alz-heimer's Association.* 2013;9(6):657–65. doi: 10.1016/j.jalz.2012.09.012. PubMed PMID: 23332672.

202. Alzheimer's Association. Alzheimer's facts and figures 2015 [cited 2015 January 1, 2015]. Available from: http://www.alz.org/alzheimers_disease_facts_and_figures.asp#prevalence.

203. Perl DP. Neuropathology of Alzheimer's disease. *The Mount Sinai Journal of Medicine,* New York. 2010;77(1):32–42. doi: 10.1002/msj.20157. PubMed PMID: 20101720; PubMed Central PMCID: PMC2918894.

204. Faden AI, Loane DJ. Chronic neurodegeneration after traumatic brain injury: Alzheimer disease, chronic traumatic encephalopathy, or persistent neuroinflammation? *Neurotherapeutics: The Journal of the American Society for Experimental Neuro Therapeutics.* 2014. doi: 10.1007/s13311–014–0319–5. PubMed PMID: 25421001.

205. Costin BN, Miles MF. Molecular and neurologic responses to chronic alcohol use. *Handbook of Clinical Neurology.* 2014;125:157–71. doi: 10.1016/B978–0-444–62619–6.00010–0. PubMed PMID: 25307574.

206. de Oliveira FF, Bertolucci PH, Chen ES, Smith MC. Assessment of risk factors for earlier onset of sporadic Alzheimer's disease dementia. *Neurology India.* 2014;62(6):625–30. doi: 10.4103/0028–3886.149384. PubMed PMID: 25591674.

207. Mattson MP. Lifelong brain health is a lifelong challenge: from evolutionary principles to empirical evidence. *Ageing Research Reviews.* 2015. doi: 10.1016/j.arr.2014.12.011. PubMed PMID: 25576651.

208. Li BY, Chen SD. Potential similarities in temporal lobe epilepsy and Alzheimer's disease: from clinic to pathology. *American Journal of Alzheimer's Disease and Other Dementias.* 2014. doi: 10.1177/1533317514537547. PubMed PMID: 24906967.

209. Lobanova I, Qureshi AI. The association between cardiovascular risk factors and progres-

sive hippocampus volume loss in persons with Alzheimer's disease. *Journal of Vascular and Interventional Neurology.* 2014;7(5):52–55. PubMed PMID: 25566342; PubMed Central PMCID: PMC4280866.

210. Gorelick PB, Scuteri A, Black SE, Decarli C, Greenberg SM, Iadecola C, et al. Vascular contributions to cognitive impairment and dementia: a statement for healthcare professionals from the American Heart Association/American Stroke Association. *Stroke: A Journal of Cerebral Circulation.* 2011;42(9):2672–713. doi: 10.1161/STR.0b013e3182299496. PubMed PMID: 21778438; PubMed Central PMCID: PMC3778669.

211. Chakrabarti M, Haque A, Banik NL, Nagarkatti P, Nagarkatti M, Ray SK. Estrogen receptor agonists for attenuation of neuroinflammation and neurodegeneration. *Brain Research Bulletin.* 2014;109:22–31. doi: 10.1016/j.brainresbull.2014.09.004. PubMed PMID: 25245209.

212. Lau CF, Ho YS, Hung CH, Wuwongse S, Poon CH, Chiu K, et al. Protective effects of testosterone on presynaptic terminals against oligomeric beta-amyloid peptide in primary culture of hippocampal neurons. *BioMed Research International.* 2014;2014:103906. doi: 10.1155/2014/103906. PubMed PMID: 25045655; PubMed Central PMCID: PMC4086619.

213. Cerajewska TL, Davies M, West NX. Periodontitis: a potential risk factor for Alzheimer's disease. *British Dental Journal.* 2015;218(1):29–34. doi: 10.1038/sj.bdj.2014.1137. PubMed PMID: 25571822.

214. Fakhoury M. Role of immunity and inflammation in the pathophysiology of neurodegenerative diseases. *Neuro-degenerative Diseases.* 2015. doi: 10.1159/000369933. PubMed PMID: 25591815.

215. Schulte EC, Fukumori A, Mollenhauer B, Hor H, Arzberger T, Perneczky R, et al. Rare variants in beta-amyloid precursor protein (APP) and Parkinson's disease. *European Journal of Human Genetics: EJHG.* 2015. doi: 10.1038/cjhg.2014.300. PubMed PMID: 25604855.

216. Blanc F, Philippi N, Cretin B, Kleitz C, Berly L, Jung B, et al. Lyme neuroborreliosis and dementia. *Journal of Alzheimer's Disease: JAD.* 2014;41(4):1087–93. doi: 10.3233/JAD-130446. PubMed PMID: 24762944.

217. Miklossy J. Chronic inflammation and amyloidogenesis in Alzheimer's disease—role of Spirochetes. *Journal of Alzheimer's Disease : JAD.* 2008;13(4):381–91. PubMed PMID: 18487847.

218. Crane PK, Walker R, Hubbard RA, Li G, Nathan DM, Zheng H, et al. Glucose levels and risk of dementia. *The New England Journal of Medicine.* 2013;369(6):540–48. doi: 10.1056/NEJMoa1215740. PubMed PMID: 23924004; PubMed Central PMCID: PMC3955123.

219. Morris MC, Tangney CC. Dietary fat composition and dementia risk. *Neurobiology of Aging.* 2014;35 Suppl 2:S59–64. doi: 10.1016/j.neurobiology.2014.03.038. PubMed PMID: 24970568; PubMed Central PMCID: PMC4107296.

220. Ding J, Eigenbrodt ML, Mosley TH, Jr., Hutchinson RG, Folsom AR, Harris TB, et al. Alcohol intake and cerebral abnormalities on magnetic resonance imaging in a

community-based population of middle-aged adults: the Atherosclerosis Risk in Communities (ARIC) study. *Stroke: A Journal of Cerebral Circulation.* 2004;35(1):16–21. doi: 10.1161/01.STR.0000105929.88691.8E. PubMed PMID: 14657449.

221. Huang Z, Sjoholm A. Ethanol acutely stimulates islet blood flow, amplifies insulin secretion, and induces hypoglycemia via nitric oxide and vagally mediated mechanisms. *Endocrinology.* 2008;149(1):232–36. doi: 10.1210/en.2007–0632. PubMed PMID: 17916634.

222. Alosco ML, Fedor AF, Gunstad J. Attention deficit hyperactivity disorder as a risk factor for concussions in NCAA division-I athletes. *Brain Injury: [BI].* 2014;28(4):472–74. doi: 10.3109/02699052.2014.887145. PubMed PMID: 24564766.

223. Raziel A, Sakran N, Goitein D. The relationship between attention deficit hyperactivity disorders (ADHD) and obesity. *Harefuah.* 2014;153(9):541–45, 57. PubMed PMID: 25507220.

224. Elkins IJ. Young children with ADHD are at increased risk of depression and suicidal behaviour in adolescence. *Evidence-based Mental Health.* 2011;14(1):15. doi: 10.1136/ebmh.14.1.15. PubMed PMID: 21266612.

225. Molina BS, Pelham WE, Jr. Childhood predictors of adolescent substance use in a longitudinal study of children with ADHD. *Journal of Abnormal Psychology.* 2003;112(3):497–507. PubMed PMID: 12943028.

226. Milberger S, Biederman J, Faraone SV, Chen L, Jones J. ADHD is associated with early initiation of cigarette smoking in children and adolescents. *Journal of the American Academy of Child and Adolescent Psychiatry.* 1997;36(1):37–44. doi: 10.1097/00004583–199701000–00015. PubMed PMID: 9000779.

227. Rakoff-Nahoum S. Why cancer and inflammation? *The Yale Journal of Biology and Medicine.* 2006;79(3–4):123–30. PubMed PMID: 17940622; PubMed Central PMCID: PMC1994795.

228. Greenfield JR, Campbell LV. Relationship between inflammation, insulin resistance and type 2 diabetes: "cause or effect"? *Current Diabetes Reviews.* 2006;2(2):195–211. PubMed PMID: 18220627.

229. Willerson JT, Ridker PM. Inflammation as a cardiovascular risk factor. *Circulation.* 2004;109(21 Suppl 1):II2–10. doi: 10.1161/01.CIR.0000129535.04194.38. PubMed PMID: 15173056.

230. Rebok GW, Ball K, Guey LT, Jones RN, Kim HY, King JW, et al. Ten-year effects of the advanced cognitive training for independent and vital elderly cognitive training trial on cognition and everyday functioning in older adults. *Journal of the American Geriatrics Society.* 2014;62(1):16–24. doi: 10.1111/jgs.12607. PubMed PMID: 24417410; PubMed Central PMCID: PMC4055506.

231. Leckie RL, Oberlin LE, Voss MW, Prakash RS, Szabo-Reed A, Chaddock-Heyman L, et al. BDNF mediates improvements in executive function following a 1-year exercise intervention. *Frontiers in Human Neuroscience.* 2014;8:985. doi: 10.3389/fnhum.2014.00985. PubMed PMID: 25566019; PubMed Central PMCID: PMC4263078.

232. Tonoli C, Heyman E, Buyse L, Roelands B, Piacentini MF, Bailey S, et al. Neuro-

trophins and cognitive functions in T1D compared with healthy controls: effects of a high-intensity exercise. *Applied Physiology, Nutrition, and Metabolism = Physiologie Appliquée, Nutrition et Metabolisme.* 2015;40(1):20–7. doi: 10.1139/apnm-2014–0098. PubMed PMID: 25525862.

233. Tamura M, Nemoto K, Kawaguchi A, Kato M, Arai T, Kakuma T, et al. Long-term mild-intensity exercise regimen preserves prefrontal cortical volume against aging. *International Journal of Geriatric Psychiatry.* 2014. doi: 10.1002/gps.4205. PubMed PMID: 25353992.

234. Fiatarone Singh MA, Gates N, Saigal N, Wilson GC, Meiklejohn J, Brodaty H, et al. The Study of Mental and Resistance Training (SMART) study-resistance training and/or cognitive training in mild cognitive impairment: a randomized, double-blind, double-sham controlled trial. *Journal of the American Medical Directors Association.* 2014;15(12):873–80. doi: 10.1016/j.jamda.2014.09.010. PubMed PMID: 25444575.

235. Friedman JE, Ferrara CM, Aulak KS, Hatzoglou M, McCune SA, Park S, et al. Exercise training down-regulates ob gene expression in the genetically obese SHHF/Mcc-fa(cp) rat. *Hormone and Metabolic Research = Hormon- und Stoffwechselforschung = Hormones et Metabolisme.* 1997;29(5):214–19. doi: 10.1055/s-2007–979024. PubMed PMID: 9228205.

236. Okonkwo OC, Schultz SA, Oh JM, Larson J, Edwards D, Cook D, et al. Physical activity attenuates age-related biomarker alterations in preclinical AD. *Neurology.* 2014;83(19):1753–60. doi: 10.1212/WNL.0000000000000964. PubMed PMID: 25298312; PubMed Central PMCID: PMC4239838.

237. Head D, Bugg JM, Goate AM, Fagan AM, Mintun MA, Benzinger T, et al. Exercise engagement as a moderator of the effects of APOE genotype on amyloid deposition. *Archives of Neurology.* 2012;69(5):636–43. doi: 10.1001/archneurol.2011.845. PubMed PMID: 22232206; PubMed Central PMCID: PMC3583203.

238. Gruber KJ. Social support for exercise and dietary habits among college students. *Adolescence.* 2008;43(171):557–75. PubMed PMID: 19086670.

239. Berryman N, Bherer L, Nadeau S, Lauziere S, Lehr L, Bobeuf F, et al. Multiple roads lead to Rome: combined high-intensity aerobic and strength training vs. gross motor activities leads to equivalent improvement in executive functions in a cohort of healthy older adults. *Age.* 2014;36(5):9710. doi: 10.1007/s11357–014–9710–8. PubMed PMID: 25194940; PubMed Central PMCID: PMC4156938.

240. Davis JC, Bryan S, Marra CA, Sharma D, Chan A, Beattie BL, et al. An economic evaluation of resistance training and aerobic training versus balance and toning exercises in older adults with mild cognitive impairment. *PLOS ONE.* 2013;8(5):e63031. doi: 10.1371/journal.pone.0063031. PubMed PMID: 23690976; PubMed Central PMCID: PMC3653911.

241. Mekary RA, Grontved A, Despres JP, De Moura LP, Asgarzadeh M, Willett WC, et al. Weight training, aerobic physical activities, and long-term waist circumference change in men. *Obesity.* 2014. doi: 10.1002/oby.20949. PubMed PMID: 25530447.

242. Avila JJ, Gutierres JA, Sheehy ME, Lofgren IE, Delmonico MJ. Effect of moderate inten-

sity resistance training during weight loss on body composition and physical performance in overweight older adults. *European Journal of Applied Physiology.* 2010;109(3):517–25. doi: 10.1007/s00421–010–1387–9. PubMed PMID: 20169360.

243. Klainin-Yobas P, Oo WN, Suzanne Yew PY, Lau Y. Effects of relaxation interventions on depression and anxiety among older adults: a systematic review. *Aging & Mental Health.* 2015:1–13. doi: 10.1080/13607863.2014.997191. PubMed PMID: 25574576.

244. Sethi JK, Nagendra HR, Sham Ganpat T. Yoga improves attention and self-esteem in underprivileged girl student. *Journal of Education and Health Promotion.* 2013;2:55. doi: 10.4103/2277–9531.119043. PubMed PMID: 24251291; PubMed Central PMCID: PMC3826026.

245. Sharma M, Haider T. Tai chi as an alternative and complementary therapy for anxiety: a systematic review. *Journal of Evidence-based Complementary & Alternative Medicine.* 2014. doi: 10.1177/2156587214561327. PubMed PMID: 25488322.

246. Wang F, Lee EK, Wu T, Benson H, Fricchione G, Wang W, et al. The effects of tai chi on depression, anxiety, and psychological well-being: a systematic review and meta-analysis. *International Journal of Behavioral Medicine.* 2014;21(4):605–17. doi: 10.1007/s12529–013–9351–9. PubMed PMID: 24078491.

247. Glass TW, Maher CG. Physical activity reduces cigarette cravings. *British Journal of Sports Medicine.* 2014;48(16):1263–64. doi: 10.1136/bjsports-2013–092525. PubMed PMID: 23709520.

248. Tsvetanov KA, Henson RN, Tyler LK, Davis SW, Shafto MA, Taylor JR, et al. The effect of ageing on fMRI: correction for the confounding effects of vascular reactivity evaluated by joint fMRI and MEG in 335 adults. *Human Brain Mapping.* 2015. doi: 10.1002/hbm.22768. PubMed PMID: 25727740.

249. Feldman HA, Goldstein I, Hatzichristou DG, Krane RJ, McKinlay JB. Impotence and its medical and psychosocial correlates: results of the Massachusetts Male Aging Study. *The Journal of Urology.* 1994;151(1):54–61. PubMed PMID: 8254833.

250. Hyman M. *The UltraMind Solution: Fix Your Broken Brain by Healing Your Body First.* New York: Scribner, 2007.

251. Gu Y, Nieves JW, Stern Y, Luchsinger JA, Scarmeas N. Food combination and Alzheimer disease risk: a protective diet. *Archives of Neurology.* 2010;67(6):699–706. doi: 10.1001/archneurol.2010.84. PubMed PMID: 20385883; PubMed Central PMCID: PMC3029147.

252. Gu Y, Schupf N, Cosentino SA, Luchsinger JA, Scarmeas N. Nutrient intake and plasma beta-amyloid. *Neurology.* 2012;78(23):1832–40. doi: 10.1212/WNL.0b013e318258f7c2. PubMed PMID: 22551728; PubMed Central PMCID: PMC3369517.

253. Colman RJ, Anderson RM, Johnson SC, Kastman EK, Kosmatka KJ, Beasley TM, et al. Caloric restriction delays disease onset and mortality in rhesus monkeys. *Science.* 2009;325(5937):201–4. doi: 10.1126/science.1173635. PubMed PMID: 19590001; PubMed Central PMCID: PMC2812811.

254. Guimaraes LR, Jacka FN, Gama CS, Berk M, Leitao-Azevedo CL, Belmonte de Abreu MG, et al. Serum levels of brain-derived neurotrophic factor in schizophrenia on a hypocaloric diet. *Progress in Neuro-Psychopharmacology & Biological Psy-*

chiatry. 2008;32(6):1595–98. doi: 10.1016/j.pnpbp.2008.06.004. PubMed PMID: 18582525.

255. Sacks FM, Bray GA, Carey VJ, Smith SR, Ryan DH, Anton SD, et al. Comparison of weight-loss diets with different compositions of fat, protein, and carbohydrates. *The New England Journal of Medicine.* 2009;360(9):859–73. doi: 10.1056/NEJMoa0804748. PubMed PMID: 19246357; PubMed Central PMCID: PMC2763382.

256. Duffey KJ, Popkin BM. Shifts in patterns and consumption of beverages between 1965 and 2002. *Obesity.* 2007;15(11):2739–47. doi: 10.1038/oby.2007.326. PubMed PMID: 18070765.

257. Moore SC, Carter LM, van Goozen S. Confectionery consumption in childhood and adult violence. *The British Journal of Psychiatry: The Journal of Mental Science.* 2009;195(4):366–67. doi: 10.1192/bjp.bp.108.061820. PubMed PMID: 19794208.

258. Dong JY, Zhang L, Zhang YH, Qin LQ. Dietary glycaemic index and glycaemic load in relation to the risk of type 2 diabetes: a meta-analysis of prospective cohort studies. *The British Journal of Nutrition.* 2011;106(11):1649–54. doi: 10.1017/S000711451100540X. PubMed PMID: 22017823.

259. St-Pierre DH, Rabasa-Lhoret R, Lavoie ME, Karelis AD, Strychar I, Doucet E, et al. Fiber intake predicts ghrelin levels in overweight and obese postmenopausal women. *European Journal of Endocrinology* / European Federation of Endocrine Societies. 2009;161(1): 65–72. doi: 10.1530/EJE-09–0018. PubMed PMID: 19369431.

260. Solomon A, Kivipelto M, Wolozin B, Zhou J, Whitmer RA. Midlife serum cholesterol and increased risk of Alzheimer's and vascular dementia three decades later. *Dementia and Geriatric Cognitive Disorders.* 2009;28(1):75–80. doi: 10.1159/000231980. PubMed PMID: 19648749; PubMed Central PMCID: PMC2814023.

261. Ahmed T, Gilani AH. Therapeutic potential of turmeric in Alzheimer's disease: curcumin or curcuminoids? *Phytotherapy Research: PTR.* 2014;28(4):517–25. doi: 10.1002/ptr.5030. PubMed PMID: 23873854.

262. Hausenblas HA, Saha D, Dubyak PJ, Anton SD. Saffron (Crocus sativus L.) and major depressive disorder: a meta-analysis of randomized clinical trials. *Journal of Integrative Medicine.* 2013;11(6):377–83. doi: 10.3736/jintegrmed2013056. PubMed PMID: 24299602.

263. Miroddi M, Navarra M, Quattropani MC, Calapai F, Gangemi S, Calapai G. Systematic review of clinical trials assessing pharmacological properties of Salvia species on memory, cognitive impairment and Alzheimer's disease. *CNS Neuroscience & Therapeutics.* 2014;20(6):485–95. doi: 10.1111/cns.12270. PubMed PMID: 24836739.

264. Ozarowski M, Mikolajczak PL, Bogacz A, Gryszczynska A, Kujawska M, Jodynis-Liebert J, et al. Rosmarinus officinalis L. leaf extract improves memory impairment and affects acetylcholinesterase and butyrylcholinesterase activities in rat brain. *Fitoterapia.* 2013;91:261–71. doi: 10.1016/j.fitote.2013.09.012. PubMed PMID: 24080468.

265. Environmental Working Group. Executive summary: Environmental Working Group; 2014. Available from: http://www.ewg.org/foodnews/summary.php.

266. Kraft BD, Westman EC. Schizophrenia, gluten, and low-carbohydrate, ketogenic diets: a case report and review of the literature. *Nutrition & Metabolism.* 2009;6:10. doi:

10.1186/1743–7075–6-10. PubMed PMID: 19245705; PubMed Central PMCID: PMC2652467.

267. Wurtman RJ, Wurtman JJ, Regan MM, McDermott JM, Tsay RH, Breu JJ. Effects of normal meals rich in carbohydrates or proteins on plasma tryptophan and tyrosine ratios. *The American Journal of Clinical Nutrition.* 2003;77(1):128–32. PubMed PMID: 12499331.

268. Logan AC, Katzman M. Major depressive disorder: probiotics may be an adjuvant therapy. *Medical Hypotheses.* 2005;64(3):533–8. doi: 10.1016/j.mehy.2004.08.019. PubMed PMID: 15617861.

269. Dinan TG, Cryan JF. Regulation of the stress response by the gut microbiota: implications for psychoneuroendocrinology. *Psychoneuroendocrinology.* 2012;37(9):1369–78. doi: 10.1016/j.psyneuen.2012.03.007. PubMed PMID: 22483040.

270. Desbonnet L, Garrett L, Clarke G, Kiely B, Cryan JF, Dinan TG. Effects of the probiotic Bifidobacterium infantis in the maternal separation model of depression. *Neuroscience.* 2010;170(4):1179–88. doi: 10.1016/j.neuroscience.2010.08.005. PubMed PMID: 20696216.

271. Brown H. A brain in the head, and one in the gut. *New York Times.* 2005;Sect. Health-science.

272. Rao AV, Bested AC, Beaulne TM, Katzman MA, Iorio C, Berardi JM, et al. A randomized, double-blind, placebo-controlled pilot study of a probiotic in emotional symptoms of chronic fatigue syndrome. *Gut Pathogens.* 2009;1(1):6. doi: 10.1186/1757–4749–1-6. PubMed PMID: 19338686; PubMed Central PMCID: PMC2664325.

ADDITIONAL READING

Ascherio A, Zhang SM, Hernan MA, Kawachi I, Colditz GA, Speizer FE, et al. Prospective study of caffeine consumption and risk of Parkinson's disease in men and women. *Annals of Neurology.* 2001;50(1):56–63. PubMed PMID: 11456310.

Ball K, Jeffery RW, Abbott G, McNaughton SA, Crawford D. Is healthy behavior contagious: associations of social norms with physical activity and healthy eating. *The International Journal of Behavioral Nutrition and Physical Activity.* 2010;7:86. doi: 10.1186/1479–5868-7-86. PubMed PMID: 21138550; PubMed Central PMCID: PMC3018448.

Bhupathiraju SN, Pan A, Manson JE, Willett WC, van Dam RM, Hu FB. Changes in coffee intake and subsequent risk of type 2 diabetes: three large cohorts of US men and women. *Diabetologia.* 2014;57(7):1346–54. doi: 10.1007/s00125-014-3235-7. PubMed PMID: 24771089; PubMed Central PMCID: PMC4115458.

Centola D. The spread of behavior in an online social network experiment. *Science.* 2010;329(5996):1194–97. doi: 10.1126/science.1185231. PubMed PMID: 20813952.

Christakis NA, Fowler JH. *Connected: The Surprising Power of Our Social Networks and How They Shape Our Lives—How Your Friends' Friends' Friends Affect Everything You Feel, Think, and Do.* New York: Little Brown and Company, 2009.

Chu YF, Chang WH, Black RM, Liu JR, Sompol P, Chen Y, et al. Crude caffeine reduces memory impairment and amyloid beta(1–42) levels in an Alzheimer's mouse model. *Food Chemistry.* 2012;135(3):2095–102. doi: 10.1016/j.foodchem.2012.04.148. PubMed PMID: 22953961.

Enriquez-Geppert S, Huster RJ, Figge C, Herrmann CS. Self-regulation of frontal-midline theta facilitates memory updating and mental set shifting. *Frontiers in Behavioral Neuroscience.* 2014;8:420. doi: 10.3389/fnbeh.2014.00420. PubMed PMID: 25538585; PubMed Central PMCID: PMC4257088.

Funk KL, Stevens VJ, Appel LJ, Bauck A, Brantley PJ, Champagne CM, et al. Associations of Internet website use with weight change in a long-term weight loss maintenance program. *Journal of Medical Internet Research.* 2010;12(3):e29. doi: 10.2196/jmir.1504. PubMed PMID: 20663751; PubMed Central PMCID: PMC2956327.

Harch PG, Andrews SR, Fogarty EF, Amen D, Pezzullo JC, Lucarini J, et al. A phase I study of low-pressure hyperbaric oxygen therapy for blast-induced post-concussion syndrome and post-traumatic stress disorder. *Journal of Neurotrauma.* 2012;29(1):168–85. doi: 10.1089/neu.2011.1895. PubMed PMID: 22026588.

Henriksen OM, Jensen LT, Krabbe K, Guldberg P, Teerlink T, Rostrup E. Resting brain perfusion and selected vascular risk factors in healthy elderly subjects. *PLOS ONE.* 2014;9(5):e97363. doi: 10.1371/journal.pone.0097363. PubMed PMID: 24840730; PubMed Central PMCID: PMC4026139.

Hollis JF, Gullion CM, Stevens VJ, Brantley PJ, Appel LJ, Ard JD, et al. Weight loss during the intensive intervention phase of the weight-loss maintenance trial. *American Journal of Preventive Medicine.* 2008;35(2):118–26. doi: 10.1016/j.amepre.2008.04.013. PubMed PMID: 18617080; PubMed Central PMCID: PMC2515566.

McChesney C, Covey S, Huling J. *The 4 Disciplines of Execution: Achieving Your Wildly Important Goals.* New York: Free Press, 2012.

Patterson K, Grenny J, Maxfield D, McMillan R, Switzler A. *Change Anything: The New Science of Personal Success.* New York: Hachette Book Group, 2012.

Ros T, Baars BJ, Lanius RA, Vuilleumier P. Tuning pathological brain oscillations with neurofeedback: a systems neuroscience framework. *Frontiers in Human Neuroscience.* 2014;8:1008. doi: 10.3389/fnhum.2014.01008. PubMed PMID: 25566028; PubMed Central PMCID: PMC4270171.

Stenzel SR, Rennert HS, G Gruber, SG. Abstract 1267: Coffee consumption and the risk of colorectal cancer. AACR Annual Meeting. 20142014.

Xie L, Kang H, Xu Q, Chen MJ, Liao Y, Thiyagarajan M, et al. Sleep drives metabolite clearance from the adult brain. *Science.* 2013;342(6156):373–77. doi: 10.1126/science.1241224. PubMed PMID: 24136970; PubMed Central PMCID: PMC3880190.

INDEX

Italic page numbers refer to illustrations